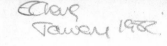

BLACKWELL'S CLASSICAL STUDIES

General Editor OSWYN MURRAY
Fellow of Balliol College, Oxford

Also in this Series

Ancient Slavery and the Ideal of Man
Joseph Vogt
Translated by Thomas Wiedemann

The Jews of Palestine
A Political History from the Bar Kokhba War
To The Arab Conquest
M. Avi-Yonah

Essays in Ancient
and Modern Historiography

Arnaldo Momigliano

Essays in Ancient
and Modern Historiography

Basil Blackwell · Oxford

First Published in Great Britain 1977
by Basil Blackwell Oxford

Copyright © Arnaldo Momigliano, 1947, 1955, 1957,
1958, 1959, 1963, 1965, 1966, 1970, 1971, 1972, 1973, 1974, 1975

ISBN 0 631 17900 3

Made and printed in Great Britain by
Richard Clay (The Chaucer Press) Ltd
Bungay, Suffolk
Set in Monotype Plantin

ALLA MEMORIA
DEI
MIEI MAESTRI
NELL'UNIVERSITÀ DI TORINO
1925-9

Contents

Foreword

The present volume is a new selection from the essays (partly in Italian, partly in English) collected in *Contributo alla storia degli studi classici* (*e del mondo antico*), of which five instalments in seven volumes have so far appeared (I, 1955; II, 1960; III, 1–2, 1966; IV, 1969; V, 1–2, 1975) and a sixth is being prepared for publication (*Edizioni di Storia e Letteratura*, Rome). A previous, entirely different, selection was published under the title *Studies in Historiography* by Weidenfeld & Nicolson in 1966. The present selection replaces the one which was due to be published by Penguin Books in 1974. Four of the essays here included (3, 4, 17, 19) were originally written and published in Italian; they were translated for this collection by Mrs Judith Landry. The translations were revised by Dr T. J. Cornell who also helped me in other ways. Each essay must be read with its original date of publication in mind. As a rule, no attempt is made to bring bibliography up to date.

I owe much gratitude to Blackwell for having undertaken the publication of this volume in difficult circumstances, and to my friend Dr O. Murray for having suggested and watched over it. I hope that the first and the last essays speak with sufficient clarity about my presuppositions and interests.

A.M.

All Souls College
Oxford, June 1976

List of Abbreviations

AJPh	*American Journal of Philology*
An. Bol.	*Analecta Bollandiana*
BiblH & R	*Bibliothèque d'Humanisme et Renaissance*
CAH	*The Cambridge Ancient History*
CQ	*Classical Quarterly*
CR	*Classical Review*
CRAcad. Inscr.	*Comptes rendus de l'Académie des Inscriptions et Belles-Lettres*
CSHByz	*Corpus scriptorum historiae Byzantinae*
DOP	*Dumbarton Oaks Papers*
GCFI	*Giornale critico della filosofia italiana*
GCS	*Die griechischen christlichen Schriftsteller der ersten Jahrhunderte*
Giorn. St. Lett. It.	*Giornale storico della letteratura italiana*
GRBS	*Greek, Roman and Byzantine Studies*
H & T	*History and Theory*
JHI	*Journal of the History of Ideas*
JHS	*Journal of Hellenic Studies*
JRS	*Journal of Roman Studies*
JWCI	*Journal of the Warburg and Courtauld Institutes*
ODCC	*Oxford Dictionary of the Christian Church*
PG	J. P. Migne, *Patrologiae Cursus, series Graeca*
PL	J. P. Migne, *Patrologiae Cursus, series Latina*
PW *or* RE	Pauly-Wissowa, *Real-Encyclopädie der classischen Altertumswissenschaft*
RAL	*Rendiconti della classe di scienze morali, storiche e filologiche dell'Accademia dei Lincei*
RPh	*Revue de Philologie*
RSI	*Rivista Storica Italiana*
TAPhA	*Transactions and Proceedings of the American Philological Association*

I

A Piedmontese View of the
History of Ideas *

WHEN I arrived in Oxford in 1939, it was enough to mention the word 'idea' to be given the address of the Warburg Institute. R. G. Collingwood, who still lectured on the history of the idea of history, was ill, isolated and discredited, and soon disappeared. Who had persuaded the English that the history of ideas was an unBritish activity? I suspect it was Lewis Namier. In the 1920s, when I was a student in the University of Turin, the history of ideas was the speciality for which English historians were most famous. This reputation went back to the days of Grote and Lecky, Freeman, Bryce and Flint. There were few books in other languages which could compete with Leslie Stephen's *History of English Thought in the 18th Century* or with J. B. Bury's *A History of Freedom of Thought* and *The Idea of Progress*. Lord Acton managed to become famous for a book on liberty he did not write. For medieval political ideas one went of course to the work in progress by the brothers Carlyle, and we were told (perhaps not quite fairly) that no Italian study of a medieval jurist could compare with C. N. S. Woolf's *Bartolus of Sassoferrato* (1913). The most significant history of an idea published in Italy in the 1920s, G. de Ruggiero's *Storia del Liberalismo Europeo*, was in method and point of view a derivation from English models. De Ruggiero was a close friend of Collingwood who translated his book into English. In the specific field of history of philosophy there was little to match Bosanquet's *History of Aesthetic* (as Croce reluctantly admitted) or Burnet's much-admired *Early Greek Philosophy*.

The situation was clearly one of change. To remain in the provincial but very alert society of the University of Turin, a distinction was becoming apparent between the Law Faculty and the Faculty of Arts.

*This essay was published in the *Times Literary Supplement*, 24 November 1972 with the title 'National Versions of an International Phenomenon'.

There were historians, indeed eminent historians on both sides. Though the study of law in Italy had a strong Germanic imprint, students of political and social ideas in the Law Faculty were in sympathy with the English tradition and with whatever American research on the history of ideas happened to be known (not very much at that time). The English translation of the book on religious liberty by Francesco Ruffini had shown that this interest was reciprocated. The masters of the Law Faculty set their pupils and, literally, their sons to work on themes of English origin and sent them to English-speaking universities. The result constitutes a little-noticed chapter of Piedmontese–Anglo-Saxon cultural relations: Mario Einaudi, the son of the future President of the Italian Republic, studied Burke and is now a professor at Cornell (and Director of the Luigi Einaudi Foundation in Turin); Edoardo Ruffini, the son of Francesco, studied parliamentary ideas of the Middle Ages and became the first cultural attaché in England after the Second World War; Alessandro Passerin d'Entrèves studied Hooker and medieval political thought under C. C. J. Webb and A. J. Carlyle in Oxford and later returned there as the Serena Professor of Italian Studies.

In the Faculty of Arts, by contrast, German *Ideengeschichte* was held in higher esteem than the English history of ideas. Federico Chabod, who had written his dissertation on Machiavelli in Turin (1924), went to Berlin to study under Meinecke; he returned to become the most influential Italian historian of his generation. Meinecke, who was recommended by Croce (the sympathy was rather one-sided), represented in many ways the most obvious alternative to the English approach to ideas. Though generalizations are precluded by the very list of names I have given above, the English approach tended to take the form of the history of the rise (and eventually of the fall) of a single specific idea, comprising its theoretical formulations and its embodiment in institutions. Even Bury's *Idea of Progress*, perhaps the most purely intellectual of all these books, deals specifically with the adoption of the idea of progress in historiography and sees connections with the social environment. Meinecke was a historian of conflicting principles: national state versus cosmopolitanism, *raison d'état* against natural rights. More and more he liked to leave these conflicts unresolved and to create an atmosphere of pathos round his books with which English prose could hardly compete.

Meinecke was only one of the facets of German *Ideengeschichte* as it emerged before Italian eyes in the 1920s. Histories of political myths, of words charged with ideological content, of class-conditioned social ideas, multiplied both from the right and the left. Among those which made an impression on me at the time of their appearance I remember F. Schneider, *Rom und Romgedanke im Mittelalter* (1926); P. E. Schramm, *Kaiser, Rom und Renovatio* (1929); A. Dempf, *Sacrum Imperium* (1929); F. Gundolf, *Caesar, Geschichte seines Ruhms* (1925); B. Groethuysen, *Die Entstehung der bürgerlichen Welt- und Lebensanschauung* (1927).

It is no accident that books on the Middle Ages played such a large part even in the formation of an ancient historian like myself. These were the 'model' books about which one spoke. K. Burdach's *Vom Mittelalter zur Reformation* (1891 ff.) seemed to be one of the supreme achievements of modern historiography. Discussions imported from Germany on the essence and chronological limits of certain periods (Middle Ages, Renaissance, Enlightenment) bordered on casuistry. Chabod wasted too much time on them. But perhaps they contributed indirectly to the notion of intellectual climate and thus rejoined the Burckhardtian *Kulturgeschichte*.

The publications of the Warburg Institute of Hamburg were of course noticed for their approach to iconography and, generally speaking, as a rallying-point for the new German currents of thought. The variety of the contributions, which included big names such as R. Reitzenstein and E. Norden among the classicists, made it difficult to separate those works by Warburg himself, F. Saxl, Edgar Wind, Erwin Panofsky and Ernst Cassirer, which represented the really original nucleus of the Institute. The wide influence of the Warburg Institute in Italy as well as in England developed only after the Second World War.

In the study of Greece and Rome, Germany made fashionable the history of 'political' words. The model analysis of the word *fides* by E. Fraenkel (1916) is often given as the starting-point of the new vogue. But this type of research prospered among scholars who were far more interested in and committed to political ideology than Fraenkel ever was. R. Heinze in his postwar *Von den Ursachen der Grösse Roms* (1921) set the tone for the new inquiry which affected Rome more than Greece and progressed from one Roman virtue to the next until it ended in implicit or explicit Nazi-Fascist propaganda. Even the study of theological words – incorporated in the monumental *Theologisches Wörterbuch zum Neuen Testament* (1933 ff.) – was marred by racial prejudice, not to mention the methodological inadequacies which J. Barr was later to expose so convincingly (1961). The total result was, however, a new archive of ancient ideas as expressed in the Greek and Roman vocabu-

3

lary which has since made much difference to research into the Classics and early Christianity.

It is difficult now to account for the poor circulation of French *histoire des idées* in Italy during the period between 1920 and 1939. Neither Croce, who disliked both French rationalism and French irrationalism, nor Mussolini, who feared French democracy, can really be made responsible for this. All the research into *représentations collectives* which characterized the Durkheim–Mauss–Halbwachs tradition was (so far as I know) practically ignored in Italy. Marc Bloch was noticed in the 1930s as a pioneer student of agricultural systems, but not as the author of *Les Rois thaumaturges*.

This ignorance of course had its limits. A masterpiece such as *Il Giansenismo in Italia* by A. C. Jemolo (1928) would hardly have been possible without the French analysis of Port-Royal. Some years later Paul Hazard's *La Crise de la conscience européenne* (1935) made an impression and Henri Bremond's *Histoire littéraire du sentiment religieux en France* (1916 ff.), though more slowly, also left its mark. More significantly, A. Omodeo, who helped Croce in editing the *Critica*, rediscovered the French liberal historians of civilization from Guizot to Tocqueville in his effort to escape from German historicism and Italian *attualismo*.

But Italian historians of ideas remained indebted to the German tradition of *Ideengeschichte* and had to settle their accounts with it. The little-known *Storia d'una mente* by E. Grasselli (1932) tells in autobiographical terms how deep this commitment went. *La lotta contro la ragione* by Carlo Antoni (1942) and some of the earliest essays by Delio Cantimori (now in *Studi di storia*) are the first signs of the disentanglement which meant the end of the Crocean era.

It seems to me that the price English historians paid in the 1930s for remaining independent of German *Ideengeschichte* was to jettison their own tradition of the history of ideas. The main exception was at Cambridge, where Herbert Butterfield manfully battled against Namier and where E. M. Butler produced that singular criticism of German humanism, *The Tyranny of Greece over Germany* (1935). But the English mood of the late 1930s was expressed – at least for the ancient historians – by Ronald Syme when, in his *Roman Revolution*, he treated the Roman political vocabulary as 'political catchwords', 'a subject of partisan interpretation, of debate and of fraud'.

It is not for me to recount the story of the increasing impact of refugee German thought on English intellectual life and its convergence with old and new native trends during the 1940s and 1950s. Today, after fifty years, English and Italian historians find themselves again at the same level – which is one of lively interest in the history of ideas in both countries. There is nothing very surprising in this. The popularity of the history of ideas is a universal phenomenon. If there is something more specifically common both to Italian and English historians, it is that they are increasingly dependent on France and on the United States for their inspiration and their methods.

Again there are exceptions. Historians of ideas like E. H. Gombrich and Isaiah Berlin have no peers elsewhere in their command of the theoretical presuppositions of their work. On the other hand there is in Italy at least one historian of ideas, Franco Venturi, who, perhaps because of his French formation, dominates his own chosen fields of work – the European Enlightenment and Russian nineteenth-century reform movements – without any concession to fashionable currents. But in neither country is there anything that can be compared with the *Annales* or with structuralism as major movements of historical research. Nor is there anything like the less sophisticated but massive and effective American exploration of ideas from sociological points of view. Young historians both in England and in Italy are more and more thinking in terms of the circulation of ideas, cultures of the lower classes, collective representations, utopias and modern myths, acculturation, position of intellectuals and of holy men, structure of scientific revolutions, and so on – all of which seem to have either a French father or an American mother (possibly with a German grandfather).

In this enthusiasm for ideas, the most difficult thing is to know what one still means by an idea; attitudes, propaganda, dreams, subconscious needs, symbolic figures are included. The traditional oppositions between ideas and institutions, between ideology and society or, quite simply, between beliefs and facts have become far too crude to define the new levels of exploration. Even the dualism between consciousness and society ably exploited by H. Stuart Hughes (1959) is inadequate. This is certainly the point which the astute Michel Foucault has grasped in trying to put across his new *'archéologie du savoir'* to replace *'l'histoire des idées'* (*'affranchir l'histoire de la pensée de sa sujétion transcendentale'*).

It explains too why pure history of ideas, in the form elaborated in America by A. O. Lovejoy's group with its organ, the *Journal of History of Ideas* (1940), seems to be unable to indicate a clear direction in the present situation. With Lovejoy – notwithstanding the extraordinary merits of the research he did or inspired – one always had the feeling of a quasi-Platonic world where ideas could be counted. The Oxford profes-sor D. S. Margoliouth had the reputation of believing in the existence of thirty Indo-European Ur-jokes from which all the others derived. Love-joy did not believe that the number of Ur-ideas was much greater.

It was already very difficult to decide whether one could separate the ideological from the institutional element in the old notions of liberty, peace, federalism, chivalry, and so on. When we come to the collective representations of belief in witches, to the parson's wife or to the English nanny – not to mention the two classical examples of French origin: the idea of childhood and the idea of madness – the distinction becomes meaningless. It is indeed the impossibility of regulating *a priori* the traditional conflict of precedence between institutions and principles or between society and ideology that gives sense and zest to the new con-fusion. The period of experiment is bound to last for some time, and so is the confusion of languages. We hear less and less of orthodox Marx-ism; notice the transition from Marxism to structuralism of the most original and internationally influential French student of Greek thought, J.-P. Vernant. Russian Marxists do not help either, at least in the field of classical studies. The latest article on Freedom in Rome by E. M. Štaer-man in the *Vestnik Drevnej Istorii* 1972, No. 2, is a warning.

I hope it is not simply an ancient historian's prejudice to say that the new exploration in the field of ideas seems up to now more rewarding when remote cultures are its primary object. The mere task of finding linguistic and conceptual equivalents to our ways of thinking in other cultures – or alternatively the necessity of acknowledging that these equivalences do not exist – throws light on ourselves and on the others. I recollect the pleasure of recognizing that the ancient Egyptian attitudes to speech and silence could be a thread to guide me in my inexperience through the various stages of Egyptian civilization. And I have no doubt that the appearance of the notion of heresy in early Christianity and late Judaism means a caesura in patterns of thought and social organization.

But when we come to our own society we need to know what we can believe rather than what is believed. There is an inescapable question of truth, if the historian is to be a responsible actor in his own society and not a manipulator of opinions. This need, incidentally, seems to be taken too lightly by the various sociologies of knowledge, including the novel one of Foucault. The resulting paradox I may perhaps put in personal terms. When I became a professor at University College Lon-don more than twenty years ago, it did not take me long to realize that the best historians of ideas in the place were two practising scientists,

J. Z. Young and Peter Medawar. But the fact that they talked about sciences I did not know not only paralysed me in regard to them (which is easy to understand), but also paralysed them in regard to me or anybody else in my position. That is, they lacked the potential public necessary for developing their scientific ideas in an historical context.

To take another less personal example, it is perhaps characteristic of our time that we have so many discussions of the religious ideas of underdeveloped countries, but so little analysis of our own religious beliefs with the simple purpose of ascertaining their credibility. During recent years in Italy more scholarly books have appeared on heretical sects than on modern Catholicism. The men who would be able to illuminate the contemporary scene by talking about truth in its historical context have not yet found their public. Therefore we are left with the English nanny and the cargo cult for the expression of our nostalgias and dissatisfactions.

2

The Fault of the Greeks *

I

CONFUCIUS, Buddha, Zoroaster, Isaiah, Heraclitus – or Aeschylus.

The list would probably have puzzled my grandfather and his generation. It makes sense now; it symbolizes the change in our historical perspective. We can face, more or less from the same angle, cultures which seemed wide apart; and we can find something in common among them. On a synchronous line the names stand for a more 'spiritual' life, for a better order, for a reinterpretation of the relation between gods and men, for a criticism of the traditional values in each respective society. These men did not know one another. No obvious external link connects the emergence of such commanding figures in different cultures between, say, the eighth and the fifth centuries B.C. Yet we feel that we have now discovered a common denominator that makes all of them – to repeat the fashionable expression – 'relevant to us'. All of them were men who by proclaiming and expounding their personal religious beliefs gave a new meaning to human life and brought about profound changes in the societies to which they belonged.

We are thus led to ask the historical questions that will interpret this relevance more precisely and consequently make it more perceptible. What conditioned the appearance of so many 'wise men' in so many different cultures within relatively narrow chronological limits? Why indeed did the cultural changes have to be brought about by 'wise men'? What is the relation between the religious stance they took and the social message they conveyed? The very nature of the questions that come spontaneously to our minds indicates that the essence of our new position towards these men is that instead of seeing *each* of them as the

*Wisdom, Revelation and Doubt: Perspectives on the First Millennium B.C., Daedalus, Spring 1975 (issued as 104, 2 of the Proceed. Amer. Acad. of Arts and Sciences), pp. 9–19.

codifier of a new religion we now see *all* of them as reformers of the existing order. Our instinctive sympathy is for the human beings who by meditation and spiritual search freed themselves from the conventions within which they were born and reoriented the activities of other men. Though questions of 'truth' can never be avoided entirely, we feel that it is almost indecent (and in any case too embarrassing) to ask whether what Zoroaster or Isaiah or Aeschylus had to say was true or false. Each of them spoke his own individual language. It takes a very great effort to translate it into our own language. But if we succeed, we shall have established a bridge to minds worth knowing. These men can explain themselves directly to us by their own words; and we do our part by commenting on their words. Given the necessary knowledge of languages and texts, we may presume that at some future date we shall understand the *Gathas* in the same way in which we now understand the *Eumenides*.

Conversely we are put off by those civilizations that at the same period and apparently under the same technological conditions failed to produce questioners and reformers. Egypt, Assyria, and Babylonia rightly or wrongly appear spiritually stagnant and almost reactionary in the first millennium. Not without repressing some impatience we wonder why they went on accepting the traditional terms of the relationship between the society of men and the society of gods. Many years ago Henri Frankfort gave expression to the impatience we now feel: 'The Hebrew prophets rejected both the Egyptian and the Babylonian views. They insisted on the uniqueness and transcendence of God. For them all values were ultimately attributes of God; man and nature were devaluated, and every attempt to establish a harmony with nature was a futile dissipation of effort.'[1] It was, however, easier for Frankfort than it is for us to utter these words in good conscience. For he was simply reiterating the Prophets' repudiation of the idols of silver and of gold. Like the first Isaiah, he was concerned with Egypt and Assyria, but he never had to consider, with the second Isaiah, the rôle of Cyrus, the anointed of God. We have to add the Indians and the Chinese. We have certainly given ourselves the pleasure of feeling that if only we knew the languages we could talk to Buddha and to Confucius and to the other wise men of the archaic age. But this mental position remains unproblematic only until we come to ask ourselves what we really expect from it. The experience of Louis Dumont who went to India to recover the full meaning of *homo hierarchicus* in history – and gave a new dimension to our conception of individualism – may be exemplary, but is by no means common. The case of Henri Frankfort is indicative of the far more common situation, in which even the most original and profound research remains conditioned by our own civilization. I am saying this not to belittle the results, but on the contrary to point out the strength of our tradition. There is an old triangular culture – composed of Jewish, Greek and Latin intellectual products – which has an immediate impact on most of us that is of a quite different order from our professional or dilettante pleasure in the amenities of more distant civilizations. This *collegium trilingue*, in academic terms, still dominates our minds. Latin culture, one of the constituent members of the *collegium trilingue*, is conspicuously absent from the set of 'wise-men civilizations' that were our starting point. If we have to add something to the essential ingredients of our civilization as a result of medieval developments, it must come from Celts, Germans and Arabs – none of whom belong to the privileged list of the original 'wise-men civilizations'. The Arabs in fact add to our difficulties. Being themselves the carriers of a prophetic civilization – if ever there was one – and therefore uniquely close to Jews and Christians, they were a menace to the Christians, if not to the Jews. Serious contacts between Christian and Arab thought mainly occurred in those areas in which Arab thinkers worked with Greek concepts. We have indeed managed to forget our precise debt to Celts, Germans and Arabs, so much so that neither Old Irish nor *Mittelhochdeutsch* nor Arabic has ever become a regular requirement in our educational establishments. But we are never allowed to forget our debt to Greece, Latium and Judea. There are powerful pressure groups (whether classicists, theologians or rabbis) to keep us, quite properly, ashamed of our failure to read the right texts in the right language.

In so far as our inheritance goes back to antiquity, it is essentially Greek–Latin–Jewish *because* it is essentially Hellenistic. The notion of Hellenistic civilization defines both the time (323–30 B.C.) and the space (Mediterranean zone) in which these three cultures converged and began to react on one another. It follows that it is not superfluous to investigate the circumstances in which a new special relationship was established between Jews, Greeks and Romans in the Hellenistic age. We have many important investigations of the re-introduction of Persian, Indian and Chinese civilizations into the mental horizon of the Europeans in the seventeenth and eighteenth centuries. But the inverse inquiry about the exclusion of Persians and Indians, not to speak of Egyptians and Babylonians, from active participation in the civilization of Europe does not seem to have made much progress. The purpose of this paper is to contribute to such an investigation. It is hoped that by implication it can also throw some light on the nature of the 'wise-men phenomenon' that we found in the earlier part of the first millennium B.C. and on the relative isolation in which each 'wise-men civilization' operated.

II

Here again we must start from a paradox. Greek was the language that dominated the Hellenistic world after Alexander the Great. Greek was the language Jews and Latins had to acquire in order to get out of their isolation and to be acceptable in the higher society of the Hellenistic kingdoms. But there was no corresponding effort by the Greeks to understand and absorb Latin or Jewish culture. The foundation of the *collegium trilingue* is primarily a Roman and Jewish affair. No doubt Greeks had the training for geographical and historical discovery that enabled them to notice the peculiarities of Latins and Jews at the beginning of the Hellenistic Age. Before Alexander there is no sign that they knew about the Jews, and their knowledge of the Romans was confined to a few legends and even fewer historical data. About 300 B.C. Hecataeus of Abdera and Theophrastus made serious attempts to investigate the religion of the Jews. About 280–270 B.C. the Roman victory over Pyrrhus impressed the Greeks and induced Timaeus – a Sicilian exile who lived in Athens – to write extensively on the history and institutions of the Latins. But when their surprise was exhausted, the Greeks did not go further. There was no detailed study of Jewish or of Roman history by Greek scholars in the third century B.C.

When the Romans effectively destroyed the power of Carthage at the end of the third century B.C. and became the greatest power of the Western Mediterranean no independent Greek historian, so far as we know, thought it necessary to analyse their victory. What was added to Timaeus was produced either by Greek historians in the service of Hannibal or by Roman historians who had mastered the Greek language and presented the Roman case to a Hellenistic audience. As for the Jews, we know (or suspect) that there were some Hellenized Egyptians who concocted a hostile version of the Exodus – a reflection of the friction between Jews and Egyptians in Alexandria, where the Jewish community was rapidly expanding. But we do not know of any ethnographical research to add to that of Hecataeus and Theophrastus. Hermippus of Smyrna, Agatharchides of Cnidus and Menander of

Ephesus, who lived in the second century, alluded to the Jews in various contexts, but did not deliberately inquire into their history. The works written in Greek about Jews and Romans between 260 and 160 B.C. seem to have been mainly polemical: the most informative was by Fabius Pictor, a Roman aristocrat (about 215–200 B.C.).

The Greeks remained proudly monolingual as, with rare exceptions, they had been for centuries. It was not for them to converse with the natives in the natives' languages. They were not acquainted with either Latin or Hebrew literature. There was no tradition of translating foreign books into Greek. The Septuagint translation of the Bible was almost certainly performed by Jews on their private initiative and only later attributed to the initiative of Ptolemy II Philadelphus. All the evidence available on the diplomatic relations between Romans and Greeks – even after the Romans had become the masters of the Greek world – points to the conclusion that the Romans spoke Greek, whereas the Greeks did not speak Latin. As for Hebrew and Aramaic, the two languages necessary for understanding the written and oral culture of the Jews, I am not aware that any Hellenistic Greek tried to acquire them.

The dialogue with the Greeks happened because the Romans and the Jews wanted it. The zeal with which the Romans learned Greek and built up their literature on Greek models is surprising. Even more surprising is the readiness of Hellenized Umbrians (Plautus), Oscans (Naevius and Ennius), Libyans (Terence) and Celts (Statius Caecilius) to write in Latin. With the partial exception of Cato, who considered himself a Sabine, archaic Latin literature is the work of men whose original language was not Latin, but who saw a future in producing Latin works inspired by Greek models. Aristocratic Romans seem to have reserved for themselves the task of composing histories, memoirs and speeches in Greek in order to impress the Greeks. The absorption of Greek culture among the Romans therefore takes the double form of offering to the non-Latin intelligentsia of Italy the means of creating a common literature in Latin on Greek models *and* of educating the Roman aristocracy to think and speak in Greek as a part of its imperial functions.

The Jews learned Greek for other reasons. They were ruled by Graeco-Macedonian kings in the third and second centuries B.C. and had to speak to officials who understood only Greek. But it is characteristic of the Jewish immigrants in Egypt that they rapidly forgot Hebrew and Aramaic, while they preserved their religious and national identity. This was made possible by translating the Bible in the third and second centuries B.C. At the same time the Jews felt the need to justify to themselves their own beliefs and ways of life in comparison with those of the Greeks. They did so both in Hebrew–Aramaic and in Greek. Ecclesiasticus, for instance, was first written in Hebrew and then translated into Greek (by a grandson of the original author) in the second century B.C. If Ecclesiastes belongs to the third or second century B.C., it can give us the measure of the sophistication with which a Jew could react to the alien wisdom.

The Romans and the Jews had this in common in their relation to the Greeks, that ultimately they were in no doubt about the superiority of their own respective ways of life. The attempt to impose Greek gods and customs on Judea about the middle of the second century was short lived and provoked deep resentment. More or less at the same time Roman conservatives, like Cato, condemned the penetration of Greek habits into Rome and succeeded in controlling and harnessing them for the benefit of the Roman ruling class. The persecution of the members of a new Dionysiac sect in Italy indicated the limits of what the Roman rulers were prepared to accept. The Romans, being polytheist and having no fear for their independence and power, could of course afford to develop in their relations with the Greeks their traditional receptiveness to foreign ideas and foreign art – provided that it did not interfere with the stability of the ruling class. The Jews had far deeper motives for their reluctance to accept the philosophy and the art of Greece. Full acceptance was equivalent to apostasy (which seems to have been rare), and partial acceptance implied, to say the least, theoretical contradictions and practical difficulties. What has to be emphasized here is that both Jews and Romans decided to learn Greek in order to compare their own ways with those of the Greeks and to shape their intellectual life in relation to the Greeks. The outcome was predictably very different in each case. But both Romans and Jews found a new sense of national identity in measuring themselves with the Greeks. The Romans soon became the aggressors and the conquerors of the Greek world in the second century B.C. The Jews could have no such ambitions, but in the circumstances of the decline of the Seleucid state, and with the help of the Romans, they expanded considerably and even violently imposed conversion to Judaism on some of their neighbours.

III

Given the indifference prevailing among the Greeks towards the Jewish and Roman cultures, any individual Greek who happened to become deeply involved with the Jews or the Romans found himself in the position of a defector: a convert if he liked Judaism, a collaborationist if he admired Roman imperialism. The phenomenon of total or partial conversion to Judaism, though to all appearances widespread, does not seem to have produced literary works in the Hellenistic period. But the collaboration of individual Greeks with the Romans left its mark on literature. Livius Andronicus, who translated the *Odyssey* and composed the first comedy and the first tragedy in Latin, had perhaps no choice: he was brought to Rome as a slave. But Polybius had a choice, even if limited. He came to Rome as a hostage in 167 B.C. and threw his lot in with the Romans, to the point of advising them in the siege of Carthage and acting as their agent in Greece before and after the destruction of Corinth. Polybius did not, however, identify himself with the Romans to the point of never criticizing them. My impression (which is not shared by the greatest living authority on him, Professor F. W. Walbank) is that as his work progressed he became increasingly anxious about the ruthlessness of Roman policy in the Greek world. But this simply proves that his identification with Roman interests made him anxious about Roman mistakes. This – even more emphatically – is the case with his continuator Posidonius, who as an aristocrat in the city of Rhodes had more room for manoeuvre. Writing after the Social War and the tyranny of Sulla, he was outspokenly critical of Roman exploitation in the provinces. Trusted and supported by powerful Roman friends, of whom Pompey was one, he could afford to speak out clearly on his and their behalf against what he considered subversive forces in Roman society.

Neither Jewish proselytism nor the attraction of Rome for stray Greek intellectuals would have made a great difference to the surrounding world if the hostility of the majority of the Greeks and Hellenized Orientals to Roman exploitation had not forced the Romans to change their methods of governing the Empire. Twice in the first century B.C. native rulers (Mithridates, King of Pontus; Cleopatra, Queen of Egypt) joined hands with dissident Roman leaders to fight the central government of Rome and found considerable support in Greek public opinion. In two other cases – the fight of Pompey against Caesar and of the

Caesaricides against the heirs of Caesar – the decisive struggles happened in Greece or Macedonia, where dissatisfaction with Rome could be expected to enlist support in anything that looked like change. Augustus recognized the implications of this half-century of unrest in the Eastern provinces. Under the cover of an alleged restoration of Italian values (which had actually never existed) he effectively reduced the oppression of the Eastern provinces: peace itself worked its wonders. The Greek East acclaimed Augustus as its saviour; and he left behind the bilingual monument of the *Res Gestae*. The Greeks *en masse* became involved in the development of a bilingual Graeco-Latin society.

It was precisely in the atmosphere of the Augustan peace that the Jews produced a sect that soon turned to Greek proselytes and to the Greek language as its main sphere of action. It may be surmised that the Christian mission appealed first to those Greek-speaking provincials who had been left cool by the reorientation of Roman imperialism. The Christians created a society that placed its values, interests and leaders outside the conventions of the Roman state. For some time there appeared to be a basic conflict between the supporters of the Graeco-Roman Empire and the followers of Christ. The philhellenic Nero was the first persecutor of Christians. But slowly the conflict was turned into collaboration. Since Clemens Alexandrinus, Christianity had claimed its share in the Greek cultural inheritance. When Constantine became a convert to Christianity he made a Greek city of the East the second capital of the Empire. The *Hellenes* turned into *Romaioi* – a word which came to imply allegiance both to the Roman Empire and to Christianity. The Greeks recognized themselves as Romans when the Roman Empire declared itself Christian.

To sum up: Latins and Jews started the building of the *collegium trilingue*, while the Greeks were uninterested in it. They learned Greek, absorbed Greek thoughts and manners, and questioned Greek values at the time when the Greeks still treated foreigners as curiosities. Slowly both Jews and Romans made proselytes in their own fashion: converts for Jerusalem, collaborators for Rome. The consequences became apparent when the *Pax Augusta* offered new terms to the Greek subjects. The Empire became a joint enterprise of Greeks and Romans. At the same time there were Jews who saw themselves in the Messianic age in which the difference between Jews and Gentiles was deleted. Christianity brought Jewish values to the Greeks in the Greek language as a *de facto* alternative to the consolidation of Graeco-Roman society that was pursued by the ruling class of the Roman Empire. The result, however, did not correspond to the initial assumption. By the beginning of the fourth century the Bible in its Greek and Latin versions (Old and New Testaments) had become the sacred book of the Roman Empire. By the end of the fourth century, thanks mainly to St Jerome, knowledge of Hebrew was recognized as a useful, if not necessary, ingredient for the understanding of the Bible. Hebrew, of course, never acquired a status comparable to Greek and Latin in Christian society. But a book that had once been written in Hebrew, the Bible, became, to say the least, an equal partner to Greek Philosophy and Roman Law. When in 1428 Giovanni Rucellai married a daughter of Palla Strozzi, Leonardo Bruni congratulated the bridegroom on having acquired a father-in-law who possessed 'tutte a sette le parti della felicità'. One of the seven parts of happiness was to be 'virtuoso et scientiato in greco et in latino'.[2] But in 1553 Caspar Stiblin in his Utopia, the *Respublica Eudaemonensium*, required 'trium linguarum peritia' of his theologians. Until Sanskrit made its appearance in the schools of the nineteenth century, these two texts might have been treated as literally representative of the cultural situation.

We can therefore correct, and improve upon, our statement that the triangle of our culture is Hellenistic. It was certainly in the Hellenistic atmosphere that the Latins and the Jews acquired the Greek language, assimilated Greek ideas, and questioned the Greek way of life. But the fusion of Greek, Latin and Jewish traditions is Christian. The Jews (and the Arabs) continued to face Greek thought in isolation. They were never deeply concerned with Latin ways of living or thinking.

IV

We have now to make explicit a situation that is implicit in the preceding exposition. The triangle was brought about by the pressure of Latins and Jews. The original reaction of the Greeks was a refusal to involve themselves deeply in foreign ways of thinking. They never had the curiosity to learn either Latin or Hebrew. This is only one of the manifestations of what we may well call the normal attitude of the Greeks to foreign civilizations as we know it from the time of Homer onwards. Whether Homer was right or wrong in taking the Trojans as Greek speakers is beside the point. What matters is that his very humane understanding of conflicts presupposes monolingualism. The Greeks were unique in antiquity in their ability to describe and define the customs of foreigners. They could analyse their institutions, religious beliefs, daily habits, even their diet. They invented what we still recognize as the valid science of ethnography. They did this with a basic sympathy for foreigners. We know how Herodotus, one of the founding masters of ethnography, was ready to declare 'barbarian' customs superior to the Hellenic ones. But it was a cool, ultimately self-assured, look at foreign civilizations. There was no temptation to yield to them. In fact there was no desire to get to know them intimately by mastering foreign languages. It was observation from outside, clever, searching, fair, occasionally humorous. In Herodotus, Scythians, Babylonians, Egyptians and Libyans are observed in turn. What emerges is the superiority of the Greek love of freedom.

There are some curious aspects of this habit of mind. We would expect the Massaliotes, Greek settlers among the Celts, to take a keen interest in the habits of their neighbours. They had their great explorers – Euthymenes (sixth century?), Pytheas (fourth century). But they explored the distant lands and seas of Africa and Northern Europe, not the Celtic hinterland. The Massaliote contribution to knowledge of the Celts seems to have been very small. The Celts really began to be known to the Greeks when they invaded Greece and Asia Minor in the third century B.C. Notice also the strange fact that Persia was less carefully observed by the Greeks in the fourth than in the fifth century B.C. Yet Greek politics were dominated by the Persian question from Lysander to Alexander. The intellectual response of the fourth century was in the harem stories of Ctesias and Dinon or in the idealization of King Cyrus by Antisthenes and Xenophon. When the foreigner was a permanent big problem (as the Celts must have been to the Massaliotes, and the Persians certainly were to the fourth-century Greeks) silence or escapism was perhaps the usual reaction.

We are therefore beginning to suspect that if Zoroaster, Buddha and Confucius have long remained separated from us, the barrier was first built up on the Greek side of the triangle. As far as the Greeks were concerned, they would have done without the Jewish prophets, too.

Such a conclusion would be a gross simplification, because in the second part of the fourth century a new interest in (and respect for) Zoroaster, the Magi, the Brahmans and Hermes Trismegistus (that is, Egyptian wisdom) becomes apparent in Greece. But an analysis of this change can ultimately only confirm the superficial impact of Oriental wisdom on the Greeks. Plato no doubt encouraged interest in Oriental wisdom. I myself doubt whether he knew much about genuine Oriental thought. I cannot take the story of Er as an authentically Eastern myth, and I do not believe that the *Alcibiades major*, the only dialogue in which Zoroaster appears, was written by Plato. Yet Plato's friend Eudoxus went to Egypt and was considered a great authority on astrology. Plato's pupil, Heraclides Ponticus, wrote a work, perhaps a dialogue, called *Zoroaster*. The Epicurean Colotes (third century B.C.) could joke about Plato's alleged borrowings from Zoroaster. In the late (first century B.C.?) pseudo-Platonic *Axiochus*, a Magus has the right information about the other world. If the attribution of a book on Magi to Aristotle is false, it came nonetheless from his school. Aristotle's friend and pupil Aristoxenus surmised that Pythagoras had been a pupil of the Chaldaean Zaratas (by whom he meant the Iranian Zarathustra). Other strange pieces of information circulated in antiquity. Pliny the Elder claimed to know that the Peripatetic Hermippus (about 200 B.C.) 'commented upon two million verses left by Zoroaster, besides completing indexes to his several works'.[3] The Byzantine Syncellus found somewhere that Ptolemy Philadelphus had Egyptian and Chaldaean, not to mention Latin, books translated for his library.[4] Much has been made of the story of the Dinkart (itself a ninth-century document) that the 'evil destined villain Alexander' had the Avesta translated into Greek.[5]

When, however, one asks what was actually known by Greeks and Latins about Zoroastrianism or any religion of India, the evidence is disappointing. I am not acquainted with any certain proof that either the *Gathas* or any other Zoroastrian text were known to Greek or Latin authors before the third century A.D. David Flusser has recently claimed that the *Oracula Sibyllina* 8, 439–55 contain an allusion to *Yasna* 44, 3–5:[6] the observation, as one would expect from such a scholar, is acute, but direct dependence does not seem to me probable. Genuine Persian lore can almost certainly be traced in the *Borysthenicus* by Dio Chrysostomus, but it is mixed with Greek speculation to such an extent as to make a written source unlikely.

What we are saying about Iranian religious texts applies even more to Indian doctrines. Asoka certainly made an effort to communicate some of the basic Buddhist truths to the Greeks, but we have no indication that his inscriptions were widely noticed, and even less that they encouraged further study. The Christianized life of Buddha, as we have it in the story of Barlaam and Ioasaph, belongs to the seventh to eighth century A.D., and has no obvious Hellenistic or Roman precedent. Megasthenes (early third century B.C.) reported with care what he saw. But the efforts of students of Indian religion (such as Allan Dahlquist) to disentangle the Indian from the Greek in Megasthenes' accounts of Dionysus and Heracles look rather pathetic. I can see no direct, widespread and influential penetration of Indian doctrines into Greek thought in the Hellenistic period. Genuine Greek developments, such as Cynicism, naturally invited attention (and sympathy) for comparable Indian phenomena, but this meant finding what one knew. Though Egypt is outside our 'wise-men civilizations', we may add that genuine religious Egyptian thought did not fare any better. Very little of the authentic Isis was left in her Greek version. Direct knowledge of Egyptian texts was rare. The Potter's Oracle, for instance, appears to have been thoroughly Hellenized, if there ever was a genuine Egyptian document behind it.

If we have to resort to a generalization about the fortunes of Oriental thought in the Hellenistic world and in its Roman prolongation, we must say that the mass of writings claiming to be translations from Oriental languages were mainly forgeries by writers in Greek. What circulated in Greek under the names of Zoroaster, Hystaspes, Thoth and even Abraham was quite simply faked, though no doubt some of the writings contained a modicum of 'Oriental' thoughts combined with Greek ideas. Porphyry was asked by Plotinus to uncover the forgery of an Apocalypse attributed to Zoroaster (*Vita Plotini* 16). This must have been less difficult than discovering the true date of the Book of Daniel – Porphyry's best known performance.

This mass of fakes provides problems for the historian of classical thought. It indicates the need for revealed, authoritative religious knowledge of a kind that was not easily available in the Greek tradition. It suggests a new 'openness' among the Greek educated classes to ideas coming from other nations. All this would seem natural enough in the social and political situation brought about by the destruction of the Persian Empire. On the other hand, the old disinclination of the Greeks to learn foreign languages is only too plainly confirmed by these products. Hardly anyone had the linguistic knowledge to recognize the swindles. True enough, after Plato Oriental wise men became real to the Greeks, as they had not been before. But what passed for their thoughts was to a great extent Greek fabrication – no genuine Buddha or Zarathustra, let alone Confucius, was known to the Greeks. Thus the change that was brought about by the Platonic and post-Platonic appreciation of 'Oriental' wisdom did not amount to genuine incorporation of Persian and Indian thought in the Greek mental world. An unreal Oriental world was created to satisfy the craving for revealed and mysterious wisdom. There was consequently no reason why a distinction should be made between the old-fashioned civilizations of Egypt and Mesopotamia and the more modern ones of Persia and India. The astrological works attributed to Abraham show that Jewish names were equally suitable carriers of such a concoction. But the existence of a Bible in Greek – even if it was not read outside the circle of Jewish and Christian proselytes – prevented the growth of a fanciful Judaism at the side of the real one. Zoroastrians and Buddhists were either less determined or less fortunate than the Jews in conveying to the Greeks the genuine thoughts of their masters.

In the *collegium trilingue* the Greeks were the only partners who had both the intellectual instruments and the dispassionate curiosity for analysing foreign civilizations in general. Their reluctance to study and grasp authentic Iranian and Indian thought was therefore decisive for the development of European culture. The Jews absorbed many Iranian ideas (as they had previously absorbed many Babylonian ideas). But they incorporated them in their own religious convictions without recognizing them as alien. The Romans in their turn knew how to exploit the Greek science of ethnography for their political purposes. As I have tried to show elsewhere, they encouraged, and even ordered, Greek experts to explore, describe and map for them the Celtic lands and Parthia. Indeed, in so far as they accepted Greek values, the Romans acquired an interest in ethnography and geography as intellectual pursuits. But they never improved on Greek methods. Strabo knew quite well that geography was a Greek science. It is therefore the Greeks who must be made responsible, if this is the word, for the barrier that for so long kept the Iranians, the Indians, and, *a fortiori* (geographically), the Chinese outside our sphere of knowledge and values.

V

The Jews broke the barrier because they wanted to break it. Otherwise they would have found themselves in the same position as the Persians and Indians in their relation to the Greeks. They were of course helped by geography. The Jews lived in organized communities in Alexandria, Rome and other centres of cultural and political life. Until A.D. 70 they had also the prestige of successful rebels. The Parthians and others merely seceded – and kept to the Hellenistic forms. The Jews revolted and presented an un-Hellenic, theocratic image of themselves to the world. The early Christians inherited this challenging attitude. To many Greeks or Hellenized Orientals, who felt the need of revealed truth and charismatic guidance, Moses and Jesus would have the direct, authentic appeal of leaders of genuine and recognizable congregations in the neighbourhood.

The Jews may also have had something in common with the Greeks, which the Persians and Indians did not have: the awareness of institutional developments in their precise historical circumstances. By translating the Bible, the Jews presented their national history in chapters full of memorable episodes. The Christians added new chapters and memorable new episodes in the New Testament. Thus to become a Jewish or Christian proselyte meant having to learn a new history – which was an operation understandable to any educated Greek. It may also be that the Jewish–Christian interpretations of the godhead were easily reconcilable with the leading philosophies of Plato, Aristotle and Zeno. At least the later history of philosophy seems to support the view that Athens and Jerusalem did not contradict one another. Even such a convinced supporter of the radical opposition between Athens and Jerusalem as Lev Isaakovich Shestov admits that history is against him: 'History would tell us that the greatest representatives of the human spirit have, for almost two thousand years, rejected all the attempts which have been made to oppose Athens to Jerusalem, that they have always passionately maintained the conjunction "and" between Athens and Jerusalem and stubbornly refused "or".'[7]

These speculations will not, however, take us very far. The fact is that the Greek wise men always operated within the *polis*, always accepted its gods and very seldom rejected its conventional morality. If we exclude the Cynics, whom nobody except themselves considered wise, the Greek image of wisdom was a higher form of civic virtue. Where religious sanction was sought (the Pythagoreans and Socrates did), it did not challenge recognized rites or sanctuaries. Socrates was notoriously approved of by Delphi: he even accepted condemnation in accordance with an ordinary law of his own city. The traditions about the Seven Wise Men, which were given coherence in the fifth century B.C., insist on the down-to-earth, albeit slightly eccentric, contents of their teaching. Confucius might have become one of the Wise Men if he had been known. But Isaiah, Zoroaster and Buddha had no chance. To begin with, they were mutually exclusive, which the Greek wise men were not. With the prophetic men of the East it was a question of who got in first. We shall not presume to say why.

References

1. Henri Frankfort, *Kingship and the Gods*, Chicago, 1948, p. 6.
2. G. Rucellai, *Il Zibaldone Quaresimale*, ed. A. Perosa, London, 1960, p.
3. *Nat. Hist.* 30.4.
4. 271 D, p. 516, Bonn.
5. Bidez-Cumont, *Les Mages Hellenisés*, II, 137.
6. David Flusser, 'A Quotation from the Ghathas in a Christian Sib Oracle', *Ex Orbe Religionum, Studia G. Widengren*, Leiden, 1972, pp. 172–
7. L. I. Shestov, *Athens and Jerusalem*, trans. B. Martin, New York: and Schuster, 1968, p. 47.

3

Eastern Elements in Post-Exilic Jewish, and Greek, Historiography *

OF the historians of our time only Eduard Meyer has attempted to assess the place of the Persian empire of the Achaemenids in the formation of the civilizations of the Jews and of the Greeks. It is no coincidence that his article on ancient Persia, written about 1911 for the *Encyclopaedia Britannica*, has not yet been superseded.[1]

The complexity of the problem is obvious; and it is also obvious that the paucity of the Persian sources puts an extremely serious limitation on any study.[2] By and large one senses that the Greeks and Jews of the fifth century B.C. were moving towards the formation of strongly national or nationalistic civilizations – or strongly political, if one prefers – in reaction to the cosmopolitan and tolerant despotism of the Persians, while themselves profiting from that cosmopolitanism and tolerance. Themistocles and Nehemiah, who feverishly supervised the building of walls that were to isolate and fortify their respective cities, were the representatives of the new culture. The intolerance towards mixed marriages in the re-established state of Judaea has its counterpart in Pericles' laws on Athenian citizenship. On the other hand both the Second Isaiah and Aeschylus recognized the moral qualities of the Persian rulers and reflected upon them.

The question is whether the reform of Jewish historiography and the formation of Greek historiography should also be placed against the background of positive and negative reactions to Persia.

As yet we have no evidence of any direct contact between Jews and Greeks in the sixth and fifth centuries B.C. With all respect for that courageous and original scholar, Franz Dornseiff, Photius was certainly

*Paper given at the Convegno Internazionale on the subject 'Persia and the Graeco-Roman World' of the Accademia dei Lincei, 11–14 April 1965. The following notes are intended purely as guidelines.

confused when, in his summary of Diodorus Book XL, he attributed a description of the Jewish religion to Hecataeus of Miletus: the Hecataeus in question was Hecataeus of Abdera, and at most one may suspect that the confusion was already present in Diodorus.[3] Jewish historiography of the post-exilic period and Greek historiography of the fifth century should therefore be considered parallel phenomena; it is legitimate to speculate whether the affinities between them should be explained in terms of similar reactions to the common background of the Persian empire.

*

In the international society of the sixth and fifth centuries B.C. stories circulated internationally. The pagan story of Achikar was already known to the Jews of Elephantine in the fifth century B.C. and reappears in the Book of Tobit.[4] The story of Otanes and Pseudo-Smerdis in Herodotus has tones which are reminiscent of those of the later (third century B.C.?) Book of Esther. Otanes encourages his daughter Phaedima, who is in the harem of Pseudo-Smerdis, to unmask the impostor. The words of Otanes: 'Daughter, you are of noble blood' – and Phaedima's reply – 'It will be very risky . . . but nonetheless I shall try' (Book III, 69) are closely reminiscent of the messages passed between Mordecai and Esther, and particularly of Esther's reply: 'And if I perish, I perish.' Similarly Holofernes in the Book of Judith gains information about the Jews in a way that is reminiscent of Atossa's questions about the Athenians in Aeschylus's *Persians*. There is no need here to discuss the date of the Book of Judith, which does not seem to have been written earlier than the second century B.C.[5] Themes of earlier story-telling are clearly included in it. When Wilamowitz made his debatable observation that the story of Judith could have had a place among the stories of Parthenius,[6] he was implicitly recognizing that, however much the heroine had by now been painted in Pharisaic colours, she belonged to the international fund of stories of the Persian empire. Thus, to quote a final example, it was easy for Nöldeke[7] to point to genuine Eastern parallels – Persian and Indian – to Herodotus' story of the wife of Intaphernes who preferred to save her brother rather than her husband and children, because she could never again have other brothers, her mother and father being dead, whereas she could still hope to find another husband and have other children (Book III, 119).

The international circulation of the themes of these stories makes it likely that the Book of Esther was the transformation into a Jewish tale

26

of a story that originally explained the source of a non-Jewish festival.[8] For the same reason it is by no means impossible that Persians and Phoenicians should have produced variants of Greek myths about the origins of the hostilities between Greeks and barbarians, as Herodotus suggests at the beginning of his *Histories*. K. Reinhardt has defended the fundamental accuracy of Herodotus' information precisely on the basis of a reassessment of the contacts between Greeks and Persians.[9] The only theory which seems incredible in the present state of our knowledge is that of Arthur Christensen, that the Eastern stories of Herodotus, Ctesias and Xenophon could have been obtained directly or indirectly from a corpus of written middle-Persian epic.[10] There is as yet no proof that this middle-Persian epic ever existed.

★

It is clear, however, that the existence of international themes of story-telling has a very limited importance for the explanation of Jewish post-exilic and Greek historiography. No doubt many features of the Books of Judith and Esther can be explained in terms of international story-telling with a Persian background; and the same is true of several stories in the first Books of Herodotus, in Ctesias and, up to a certain point, in the *Cyropaedia* of Xenophon. This interpretation may also be extended to the stories of Xanthus the Lydian and the *Persica* of Hellanicus of Mytilene, as far as we can tell from the fragments. But the substance of the work which we conventionally divide into the Books of Ezra and Nehemiah, like the substance of Herodotus, can clearly not be interpreted in terms of story-telling. At this point we must completely separate post-exilic Jewish historiography from the emergent Greek historiography and ask ourselves what the contact with Persian culture and the Persian state meant for each of them.

In a way post-exilic Jewish historiography continues the traditional chronicles of the two kingdoms. But with the arrival of Ezra and Nehemiah a new voice is heard: it is represented by the autobiographical fragments of the two founders of Judaism – fragments which now form the most characteristic part of the Books of Ezra and Nehemiah.

From the point of view of our problem it is not very important to decide if Nehemiah, as seems probable, preceded Ezra in his activities in Jerusalem,[11] nor what part the compiler of Chronicles played in putting together the existing text on the basis of the autobiographies of Ezra and Nehemiah and of other documents. What matters to us is that Ezra and Nehemiah should have written contemporary history, not organized in an impersonal chronicle form, but centred autobiographically around the political and religious activity of the writer. The historian is here the actor; he talks of direct experiences and events he has lived through. The nocturnal visit of Nehemiah to the ruined walls of Jerusalem is unforgettable: 'And I arose in the night, I and some few men with me; neither told I any man what my God had put in my heart to do at Jerusalem. . . . And I went out by night by the gate of the valley . . . and viewed the walls of Jerusalem, which were broken down, and the gates thereof were consumed with fire' (Nehemiah ii, 12–13).

It is most improbable that this narrative in the first person had a parallel in the chronicles of the kings of Persia. Royal chronicles naturally existed in Persia: Ctesias boasted of having examined them; according to the Book of Esther, they were consulted by King Ahasuerus one night when he could not sleep; and, conclusively, they were invoked by the enemies of the Jews in a document quoted by the Book of Ezra (iv, 15). But there is no reason to believe that these Persian chronicles departed from the usual impersonal style of Eastern annalistic writing.

As was seen, possibly for the first time, by Sigmund Mowinckel, the style of the memoirs of Ezra and Nehemiah must be compared with the style of the Assyro–Babylonian and Persian inscriptions of kings and princes who narrated their own deeds in autobiographical form.[12] However, G. von Rad has recently noted, perspicaciously, that Asiatic models offer no parallel for the tone of self-recommendation which is so characteristic of the fragments of Nehemiah's memoirs: 'Think upon me, my God, for good, according to all that I have done for this people' (Nehemiah, V, 19). On the other hand, a closer parallel for this justification of the writer in the face of God is provided, as von Rad observes, by the Egyptian autobiographical inscriptions which begin with the Twenty-Second Dynasty and continue until the Roman period.[13]

It is not difficult to accept that the style of Ezra and Nehemiah was influenced, directly or indirectly, by numerous Oriental models of Babylonian, Egyptian or Persian origin, made accessible by translations into Aramaic. It is known, for instance, that an Aramaic version of the Behistun inscription was read by the Jews of Elephantine in Egypt more or less at the time of Ezra and Nehemiah.[14] But something remains which at least in the present state of our knowledge cannot be traced to any model and constitutes the original reaction of the two Jewish reformers. They faced up to the politico-religious problems of a new community, and implied and expounded the legislative activity of a representative assembly. Above the writer there was certainly a god to whom he must justify his own actions; but before the writer there was a people with its own will, which reacted to the reformer's initiatives and ultimately made the decisions. The actions of Ezra and Nehemiah culminate in a new pact between God and Israel, not between God and the writer. For this reason the autobiographical style is bent to a new aim, to recounting the formation of a community built not on autocratic foundations, but on the principle of the pact between God and people through the intermediary of a reformer who paradoxically derives his powers from the King of Persia. In Ezra and Nehemiah an autobiographical form originally destined to extol an individual is used to narrate the birth of a new politico-religious organization.

*

We must naturally approach the origin of Greek historiography from another point of view.

The first Greek geographer, Scylax of Caryanda, was in the service of King Darius in his explorations of the regions of the Indus (Herodotus, Book IV, 44), but it is possible that later on he went to Athens.[15] The first critical student of genealogies and periegeses, Hecataeus of Miletus, was a rebel against Persia. Herodotus himself was born within the Persian empire. The geographical and ethnological exploration which characterized the beginnings of Greek historiography (the interest in foreign peoples, in differing customs, in geographical discoveries) originated in the Persian empire and was made easier by the empire itself. In the case of Scylax, exploration was paid for by Persia. In this context an awareness of the differences between the Greek and the Eastern traditions developed – not always to the advantage of the Greeks. Hecataeus discovered that the tales of the Greeks were many and ridiculous, and was humiliated by Egyptian priests when in the normal fashion of a Greek aristocrat he recited his family tree which linked him, over fifteen generations, to a god (Herodotus, Book II, 143).

Herodotus in his turn organized all his ethnographical exploration in relation to the war between Persia and Greece and explained the victory of the Greeks as due to the superiority of their way of life, and more especially to the democracy of Athens.

For Hecataeus and Herodotus contact with the Persian empire was above all an experience of critical rediscovery of their national tradition in comparison with other traditions. In the same conditions, and with the direct example of the Greeks, a Lydian historian writing in Greek, Xanthus, carried out a similar exploration of his own national tradition.

As in the case of Ezra and Nehemiah, though in entirely different ways, contact with Persia reactivated national consciousness.

The atmosphere of vigorous personal initiative which Persia aroused and partly encouraged was probably responsible for the attention paid by Herodotus – and presumably by Scylax and Hecataeus – to their own and other people's personal experiences. We know that Scylax wrote the biography of Heraclides of Mylasa, a tyrant under the Persian regime who later (it seems) fought against the Persians at the Battle of Artemisium. The tone of an autobiographical memoir was certainly lacking in Herodotus, and must also have been lacking in Hecataeus. Personal recollections or judgements in the first person are relatively rare (although they are very significant when they occur). There are other reasons for believing that the taste for biography, which is so conspicuous in Herodotus, comes from the Orient. Herodotus does not have many personal stories about Greeks from Greece. Even the most interesting heroes of the Persian Wars have no biography. There is no story about Themistocles. Clearly the Greek setting of Athens or Sparta did not provide Herodotus with the necessary material. But the Eastern section of his history is rich in biographical accounts. In some cases there can be no doubt that the story actually goes back to a family tradition or indeed to autobiographical accounts of the protagonist. Unfortunately the biography of the tyrant of Mylasa, Heraclides, is entirely lost; it was written, as we said, by Scylax of Caryanda, and must have been a model for such Graeco–Persian experiments. But several episodes in Herodotus may give us an idea of what it was like. The story of Democedes in Book III is a well-known example. A doctor at the Persian court, as the historian Ctesias was to be a hundred years later, Democedes exploited his position to return to his native land, just as Nehemiah exploited his position as cup-bearer. The authenticity of the situation is confirmed by one of the Egyptian autobiographical inscriptions, which tells of the benefits accruing to an Egyptian temple from the intimacy of the protagonist, also a doctor, with the King of Persia.[16] Democedes, like Nehemiah, had a political mission, but differed from Nehemiah in being divided in his loyalties: nostalgic attachment to his native Croton made him abandon the King of Persia. Herodotus' information must go back directly or indirectly to a tale told by Democedes. Only Democedes could tell of the illnesses of Darius and Atossa, which marked the beginning of his successful career. A little further on in the same book Herodotus tells another of his more adventurous stories, the one about Zopyrus who betrayed the rebel city of Babylon to Darius. Herodotus implies (Book III, 160) that the story was told him by a grandson of this Zopyrus, who had fled to Athens. The accuracy of this story, already contested by Ctesias, does not concern us.[17] In this case, too, a personal anecdote with a political background is placed on the Graeco–Persian borders, and comes from people who had lived in Persia or were actually Persians. It is significant that two of the very few personal stories told by Thucydides were also stories from the Graeco–Persian borderland: the adventures of Pausanias in Byzantium and the flight of Themistocles. Later the personal adventure was to be formalized into a traditional pattern of biography or memoir, while Ctesias was to exaggerate its more irresponsible and fictional aspects. It would be interesting to know more about the autobiographical memoirs of Ion of Chios, from which some delightful details about his friend Sophocles have come down to us. What model, if any, could have inspired them?[18]

For the moment it is enough for us to note that, within the Persian empire, the Greeks were beginning to gain a scientific knowledge of geography and of the features of their own history, and to take an interest in personal events of a political nature. Possibly through contact with the Persians and other Eastern peoples, their capacity to express themselves autobiographically, already demonstrated in poetry, was increasing.

*

Before concluding, there is one further aspect that is worth at least a mention.

The Persian state was bureaucratic, and took care of its archives. Already Herodotus (Book III, 128; *cf.* Book I, 99) implicitly and Hellanicus (fr. 178 Jacoby) explicitly knew that the Persian kings communicated by letter. The documents quoted in the Books of Ezra and Nehemiah are of Persian origin and presuppose archives in some sort of order, but not too well ordered (Ezra vi, 1–2). After the studies of Eduard Meyer, Elias Bickerman (*quem honoris causa nomino*) and others, one can no longer doubt the authentic origin of these documents.[19] It is also probable that in the matter of quoting documents the Books of the Maccabees followed the example of the Books of Ezra and Nehemiah, just as Flavius Josephus was later to follow the example of the Books of the Maccabees. In Jewish post-exilic historiography the liberal use of documents reflects, directly or indirectly, the importance that the Persian state and its successors attributed to documents for establishing rights. It is possible that documents had already been quoted by Persian chronicles, if the uncertain interpretation of Ezra iv, 15, can be a guide:

31

'That search may be made in the book of the records of thy fathers.' But even if the Persian chronicles did not in fact contain verbatim quotations of documents, Jewish historiography would nonetheless reflect the conditions of a political organization in which documents had assumed particular importance.

The origin of the use of documents in Greek historiography of the fifth century B.C., however, is still an open question. The first Greek historians who have come down to us appear to have been little interested in the use of archival documents to reconstruct events in Greek history. If indeed there existed an authentic decree of Themistocles for the evacuation of Attica, Herodotus did not bother to quote it. Herodotus used translations or presumptive translations of Eastern inscriptions as best he could, such as that of Sesostris (Book II, 106), or of the Pyramids (Book II, 125). Furthermore, he used documents of Persian origin whose nature is not easy to define, such as the list of Satrapies (Book III, 89 ff.), the description of the Persian road system (Book V, 52) and the information on the troops of Xerxes (Book VII, 61 ff.). He does not seem to quote any authentic letter from an Eastern sovereign: the letter from Amasis to Polycrates in Book III, 40 is part of the story of Polycrates' ring. Whether, and in what way, Herodotus was influenced in his manner of using documents by Eastern bureaucratic or historiographic usage it is impossible to say.[20]

The same is true of Thucydides. It is curious that of the eleven documents quoted by him word for word, five should have a Graeco–Persian content: the two letters exchanged between Xerxes and Pausanias (one probably authentic, the other certainly a forgery), and the three versions of the Spartan–Persian agreement of 411. But it is impossible to say whether Thucydides was following the example of some Ionian historian, who in his turn could have derived his concern with archival documents from Persian models. Archival documents are certainly rare in Greek historians, so much so that eminent students of historiography, such as E. Schwartz and Wilamowitz, have postulated, or rather invented, a stylistic law which would have prevented the verbatim quotation of documents; and they explain what they believe to be the exception of Thucydides by the incomplete and provisional character of his text. The fact remains that we do not know in what circumstances and under what influences Greek historians chose to quote archival documents.[21] In fictionalized historiography with an Eastern background the quotation of documents or pseudo-documents seems to have been frequent, as a papyrus of Oxyrhynchus confirmed a few years ago in the case of Ctesias (*Pap. Ox.* 2330 = Ctesias Fr. 8b Jacoby). In short, it is legitimate to wonder if the first Greek historians learned from the Persians, directly or indirectly, to quote the text of archival documents. But no answer is possible.

In conclusion:

(1) Elements of Eastern, and particularly Persian, story-telling certainly penetrated both into Jewish post-exilic historiography and into Greek historiography of the fifth century B.C.

(2) The Jewish memorialists of the fifth century B.C. – Ezra and Nehemiah – echoed certain stylistic and religious motifs of Eastern autobiographical inscriptions, Persian included; but their politico-religious bias was rather one of reaction to the egotism of these autobiographical inscriptions and reveals a different notion of collective life.

(3) Contact with the Persian world made the Greeks more conscious both of the world around them and of their own cultural heritage: it was one of the stimuli that created Greek historiography. Furthermore it is probable that Oriental biographical tales like that of Zopyrus, or Graeco–Oriental ones like that of Democedes, played their part in refining, and perhaps even in creating, the interest of Greek historians in the biographies of politicians.

(4) In the use of archival documents Jewish historians were certainly influenced by Persia. The origin and limits of the use of documents by the first Greek historians – and in particular of their use of archival documents – are still unexplained. In this context also we cannot exclude the possibility of Persian influences, at least in Herodotus.

References

---

1. For fresh and up-to-date information, R. N. Frye, *The Heritage of Persia*, London, 1963. Important for its detailed discussion of sources and for religious and social movements, M. A. Dandamaev, *Iran pri pervych Achemenidach*, Moscow, 1963. See both of these for earlier bibliography.

2. The main texts in R. Kent, *Old Persian*, New Haven, 1953. For translations also J. B. Pritchard, ed., *Ancient Near Eastern Texts Relating to the Old Testament*, Princeton, 1950. C. Clemen, *Fontes Historiae Religionis Persicae*, Berlin, 1920, has not yet been superseded. Also G. G. Cameron, *Persepolis Treasury Tablets*, Chicago, 1948, and E. Schmidt, *Persepolis*, I–II, Chicago,

1953–7. *Cf.* also F. Altheim–R. Stiehl, *Die aramäische Sprache unter den Achaimeniden*, I, Frankfurt, 1961. In general M. Forderer, *Religiöse Geschichts-deutung in Israel, Persien und Griechenland zur Zeit der Persischen Expansion*, diss., Tübingen, 1959, which I was unable to consult again when writing the present article.

3. *Echtheitsfragen antik-griechischer Literatur*, Berlin, 1939, pp. 52–65.

4. *Tobit*, 14, 10, and elsewhere. For Elephantine, E. Meyer, *Papyrusfund von Elephantine*, 1912, p. 202; A. Cowley, *Aramaic Papyri of the Fifth Century B.C.*, 1923, p. 204.

5. The earliest date, about 360 B.C., suggested by Y. M. Grintz, *Sefer Yehudith*, Jerusalem, 1957 (in Hebrew), does not seem convincing. For this and other Biblical passages referred to in the text, see O. Eissfeldt, *Einleitung in das Alte Testament*, 2nd ed., Tübingen, 1956, and C. Schedl, *Geschichte des Alten Testaments*, V, Innsbruck, 1964 (often somewhat daring). *Cf.* K. Galling, *Studien zur Geschichte Israels in persischer Zeit*, Tübingen, 1963; A. M. Dubarle, *Rev. Bibl.*, 66, 1959, pp. 514–49. On Jews and Persians *cf.* also B. Meissner, *Sitzb. Preuss. Akad.*, 1938, pp. 6–26, all the more remarkable given the time of its publication. On Jews and Greeks F. M. Heichelheim, 'Ezra's Palestine and Periclean Athens', *Zeitschr. für Religions- und Geistesgeschichte*, 3, 1951, pp. 251–3, is not convincing. Nor is A. Marmorstein, *Jewish Quarterly Rev.*, 37, 1946–7, pp. 169–73.

6. 'Griech. Literatur', in *Kultur der Gegenwart*, 1st ed., p. 122.

7. *Hermes*, 29, 1894, pp. 155–6 and bibliography. S. Trenkner, *The Greek Novella in the Classical Period*, Cambridge, 1958, gives the essential bibliography.

8. *Cf.* (apart from the information given in n. 5) R. Stiehl, *Wiener Zeitschrift f. die Kunde des Morgenlandes*, 53, 1957, pp. 4–22; H. Cazelles, *Festschrift H. Junker*, Trier, 1961, and the commentary by H. Bardtke, Gütersloh, 1963. The essay by R. Stiehl is reprinted in *Die aramäische Sprache*, quoted in n. 2.

9. 'Herodotos Persergeschichten' in *Von Werken und Formen*, 1948, pp. 190–93. *Cf.* also O. Regenbogen, *Kleine Schriften*, 1961, pp. 101–24.

10. A. Christensen, *Les gestes des rois dans les traditions de l'Iran antique*, Paris, 1936; *cf.* also (apart from the classic work by T. Nöldeke) W. Barthold, 'Zur Geschichte des persischen Epos', *Zeitschr. d. Deutsch. Morgenländ. Gesell.*, 98, 1944, pp. 121–57. For later Persian historiography *cf.* H. Lewy, *Journ. Amer. Or. Soc.*, 1944, pp. 197–214; J. Suolahti, *Studia Orientalia*, 13, Helsinki, 1947, 9: a study being produced at the University of London by Averil Cameron will bring new light to bear on the relationship between Agathias and the Persian sources (see now: *Dumbarton Oaks Papers* 23–4, 1969–70, pp. 69–183). For general information on popular Persian epic *cf.* also J. Cejpek in J. Rypka, *Iranische Literaturgeschichte*, Leipzig, 1959, pp. 470–98 (bibliography pp. 628–37), and A. Pagliaro and A. Bausani, *Storia della letteratura persiana*, Milan, 1960, p. 63. A more recent edition of Rypka's handbook exists in Czech, Prague, 1963.

11. For general guidance in this connection *cf.*, among recent commentaries, those of W. Rudolph, 1949; K. Galling, 1954; H. Schneider, 1959; J. de Fraine, 1961. Also: V. Palovsky, *Biblica*, 38, 1957, pp. 275–305, 428–56; G. Da Deliceto, *Laurentianum*, 4, 1963, pp. 431–68; S. Mowinckel, *Studien zu dem Buche Ezra-Nehemia*, I, Oslo, 1964. But it is impossible not to give at least a reference to the book that reinterpreted Ezra for my generation: H. H. Schaeder, *Ezra der*

Schreiber, 1930. For Deutero-Isaiah and Persia, M. Smith, *Journ. Am. Or. Soc.*, 83, 1963, pp. 415–21. I assume that there is an authentic nucleus in the auto-biography of Ezra.

12. 'Die Vorderasiatischen Königs- und Fürsteninschriften', *Eucharisterion H. Gunkel*, Göttingen, 1923, pp. 278–322; cf. H. Gese, *Zeitschr. f. Theologie und Kirche*, 55, 1958, pp. 127–45. The collective volume *The Idea of History in the Ancient Near East*, New Haven, 1955, and B. C. Brundage, 'The Birth of Clio' in *Teachers of History. Essays in Honor of L. Bradford Packard*, Ithaca, 1954, pp. 199–230, are perhaps the best introductions to Eastern historiography. *Cf.* also A. Millard, 'Another Babylonian Chronicle Text', *Iraq*, 26, 1964, pp. 14–35 and J. J. Finkelstein, *Proceed. Amer. Philosophical Society*, 107, 1963, pp. 461–72.

13. G. von Rad, *Zeitschr. Alttestam. Wiss.*, 76, 1964, pp. 176–87.

14. E. Meyer, *Papyrusfund von Elephantine*, p. 99; A. Cowley, *Aramaic Papyri*, p. 248; E. G. Kraeling, *The Brooklyn Museum Aramaic Papyri*, 1953, p. 29.

15. H. Bengtson, *Historia*, 3, 1954, pp. 301–7, is fundamental. On Greeks in Persia G. M. A. Richter, *Amer. Journ. Arch.*, 50, 1946, p. 16; C. Nylander, ibid., 69, 1965, p. 49. [See now A. Momigliano, *The Development of Greek Biography*, Cambridge, Mass., 1971.]

16. E. Otto, *Die biographischen Inschriften der ägyptischen Spätzeit*, 1954, p. 169 (inscription of Udjahorresnet of the time of Cambyses and Darius).

17. *Cf.* F. M. T. de Liagre Böhl, *Bibl. Orient.*, 19, 1962, pp. 110–14, for a recent discussion. The various extremely penetrating studies by J. Morgenstern on the significance of the year 485 B.C. for Jewish history (indications in *Hebrew Union College Annual*, 31, 1960, pp. 1–29) have not convinced me.

18. A. von Blumenthal, *Ion von Chios*, 1939; F. Jacoby, *Class. Quart.*, 41, 1947, pp. 1–17. L. Pearson, 'Real and Conventional Personalities in Greek History', *Journ. Hist. Ideas*, 15, 1954, pp. 136–45, contains important observations.

19. E. Meyer, *Die Entstehung des Judentums*, 1896; E. Bickerman, *Journ. Bibl. Lit.*, 65, 1946, pp. 249–75. Methodologically fundamental, also by the same author, *Mélanges I. Lévy*, 1953, pp. 11–34.

20. For a careful analysis of the material cf. H. Volkmann, *Convivium* ('Festschrift K. Ziegler'), Stuttgart, 1954, pp. 41–65, and also A. E. Raubitschek, 'Herodotus and the Inscriptions', *Bull. Inst. Class. Studies*, 8, 1961, pp. 59–62. According to Dionysius of Halicarnassus – *De Thucyd.* 5 – the earliest Greek historians used texts preserved in archives: T. S. Brown, *Am. Hist. Review*, 59, 1954, p. 938, is sceptical about this unverifiable statement. I shall here avoid discussing the problem of whether Herodotus and Thucydides in quoting few Greek documents reflect the poverty or indeed the non-existence of archives in Greek cities. I do not know of any adequate study of Greek archives of the archaic age and of the fifth century B.C. *Cf.* for Athens A. R. W. Harrison, *Journ. Hell. Studies*, 75, 1955, pp. 26–35, and bibliography quoted. (See now E. Posner, *Archives in the Ancient World*, Cambridge, Mass., 1972.)

21. Bibliography in A. Momigliano, 'La composizione della storia di Tucidide', *Mem. Accad. Torino*, 67, 1930, pp. 32–41, and C. Meyer, *Die Urkunden im Geschichtswerk des Thukydides*, Munich, 1955. On the subject of this article cf. now also V. Martin, *Mus. Helvet.*, 22, 1965, pp. 38–48.

4

Athens in the Third Century B.C. and the Discovery of Rome in the Histories of Timaeus of Tauromenium*

To Augusto Rostagni
φιλοτιμαίῳ

THE ARRIVAL OF THE EXILE

FOR a few months in 318 B.C., Athens had a democratic government which people hoped would be protected by the Macedonian sarissae of Polyperchon. Towards the end of the year a naval battle destroyed Polyperchon's power. His rival Cassander re-established a government of wealthy citizens at Athens and kept a garrison at Munychia to support it; but, made cautious by events, he reduced by half the property qualification necessary for full rights of citizenship which had been imposed by Antipater in 322. The admiral in command of Cassander's fleet was Nicanor, the son-in-law and adopted son of Aristotle; with his triumphant landing at the Piraeus the Peripatetics obtained power.[1] For ten years Athens was ably administered – on behalf of Macedonia, but with considerable deployment of Peripatetic theories – by Demetrius of Phalerum, a pupil of Theophrastus.[2]

A few months after Demetrius' assumption of power another of Theophrastus' pupils, Menander, received the prize at the Lenaean games of 317/16 B.C. for his comedy The Misanthropist (the 'Dyscolos'); whether by chance or not, all the humanity and domestic virtues of the play conformed to the tone affected by the libertine Demetrius.[3] But the character who gave the play its name was not exactly a model of the civic virtues. On the contrary, he was a man who hated the human race, and

* This essay was first published in Rivista Storica Italiana, 71, 1959, pp. 529–56.

fled the *agora* for the solitude of Mount Parnes, frequented by Pan and graced by the presence of a charming daughter; and he reformed himself only as much as was necessary to allow the play to reach its happy conclusion.[4] Theophrastus himself, with the sharp eye of the only half-assimilated foreigner, depicted in his *Characters* more than one of these restless and introspective inhabitants of Athens, so unwilling to play the part of political animals.[5]

It must have been during the administration of Demetrius of Phalerum that another misanthropist, a second learned '*Dyscolos*', arrived to settle in Athens: Timaeus, the son of Andromachus, from Taormina in Sicily.[6]

Almost everything about Timaeus is obscure, even the date of his arrival in Athens. The known facts are briefly as follows. He was exiled by Agathocles. We know from direct evidence that when he was writing the thirty-fourth book of his Sicilian history, which comprised a total of thirty-eight books, he had already lived in Athens for fifty years. After the Sicilian history, the last five books of which dealt with his father's enemy Agathocles, he wrote another work on Pyrrhus in which he reached the First Punic War (264 B.C.), thus providing the starting point for Polybius' history.[7] It is only modern conjecture that makes him go back to his native Sicily after half a century – not that the conjecture is necessarily wrong.[8] Even if we agree to give Timaeus all the ninety-six years of life attributed to him by an unreliable statement in the *Macrobii* of Lucian (or pseudo-Lucian), we cannot make him arrive in Athens much before 317 B.C.[9]

The vicissitudes of Timaeus' family make a date not earlier than 317 inevitable. His father was the Andromachus who in 358 occupied Taormina (Tauromenium) with a group of men from Naxos who had survived the destruction of their city by Dionysius the Elder. Andromachus came to an agreement with Timoleon and helped him to establish himself in Syracuse in 345; in this way he associated himself with the cause of restoration of democratic freedom in Syracuse, though he was not able to avoid the obvious accusation of being a tyrant in his own town. We do not know if he lived long enough to see Taormina fall into the hands of Agathocles of Syracuse, between *c.* 316 and 312 B.C.[10] But it is clear that the exile of his son Timaeus must have begun in those years. It is a rather pointless way out to conjecture that the young Timaeus was surprised by the fall of Taormina while he was occupied with his studies in Athens and decided not to return home. In any case his fifty years in Athens, which preceded the end of the Sicilian history and still left him time to write (in Athens or in Sicily) the history of Pyrrhus, can plausibly be placed in the period of about 315–264 B.C., with a few years of uncertainty at either end.

His father was an aristocrat, a semi-tyrant, a supporter of the Syracusan democracy of Timoleon, and ultimately a victim of the bare-faced tyranny of Agathocles. With this background Timaeus was heir to a difficult position. In addition he had to spend at least fifty years of exile in a city disturbed by frequent changes of regime, where foreigners were sometimes admired but always critically watched. The fact that his teacher Philiscus had been a pupil of Isocrates did not create a place in society for him. Timaeus retired into himself, concentrating on the books that reminded him of his far-away country and the barbaric West; his hatred for the tyrants of Syracuse and for the Carthaginians intensified in a city wrapped up in other affairs. He became the withdrawn, pedantic, superstitious and malicious scholar described by tradition and in particular by Polybius. The Athenians called him Timaios-Epitimaios, 'Timaeus the fault-finder', a name repeated, possibly when he was still living, by the learned Ister Callimacheus in an attack whose details are unfortunately unknown. Another of his nicknames was 'the gossip'.[11] Among his victims were Thucydides, Isocrates, Theopompus, Ephorus, Philistus, Plato, Aristotle, Callisthenes, Theophrastus and Demochares. He in his turn naturally had bitter adversaries, but it is interesting that, apart from Ister, the ones we know of belong to later centuries: Polybius, and the second-century antiquarian Polemon, whose *Against Timaeus* was at least twelve books long.[12]

The tone, the precise note of denigration in Timaeus' histories will probably never be recovered. It is certainly difficult to draw any clear deductions from Polybius, whose account is the only one to survive; Polybius was too concerned with himself and his own method to steep himself once more in the atmosphere of declining Athenian freedom, as would have been necessary to be fair to Timaeus. In any case Timaeus' attacks were formally of the usual kind. Uppermost was the desire to discredit his adversaries by revealing their minor errors of scholarship and their considerable private vices. Against Aristotle he made insinuations of arrogance, ignorance, sycophancy, sensuality and gluttony (Fr. 156–7). Against the historian and politician Demochares, the nephew and spiritual heir of Demosthenes, he repeated in cold blood, certainly after 289 and probably after 270, the accusations of immorality which had been levelled at him by orators and comic poets in the heat of political struggle (Fr. 35).

But one need only name Aristotle and Demochares to realize the strangeness of a historian who inveighs, at one and the same time, against the master of the pro-Macedonian philosophers and against the enemy of the pro-Macedonian philosophers. Here we have the first sign of Timaeus' radical isolation, and consequently of his singular position in the cosmopolitan culture of Athens in the first half of the third century B.C. In a certain sense, as is natural in the work of an exile concentrating on the history of his native Sicily, he represents the most extreme departure from the premises of the Hellenistic political system. In another sense, new and as yet indistinct situations which were emerging from this system are reflected in him. He was not only the historian of Pyrrhus, but also a prelude to Pyrrhus; a crucial achievement of his historical writing was that in his lonely meditation at Athens he discovered, or helped to discover, the political importance of Rome.[13]

It is no coincidence that the scarcity of information about Timaeus should be linked with our ignorance about the fifty years of Athenian history from the regime of Demetrius of Phalerum to the desperate revolt against Macedonia which is called the Chremonidean War. We still do not know the exact chronology of the main events, and we have very little information about the careers of the leading politicians (for instance Lachares, Demochares, Phaedrus of Sphettus, Olympiodorus). We know even less about the changes in the social structure and the precise variations of the intellectual atmosphere. We do not know how quickly or at what intervals Timaeus published the first thirty-three books of his history. Furthermore, we do not know whether the attack on Demochares in the thirty-eighth and last book of the Sicilian history was composed later than 270, and therefore after the death of Demochares, which occurred between 280 and 270; even if it was, we still do not know if it was written before, during or after the Chremonidean War (267–263?), in Athens or in Sicily. In other words we cannot use the *terminus post quem* to identify a precise political situation.

Examples of our twofold uncertainty could be multiplied. Nonetheless it is obvious that Timaeus will remain even more incomprehensible if we do not try to see him in the streets of the city which he never regarded as his, and among the men he loathed or for whom he had no sympathy, but towards whom he was never indifferent. In short, for at least fifty years Timaeus shared the Athenians' alternating periods of peace and war, and he met or avoided meeting the men who governed Athens, the philosophers who made her the centre of a new culture. He declared Syracuse to be the greatest and most beautiful of all the Greek cities, if we are to believe Cicero.[14] This implicit challenge to Athens contained the nostalgia, arrogance and polemical vigour of the historian whose dogged work during fifty years of exile presented a new image of the West.

ATHENS AT THE TIME OF TIMAEUS

The government of Demetrius of Phalerum, which had seemed near its end in 312 because of the successes of Antigonus Monophthalmus, fell in 307 and was replaced by some sort of democracy supported by Demetrius Poliorcetes. The game of the parties was dependent on the permanent reality of foreign control, in this case control by sea. But Demetrius did not hold Macedonia, and it soon became clear that Athens could be held for long only by someone who was solidly installed in the north. For this reason the new regime was weak and soon broke up into factions. The law prohibiting the running of schools without the specific permission of the council and people of Athens – a measure against the Peripatetics who supported Demetrius of Phalerum – was first passed and then repealed. The situation deteriorated after 304 when Athens was in danger of falling, by siege, into the hands of Cassander. Demetrius Poliorcetes arrived in time to save Athens, but discredited himself and his closest followers with months of loose living at the Athenians' expense. Stratocles of Diomeia remained his instrument of government. Demochares was forced into exile about 303; the repeal of the law against the philosophers, which he had backed, had already demonstrated the weakness of his position.[15]

In 301 Antigonus Monophthalmus died in battle, and Demetrius was forced to flee. Athens was slipping from his hold. The Athenian government, in its rather unsuccessful attempts to withdraw into neutrality, changed hands in circumstances of which we know little. It seems that even before Demetrius' defeat at Ipsus, towards the later summer of 301, one of the Athenian generals, Lachares, was causing trouble. It is indeed possible that he had already seized effective control of the state while leaving Stratocles as the nominal head. What is certain is that after Ipsus Stratocles lost even nominal control. Between 300 and 297 (?) Lachares and another general, Charias, were battling for supremacy. At some point Charias took possession of the Acropolis, but was dislodged and killed by Lachares, who had already acquired or was later to acquire the support of Cassander. It seems that Lachares soon lost possession of the Piraeus. The hostility which Lachares aroused in the Piraeus (i.e.

among the maritime proletariat) was exploited after the death of Cassander by Demetrius Poliorcetes for the purpose of engineering his own return between 296 and 295. Lachares must have lost power in 295, when Demetrius occupied Athens and left a garrison at the Museum.[16]

Shortly afterwards Demetrius obtained the throne of Macedonia. His control of Athens took on a different complexion. Stratocles returned to the government of Athens in a coalition which included Philippides and Olympiodorus. Apparently the archonship had once again become elective, and for two years remained in the hands of the forceful Olympiodorus (294/3 and 293/2). Even after the disappearance of Stratocles about 291 the prevalent tendency seems to have been one of conciliation between the various factions among the wealthy classes, excluding the most active nationalist elements. The oligarchs returned (292/1), including the orator Dinarchus, who had been in exile since 307; but Demochares stayed out of the country. The popular mood was hostile to Macedonia, and there was no lack of invitations to rebellion from the Ptolemies in Egypt and Lysimachus in Thrace. It would be interesting to know what lies beneath the vague allusion in an inscription to a threat against 'democracy' in the archonship of Cimon (288/7?).[17] But only with the collapse of Demetrius' fortunes in Macedonia did Athens, led by Olympiodorus, declare herself free. Demochares was recalled during the archonship of Diocles, which seems to correspond to 286/5 B.C.[18] The Macedonian troops had to abandon the Museum and Eleusis. However, they still retained the Piraeus, and from there, even after the failure of an attempted siege of Athens, they continued to threaten the city. A body of Athenians sent to free the Piraeus was mown down. Command of the Piraeus was transmitted by Demetrius, even after his final downfall and death (283?), to his son Antigonus Gonatas. If there was a liberation of the Piraeus, it must have happened between c. 280 and 277; it could have taken place during the years when, at the request at Demochares, the Athenians put up a monument to the memory of Demosthenes.[19]

The short period of Athenian independence was directly related to the crisis in Macedonia and the chaos created everywhere by the invasion of the Celts. Athens played her part in the defences of Greece. But from the rebuttal of the Celtic invasion there emerged the new Macedonian kingdom of Antigonus Gonatas and the restoration of Macedonian control over Greece (c. 277). For some years Athens was in fact the Greek capital of Antigonus Gonatas. Political passions seemed to die down in the impoverished city, where the political leaders of the older generation, such as Demochares, were gradually disappearing. Yet a subterranean vein of political initiative and love of independence persisted. In contemporary decrees the political tradition of freedom and democracy continued to be expressed. The Egypt of Ptolemy Philadelphus encouraged rebellion. Antigonus Gonatas was becoming unpopular all round, and for this very reason had to have recourse to tyrants to maintain local situations. We do not know what triggered off the rebellion in the archonship of Peithidemos (268/7–265/4?). Whatever the compromises to which it had had to adapt in the last fifty years and whatever the advantages derived from Macedonian protection, the Athenian ruling class, which consisted of landowners, had not lost its taste for being master in its own house. Sparta joined in the same spirit. The appeal to rebellion against the foreigner in the name of the old Hellenic tradition echoes even today in the decree inspired by Chremonides, a politician originally linked with the Stoic group.[20] The war turned out badly for both Athens and Sparta. After the vicissitudes of a prolonged siege Athens capitulated during the archonship of Antipater, which is now reckoned at 264/3, or better still at 263/2, B.C. Timaeus was probably finishing his last work. The Macedonians returned to Athens where they remained for over thirty years (i.e. until 229).

Political corruption, shortage of provisions and decline in trade were inevitable in the conditions which obtained in Athens between 317 and 268. More than once, especially in the period 300–280, the Athenians felt famine near at hand. But what is remarkable in Athens in the first half of the third century is that the almost impossible political conditions were not reflected in either economic ruin or profound demoralization.[21]

At that time Athens was more than a city yearning for political freedom: she was a city creating intellectual freedom. The historians kept alive the sense of her political tradition, her glories, her independence. Diyllus, a continuator of Ephorus who wrote the history of Greece from c. 356 to 296, still remains a shadow without substance. Plutarch regarded him as a by no means negligible historian, and his information on Herodotus (Fr. 3) reveals his talent as a researcher into archives.[22] Demochares on the other hand is recognizable even from the few remaining fragments.[23] His innate qualities of courage, independence and loyalty to the suspicious and anti-intellectual Athenian democracy shine through even amid the almost total destruction of his work. Demosthenes' nephew was the first historian to be distinguished by his freedom of speech.[24] He despised both Demetrius Poliorcetes and his flatterers and passed a negative judgement on the prosperity without dignity or freedom of the government of Demetrius of Phalerum. The absence of precise documentation does not permit us to be certain even about the length of his exile. But if he lived for at least eighteen years away from his homeland and returned there with enough prestige and vigour to direct Athenian politics for some years as an old man, the fact speaks for itself. Between the mild freedom of speech ($\pi\alpha\rho\rho\eta\sigma\acute{\iota}\alpha$) of the Epicurean who cultivates sincere friendship, and the rude freedom of speech of the Cynic who despises polite manners, Demochares interposed the freedom of speech of the historian who sets his own frankness against the adulation of others. With the invective and exhortation of the *oratorium genus*, to which Cicero ascribed his history (*Brut.*, 286), Demochares translated Demosthenian eloquence into history. Demochares' $\pi\alpha\rho\rho\eta\sigma\acute{\iota}\alpha$ is connected with the *libertas* of Tacitus, however tenuous the historical link between the two. Like Tacitus, Demochares was suspicious of philosophy (which he had persecuted at the beginning of his political career) and preferred eloquence, but he was paradoxically close to the free philosophers of his time.

Side by side with the rhetorical and combative history of Demochares (which seems to have gone back to at least 350 B.C.) we have the learned research of Philochorus. He worked doggedly to preserve and codify the history and customs of Athens in an *Atthis* and other learned studies.[25] As 'a prophet' ($\mu\acute{\alpha}\nu\tau\iota\varsigma$) at the service of the Athenian state he had the opportunity of predicting the future in a liberal-conservative direction, pointing out that no danger would ensue from the return of the oligarchic exiles (Fr. 67). He was clearly an anti-Macedonian patriot, and when Athens fell about 263 B.C., Antigonus Gonatas set an ambush for him and had him killed. Despite its antiquarian tone, an unusually large part of his *Atthis* was devoted to contemporary events. If he adapted the traditional genre of the *Atthis* to the more modern exigencies of Alexandrian learning, he set himself apart from the cosmopolitan scholars of Alexandria by concentrating on the past and present of his small Athenian homeland.

As we have already indicated, in insisting on the freedom of Athens the historians were ultimately also of use to the philosophers who gathered there. Four great philosophical schools were established there, and developed and prospered in peaceful competition in a situation unique in the history of the ancient world. These schools were run sometimes by Athenians and sometimes by foreigners; being a foreigner did not constitute any essential difficulty.[26] As a centre of philosophy, Athens attracted visitors, and philosophy helped to offset the decline in trade and the falling off of political prestige because of its intellectual appeal or simply as a tourist attraction. The creation of an international society of this kind in Athens was undoubtedly connected with political decadence and offered scholastic affiliation as an alternative to political association. But it would be wrong to be satisfied with such a simple formula to explain the transitional situation in which Theophrastus, Epicurus, Zeno, Xenocrates and Archesilaus developed their influential teaching. It is typical that the philosophical schools did not remain isolated and indeed that men of culture (in particular Archesilaus and Crates of the Academy) were used as ambassadors and spokesmen of the state.[27]

On the other hand, while the various schools enjoyed the protection of influential foreigners, they manoeuvred with sufficient ability to maintain freedom of research and to keep the respect of the Athenians. The absolute identification of a school with a regime had provoked the reaction of 307; but after the fall of Demetrius of Phalerum this mistake was avoided. Straton the Peripatetic was in contact with the court of Alexandria. His successor Lycon, if he enjoyed the patronage of Antigonus Gonatas, also enjoyed that of Eumenes and Attalus of Pergamum. Hieronymus of Rhodes, a rival of Lycon but supported by Antigonus, maintained friendly relations with philosophers of freer sentiments.[28] The way the philosophers restrained each other is indicated by an anecdote in Diogenes Laertius: 'Eurylochus of Cassandria, invited to court by Antigonus . . . declined the invitation because he feared that Menedemus, caustic and freely spoken as he was, might come to hear of it.'[29]

Epicurus hovered adroitly between the support of Demetrius Poliorcetes and that of the more distant Lysimachus. Craterus, Antigonus' half-brother, was a friend of the Epicureans; but Epicurus himself, it seems, in the archonship of Euthios (now reckoned at 283/2), expressed indignation against the Macedonians.[30] Zeno had his moment of power and influence with Antigonus Gonatas, his pupil, having made himself the spokesman of the Athenians. We know, however, that both he and Cleanthes formed personal, and even erotic, relations with anti-Macedonian patriots. Zeno boasted of knowing how to hold his tongue.[31]

It is noteworthy that even in the Academy, which was so directly connected with the Athenian aristocracy, Archesilaus was a friend of the commander of the Macedonian garrison in the Piraeus, taught Antigonus's half-brother Demetrius the Fair, and earned himself the goodwill of the kings of Pergamum; the friendship with the commander of the

Piraeus was unfavourably commented upon in Athens.[32] These men concerned themselves above all with their own schools.

But although they were often not even Athenian citizens – this was the case with Zeno, Archesilaus, Straton, Cleanthes, Lycon and Hieronymus, among those quoted – they preferred Athens to other calmer places of residence. With all its attractions and opportunities Alexandria did not succeed in luring the philosophical schools away from Athens. Offers also came from Syria.[33] The philosophers remained in Athens, as did Menander.[34] They were faithful to a city several times besieged and starving, and were listened to and respected there. In a strange, instinctive cooperation, the Athenians defended the freedom of this cosmopolitan society of philosophers and were helped by it in delicate dealings with the Hellenistic kings and, more generally, by the new prestige that philosophy gained for the city.

TIMAEUS AND THE WEST

Timaeus not only absorbed the freedom of Athens, but in a certain way he also acknowledged his debt. He wrote that Demosthenes and the other orators had acted in a manner worthy of Greece by refusing to accord divine honours to Alexander. He added, alluding to Callisthenes, that the philosopher who conferred *aegis* and thunderbolt upon an ordinary mortal was justly punished by the gods.[35]

The simple piety of the provincial was combined with veneration for the civic tradition of Athens. Timaeus thus shared with the Athenian historians the basic attitude of turning his back on Alexander and his Diadochi, and steeping himself in a past age of civil liberties. His respect for Demosthenes was no less than that of Demochares. His hatred of the tyrant Dionysius corresponded to Athenian feelings. With Philochorus in particular he shared a romantic antiquarianism, an erudite curiosity. His world was the *polis*, not the Hellenistic monarchy. His lack of interest in the Orient was, it seems, absolute. The exception of Phoenicia is only apparent because of its relation to Carthage. Much of his polemic was directed against pro-Macedonians or, at any rate, supporters of despotic governments. Aristotle, Callisthenes and Theophrastus came into this category. Plato, apart from having been the teacher of Aristotle, had compromised himself with the tyrants of Sicily. Above all, the hostility towards Aristotle, which descended to trivialities of learning and personal gossip, cannot be explained without reference to the political background of the philosopher's collaboration with Alexander. The coolness towards Theopompus, the historian of Philip of Macedon (Fr. 117), can probably be attributed to the same cause; and politics entered equally into the criticism of Ephorus, though this, as we shall see, has more definite historiographical explanations. Timaeus' anti-Macedonian and anti-Hellenistic bias is obvious.

Yet Timaeus did not become an Athenian. However much he admired Demosthenes, we know from Polybius that his ideal politician was Timoleon, the Corinthian who became the 'liberator' of Syracuse.[36] If it is pointless to attempt to use Plutarch's biography to reconstruct the picture that Timaeus gave of Timoleon in his histories, it is certain that Plutarch's uncritical enthusiasm for Timoleon reflects Timaeus' thought. The extravagant section devoted by Plutarch to Timaeus' father would be enough to suggest this.[37] Timoleon is the model of the deliverer from tyranny and of the city magistrate. And before Timoleon there was Hermocrates, whom Timaeus idealizes even more than Thucydides had already done, making the Athenian aggression against Syracuse (Fr. 100–102) more odious still. He attributed to Hermocrates a hymn to peace for which Polybius was to have words of scorn. Furthermore he claimed Syracuse as the birthplace of rhetoric, the instrument of democracy (Fr. 137). In dwelling on the history of rhetoric he has anti-Isocratean tones that sound strange in a pupil of a pupil of Isocrates (Fr. 139). But he must have been strongly tempted to note that the pro-Macedonian Isocrates had spent more time composing his *Panegyric* on the war against the Persians than it had taken Alexander to conquer Asia. Nor can it have been without irony, for a man who enjoyed the ironies of history, that he emphasized that Thucydides had been an exile in Italy (Fr. 135–6) as he, Timaeus, had been in Athens. The Syracusan, not the Athenian, tradition of democracy, freedom and peace had a paradigmatic value for Timaeus. This is all the more comprehensible in that he did not recognize any successors of Demosthenes among his own contemporaries, as is shown by his attack on Demochares, whom public opinion in Athens rightly considered the representative and defender of Demosthenic ideals.

The precise reasons for this attack remain unknown. Since it occurred in the last book of the histories concerning Agathocles, it was probably provoked by some opinion of Demochares which, to Timaeus, seemed too favourable to Agathocles. We certainly know that Demochares talked of Agathocles[38] in his historical work. We must also remember that towards the end of his life Demochares provoked at least one other hostile comment because of his political inconsistency. Diogenes Laertius has an ambiguous story from which it appears that Demochares tried to avail himself of Zeno's authority over Antigonus Gonatas to obtain some benefit from the latter and aroused the indignation of Zeno.[39] The basic fact remains that Timaeus hated Demochares deeply even after Demochares' death. Hatreds of this kind develop on a basis of long-standing mutual incomprehension and antipathy. Even admitting that Demochares had provoked Timaeus with an out-of-place apologia of Agathocles, the problem is simply put elsewhere. Demochares, who could not fail to have known Timaeus personally in Athens, must have realized what he was doing by siding with the commenders of Agathocles, i.e. against Timaeus. To hate Demochares meant cutting oneself off from the democratic current; it meant separating Demosthenes from contemporary Demosthenism and despairing of the future of Athens. From 280 to his death Demochares was cared for in the Prytaneum as a descendant of Demosthenes. In point of fact his Athenian contemporaries, whether pro-Macedonian or anti-Macedonian, remained equally distant from the historian who, in Athens, was idealizing Timoleon and keeping his eyes fixed on his distant homeland. Hermocrates the Syracusan's hymn to peace must have had a personal significance for someone who had seen Athens involved in so many wars.

We may add, and the whole of the following exposition will confirm it, that Timaeus also remained a stranger to the great Athenian philosophical schools of his time. Their doctrines did not influence him either directly or indirectly. Their masters (Plato, Aristotle, Theophrastus) appear only to be criticized. But on the other hand Timaeus idealizes the ancient philosophers of Sicily and Magna Graecia, and indeed one wonders if this might not perhaps be the result of a conscious distaste for the philosophy of his time.[40] Polybius accused Timaeus of 'making events in Sicily finer and more illustrious than those in the rest of the world', of putting 'the wisest of the wise' in Sicily and the 'most skilled and marvellous of politicians' in Syracuse.[41]

As F. Jacoby saw clearly, Timaeus' originality lay in his determined refusal to take on the role of the historian of Eastern Hellenism. But one should perhaps add that equally decisive was his refusal to allow himself to be caught up in the politics and philosophy of the city in which he was living. He preferred to be a provincial. He recognized the complex nature of his Western Hellenistic province and divined the importance of the non-Greek factors. Sicily was merely the centre of his narrative. He included the whole political and cultural history of the Western Greeks in the framework of a geographical–ethnographical description of Italy,

Gaul, Spain, Britain, Libya, Corsica, Sardinia and the smaller islands of the Western Mediterranean. Not surprisingly, he was not the only one in these years, about 300, to plan a work on Sicily. In Alexandria, about 300 or soon afterwards, Lycus of Rhegium, the presumed father or step-father of Lycophron, was engaged on two works on Sicily and on Libya, which must have contained much ethnographical information about the Western Mediterranean. But Lycus was only an ethnographer, not an historian. Furthermore it is uncertain whether he preceded Timaeus and in any way influenced him.

Timaeus' real history was preceded by an introduction which dealt, according to Polybius (XII, 26 d, 4), with colonies, foundation of cities, and relationships (or histories of families). Between the introduction and the narrative part Timaeus inserted a discussion on the nature of history, at the beginning of the sixth book; the introduction therefore consisted of five books. Information about customs of Etruria and Corsica are explicitly attributed to it. The more exact distribution of the material within these five books is unknown to us. However, J. Geffcken was probably right to suggest that the first two of the five books were more specifically geographical. The description of the islands in the Western Mediterranean and the Ocean in Diodorus, V, 2–23, which almost certainly goes back to these books by Timaeus,[42] can give us some idea of what they may have been like.

From Book VI to Book XXXIII the work became predominantly Sicilian, with considerable reference to Magna Graecia. The main lines of the Sicilian historical narrative were the struggles for tyranny and the conflict between Greeks and Carthaginians. With love, but not without detachment, Timaeus described the period of great Sicilian prosperity, lingering over Agrigentum, whose monuments in the third century were still the most impressive sign of past greatness. He distinguished between Gelon, not a real tyrant, but a liberator (Fr. 20, 94), and Diony-sius, a tyrant in the worst sense. He watched out for corruption through indulgence and extravagance, and thus gave classical formulation to the legend of the lasciviousness of the Sybarites. His account of the affairs of Empedocles, Pythagoras and the Pythagoreans must have extended, at least, intermittently, over several books.[43]

The history was constructed according to the requirements of third-century scholarship. It was founded on a preliminary study of Olympic chronology, for which, according to reliable evidence given by Polybius, he visited Olympia and examined the lists of the winners of the games.[44] The list of Olympic victors obtained by him was accompanied by parallel lists of the ephors and kings of Sparta, the archons of Athens and the priestesses of Hera at Argos; it thus amounted to a comprehensive treatise on Greek chronology in the apparently new form of comparative tables. Aristotle had already studied the lists of Olympic victors and, as far as we can tell, Philochorus followed rather than preceded Timaeus in a further revision. It is pointless to speculate about the relative importance of their researches. There was clearly scope for everyone in this tricky field. Furthermore Timaeus went to Eastern or Western Locris in Greece to study documents, while it seems that he made do with information given him by a native for Locris in Italy.[45] We do not know to what extent he personally visited the countries of the Western Mediterranean. He certainly saw Agrigentum, where he noted the statues to the racehorses and pet birds.[46] As in the case of Locris, it is clear that he met and questioned somewhere natives of Lavinium about the Roman Penates.[47] His accuracy in chronological details and in the study of documents was famous.[48] Here once again he adhered to the contemporary methodology of autopsy, which went back ultimately to Herodotus.[49]

For contemporary scholars autopsy was also subordinate to the gathering of material from books. For this reason, in his preface to the sixth book, which was the beginning of the actual history, Timaeus boasted of having spent considerable sums to buy the necessary books for writing about Tyre and to obtain information, written and oral, on Celts, Ligurians and Iberians. He never made a secret of the fact that he was an armchair historian, and it seems that he even admitted (if the text of Polybius is thus to be interpreted) that he lacked military experience. Hence Polybius' accusation that he preferred hearing, i.e. reading, to sight, i.e. travelling.[50] In the same preface Timaeus declared against Ephorus that the superiority of history over eloquence lay in concern for the truth and in the effort and expense necessary to amass the facts. He clearly assumed the position of spokesman and theoretician of an erudite historiography, a fact which was to arouse the wrath of Polybius.[51]

Polybius considered that Timaeus' accounts were full of dreams, miracles and incredible fables, and, in short, of ignoble superstitions and womanish love of the marvellous.[52] But he had to admit, among other things, that his discussion of colonization, of foundations of cities and of genealogies inspired respect.[53] Indeed, in Timaeus both elements were to be found. He was sufficiently subtle and perceptive to realize the significance of Pytheas' reports for the geography of the West, and he was not lacking in critical sense in the choice of sources.[54] However much he despised Philistus as subservient to Dionysius the Elder and extended his distrust to Thucydides as the favourite model of Philistus, he nonetheless used them both.[55] He tended constantly to reduce extravagant army numbers.[56] In one case – the death of Empedocles – he refused to believe in a miracle.[57] He was even sceptical about the existence of so famous and popular a figure in the archaic history of Magna Graecia as Zaleucus; and in this he has found followers among the moderns.[58] In the case of Lycurgus he had recourse to the by no means unworthy expedient of dividing him into two persons (Fr. 127).

On the other hand his love of coincidences was notorious: the contemporaneous founding of Rome and Carthage (Fr. 60); the simultaneous death of Euripides and birth of the tyranny of Dionysius (Fr. 105); the birth of Alexander on the day of the burning of the temple of Artemis at Ephesus (Fr. 150); the connection between the profanation of the Apollo of Gela by the Carthaginians and the capture of Tyre by Alexander (Fr. 106). A liking for the erudite, the ironic and the superstitious made Timaeus dwell on dreams and auguries. The distinction between the mythical period and the historical, though reflected in the distinction between introduction and history proper, was even vaguer and more blurred in him than in Ephorus, from whom he had taken it.[59]

Not everything was frivolous even in the weaker part of Timaeus' work. The passion for coincidence was a way of intuitively establishing invisible historical links, and, in at least one case which we shall examine presently, it served its purpose. The essence of Timaeus' scholarly method is naturally present also in Philochorus, and it undoubtedly recurred in hundreds of historical works whose very names we scarcely know today. Whether Timaeus was one of the first to give an example on a large scale of this type of history – bookish yet anxious for first-hand information – is another question. Our ignorance of the relative chronology of historical production in the first decades of the third century makes a reply impossible. For the moment it is as well to limit ourselves to what is absolutely clear. For us, Timaeus is characterized not by the novelty of his method, but by his choice of subject, and by a certain unmistakable tone in his treatment of details.

As often happens with people who live in isolation, he saw something that others did not see. He grasped a tendency, an aspect of contemporary life less conspicuous than the struggles between the Hellenistic states, less dramatic than the effort of dying Athens to survive. He focused on the rapid disintegration of Western Hellenism and gave direction to the interests and desires for intervention which are clear, even if intermittent, in the politics of the third century B.C. His hatred of tyrants prevented him from idealizing the Sicilian present.

Here we may leave aside the question of whether Alexander the Great had formulated a plan to conquer the West and whether this plan – authentic or not – had already been accepted as authentic by a historian as serious as Hieronymus of Cardia.[60] The question is too uncertain to be of any use for our purpose. But about 309, Ophellas, ruler of Cyrene, and Agathocles, ruler of Syracuse, reached an agreement to fight together against Carthage and to create a Greek empire in Africa. The venture ended in discord between the two associates: Agathocles first assassinated Ophellas and was then defeated. The plan had aroused interest throughout Greece: many Athenian mercenaries and their families had taken part in it, and Ophellas himself was accompanied by his wife, Eurydice, a descendant of Miltiades and therefore a member of the highest Athenian aristocracy. Furthermore, Diodorus tells us in a sibylline phrase that Ophellas had asked for an alliance with Athens. Economic pressures among the common people, who had not yet recovered from the dissolution of the cleruchy of Samos, and the restless ambitions of aristocrats combined during the last years of Demetrius of Phalerum suddenly to recall the Athenians to the possibilities of the West, and equally suddenly to disappoint them. The affair became even more sensational when in 306 the new master of Athens, Demetrius Poliorcetes, married the widow of Ophellas or made her his concubine, after she had returned to her father's family.[61] One would like to know what Timaeus thought of the Athenians who placed their trust in Agathocles at this time. We may even be tempted to imagine that the episode had some connection with Timaeus' decision to devote his life to a history which would enlighten the ill-informed on the realities of Carthage and Syracuse. A few years later, in 303, Cleonymus, uncle of a king of Sparta, went to Italy to defend the Tarentines against Lucanians and Romans. He too gathered mercenaries from all parts of Greece. The account that Timaeus later gave of these campaigns, in which Agathocles was involved, seems to have been the source for the curious information that a certain Gaius (a Roman) and an Aulus Peucestius (?) tried to poison Cleonymus.[62] The later interventions of the Hellenistic sovereigns in the Italiot and Sicilian world belong to general history. About 291 Demetrius Poliorcetes went to the assistance of Lanassa, daughter of Agathocles, and took possession of Corcyra. Then Pyrrhus came to the rescue against Rome (280). Demetrius Poliorcetes himself had been fleetingly interested in Rome and its origins (which he believed to be Greek), when he sent an embassy there to protest against the pirates of Antium.[63]

But the course of events was in itself beginning to indicate that the Greeks of Italy were weakening; that the tyranny of Agathocles was losing its function as bulwark against the Carthaginians and Italic tribes; that the metropolitan interventions with mercenary armies (from Ophellas to Cleonymus and Pyrrhus) were of little avail; and lastly, that in contrast Rome was emerging as the new great power in Italy. Something of this process must have been registered in contemporary historical works such as that of Hieronymus of Cardia.[64] Moreover, it is certain that other historians wrote on Rome before Timaeus or at the same time; for instance, Theophrastus and Callias of Syracuse. But Timaeus was the first to go into details, as is apparent from the traces left in the tradition. More important, he was the first to grasp the consequences of the situation and to devote a special monograph to a war in which Rome had fought and defeated a Greek army. Merely by observing the Graeco–Hellenistic intervention in Italy Timaeus came to appreciate the strength of Rome. His indifference to territorial monarchies and his hatred of tyrants led him in the direction of a city that was governing itself in a republican fashion.

TIMAEUS AND ROME

Timaeus wrote about Rome twice, once in his general history of Sicily and once in the account of the expedition of Pyrrhus.[65] The few remaining fragments on Rome cannot now be apportioned exactly between the two works, and we must frankly admit that the precise physiognomy of both accounts escapes us. On both occasions he lingered over the origins. The fragment concerning the contribution of Servius Tullius to the coinage (Fr. 61) seems to belong to the account of Pyrrhus. A detail like this presupposes that the single kings were mentioned and at least briefly characterized.[66] The same monograph went back to the Trojan origins and cited as evidence the rite of the October Horse in the Campus Martius.[67] It is therefore probable that the work on Pyrrhus amplified and corroborated the sketch of Roman history given in the history of Sicily with the addition of further details. This is confirmed by Aulus Gellius, if he is referring to the book on Pyrrhus when he ascribes to Timaeus 'historiae ... de rebus populi romani' (nor is it easy to see to what else Gellius could have been alluding).[68] Even without going beyond the attested fragments, one can see that Timaeus' knowledge of the origins of Rome was considerably superior to that of his predecessors. The research on the Penates of Lavinium proves that he was in contact with the local tradition. Through the study of their origins he grasped, more or less, the national physiognomy of the Latins. And it cannot have been by chance that he was particularly well informed about Lavinium, where contacts with Greece had already existed for some time, as has now been proved by the recently discovered inscription of the Dioscuri.

It is also of essential importance that Timaeus, having become aware of Rome, should have followed the fortunes of the city until 264. He examined the consequences of the conflict between Pyrrhus and Rome up to the point when they coincided with the beginning of the First Punic War. Even if the details escape us once again, it is clear that Timaeus with his Siceliot sensitiveness realized that Rome, through her victory over Pyrrhus, was replacing the Greeks in the position of adversary of Carthage. In other words, Timaeus did not write, or at least did not complete, his history of Pyrrhus in the years in which Rome had consolidated and renewed her friendship with Carthage to save herself from Pyrrhus, but during the years when that friendship had turned almost unexpectedly into war. Not only did he understand the significance of the war with Pyrrhus, but in a way he grasped the connection between it and the First Punic War.

This observation has its importance for understanding the problems which are implicit in the famous and fanciful synchronism of the foundations of Rome and Carthage, both ascribed to the year 813 B.C. Here a common destiny was certainly implied: but a destiny of hatred or of friendship? If the synchronism was formulated for the first time in the work on Pyrrhus, i.e. after 264, the destiny was one of hatred. But this hypothesis implies that in his first work Timaeus had not yet thought of the synchronism and had therefore implicitly or explicitly dated the founding of the two cities in two different years. The almost over-watchful Polybius would have pounced on this contradiction. And it was moreover a contradiction unlikely to escape Dionysius of Halicarnassus. One must admit that the hypothesis of a synchronism discovered or invented by Timaeus only in relation to the First Punic War has its problems. On the other hand the hypothesis that the synchronism had already been formulated in the first history is itself not without ambiguities and problems:

(1) although probable, it is not in fact certain that Timaeus finished his Sicilian history before 264 and therefore cannot have included in it a synchronism signifying hostility;

(2) it is in any case obscure how Timaeus could reconcile a foundation of Rome in the year 813 with his assertion that the Trojan War took place about 1200.[69] All in all, I should like to leave the question open. We cannot exclude the possibility that the synchronism originally referred to the unusual length of the alliance between Rome and Carthage.[70] Once again one should not underestimate what is uncertain, but it is equally important not to lose sight of the fact that the essential contribution was in the synchronism itself. Timaeus recognized that Carthage and Rome were on the same level. The Greeks, accustomed to respecting Carthage, now had to attribute the same importance to Rome. Within the strange symbolism of a coincidence a historical discovery of the first importance was concealed: the rise of Rome to the position of a great power in the West.

Only one contemporary can contend the primacy of this discovery with Timaeus, and he was not a historian, but a poet: Lycophron. This means that the doubt concerns not the historical exposition, in which Timaeus was unrivalled, but who had the first intuition of the new historical situation. The problems are well known[71] and can be recalled here in their barest outlines. The poet Lycophron may have been educated in Athens, but lived for a long time at the court of Ptolemy Philadelphus. His extant poem, the *Alexandra*, presents the Romans in their struggle with Pyrrhus as a great power inheriting and vindicating the greatness of Troy. In certain ethnographical details the poem depends without the slightest doubt upon Timaeus; on the other hand, it does not allude to the First Punic War and must therefore be dated before 264. An opinion already expressed by an ancient grammarian, and taken up on various occasions from Niebuhr onwards, implies that so early a date for a poem full of the glory of Rome is unlikely, and tries to take the *Alexandra* away from the poet of Ptolemy Philadelphus and to assign it instead to a writer who was a flatterer of Flamininus (c. 196). This opinion has against it both tradition and the actual play of erudite reflections and cultural contracts which all take us back to the time of Timaeus.[72]

The real problem is whether the *Alexandra*, composed, for the reasons I have mentioned, before 264, and already utilizing part of the Sicilian history of Timaeus, nonetheless anticipated Timaeus in his assessment of Rome. In my opinion the problem remains open. While it is certain that Lycophron's imagination was drawn in the general direction of the Western Mediterranean by the appearance of the work of Lycus and the first sections of Timaeus' history, it is impossible to say exactly how far Timaeus and Lycophron influenced one another in their assessment of Rome. Everything depends on two unknown factors: the date of publication of the Sicilian history and the exact position within it of the section on Rome. At all events the feeling of the dawning greatness of Rome was immediately shared by at least one contemporary of Timaeus: Lycophron.[73]

Thus we are brought back to the last remaining aspect of the question, namely the vividness of the exposition in Timaeus' histories and his effectiveness in drawing the attention of his contemporaries to the West. As far as we can judge from the fragments, Timaeus was a pedant with imagination. His pedantry and polemical zeal cut him off completely from the simple joy of seeing and discovering that had characterized Herodotus, but from Herodotus he learned the subtle economy of a well-told anecdote. In changed circumstances he gave a description of the West for which Herodotus had provided a model with his books on the East. It is full of almost contemporary episodes, such as the very beautiful description of the banquet at the court of Dionysius the Younger, in which the philosopher Xenocrates beats everyone in the drinking contest and goes away without collecting the prize (Fr. 158), or the little story of the flatterer of this same Dionysius with the ready retort (Fr. 32), or the scene of the madmen who thought they were on a trireme (Fr. 149). Personalities, such as the courtesan Lais (Fr. 24), are rapidly sketched in, and there are delightful references to local lore in the manner of Herodotus, such as the description of the cicadas on the River Halex which sang on the Locrian shore but not on that of Rhegium (Fr. 43). Primitive customs are minutely described. The picture of social development in the Liparic islands (in Diodorus, V, 9) must go back to Timaeus. Proverbial phrases – such as the 'sardonic laugh' – are explained (Fr. 64). Fauna and flora of inhospitable regions are described. New biographical information is given even for such well-known men as Thucydides. Knowledge of the myths of the West is renewed. For Greece, too, Timaeus manages to clarify episodes most authoritatively. The interest of the poets, and possibly also of the politicians of the third century, in the strange custom of the expiatory sending of virgins from Locris to Troy is inseparable from the account of it given by Timaeus.[74] Just as he sometimes quoted documents, so on other occasions he liked to adorn his prose with the verses of a classical writer: Pindar (Fr. 92, 142) or Sophocles (Fr. 119). But usually he found within himself the imaginative impetus which has made it possible even now for the life of

Agrigentum and Sybaris in the archaic period, or the beginning of the career of Empedocles (Fr. 134), to appear before us as he intended they should.

All this, culled from a variety of sources during fifty years of activity, had its effect even on a generation accustomed to the marvels of Alexandrian learning. It would be naïve to think that anyone like Callimachus, let alone Lycophron, would have depended slavishly upon Timaeus for their own information on the West. Callimachus knew how to seek information quite as well as Timaeus. But the dependence of Callimachus on Timaeus is demonstrable in a number of fragments which must be considered large in proportion to the small amount of their works that has come down to us.[75] And in other cases too, for example the anecdote about Gaius revealed to us by the Milan papyrus, such a derivation seems probable.[76] The link between Timaeus, Callimachus and Lycophron is not only a question of sources, but also an indication of a common cultural grounding, nostalgic, learned, keenly exploratory and therefore politically aware. In this situation it was certainly Timaeus who took the initiative for the West and attracted the attention of contemporaries to it. His erudition was genuine, and capable of arousing the interest of poets.

In the present state of our knowledge it is impossible to say how Timaeus, who was never unresponsive, reacted to the successes of the Romans. Antipathy is certainly excluded because otherwise Polybius would not have lost the opportunity of emphasizing it. Benign curiosity seems implicit in the few fragments where Roman customs are referred to: but we must not forget that the paternity of Callimachus' anecdote about Gaius, clearly pro-Roman in tone, has been attributed to Timaeus only *ex hypothesi*. We would be able to say more if we knew Timaeus' attitude towards Pyrrhus and if we could be certain that he was hoping that the Greeks of Sicily would gain something from the duel between Rome and Carthage which had begun in 264.

The Romans were still enjoying his histories of Sicily and Pyrrhus at the time of Varro and Cicero.[77] It is reasonable to conjecture that these histories soon made their way to Rome in the third century, with the conquest of Sicily, and represented required reading for the growing minority of educated aristocrats able to understand Greek. In Timaeus the Romans found a summary of their own history, an analysis of their own customs and an account of their victory over Pyrrhus, all calculated to arouse feelings of emulation. We know nothing about the education of the first historian of Rome – Fabius Pictor. But he must have read

Timaeus to be able to write, in Greek, his own version of the history of Rome. His attention to chronology, his interest in Roman customs, beyond the mere pragmatic narration of events, seem to be derived from the example of Timaeus. Who else about 215 B.C. was better equipped to teach a Roman how to write Roman history in Greek?[78]

A century after Timaeus, Polybius was still faced with him as the most authoritative historian of the West, so authoritative that it seemed obvious to him to begin where Timaeus had left off. But Polybius also recognized that in order to establish himself and to have the originality of his method acknowledged by Greek and Roman readers, he would have to undermine the authority of his predecessor. For this reason he emphasized all the weaknesses (and indeed some things that were not weaknesses, but simply differences) without admitting that the way to Rome had been opened up for him in Athens by the exile from Taormina. Timaeus, disdaining homage to Alexander and his diadochs, uninterested in cosmopolitan philosophies, without hope or faith in the contemporary politicians of the city which was offering him hospitality, gazed fondly towards the West with a nostalgic eye. He celebrated the glories, often real, sometimes imaginary, of his ancestors, but did not lose himself in the past. Timaeus observed that the power of Rome was rising over the present misfortunes of the Greeks and that Rome was preparing for war with Carthage. Possibly he also sensed that Rome had by now replaced Greece in the duel with Carthage and was threatening the balance of the Hellenistic states.

Bibliographical Note

The collection of the fragments in F. JACOBY, *Fragmente der griechischen Historiker*, III B, 1950, No. 566, with the commentary of 1955, is the sure guide to the understanding of Timaeus. It is taken for granted at every point in my article with a deep sense of debt and admiration. The judicious and informative work of T. S. BROWN, *Timaeus of Tauromenium*, Berkeley and Los Angeles, 1958, was written without the knowledge of Jacoby's commentary and is not a piece of research of great novelty. The lectures of G. DE SANCTIS, 1947, now printed under the title *Ricerche sulla storiografia siciliota*, Flaccovio, Palermo, 1958, pp. 43–69, are of considerable interest: they should of course be judged as lectures, not as a study.

Like Jacoby and Brown I base my exposition only on the fragments. The question of how far one can utilize Diodorus, Plutarch and other authors who probably used Timaeus as evidence in a study of his history remains open. So far definite results have not been obtained. R. LAQUEUR in the article *Timaios* in PAULY-WISSOWA, 1936, tackled Diodorus squarely and arrived at the conclusion that for his account of Sicilian history Timaeus was only a secondary source (*cf.* also *Hermes*, 86, 1958, pp. 257–90). But in individual passages the distinction between the sources is so uncertain as to make it impossible to attribute a precise point of view to Timaeus: *cf.*, apart from the observations by JACOBY, *Kommentar*, p. 529, the criticisms of T. S. BROWN, *Am. Journ. Phil.*, 73, 1952, pp. 337–55. For example, it is impossible to prove in a strict sense that the speech of Theodorus in Diodorus, XIV, 65–9, is copied from Timaeus. It is therefore impossible to be certain that Timaeus elaborated the theme of the dismal temptation for lovers of freedom to yield to the foreigner (Carthage) in order to free themselves from the tyrant – though this is certainly a theme that should have been his. Other attempts, both ancient and modern, to isolate the material of Timaeus in Diodorus and Plutarch cannot be said to be any more successful, even if their correctness on certain points is not to be excluded. *Cf.* N. G. L. HAMMOND, 'The Source of Diodorus Siculus, XVI', *Class. Quart.*, 32, 1938, pp. 137–51; H. BERVE, *Sitzungsb. Bayer. Ak.*, 1952, 5, pp. 4–21, for Agathocles (*cf.* also *Abh. Ak. Mainz*, 1956, No. 10, pp. 752–7); K. F. STROHEKER, 'Timaios und Philistos', *Satura* ... *O. Weinreich*, 1952, pp. 139–61; idem, *Dionysios I*, Wiesbaden, 1958, pp. 11–31, which has important observations on the anti-tyrannical tradition of Athens; P. LÉVÊQUE, *Pyrrhos*, 1957, pp. 32–7; H. D. WESTLAKE, *Class. Quart.*, 32, 1938, pp. 65–74 (on Timoleon); R. LAURITANO, *Kokalos*, 2, 1956, pp. 206–16 (Diodorus, XI–XVI). On the organization of the work, J. K. BELOCH, *Jahrb. f. Philol.*, 123, 1881, p. 697; idem, *Gr. Geschichte*, III, 2nd ed., 2, 1923, p. 43; E. SCHWARTZ, *Hermes*, 34, 1899, p. 481 = *Ges. Schriften*, II, 1956, p. 175. *Cf.* also H. KOTHE, *Jahrb. f. Philol.*, 137, 1888, p. 815; H. D. WESTLAKE, *Historia*, 2, 1953, p. 288.

The older or less important bibliography is easily available in Jacoby and in F. SUSEMIHL, *Lit. d. Alexandrinerzeit*, I, 1891, p. 563, as well as in SCHMID-STÄHLIN, *Griech. Lit.*, II, 1, 1920, p. 218. Fundamental for Hellenistic historiography in general, P. SCHELLER, *De hellenistica historiae conscribendae arte*, Leipzig, 1911.

Note also (a brief selection): C. A. VOLQUARDSEN, *Untersuchungen über die Quellen d. griech. und sizil. Geschichten bei Diodor*, diss., Kiel, 1868; K. MÜLLENHOFF, *Deutsche Altertumskunde*, I, 1870 (reprint 1890, p. 429); H. KOTHE, *De T. T. vita et scriptis*, Breslau, 1874; A.

ENMANN, *Ueber die Quellen des Pompeius Trogus für die griech. und sicil. Geschichte*, Dorpat, 1880; C. CLASEN, *Unters. über T. von Taur.*, Kiel, 1883; P. GÜNTHER, *De ea quae inter T. et Lycophronem intercedit ratione*, Leipzig, 1889; W. ZINZOW, *De T. Taur. apud Ovidium vestigiis*, diss., Greifswald, 1906; K. TRÜDINGER, *Stud. zur Gesch. d. griech.-röm. Ethnographie*, 1918, pp. 108–11; M. A. LEVI, *Raccolta Scritti in onore di F. Ramorino*, 1927, p. 65; M. SEGRE, *Historia* (of Milan), I, 1927, fasc. 4, p. 18–42 (Celtic invasion); R. VAN COMPERNOLLE, *Rev. Belge de Philologie*, 32, 1954, pp. 395–421 (Agathocles); A. RAUBITSCHEK, *Classica et Mediaevalia* 19, 1958, pp. 93–5 (ostracism); L. MORETTI, *Riv. Fil. Class.*, N.S. 30, 1952, pp. 289–302 (T. and Cato); L. MENDELSSOHN, *Acta Soc. Phil. Lipsiensis*, 2, 1872, pp. 159–96 (synchronisms); L. RADERMACHER, *Rhein. Mus.*, 52, 1897, pp. 412–19 (origin of rhetoric); F. REUSS, *Philologus*, 45, 1886, pp. 271–7 (Aristodemus of Cumae), and, a contrary view, W. CHRIST, *Sitz. Bayer. Ak.*, 1905, I, pp. 59–71. For Timaeus' reputation in later times, J. GEFFCKEN, *Timaios' Geographie des Westens*, 1892, pp. 177–85, is still fundamental.

Furthermore M. SORDI, *I Rapporti Romano-Ceriti*, Rome, 1960, pp. 143–82; F. W. WALBANK, *Journ. Rom. Studies*, 52, 1962, p. 3, and 53, 1963, p. 3; F. W. WALBANK, *Miscellanea di Studi Alessandrini in memoria di A. Rostagni*, Turin, 1963, p. 203; M. A. LEVI, ibid., p. 195.

References

1. Nicanor, however, soon entered into personal conflict with Cassander and came to a bad end: Diodorus, XVIII, 75, 1; Polyaenus, IV, 11, 2; Trogus Pompeius, *prol.* 14.

2. Bibliography in F. Wehrli, *Die Schule des Aristoteles*, IV, *Demetrios von Phaleron*, Basle, 1949. The most recent monograph known to me is by E. Bayer, Stuttgart, 1942. The bibliographical references in the present article are limited to recent literature. *Cf.* in general the histories of Glotz-Roussel and H. Bengtson.

3. *Cf.* my note in *Riv. Stor. It.*, 71, 1959, p. 326. Also the important essay by A. Barigazzi, *Athenaeum*, 37, 1959, pp. 184–95, whose doubts on the date of the *Dyscolos* (p. 195n) do not seem to me to be well founded. *Cf.* also along the same lines W. Schmid, 'Menanders Dyskolos und die Timonlegende', *Rh. Museum*, 102, 1959, pp. 157–82, esp. p. 172. Also M. Pohlenz, *Hermes*, 78, 1943, p. 274; G. Zuntz, *Proceed. Brit. Acad.*, 42, 1956, p. 209. The interesting page by E. G.

Turner, *Bullet. John Rylands Library*, 42, 1959, p. 257, does not interpret my own thought exactly and is open to historical objections.

4. Barigazzi's observation that philanthropy triumphs over misanthropy in the play (p. 193) is perhaps not entirely acceptable.

5. On the date of the *Characters* C. Cichorius in *Theophrasts Charaktere*, Leipzig, 1897, LVII–LXII. But P. Treves is probably right to transfer the date of Character 8 from 319 to 317 B.C.: *Rend. Ist. Lombardo*, 92, 1958, pp. 367–74. *Cf.* A. L. Boegehold, *Trans. Am. Phil. Assoc.*, 90, 1959, pp. 15–19.

6. See bibliographical appendix. All the data on Timaeus are collected in F. Jacoby, *Die Fragmente der griechischen Historiker*, IIIB, 1950, no. 566, with the commentary (text and notes) of 1955. The references in my text are of course to the *testimonia* (T.) and fragments (Fr.) of this edition.

7. Polybius I, 5, 1 is to be taken literally (*cf.* XXXIX, 8, 4). For Timaeus and Polybius see in general F. W. Walbank, *A Historical Commentary on Polybius*, I, 1957, index s.v. Timaeus.

8. To say that Timaeus returned to Syracuse because Diodorus calls him Syracusan in XXI, 16, 5 (as for instance Croiset, *Litt. grecque*, 5, 1899, p. 109), is of course arbitrary. The essential evidence is Polybius, XII, 25d. Little is to be made of Plutarch, *de exil.*, 14, p. 605 C, according to which Timaeus wrote (all?) his histories in Athens. The perceptive judgement of E. Schwartz (1899), now in *Ges. Schriften*, II, p. 187, should be noticed: 'Diese geistige Luft des politisch verfallenden, von der Vergangenheit träumenden Athen hat auf den Sikelioten gewirkt'.

9. *Macrob.*, 22. For approximative calculations *cf.* G. M. Columba, *Riv. Fil. Cl.*, 15, 1886, p. 353; R. Laqueur, Pauly-Wissowa, s.v. *Timaios*, 1077; T. S. Brown, *Timaeus of Tauromenium*, p. 6. Jacoby, *Kommentar, Text*, pp. 531–2 is preferable. E. Bayer, *Demetrios Phalereus*, 73, fixes the date at 317, but without foundation.

10. *Cf.* Diodorus, XIX, 65, and XIX, 102, and Jacoby, *Kommentar, Noten*, p. 316. Also Marcellinus, *Life of Thucydides*, 27 (T. 13).

11. Athenaeus, VI, 103, p. 272 B (T. 16). *Cf. Suda*, s.v. *Timaios* (T.1).

12. *Cf.* Müller, *Fr. Hist. Graec.*, III, p. 126; K. Deichgräber, Pauly-Wissowa, s.v. *Polemon*, 1307. The view of J. Geffcken, *Timaios' Geographie des Westens*, 1892, p. 175, that Timaeus 'bleibt dem Quietismus des Isokrates treu', is frankly incomprehensible to me.

13. The essentials on this are in Jacoby, *Kommentar, Text*, p. 535, 'Karthager und später Römer sind ihm – um es zugespitzt zu sagen – wichtiger als Alexander. die Welt des Ostens, die Kämpfe der Diadochen, und das Schicksal des Mutter. landes'. The statement in the *Suda* that Timaeus wrote on Syria is due to some confusion. Jacoby, *Kommentar*, p. 546.

14. Cicero, *de rep.*, 3, 43 (Fr. 40).

15. Demochares was exiled before 301 according to Plutarch, *Dem.*, 24. G. De Sanctis, following Droysen, has contested this (*Contributi alla storia ateniese dalla guerra lamiaca alla guerra cremonidea*, 1893, p. 50) and is followed, for instance, by E. Manni, *Demetrio Poliorcete*, 1951, p. 89. P. Treves, *Euforione e la storia ellenistica*, 1955, pp. 113–14, who takes a similar view, has added a new argument, which leads me to believe that he has misunderstood Plutarch's text. Plutarch writes that 'since they had freed themselves from the garrison the

Athenians thought that they were free'. The garrison to which Plutarch is referring is that of Cassander, at Phyle and at Panactum, from which Demetrius freed the Athenians (cf. the same Life of Demetrius, 23, 3). Plutarch is therefore unequivocally of the opinion that Demochares' exile preceded the fall of Demetrius, and I have not yet managed to persuade myself that he is unworthy of belief.

16. The extremely obscure history of this period has been reconstructed, in my opinion with the greatest respect for the sources, by W. S. Ferguson, Class. Phil., 24, 1929, pp. 1–31. The different reconstruction of G. De Sanctis, Riv. Fil. Class., 56, 1928, pp. 53–77; 64, 1936, pp. 134–52, 253–73, does not give sufficient weight to Pap. Ox., 10, 1235; nor does it seem to me to be backed by the essential document Pap. Ox., 17, 2082. But differences are inevitable amid such obscurity (cf. also Plutarch, Dem., 33; Polyaenus, Strat., 4, 7, 5; Pausanias, I, 25, 7; I.G. II², 1, 646); De Sanctis is followed by P. Treves, Riv. Fil. Class., 59, 1931, pp. 73–92, 355–74 (see also his article Philippides, in Pauly-Wissowa); Manni, Demetrio, and A. R. Deprado, Riv. Fil. Class., N.S. 32, 1954, pp. 290–302. Cf. Glotz-Roussel, IV, 1, p. 351.

17. Dittenberger, Syll.³, 409 ll. 31–40. For the chronology I have used W. B. Dinsmoor, Hesperia, 23, 1954, pp. 284–316, while awaiting his promised book. One should, however, bear in mind E. Manni's disagreement, in Athenaeum, 33, 1955, p. 256, and elsewhere earlier; note also the factual correction made by B. D. Meritt, Hesperia, 26, 1957, p. 53.

18. Cf. also E. Manni, Athenaeum, 27, 1949, pp. 102–21; A. R. Deprado, Riv. Fil. Class., N.S. 31, 1953, pp. 27–42; M. Chambers, Amer. Journ. Phil., 75, 1954, pp. 385–94.

19. For the notorious question of the liberation of the Piraeus by Olympiodorus attested by Pausanias, I, 26, 3, cf. B. D. Meritt, Hesperia, 7, 1938, p. 103. De Sanctis' opinion differs, e.g. Riv. Fil. Class., 55, 1927, pp. 487–500; ibid., 64, 1936, pp. 144–7. The memorial to Demosthenes, X Orat. Vitae, 850 F. For the date (280/79) cf. ibid., 847 D. Cf. also W. Hoffmann, Pauly-Wissowa, s.v. Phaidros, 1553. For the personality of Olympiodorus cf. a possible connection with Theophrastus in Diogenes Laertius, 5, 57.

20. Dittenberger, Syll.³, pp. 434–5. For the possible dates of the archon Peithidemos, cf. Dinsmoor, Hesperia, 23, 1954, p. 314; Manni, Athenaeum 33, 1955, p. 257; Meritt, Hesperia, 26, 1957, p. 97. For the connection with the loss of the Piraeus, W. W. Tarn, J.H.S., 54, 1934, pp. 26–39. On the date of the archon Antipater, Apollodorus, Fr. 44 Jacoby, seems decisive for 263/2. Cf. Jacoby, Fragmente III B (Supplement), I, 1954, p. 220 and notes.

21. Cf. in general J. Day, An Economic History of Athens under Roman Domination, 1942, pp. 1–28, and of course M. Rostovtzeff, Soc. and Econ. Hist. of the Hell. World, I, pp. 163, 211, 215.

22. Fragments in Jacoby, No. 73. Also P. Ox., 2082 (Jacoby, No. 257 a), and A. Momigliano, Rend. Ist. Lombardo, 65, 1932, p. 573, for bibliography.

23. Jacoby, No. 75, with bibliography, to which should be added the essay by Droysen, Zeitschr. f. Altertumswiss., 3, 1836, pp. 161–70 (not in Kleine Schriften), and A. Wilhelm, Abh. Preuss. Ak., 1941, No. 4. In general E. Cappellano, Il fattore politico negli onori divini a Demetrio Poliorcete, Turin (Facoltà Lettere), 1964.

24. Seneca, *De Ira*, III, 23, 2: 'Demochares . . . Parrhesiastes ob nimiam et procacem linguam appellatus' (not in Jacoby).

25. *Cf.* mainly Jacoby, No. 328, 1954, a monumental commentary; also R. Laqueur, Pauly-Wissowa, s.v. *Philochoros*, 1938.

26. Wilamowitz, *Antigonos von Karystos*, pp. 263 ff.; A. G. Roos, 'Van groote Mogendheid tot Universiteitsstad', *Mededel. Nederl. Ak.*, 1945, pp. 15 ff. But *cf.* the earlier and vigorous pages of J. Bernays, *Phokion*, 1881, pp. 35–44, 107–11, etc. Specific studies on the various schools (for instance the article *Peripatos* in Pauly-Wissowa, Supplement VII, and M. Pohlenz, *Die Stoa*) overlook the problems referred to here. More in such works as W. S. Ferguson, *Hellenistic Athens*, and W. W. Tarn, *Antigonos Gonatas*.

27. Diogenes Laertius, 4, 39; Plutarch, *Dem.*, 46.

28. Diogenes Laertius, 5, 58; 5, 67; 4, 41 (*cf.* 5, 68). *Cf.* G. Arrighetti, 'Ieronimo di Rodi', *Studi Classici e Orientali*, 3, Pisa, 1955, pp. 116–17; F. Wehrli, *Die Schule des Aristoteles*, 10, 1959, p. 29.

29. Diogenes Laertius, 2, 127.

30. *Cf.* A. Momigliano, *Riv. Fil.*, 13, 1935, pp. 302–16. For Craterus *cf.* W. S. Ferguson, *Hell. Athens*, 169, n. 3; C. Diano, *Lettere di Epicuro*, 1946.

31. Diogenes Laertius, 7, 24.

32. Diogenes Laertius, 4, 30, 38, 40, 41.

33. Diogenes Laertius, 5, 68; 7, 185, etc.

34. Alcyphron, *ep.* 4, 18; 19. Pliny, *N.H.* 7, 111, 'regiae fortunae praelata litterarum conscientia'.

35. Polybius, XII, 12 b. 2 = Fr. 155. For the interpretation, *cf.* Jacoby, 124, T. 20. *Cf.* also F. Taeger, *Charisma*, I, 1957, p. 382.

36. Polybius, XII, 23, 4 = Fr. 119.

37. Plutarch, *Timol.*, 10, 4 (T. 3): 'Andromachus the father of Timaeus the historian was the most powerful of those who were governing Sicily at that time, and he led his fellow-citizens along the paths of law and justice and was always openly adverse and hostile to tyrants'. Differently Marcellinus, *Vita Thucyd.*, 27 (T. 13).

38. Jacoby, 75, Fr. 6. De Sanctis' hypothesis, put forward in university lectures (*cf. Ricerche sulla storiografia greca*, Palermo, 1958, p. 47), that the attack on Demochares was part of a general memoir of the time spent in Athens, should not be disregarded; but such a hypothesis presupposes among other things that Timaeus had already left Athens.

39. Diogenes Laertius, 7, 14. The passage, incidentally, is misunderstood by Droysen, *Hist. de l'Hellénisme*, III, p. 223, n. 1.

40. *Cf.* A. Rostagni, *Pitagora e i Pitagorici in Timeo*, 1914, now in *Scritti minori*, II, I, 1956, pp. 3–50; K.v. Fritz, *Pythagorean Politics in Southern Italy*, New York, 1940. *Cf.* also A. Delatte, *Essai sur la politique pythagoricienne*, Liège, 1922. But the question I have referred to in the text would merit investigation: *cf.* also Jacoby, Commentary on Fr. 13–17 (p. 550), and J. S. Morrison, *Class. Quart.*, N.S. 6, 1956, pp. 134–56.

41. Polybius, XII, 26b = Fr. 94.

42. Jacoby puts Diodorus in his 'Anhang' to Timaeus and admirably comments upon him; he admits that descent from Timaeus cannot be *proved*. *Cf.* his commentary on Fr. 164 (p. 593). Geffcken's theory (*Timaios' Geographie*

des Westens, 1892) is discussed unconvincingly by M. A. Levi in 'Timeo in Diodoro IV e V', *Raccolta* . . . *G. Lumbroso*, 1925, p. 153, where the passage in Diodorus, V, 1, is misunderstood. Note also B. Niese, *Gött. Gel. Anz.*, 1893, pp. 353–60. The linguistic criterion of O. Meltzer, *Jahrb. class. Phil.*, 107, 1873, pp. 234–7, is more ingenious than persuasive.

43. *Cf.* Jacoby's commentary to Fr. 13–17.

44. Polybius, XII, 11, 1 = T. 10.

45. Polybius, XII, 9, 2; 10, 7 = Fr. 12.

46. Diodorus, XIII, 82, 6 = Fr. 26.

47. Dionysius of Halicarnassus, *Ant. Rom.*, I, 67, 4 = Fr. 59.

48. Polybius, XII, 26d = T. 19.

49. *Cf.* G. Nenci, *Studi Classici e Orientali*, 3, 1955, pp. 14–46. Also F. Susemihl, *Gesch. Griech. Lit. in der Alexandrinerzeit*, I, 1891, p. 565. For a typical episode of autopsy in Timaeus (the bull of Phalaris) *cf.* F. W. Walbank, *Class. Rev.*, 59, 1945, pp. 39–42.

50. Polybius, XII, 27 = T. 19. *Cf.* the observations in Jacoby's commentary, p. 532.

51. Fragments collected by Jacoby, 151–58, and commentary: *cf.* also Fr. 7 (from Polybius, XII, 28).

52. Polybius, XII, 24, 5 = T. 19.

53. Polybius, XII, 26 d, 2 = T. 19.

54. Fr. 73–5. *Cf.* Pliny, *N.H.* 37, 36; 'huic (Pytheas) et Timaeus credidit'. H. J. Mette, *Pytheas von Massalia*, 1952.

55. This emerges from Plutarch, *Nicias*, 1 (T. 18), and is obvious in any case. Timaeus had a theory that one could deduce certain peculiarities of an author's character from the insistence on certain themes in his books (Fr. 152 = Polybius, XII, 24).

56. For instance Fr. 25 (Diodorus, XIII, 80, 5). *Cf.* C. Clasen, *Unters. über T.*, 1883, p. 58.

57. Diogenes Laertius, 8, 71 (= Fr. 6).

58. Cicero, *de leg.*, 2, 15 (Fr. 130); but see Jacoby's commentary.

59. Jacoby, *Kommentar*, p. 529.

60. *Cf.* for opposing theories W. W. Tarn, *Alexander the Great*, II, 1948, p. 378; F. Schachermeyr, *Alex. der Grosse*, 1949, p. 451. The most recent discussion known to me is by G. Nenci, *Introduzione alle guerre persiane e altri saggi*, Pisa, 1958, pp. 215–57, with bibliography.

61. Diodorus, XX, 40, 5; Plutarch, *Dem.*, 14. *Cf.* V. Ehrenberg, *Riv. Fil. Class.*, 66, 1938, pp. 144–51; H. Berve, 'Die Herrschaft des Agathokles', *Sitzungsb. Bayer. Ak.*, 1952 (1953), pp. 52 ff. (which overlooks Ehrenberg and makes little use of De Sanctis, *Riv. Fil. Class.*, 23, 1895, p. 289, reprinted in *Per la scienza dell'antichità*, 1909, and is superficial). For the cleruchy of Samos, Diodorus, XVIII, 18, 9; Philochorus 328 Fr. 154 Jacoby, and C. Habicht, *Ath. Mitt.*, 72, 1957, p. 155.

62. *Cf.* P. Meloni, *Giorn. Ital. Filologia*, 3, 1950, pp. 103–21. On (Ps. Arist.) *De Mirab. ausc.*, 78, E. Pais, *Storia di Roma*, 3rd ed., V, 1928, p. 352, n. 2; but *cf.* also K. Müllenhoff, *Deutsche Altertumskunde*, I, reprint 1890, p. 429. *Cf.* also H. Bengtson, *Parola del Passato*, 48, 1956, pp. 161–78; E. Manni, ibid., pp. 179–90.

63. Strabo, 232. On the doubtful passage Pausanias, I, 29, 14, see the doubt-

ful commentary by E. Pais, *Ricerche storiche e geografiche sull'Italia antica*, Turin, 1908, pp. 437–49.

64. For this topic it is sufficient to refer to W. Hoffmann, *Rom und die griechische Welt im 4. Jahrh.*, Suppl. *Philologus*, 27, 1934; G. Pasquali, *Terze pagine stravaganti*, 1942, pp. 25–38; M. Ninck, *Die Entdeckung von Europa durch die Griechen*, 1945, pp. 159–71. On J. Perret, *Les origines de la légende troyenne de Rome*, 1942, pp. 440–50, cf. my observations in *Journ. Rom. Studies*, 1945. For A. Alföldi, *Die Trojanischen Urahnen der Römer*, Basle, 1957, my review in *Riv. St. Ital.*, 1958. Alföldi makes a number of statements about Timaeus which cannot be proved. Cf. also G. Wissowa, *Ges. Abhandlungen*, 1904, p. 95; M. Pallottino, *Studi Etruschi*, 26, 1958, p. 336. Of the various studies by F. Altheim note *Welt als Geschichte*, 2, 1936, pp. 86–90. Now also S. Weinstock, *J.R.S.*, 49, 1959, p. 170.

65. There is explicit evidence for this in Polybius, XII, 4 b (Fr. 36).

66. Pliny, *N.H.*, 33, 42–3 (Fr. 61): 'populus Romanus ne argento quidem signato ante Pyrrhum regem devictum usus est . . . Servius rex primus signavit aes; antea rudi usos Romae Timaeus tradit'. If the connection between Pyrrhus and Servius goes back to Pliny's source (which is of course uncertain), Timaeus was talking of Servius in connection with Pyrrhus.

67. Fr. 36 (Polybius, XII, 4 b).

68. Gellius, *N.A.* 11, 1, 1 (T. 9), which seems to be dependent on Varro for its information. The inscription from Lavinium has been published with an excellent commentary by F. Castagnoli, *Studi e Materiali di storia delle religioni*, 30, 1959, p. 109.

69. Censorinus, *De d. nat.*, 21, 3 (Fr. 125), with Jacoby's commentary. The contradiction with Fr. 80 (*Schol. Apoll. Rh.*, 4, 1216), to some degree supported by Fr. 146 b, has not yet been adequately explained. A. M. Panaro, *Giorn. Ital. Fil.*, 4, 1951, pp. 8–32, is unsatisfactory.

70. See the perceptive judgement in the opposite direction by K. Hanell, 'Zur Problematik der älteren römischen Geschichtsschreibung' in *Histoire et historiens dans l'Antiquité*, Vandoeuvres–Geneva, 1958, p. 152.

71. An up-to-date bibliography can be found in the reprint of my two essays on Lycophron (*Journ. Rom. Studies*, 32, 1942, and *Class. Quarterly*, 39, 1945) in *Secondo Contributo alla storia degli studi classici*, Rome, 1960. The inscription from Chios in which Rome is celebrated and knowledge of the legend of Romulus and Remus is already taken for granted (partial edition by N. M. Kontoleon in *Prakt. Arch. Etair.*, 1953 (1956), p. 271, though I am acquainted with the complete and as yet unpublished text) confirms that the Greeks were well acquainted with Roman legends towards the end of the third century, but it cannot be used to date Lycophron. For a different opinion on Lycophron, W. W. Tarn, *Alexander the Great*, II, 1948, p. 28; P. Treves, *Euforione e la storia ellenistica*, 1955, but cf. P. Lévêque, *Rev. Et. Anc.*, 57, 1955, p. 36; idem, *Rev. Et. Grecques*, 71, 1958, p. 437 n. 34. Jacoby, *Kommentar*, p. 536, and relevant notes (cf. in particular 319–20) is neutral. For the historical background L. H. Neatby, *Trans. Am. Phil. Ass.*, 81, 1950, pp. 88–98. For the European (Athenian?) origin of the *Alexandra*, Wilamowitz, *Hell. Dichtung*, II, p. 144. Cf. P. Fraser, *Class. Rev.*, N.S. 9, 1959, p. 64. Cf. also N. M. Kontoleon, *Akte des IV. Intern. Kongresses für . . . Epigraphik*, 1964, p. 192.

72. On this *cf.* R. Pfeiffer, *Callimachus*, II, 1953, p. xliii; S. Weinstock, *Harv. Theol. Rev.*, 50, 1957, p. 257, with bibliography. Pfeiffer says 'Si respicias quot res et vocabula Lycophro et Callimachus ex iisdem fontibus prompserint, Alexandram potius tertio saeculo tribuas quam altero.'

73. On Timaeus as a source for Lycophron see Jacoby's note in his commentary, *Noten*, 312. However, Timaeus' influence is certain in Lycophron, 1050, 1135 ff. (*cf.* Fr. 55 and 56 of Timaeus). *Cf.* W. Ehlers, *Mus. Helv.*, 6, 1949, pp. 166–75. An example of pre-Jacoby reasoning about Lycophron and Timaeus in F. Schachermeyr, *Wiener Studien*, 47, 1929, pp. 154–60.

74. Fr. 146 with the commentary giving the recent bibliography.

75. Callimachus' dependence on Timaeus is particularly clear in Fr. 96 and D. 201 Pfeiffer as well as in Fr. 407, 20. *Cf.* Pfeiffer's index s.v. Timaeus, and notes. Pfeiffer's argument in *Sitz. Bayer. Ak.*, 1934, No. 10, p. 16, is essential. On the chronology of Callimachus see Pfeiffer in his 2nd ed., p. xxxviii. *Cf.* also W. Ehlers, *Die Gründung von Zankle*, diss., Berlin, 1933, p. 26.

76. G. Pasquali, 'Roma in Callimaco', *Studi It. Fil. Class.*, 16, 1939, pp. 69–78 = *Terze pagine stravaganti*, 1942, pp. 95–106, is unconvincing in its details, but only Timaeus seems to have had the opportunity of collecting Roman anecdotes of an ethico-military character. *Cf.*, however, Jacoby, notes to *Kommentar*, p. 331. J. Andor, *Acta Ant.*, I, 1951, pp. 121–5, has not much to add.

77. Varro, *De r. r.*, 2, 5, 3 (Fr. 42). Cicero, *ad Att.* 6, 1, 18, 'a Timaeo tuo familiari' (T. 29). Cicero himself quoted Timaeus freely: *Brutus*, 63 (Fr. 138). Note also the anonymous *On the Sublime*, 4 (T. 23), with its reference to Caecilius of Calacte. *Cf.* U. Wilamowitz, *Hermes*, 35, 1900, pp. 44–6.

78. Tersely formulated by K. Hanell, *Histoire et historiens dans l'Antiquité*, op. cit., p. 152: (Timaeus) 'der Urvater der römischen Historiographie'. *Cf.* also my own essay on Fabius Pictor (*Terzo Contributo*). For Polybius' criticisms of Timaeus *cf.* also M. Isnardi, *Studi Classici e Orientali*, 3, 1955, pp. 102–10. For the moment I shall not discuss Timaeus' influence on Cato. But his influence on Silenus of Calacte, the historian of Hannibal (Jacoby, No. 175), is evident from the fragments.

5

The Historian's Skin*

ON 22 June, 168 B.C., in about one hour, the Macedonian phalanx was destroyed near home, on the fields of Pydna, by the Roman legions. In the Greek East there was no longer any organized force that could check the winners. The old monarchy of Macedon was split into four republics, vassals of Rome; its ruling class was systematically uprooted. The inhabitants of Epirus, who had supported their neighbours, were sold into slavery, and their towns were destroyed.

'Allies' of Rome who had shown less than the required enthusiasm during the campaign were punished. The most important Greek state, the Achaean League (which included Arcadia), had to surrender a thousand young members of its upper class – that is, the greater part of it.

The thousand Achaean hostages were distributed among the cities of central Italy. A few managed to slip away, but most withered in Italy. When, seventeen years later, the three hundred survivors were allowed to go back to Greece, Cato the Censor commented that they could by now safely be left to the care of Greek undertakers.

*

Only one of the thousand had emerged as a personality in his own right during those seventeen years, and this in the service of the Romans. Polybius, a native of Megalopolis in Arcadia, was the son of Lycortas, one of the Achaean politicians who had never wholeheartedly embraced the Roman cause. He himself, as commander of the Achaean cavalry during the year 169, had been only moderately efficient in helping the Romans against the Macedonians. When he arrived in Italy in 167 at the age of about thirty or thirty-two, however, he was soon accepted by the Roman upper class, was exceptionally allowed to live in Rome, was given freedom to travel, and became an unofficial tutor to the future destroyer of Carthage, Scipio Aemilianus (by birth the son of Paulus

*The New York Review of Books, 21, 12, 18 July 1974, pp. 33–5, a review of F. W. Walbank, Polybius, 1972.

Aemilius, the victor at Pydna, by adoption the grandson of the general who had beaten Hannibal).

No wonder that the Romans appreciated him. Polybius was a man of parts: a budding historian who had already written an encomiastic biography of the Achaean leader Philopoemen, he was also a military expert with technical inventions to his credit, a competent geographer who later turned into an audacious explorer – and a brilliant secret agent. Polybius himself tells the story of how he helped the Syrian prince Demetrius to flee from Rome and to recover the throne. He does not add the obvious, namely that he was acting on behalf of a senatorial group. He was at the siege of Carthage with Scipio Aemilianus. When the Macedonians and Achaeans, who had attempted a poorly coordinated rebellion against Rome, were smashed for good in 146, Polybius advised on the reorganization of Greece.

We may believe Polybius when he claims that he was able to obtain concessions from the Romans on behalf of the Greeks. They cannot have amounted to much, because the centre of the rebellion, Corinth, was sacked and reduced to a heap of ruins. As Greece was never to be free again until A.D. 1827, Polybius had time to find compatriots who would appreciate what he had done for them. In the second century A.D. the traveller and antiquarian Pausanias saw many monuments in honour of Polybius. One declared that 'Greece would not have fallen at all, if she had obeyed Polybius in everything, and when she met disaster, her only help came from him'. Another, slightly more realistic, inscription praised Polybius who 'roamed over every land and sea, became an ally of the Romans, and stayed their wrath against the Greeks'.

Polybius must have had an instinctive understanding of the state of mind of those Roman aristocrats who, though Hellenized in culture, employed much of their time in sacking and destroying centres of civilization. In one of the few autobiographical details provided by his history, we are told that a common interest in books had put Polybius in touch with the eighteen-year-old Scipio Aemilianus and his elder brother. The books may have been those of the king of Macedon which Paulus Aemilius had transferred to his house in Rome as part of his booty. The friendship with Aemilianus developed into platonic love, with Polybius self-consciously playing Socrates to a better Alcibiades. Twenty years later Polybius stood beside Scipio Aemilianus as he contemplated Carthage burning. With tears in his eyes, 'turning round to me at once and grasping my hand, Scipio said: "a glorious moment, Polybius, but I have a dread foreboding that some day the same doom will be pronounced upon my own country" '. (Translated by W. R. Paton, Loeb Library edition.)

*

Having decided that it was foolish to question Rome's rise to world power, Polybius saw deeply enough into his own masters to realize that ruling the world was a perturbing business. The more so if you belonged to an aristocracy like the Roman one, for which glory was real only if one's ancestors had contributed to it and the generations to come could be expected to share in it. Such understanding immediately made Polybius a good educator and adviser of Roman leaders. It would not have been enough to make him the unique historian of Roman imperialism he is if it had not been supported by a penetrating study of the means by which power is gained and lost.

There was professional care and pride in the way in which Polybius went about preparing his historical work. He even suggested that one of the advantages of the new political situation was that it provided the Greeks with greater leisure for intellectual activities. He believed in the use of intelligence for practical purposes. He would certainly not imitate the emotional, theatrical accounts of his predecessor Phylarchus, nor – unlike the first Greek historian of Rome, Timaeus, a century before – would he be satisfied with what he could learn in libraries. Direct experience of war and diplomacy, first-hand acquaintance with places and men, consummate skill in cross-questioning witnesses, and finally a sober investigation of causes, with due allowance for chance and luck, were the qualities which Polybius claimed for his work. His heavy-going and intermittently boastful pages reflect his uneasiness in writing for two publics: the more sophisticated, but not necessarily more sympathetic, Greek readers, and the select, far from homogeneous, group of Hellenized Roman masters who could not be trusted to take a point quickly.

Polybius' education in Arcadia had obviously been very good according to local standards, but he had nothing of the Alexandrian finesse. He knew his historians, especially Thucydides, and may have read some Plato and Demosthenes. But fifth-century Athens was to him a distant, unattractively democratic world. One wonders whether he ever read a whole Athenian tragedy or comedy. He had the stamina of a keen hunter and horseman. From his arrival in Italy in 167 until his death at the age of eighty-two after a fall from his horse, c. 118 B.C., he worked on the history of the rise of Rome to a world power beginning in 220 B.C. He planned it first in thirty books, to reach 168 B.C. (with books 1 and 2 serving as an introduction to the events between 264 and 220 B.C.). Then he enlarged the work to forty books to include the events of 168–145 B.C.; and explained in a second preface in book 3 that this was necessary in order to judge Roman rule by its effects. Finally, he wrote a separate account of the Roman war in Spain which ended with the fall of Numantia in 133 B.C., the last triumph of Scipio Aemilianus. A treatise on tactics may belong (like the life of Philopoemen) to the pre-exilic, Achaean, period.

*

It was Polybius' most original thought that the virtual unification of the known world under Rome made a new genre of historiography both possible and necessary. For the first time a historian could write authentic universal history with a unified theme – Rome's ascent to world power. What in the fourth century Ephorus had presented as a universal history was to Polybius a mere conglomeration of special histories. The new epoch required a new historiography, and this in turn implied new narrative techniques in order to register the convergence of events. Chronology had to be kept tight; and the developments in different areas had to be correlated without creating confusion in the minds of readers who could not be expected to have maps at their disposal.

The texture of Polybius' history has been very satisfactorily analysed by the scholar most qualified to do so. Professor F. W. Walbank, as the author of a monumental commentary on Polybius (of which two volumes have appeared and the third and last is in an advanced stage of preparation), has a unique knowledge of Polybius' craftsmanship. The invitation to deliver the Sather Lectures at Berkeley in 1971 gave him the opportunity to present a comprehensive view of the historical art of his author. His emphasis on the craftsmanship of a historian represents a departure from the subjective style of historical analysis made fashionable among students of ancient historiography by Sir Ronald Syme's brilliant books and articles. Syme attributes his own moods and tastes to the historians he studies. His images of Thucydides, Sallust, Livy, Tacitus and the anonymous author of the *Historia Augusta* have a common denominator which is Syme himself. By contrast Walbank never identifies himself with Polybius. He keeps him at a distance and even accentuates his obscurities and logical weaknesses. If one compares his book with a French counterpart which appeared a few years ago

70

(P. Pédech, *La méthode historique de Polybe*, Paris, 1964), it becomes immediately apparent that Walbank is much less systematic and therefore much closer to the spirit of Polybius.

Walbank goes so far as to see a break in the continuity of Polybius' historical interests and hence in his method of working. Whereas in the original plan for thirty books Polybius had a clear thesis to develop – how Rome reached world power – the last ten books, according to Walbank, were lacking in direction and amounted to personal memoirs. If there was something that kept the last ten books together, it was his unconditional support of the policies of Rome, even of the destruction of Carthage and Corinth. 'What I am suggesting [says Walbank in his conclusion] is that Polybius wrote his main Histories under the stimulus of an idea, but that he wrote the last ten books mainly because he had material to hand and a personal story to tell . . . The Histories begin by being focused on Rome. They end by being focused on Polybius, perhaps an anti-climax, but one which throws some light on the man who wrote them.'

Here there is perhaps place for disagreement both on the function of the last ten books and on the political attitude which they represent. We shall soon see that the question involves the whole of Polybius' historical outlook.

*

Two circumstances make the interpretation of Polybius' thought very hazardous. The first concerns the transmission of his work. The second touches upon the very nature of it.

The Greek readers never reckoned Polybius in the same class as Herodotus, Thucydides and Xenophon. One influential Greek critic (Dionysius of Halicarnassus, who admittedly treated Polybius as something of a competitor, though he had been dead for a century) classed his History among the works nobody can read to the end. In a literary tradition where style came first, his clumsy, overheavy sentences were a handicap. But the main obstacle to popularity was the subject itself. It was one thing for the Greeks to recognize the benefactions of Polybius; it was quite another thing to have to read how Greece had been enslaved.

Educated Romans were affected by the inverse consideration and therefore for a while studied Polybius with care. He was Livy's main source for the period 220–146 B.C. As Cicero shows, Polybius' interpretation of the Roman state as a mixed constitution and his general theory about the cycle of the forms of government attracted much

71

attention in Rome. But after Augustus the Roman aristocracy progressively lost interest in the problems with which Polybius had been concerned; and knowledge of Greek declined in the West. Ultimately the survival of Polybius depended on the Eastern, Greek-speaking readers of the Byzantine period.

Here the reactions (as far as our very incomplete knowledge of the facts goes) were mixed. In the sixth and seventh centuries Polybius found many admirers. Zosimus, a pagan, took him as a model for his history of the decline of Rome which he attributed to the introduction of Christianity. But Republican Rome was not the most urgent historical theme for later Byzantine readers. Polybius' work was of greater interest as a collection of stock examples for soldiers, diplomats and rhetoricians.

By the time the manuscripts of Polybius were brought back to Western Europe in the fifteenth century, only the first five books had been preserved in their entirety. Even the fundamental sixth book on the Roman constitution was mutilated. A few books (the concluding one among them) had been entirely lost. The rest was partially transmitted in an anthology of books 1–16 and 18 and in those sections of the excerpts made by Constantine VII which had survived in their turn. It has been calculated that we have about one third of the original text. The most grievous lacunas are in books 31–40, which gave Polybius' judgement on the effects of Roman imperialism after 168 B.C. Much of the disagreement among modern scholars is due to our insufficient knowledge of Polybius' last writings.

*

But the main difficulty about interpreting Polybius is that our evaluation of him depends on our evaluation of Roman imperialism, and our evaluation of Roman imperialism depends on our evaluation of Polybius. Inscriptions and later accounts no doubt serve to check what Polybius says, but he is the only contemporary witness we have and in all probability the only contemporary who took the trouble to collect the facts of Roman conquest and to think steadily and sharply about them. Can we find a way out of this vicious circle?

Polybius' field of inquiry is fairly well defined by a chain of implicit or explicit assumptions. The assumption that the Roman urge to rule was natural and as such not to be questioned depended on the other assumption that conquests did not produce a serious conflict of interests within Roman society. In its turn the (alleged) absence of conflicts was explained by the assumption that Rome had a particularly stable constitution. At this point Polybius began to proceed analytically. He described the Roman state as a mixed constitution which would not easily degenerate. He showed in detail how well the Roman leaders managed the affairs of their own country while their opponents fell into all the possible traps – with the exception of Hannibal, a great man who was, however, unable to save his erratic fellow citizens.

Religion was one of the instruments in the hands of the Roman aristocracy for controlling the masses. Polybius had no hesitation in recognizing a Roman mistake when he saw one. He even admitted that the Roman conquest of Sardinia, by then in the remote past, was patently unjust. What he did claim was that the Roman system was in theory and in practice more resilient and ultimately more successful than any other political system. Few could deny that he was right.

Polybius' position would have been impregnable if, as a Greek, he had not had to convince himself that what the Romans had done was beneficial for the conquered as well as for the conquerors. This in a sense was not too difficult. It must by now be evident that Polybius was one of those Greeks who, if they had to choose between social reforms and Roman rule, would unhesitatingly choose the Romans. The situation had changed after 168. In the decade 156–146 B.C. the opposition of the Greek democrats to Rome had become increasingly radical, with the liberation of slaves and a moratorium for debts: the old cry for the redistribution of land was heard again. Polybius therefore treated the rebels against Rome as madmen: 'the whole country was the prey of an unparalleled attack of madness with people throwing themselves into wells and over precipices'. He was too indignant to pause to consider that the far more traditional and conservative Macedonians shared in this hatred of Rome.

*

But the destruction of Corinth and the obliteration of Carthage were not events a civilized man could dismiss by imputing madness to the victims. As a Roman agent Polybius was also bound to consider what the survivors of the massacres of 146 B.C. were likely to think of Rome. It was part of his realism (and of the realism he attributed to the Romans) to take public opinion into account. Nor was he blind to the coincidence of the increasing unrest among Macedonians, Greeks and Carthaginians before 146 and the increasing ruthlessness of the Romans. He knew and stated that the Romans had decided to eliminate Carthage long before the Carthaginians gave them the 'suitable pretext which would appear decent to foreign nations'.

This explains why he went out of his way to report at length the reactions of the Greeks to the destruction of Carthage. He recorded four different opinions of the Greeks. With skill he sandwiched the second and third opinions, which are a devastating denunciation of Roman ruthlessness and treachery, between the first and the fourth opinions, which accept the Roman action as necessary or at least as understandable. As the fourth opinion substantially repeats the legalistic arguments for destroying Carthage which Polybius elsewhere declares a mere pretext, I cannot, as Professor Walbank does, take it to be Polybius' personal and final justification of the destruction of Carthage.

Indeed none of the four opinions can be identified as Polybius' own. The whole debate is meant to underline the enormity of the event itself by indicating the reactions of Greek public opinion to a war which did not touch the Greeks directly. If Polybius had produced a similar debate on the destruction of Corinth he would have risked his own skin – which was not the purpose of his historical work. But at least his Greek readers would have noticed that he had previously condemned the Macedonian destruction of a Greek city with the words: 'good men should not make war on wrongdoers with the object of destroying and exterminating them' (5, 11, 5).

*

The vicious circle by which our understanding of Polybius depends on our understanding of Roman imperialism and vice versa is broken as soon as we appreciate his real position. He was caught in the system he attempted to describe. He was not free – in the least metaphysical sense of the word. To disapprove of Rome was to perish. But by the mere effort of studying the causes and consequences of his masters' victories Polybius created a space for himself. He never accepted the Romans wholeheartedly. He distrusted their Hellenization. He paints in a hostile way the adoption of Greek customs by their younger generation. He sympathizes with Cato's jokes against those Romans who wrote bad Greek as if they were obliged to do so by a federal decree. He seems to be unaware that under his very eyes, and with the patronage of his own friends, gifted Roman writers were using Greek models to create an original literature in Latin. Polybius was by no means certain that the conquest of Greece would improve the minds of the conquerors.

Though we can seldom check against independent evidence what he

74

tells us about his contemporaries, there are at least two basic facts which he underrates. One is the Roman conquest of Spain and the other is the Roman organization of Italy. In either case we may suspect that he was misled by his Greek preoccupations and prejudices.

Polybius visited northern Italy, southern Gaul and Spain, and was certainly aware of the energies that the Romans were expending there. He could not know, as we do, that it would take the Romans two centuries (the first and second B.C.) to obtain complete control of Spain and that the conquest of Spain would lead to the occupation of the whole of Gaul, with the resulting destruction of Celtic culture in continental Europe. But it was already evident in Polybius's time that after the elimination of the Carthaginians Spain could not possibly count even as a remote danger to Rome. The decision to remain in Spain and to control it was a compound of economic considerations (mines to explore and land to colonize) and of instinctive pleasure in power.

The Romans never bothered to learn the native languages of Spain and Gaul and never cared for Celtic and Iberian art. They were not faced there by a language and a culture they knew and respected, as was the case with Greece. But if there was inducement to plunder and massacre at pleasure, there was also a danger of demoralization of which the Romans themselves soon became aware. It was to fight corruption in dealing with the Spanish provinces that they first instituted special tribunals for malversation in 149 B.C., and there are other signs that they became uneasy about the behaviour of their generals in the Peninsula. Unless we are misled by the lacunas in Polybius' text, he appears to be insensitive to the problems presented to Rome by the conquest of Spain. There is no sign that he realized that the destruction of Numantia by his friend Scipio raised the same moral problems as the destruction of Corinth and Carthage.

*

Even more characteristic is his treatment of the Italian confederation, which was the force behind Roman expansion. Whatever may have been the origins of this confederation, which existed in its essential features by the beginning of the third century B.C., it was founded on a series of treaties between Rome as the hegemonic state and the various populations of central and southern Italy as vassal nations. They provided Rome with a fixed number of auxiliary troops for any war. In return Rome supported the local aristocracies. Social stability was reinforced by the expansion of Italian trade and by some share in colonization.

Polybius knows and expounds the military aspects of this organization but seems to be indifferent to its political and social aspects. Though he is particularly concerned with identifying the sources of Roman strength he misses the most important one, the cooperation between aristocracies in Italy. He applied to Rome a Greek constitutional scheme (derived, with modifications, from Plato and Aristotle) which can do no justice to the novelty of the Italian confederation. He interprets the Roman state as a city of the Greek type with a mixed constitution controlled by the Senate.

Mommsen poured on this theory well-deserved contempt, which has not prevented later scholars from repeating and expanding Polybius. It is difficult to say whether excessive confidence in Hellenic theories or excessive admiration for his Roman friends led Polybius to underrate the political importance of the Italian organization. He was too pre-occupied with the policies of the Romans in the East to study with equal care their problems and achievements in Spain and in Italy.

What limited Polybius as a historian of ancient Rome – his excessive confidence in the theory of the mixed constitution, his emphasis on military technicalities, his preference for the civilized East – recommended him to the politicians and soldiers of the Renaissance. The men who among the ruins of the feudal system were searching for a new political and military machinery were anxious to get all the advice they could from the classical thinkers. What is surprising is not that this should happen, but that it should go on for four centuries. Polybius was one of the first to be exploited and one of the last to be returned after exploitation to the museum of classical philology. He was re-imported into Western Europe by the future chancellor of the Florentine Republic, Leonardo Bruni, about 1418. He became a model for military and political history before Thucydides was known. One century later Machiavelli used Polybius (whom he was unable to read in the original) both for his institutional and his military theories. About the middle of the sixteenth century Jean Bodin delighted in Polybius as a great master of historical wisdom.

*

At the end of the century Justus Lipsius – a Christian Stoic who moved between Protestants and Catholics without losing respectability on either side – produced his *De Militia Romana*, a theory about a modern army on the lines suggested by Polybius. He considered the advice of Polybius especially useful against the Turks, but of course did not exclude his employment against fellow Christians. The military reformer Maurice of Nassau, Prince of Orange (1567–1625), was Lipsius's pupil. Another Nassau, Wilhelm Ludwig, had the account of the battle of Cannae by Polybius retranslated because the Latin translation by N. Perotti did not make sense to him as a piece of technical writing. The recent publication of the 'Book of War' by a third Nassau, Johann von Nassau-Siegen (1561–1623), adds a fascinating document to this dossier.

The prodigious popularity among professional soldiers of Lipsius' *De Militia Romana* was later matched by the success of the *Considérations sur les causes de la grandeur et de la décadence des Romains* (1734) and of *L'Esprit des Lois* (1748) by Montesquieu, who theorized the separation of powers on the model offered by Polybius. It is a well-known matter for regret by classical scholars on both sides of the Atlantic that Polybius should never have been recognized as one of the founding fathers of the USA. Evidence is available that he was read in the right places.

Alas, his career was interrupted by the Romantic movement. He had none of the qualities that could endear him to the Byronic age. He did not like rebels, he felt no nostalgia for simpler societies, he understood religion almost exclusively as a way of controlling the lower classes. And he wrote as badly as the professors who studied him. Our age, perhaps for contradictory reasons, is clearly returning to him with sympathy. He saved his skin and his intelligence. To be more precise, if he lost some of his intelligence in his successful effort to save his skin, what was left was enough to keep many later historians and political philosophers in business through the centuries.

6

Polybius' Reappearance in Western Europe*

I

POLYBIUS arrived twice in Italy, the first time in 167 B.C., the second time at an uncertain date about A.D. 1415. In both cases he had some difficulty in establishing his credentials. He was born too late to be a classic, too early to be a classicist. Furthermore, he had committed the unpardonable sin of having underrated Sparta and Athens, the two pillars of classicism. There was also the suspicion, never definitely dispelled, that he was something of a bore. Only Dionysius of Halicarnassus (*Comp.*, 30) was courageous enough to list him among the authors one does not read to the end, but the silence of Quintilian was even more deadly. Yet Cato the Elder respected him; Sempronius Asellio learnt from him what pragmatic history was about; Varro, Nepos and Cicero – that is, the greatest authorities of the Caesarian age – recognized his worth. Livy praised and plundered him. Pliny the Elder quoted him twelve times on geographic matters, and presented him as a great traveller (*Nat. H.*, V, 9). Ammianus Marcellinus shows that Julian the Apostate was acquainted with Polybius (XXIV, 2, 16) and St Jerome repeated Porphyry's opinion that Polybius was one of the authors necessary for the understanding of the last part of the Book of Daniel (*In Dan.*, in *PL*, XXV, 494A), and Orosius quoted him twice, once very prominently (*Hist.*, IV, 20, 6; V, 3, 3).

For the reputation of Polybius in the Renaissance not all these testimonials were of equal value. Cicero's praise in *De republica* was wasted on an age *de libris quidem rei publicae iam desperans*, to repeat Petrarch's words (*Sen.*, 16, 1). This, however, made the same Cicero's definition of Polybius as *bonus auctor in primis* in *De officiis* (III, 32, 113) all the more valuable. Again, the reference to Polybius in Livy, XLV, 44,

*Polybe – Entretiens sur l'Antiquité Classique, XX (1973), Fondation Hardt, Vandoeuvres-Genève, 1974, pp. 347–72.

19, became known only in 1527, but since Petrarch had put together Livy's first, third and fourth decades in the present cod. Harleianus 2493 – that is by A.D. 1329 – humanists were aware that for Livy Polybius was *haudquaquam spernendus auctor* (XXX, 45, 5); *non incertum auctorem cum omnium Romanarum rerum tum praecipue in Graecia gestarum* (XXXIII, 10, 10). With the spread of Plutarch in the Quattrocento nothing could be more impressive than the knowledge that Brutus had been hard at work on an epitome of Polybius on the eve of the battle of Pharsalus: ἄχρι τῆς ἑσπέρας ἔγραφε συντάττων ἐπιτομὴν Πολυβίου (*Brut.*, 4, 8). The rediscovery of Pausanias added new elements to Polybius' posthumous glory. But we must remember that, i the *editio princeps* of Pausanias by Marcus Masurus goes back to 1516, what counts are the two Latin translations by Romulus Amasaeus and Abramus Loescher which appeared respectively in 1547 and 1550. Scholars of the second part of the sixteenth century could not fail to be touched by the decree of the Megalopolitans which praised their fellow-citizen Polybius as one who 'roamed over every land and sea, became an ally of the Romans, and stayed their wrath against the Greeks'. Indeed (Pausanias went on to report) 'whenever the Romans obeyed the advice of Polybius things went well with them, but whenever they would not listen to his instructions they made mistakes' (VIII, 30, 8–9). From Pausanias scholars learnt furthermore that in the temple of the Despoina near Arakesion an inscription roundly declared that 'Greece would not have fallen at all, if she had obeyed Polybius in everything, and when she met disaster, her only help came from him' (VIII, 37, 2). Here one found a historian *magister vitae*.

I am not aware of any quotation of Polybius in the Latin writers of Antiquity after St Jerome and Orosius. When Petrarch wrote his letter to Livy he asked him to convey his greetings to 'Polybius and Quintus Claudius and Valerius Antias and all those whose glory thine own greater light has dimmed' (*Fam.*, XXIV, 8): he had in mind Orosius, *Hist.*, V, 3, 3, where Polybius is found together with Claudius and Antias. To Petrarch all these gentlemen were mere names. What, so far, remains obscure is the extent of the knowledge and reputation of Polybius in his own Greek world between the fifth and the fifteenth centuries. This obscurity also conditions our appreciation of the reappearance of Polybius in the West at the beginning of the fifteenth century.[1]

Leaving Zosimus aside, I am insufficiently informed about what Polybius meant to Byzantine historians. Imitations of individual passages have been identified in Procopius and Agathias.[2] It would be surprising if Procopius' notion of Tyche and his emphasis on the technical factors in warfare had not been affected by Polybius. He may have thought of the comparison between the Macedonian phalanx and the Roman legion in Polybius XVIII 28 ff. when in the procemium to the *Persian War* he compared the bowmen of his time with the archers of the past: but I do not find Polybius' influence self-evident. The stylistic models of Procopius and Agathias are Herodotus, Thucydides, Xenophon, Diodorus, Arrian and even Appian, but not Polybius. Photius, strangely enough, took no notice of Polybius. In the tenth century Constantine VII Porphyrogenitus redistributed Polybius' history among his collections of excerpts – that is, he reduced the history to the function of *exempla*. Somebody else, not later than the tenth century, made excerpts of a less systematic nature from Books I–XVI and XVIII: which we now call the *Excerpta antiqua*. Book XVII may already by then have been lost. It is pleasant to remember that Casaubon did not think it impossible that the *Excerpta antiqua* went back to the epitome of Polybius by Brutus! The influence of Polybius has been noticed in the biographies of Theophanes Continuatus, in Anna Comnena, in Byzantine treatises on fortifications and, no doubt, in many other places.[3] In the late eleventh century Xiphilinus preferred Polybius to Dio Cassius because he was less inclined to report portents (LI, p. 506 Boiss.). Xiphilinus obviously knew what sort of historian Polybius was. Polybius' status in the history of Byzantine thought – and especially in Byzantine historiography – still needs to be clarified by an expert.

To all appearances, Polybius was not one of the Greek authors most prominently exhibited by Byzantine scholars when they came to the West either as ambassadors or as refugees, or both. The first Byzantine scholar to produce an edition and translation of Polybius (a partial text of Book VI), Janus Lascaris in 1529, did so in response to the increasing interest by Italian scholars and politicians in this author. How the MSS. of Polybius reached Italy is only partially known. John M. Moore has done much in recent years to reclassify *The Manuscript Tradition of Polybius* (Cambridge 1965) but we need a Billanovich to tell the true story of Polybius' reception. The most important codex for Books I–V, A, *Vaticanus Gr.* 124 – written in A.D. 947 by Ephraim the Monk – was almost certainly in the Vatican Library in 1455 under Pope Nicholas V.[4] Moore believes that B – *Londiniensis, Mus. Brit., Add.* MS. 11728 – was directly copied from A. If so, there are some interesting inferences to be made for both B and A. B was copied by a monk, Stephanus, in the monastery of John the Baptist in Constantinople in 1416: the same MS.

was in the Badia of the Benedictines in Florence by 1437; and it came to the Badia from the library of Antonio Corbinelli,[5] who had died in 1425. It follows that A was still in Constantinople in 1416, and that B reached Florence between 1416 and 1425. Indeed B was transferred to Siena in 1435, when Antonius Athenaeus made a copy of it for Francesco Filelfo, the present *Mediceus Laurentianus Plut.* 69, 9, or B3. From B3 descended B4 and B5, both now in the Marciana, one as *Marcianus Gr.* 371, the other as *Marcianus Gr.* 369, both belonging to the library of Cardinal Bessarion: the subscription of B5 makes it clear that it was copied at Bessarion's command, and this is also probable for B4. The name of Filelfo is particularly interesting. He had been trying hard to get hold of manuscripts of Polybius. In a letter of 1428 to Traversari, after his return from Constantinople, he said that he had (or was expecting) a MS. of Polybius.[6] But Filelfo, not to speak of Bessarion, had apparently begun to take an interest in Polybius only when his reputation had already been solidly re-established in Florence.

The location of Polybius' rediscovery is not in any doubt: Florence. The discoverer does not seem to be in doubt either: Leonardo Bruni Aretino. The date was about 1418–19 – when Bruni wrote his history of the first Punic War and of the subsequent Illyrian and Gallic Wars, a free translation from Polybius, I–II, 35.

J. E. Sandys – a name one always utters with respect – thought he had found some evidence that about 1403 Pier Paolo Vergerio had chosen Polybius as an example of a Greek historian who knew Roman history better than the Romans (or at least than the Italians) themselves.[7] But Vergerio's speech *De ingenuis moribus* has no definite allusion to Polybius and may allude, for instance, to Plutarch: *Et est eo deventum ut Latinae quoque historiae et cognitionem et fidem a Graecis auctoribus exigamus.*[8] The name of Vergerio may be left out of the story. We still do not yet know where and how Bruni found a manuscript of Polybius with an account of the first Punic and of the Illyrian and Gallic Wars. I am not aware of any evidence suggesting that when his teacher Manuel Chrysoloras came to Florence in 1397 he brought with him a manuscript of Polybius.[9] We can, however, be sure that about 1418 there was nothing Leonardo Bruni needed except a manuscript to enable him to appreciate the importance of Polybius as a historian. The present *Londiniensis* 11728 may already have been in Florence at that time.

Bruni himself tells us in his *Commentaria rerum suo tempore gestarum* how at the turn of the century the war between Giangaleazzo Visconti and Florence had represented a revolution in the intellectual life of Italy

– the rediscovery of Greek language and literature: *Litterae per huius belli intercapedines mirabile quantum per Italiam increvere, accedente tunc primum cognitione litterarum graecarum quae septingentis iam annis apud nostros homines desierant esse in usu. Rettulit autem graecam disciplinam ad nos Chrysoloras, Byzantius vir domi nobilis ac litterarum Graecarum peritissimus.*[10] Hans Baron's admirable work on Leonardo Bruni and his time can be said to be an extensive commentary on this theme formulated by Bruni himself.[11] The young man, who, about 1403, had modelled his *Laudatio Florentinae Urbis* on Aristides' *Panathenaicus,* was a mature statesman and historian fifteen years later.[12] He had come back to Florence in 1415 after long and disappointing service in the papal Curia. He was more than ever certain that Florence belonged to the line of direct descent from the ancient republics of Greece and Rome. He had started the *Historiae Florentini populi.* More or less together with the *Commentaria tria de Primo Bello Punico* he wrote in 1419 the preface to the new Statute of the *Parte Guelfa* in which he reasserted the idea of republican liberty. Even more significantly he composed in 1421 the pamphlet *De militia.* It is the merit of the edition and commentary by C. C. Bayley in 1961 to have revived interest in this little work. Criticisms of this edition have not always been fair.[13] Professor Bayley did understand that *militia, miles* meant to Bruni 'cavalry, knight'. He did not interpret the pamphlet as an attack against mercenaries on behalf of civic armies – as if Bruni were Machiavelli. Bruni of course intended to glorify the equestrian order and to trace it back to ancient – and therefore honourable – origins. In such a context the Polybius Bruni knew could be of little use, since Bruni was certainly not acquainted with Book VI. Yet it is not an accident that the man who discovered Polybius as a historian was also especially interested in military problems. In various forms and situations the combination of admiration for Polybius as a historian and the interest in military problems was to remain characteristic of the whole debate on Polybius from Machiavelli to Justus Lipsius and Casaubon, not to mention the later Montesquieu.

Contemporaries sensed that Bruni was producing something important in his *Commentaria de Primo Bello Punico.* While he was still writing it in or about 1419, Ambrogio Traversari wrote to Francesco Barbaro: *Leonardus Arretinus commentaria scribere de primo bello poenico ex Polybio coepit, opus, ut audio, egregium; nam ipse non vidi.*[14] We must bear in mind that Bruni did not intend his work as a simple translation of Books I–II, 35 by Polybius. He intended to write history, more precisely that history of the first Punic War and of the Gallic War

225–222 B.C. which was missing in Livy. It must have given Bruni and his Florentine readers enormous pleasure to end with the occupation and humiliation of Milan by the Romans. Bruni paraphrased and freely supplemented his Polybius to make him look like Livy. The Sallustian component in Bruni's historical style which Antonio La Penna so acutely recognized in Bruni's *Historiae Florentini populi* and elsewhere does not seem to figure – at least to my untutored eye – in the history of the Punic War.[15] Bruni's success in Livianizing Polybius may be indicated by a story we owe to Gianni Gervasoni (he published it in 1925). According to this story in 1783 Lorenzo Mascheroni, 'insigne matematico, leggiadro poeta e ottimo cittadino' (as Vincenzo Monti later defined him), thought he had discovered in an old MS. Livy's account of the first Punic War. After having transcribed the greater part of the MS. he revealed its contents to his fellow-citizen of Bergamo, the learned Canonico Conte Camillo Agliardi. Agliardi immediately recognized the nature of the text: Leonardo Bruni's *De Primo Bello Punico*, of course. Mascheroni turned to his Muse for consolation:

> Mio venerato Monsignor Canonico,
> Affè, m'avete fatto il bel servizio
> Da farmi per un anno malinconico.
> Che v'è venuto in cor di darmi indizio
> Di quel volume, ch'io non voglio dire,
> Che allegro io mi copiava a precipizio?[16]

Two points are relevant in Bruni's historical method. First of all he thought that there were only two ways of writing history: one was to observe and recount contemporary facts, the other to discover new sources and to present their accounts in one's own appropriate language. As he wrote in his preface to his translation of Plutarch's life of Marc Antony – perhaps before 1405: *In historia vero, in qua nulla est inventio, non video equidem, quid intersit, an ut facta, an ut ab alio dicta, scribas. In utroque enim par labor est, aut etiam maior in secundo.* In perfect accord with these principles, he went on producing, as his own histories, what we would treat as translations or paraphrases of ancient texts: his *Commentaria rerum graecarum* of 1439 are a paraphrase of Xenophon's *Hellenica*, and the *De bello Italico adversus Gothicos libri IV* of 1441, his last big work, are almost undiluted Procopius. He never concealed his sources: Polybius is mentioned specifically in the introduction to his history of the Punic War. But he thought he had done the day's work if he put his sources into his own prose. At the same time (and this is my second point) he was well aware that ancient writers contradicted each other because they followed different sources. He thought he was imitating the ancients in so far as the ancients themselves blindly followed their sources; he knew that this situation created difficulties, but as far as I am aware he never formulated any general principle about the solution of such difficulties. He came very near to the root of the problem in a letter to Cardinal Colonna who had asked questions about a contradiction between Livy and Polybius concerning *de legione illa quae Regium occupavit*: the references must be Polybius, I, 7 *versus* Livy, XXVIII, 28, 2 and XXXI, 31, 6. Bruni admits of course the existence of this contradiction between ancient authorities and appeals to the authority of Polybius as justification for the version he had preferred: *ego igitur in commentariis illis, quos tu legisti, Polybium Megalopolitanum secutus sum magnum profecto virum, et scriptorem egregium, ac summae apud Graecos auctoritatis.*[17] Having translated Polybius' Book I, Bruni knew what Polybius thought about the bias of Fabius Pictor and Philinus. In fact he deduced rather perversely from his author that Livy had followed Fabius Pictor, but Polybius had preferred Philinus as his source. If he, Bruni, had followed Polybius, and therefore by implication Philinus, the explanation was simple: Livy's account was lost, *cuius libri si extarent, nihil opus erat novo labore.*[18]

This mixture of uncritical repetition of ancient sources and of very critical awareness that the ancient authorities themselves were conditioned by their own sources is the real beginning of historical criticism. Thus Bruni had discovered a missing chapter of Republican Roman history and had suddenly presented Polybius as an authority on Republican Rome. This was very little compared to what he gave his contemporaries with his translation of Aristotle's *Politics*. From Aristotle he derived the interpretation of the Florentine constitution as a mixed constitution, which he was able to present in Greek to his Greek friends about 1438 in his wonderfully fresh pamphlet Περὶ τῆς τ ῶν Φλωρεντίνων πολιτείας.[19] But the link between Polybius and Aristotle was to become clear later with the rediscovery of Book VI. In 1437 Sicco Polenton had concluded in Padua the second edition of his *Scriptorum Illustrium Latinae Linguae libri XVIII*. There (but not in the first draft of 1426 which is preserved in *Cod. Ricc.* 121), Polybius is taken for granted as the authority for the first Punic War. He is also specifically mentioned as one of the Greek authors whom the Italians have lately made accessible: *Illud autem iam est horum beneficio, industria, opera factitatum quod Plutarchum, quod Polybium, quod Basilium, quod Ptolemaeum, quod alios plures ne singulos nominem, Graecos ac doctos scriptores, quos Latini homines ignorarent, traductos a Graeco latinas in litteras ac cognitos habeamus.*[20] Bruni had started his Greek studies with a translation of Basilius. Plutarch and Polybius were his authors. The allusion of Sicco Polenton to him is obvious: Ptolemy had been translated by one of Bruni's fellow students under Chrysoloras, Giacomo da Scarparia.

The new status of Polybius was recognized by Pope Nicholas V, about 1450, when Polybius was included among the Greek historians to be translated into Latin. Niccolò Perotti, who was chosen for the translation, was in the service of Bessarion, and there can be little doubt that his name was suggested by Bessarion and that he used one of the manuscripts owned by his protector. As *Marcianus Graecus* 369 was written later in 1470, *Marcianus* 371 is a strong candidate for identification with the codex used by Perotti.[21] But as one of his letters to the Pope's librarian Giovanni Tortelli shows, he found it a difficult MS. to work on and asked to see *Polybium summi pontificis qui olim d. episcopi Coronensis fuit.* The allusion, as so much else concerning Perotti, was clarified by Cardinal Mercati, who recognized in it MS. *Vat. Gr.* 1005 of the fourteenth century originally owned by Cristoforo Garatone, Bishop of Corone, who died in 1448.[22]

Perotti finished the translation of Book V, the last available to him, in the summer of 1454. Besides 'interim' rewards, he received five hundred golden 'ducati', for which he expressed gratitude in an epigram. In the next century the translation was found to be incompetent and it was finally denounced by Casaubon in words which ruined Perotti's reputation. But for the rest of the fifteenth century – and indeed even in the sixteenth century – Perotti's translation was the vehicle by means of which Polybius circulated in Europe. Unlike Bruni, Perotti did not believe that Polybius was useful only where Livy was missing. A passage of one of his letters to Tortelli contradicts Bruni's opinion:

> *Scribit etiam in eodem libro [III] secundum bellum punicum usque ad pugnam Cannensem, quod et si scribatur a Tito Livio nostro, tamen, mihi crede, non penitebit etiam hunc legisse, nam et gravius fortasse scribit, et lectione eius intelliguntur apertissime multa, quae apud Livium aut nullo modo aut vix intelligebantur.*[23]

What the almost simultaneous translation of the greatest Greek historians under Pope Nicholas V meant to European historiography is a point beyond our terms of reference today. We are still left with the curiosity to know what was happening to the rest of the preserved text of Polybius while the first five books were circulating in Latin. Hans Baron has repeatedly stated that when Leonardo Bruni in one of his letters (8, 4) distinguishes between panegyric and history – *aliud est enim historia, aliud laudatio* – he follows Polybius X, 21, 8 who opposes *encomium* to history. This would imply knowledge of the *Excerpta antiqua* and make it necessary to ask why Bruni seems to be unaware of Book VI with its discussion of the Roman constitution. But the distinction between *encomium* and history is in Cicero. It may have been reinforced by the teaching of Chrysoloras, with or without any specific reference to Polybius. I should like, however, to leave the question open, because we know at present too little about the circulation of the materials contained in the *Excerpta antiqua*.[24]

What is now the main MS. for the *Excerpta*, F, *Vat. Urbinas Gr.* 102 of the tenth or eleventh century, was in the library of Urbino at least from 1482 onwards. Copies circulated in Italy during the early sixteenth century. More precisely, F2, *Vaticanus Gr.* 1647, which was derived from F, belonged to Andrea Navagero at the beginning of the sixteenth century.

The first clear sign of acquaintance with the excerpts of Book VI was discovered not long ago by Carlo Dionisotti in one of those obvious printed texts to which few turn. Bernardo Rucellai who died in 1514 refers to Polybius' sixth Book in his *Liber de urbe Roma* first printed in Florence in the eighteenth century.[25] We know in fact that the *Liber de urbe Roma* was written before 1505 because it is mentioned in the *De honesta disciplina* by Pietro Crinito who died in 1505.[26] Rucellai wrote:

Me certe haud poenitet Polybii Megalopolitani sententiae esse, quippe qui romanam non modo praecellere ceteras omnes respublicas adserit, sed nihil eo rerum ordine excogitari posse perfectius ... Qui si Polybii sextum volumen recte interpretati sint, profecto longe aliter ac senserant de romana gravitate iudicabunt.

Thus in the first years of the sixteenth century Polybius' Book VI was discussed in Florence though no formal Latin translation of it was as yet in circulation. Machiavelli did not have to go far to learn about the cycle of the constitutions. There is no need to suppose that he had to wait for Janus Lascaris or anybody else to come to Florence to translate for him the Greek he was unable to read. The substance of Book VI had been known in Florence for several years when, to all appearances in 1513, he started writing his *Discorsi*.[27] Seldom has so much ingenuity been misused as in J. H. Hexter's paper *Seyssel, Machiavelli and Polybius VI:*

the mystery of the missing translation (*Studies in the Renaissance* 3, 1956, pp. 75–96). What remains memorable is that Machiavelli was the first to appreciate Polybius as a political thinker. Machiavelli also availed himself of Polybius in the *Arte della Guerra* about 1520 and was certainly confirmed by him in his admiration for the Roman military model, but his actual use of Polybius' texts (never explicitly quoted) is very restricted.[28]

As we have seen, it was in Florence that Polybius was rediscovered, first by Leonardo Bruni as a historian, then by Machiavelli and his contemporaries as a political thinker. It was probably also in Florence that Polybius was first studied philologically. Politian not only made extracts from Polybius (which are preserved in the famous MS. of the Bibliothèque Nationale, MS. Gr. 3069, and perhaps in the Turin MS. I, III, 13$^{1-2}$); he also used Polybius critically in his *Miscellaneorum Centuria Secunda* recently published by Vittore Branca and Manlio Pastore Stocchi. At no. 38 of the new *Centuria* Politian discusses the meaning of *Catorthoma* and leaves an empty space to be filled by quotations of the relevant Greek texts. In the margin he adds: *ex Thucydide aliquid et Polybio*. He intended to turn to Thucydides and Polybius for examples. Κατόρθωμα is not a word used by Thucydides, but is used by Polybius. The excellent editors have failed to notice, if I am not mistaken, that Polybius did not appear in Politian's *Centuria Prima*. His appearance in the second *Centuria* is therefore an event. But we must remember that Polybius was by then read in some universities. Rudolphus Agricola may have become acquainted with Polybius in Ferrara about 1475.[29]

II

After Machiavelli translations of the military chapters of Book VI multiply. There are at least four between 1525 and 1550. One was made by Machiavelli's admirer and disciple, Bartolomeo Cavalcanti, an exile from Florence. From 1537 to 1548, he served the Duke of Ferrara, Ercole II, who was not interested in republics, but was very ready to improve his army. For him Cavalcanti translated from Polybius a *Discorso circa la milizia romana* in 1539. In the following year Cavalcanti translated from Polybius XVIII, ch. 28–33, *La comparazione tra l'armadura e l'ordinanza de' Romani e de' Macedoni*. Finally, he wrote a dissertation on the Roman Camp, *Calculo della castrametatione*, which was printed, together with the *Comparazione*, in 1552 in a collection of pamphlets *Del modo dell'accampare*. Later, perhaps when he was old and poor in Padua about 1560, Cavalcanti went back to Polybius in the context of his *Trattati sopra gli ottimi reggimenti delle repubbliche antiche e moderne*. Here he used Polybius to support Aristotle on the mixed constitution, though he remarked drily that Polybius did not know Aristotle's *Politics* 'perchè nei tempi di Polibio, i libri di Aristotele non erano ancora stati trovati, nè i Romani ne potevano aver notizia'. Cavalcanti had obtained a complete transcription of the *Excerpta antiqua* of the *Cod. Urbinas* 102. His letters, which were made accessible by Mrs Christina Roaf in 1967, contain many details, new to me, about plans to publish the *Excerpta antiqua* in Italy. In a letter of 1540 to Pier Vettori he speaks of a projected publication by Paolo Manuzio. He also explains by implication why he did not go on with the complete translation of the *Excerpta* which he had promised. 'Giorgio greco', that is, Giorgio Balsamone who used to check Cavalcanti's translations of Polybius word by word, died about that time.[30] Certainly no one was in any hurry to print the Greek text of Polybius. Aldus Manutius significantly did not handle him. When in 1529 Janus Lascaris at last edited in Venice a fragment of Book VI, the Latin preceded the Greek and the publisher Joannes Antonius de Sabio felt obliged to explain: *Graeco libro ut omnia conferri possint adiuncto*.

Meanwhile, in accordance with the general trend, Polybius was being edited in Greek outside Italy. The text of Books I–V was first published at Haguenau in 1530 by Vincentius Opsopaeus (Heidnecker) who used a MS. sent to him by Jacobus Ottonis Aetzelius of Nuremberg. The MS. was the present *Monacensis Gr.* 157 (C), a fourteenth-century MS. brought from Constantinople after 1453 which for a while was in the library of Matthias Corvinus, King of Hungary. Later, in 1577, we find this MS. in the hands of Joachim Camerarius who gave it as a present to Albrecht V of Bavaria – hence its present location in the Bayerische Staatsbibliothek. Opsopaeus' introduction is important for its eulogy of Aldo Manuzio, its attack on the Thomist theologians and its high appreciation of Polybius himself (*historiae tam graecae quam latinae facile principatum obtinens, si omnia eius scripta ad memoriam nostram salva pervenissent*). In 1549 Johannes Hervagius published in Basle the *editio princeps* of the *Excerpta antiqua*. The text of the *Excerpta antiqua* came from a MS. in the possession of Don Diego Hurtado de Mendoza which was later burned in the fire of the Escorial in 1671. The translation into Latin was by Wolfgang Musculus.

Translations into modern languages were meanwhile in demand: L. Maigret published a French translation of Books I–V in 1545(?) and of Book VI in 1546(?). The Italian translation by L. Domenichi, notoriously incompetent, belongs to the same year, 1546. The English came a bad third in 1568 with a meagre translation of Book I by Christopher Watson of St John's College, Cambridge. The arrival of Polybius in England was, however, celebrated in a poem by R. W. which ends thus:

> Then Vertue learne
> That thou mayst earne
> Such glorie for to have
> As Momus sect
> Can not reject
> When thou arte closde in grave.

In 1574 Guil. Xylander published his German translation which Casaubon considered good. In 1582 Fulvio Orsini published in Antwerp the Polybius contained in the *Excerpta de legationibus* on a MS. sent to him by the great Antonius Augustinus, Bishop of Tarragona, the present U, now split between *Vat. Gr.* 1418 and *Neapolitanus Gr.* III, B, 15, which is a copy by Andreas Darmarius of a lost MS. of the Escorial.[31] Another edition of the *Eclogae legationum* by D. Hoeschel was published in Augsburg in 1603. They were the texts which paved the way for Casaubon's Paris edition of 1609. Casaubon, however, benefited from the acquaintance with other MSS. and especially from the readings communicated to him by Andreas Schottus from a MS. in his possession of the *Excerpta de legationibus*, the present *Bruxellensis* 11301/16.

The removal of the centre of the classical scene to France, Germany and the Low Countries only served to increase the interest in Polybius as a historian and as a theoretician of political and military organization. The humanistic national history which the Italians had diffused throughout Europe (Polydorus Virgilius, Paulus Aemilius, etc.) was beginning to lose favour. History was becoming the repository of prudence and wisdom in an age of religious conflicts and political absolutism. *Historia si adsit ex pueris facit senes: sin absit, ex senibus pueros.* These words by Juan Luis Vives, *De tradendis disciplinis* (*Opera*, I, 1555, p. 505) are echoed in endless variations by all sixteenth-century writers on history and the art of history writing. Prudence, direct experience, travels, geography, technical expertise and a general respect for truth were the virtues required of the historian; and Polybius seemed to have all of them. He lacked style, but translation into Latin would improve him. About 1550 Benedetto Varchi declared in the 'Proemio' to the *Storia Fiorentina*: 'Polibio, il quale de' Greci avemo preso a dover imitare, siccome Cornelio Tacito fra' Latini'. In 1552 Roger Ascham rather improbably associated Polybius with Commynes in his praise: they 'have done the duties of wise and worthy writers'. In 1566 Bodin thought that Paolo Giovio could not compete with Polybius in direct experience of military and political affairs: *ille (Polybius) in sua republica princeps, hic (Giovio) privatus.*[32]

Francescus Balduinus saw in Polybius the ideal combination of the historian and of the lawyer: *immo vero Polybius, cum fieret historicus, factus etiam iurisconsultus est.* Not by chance had Marcus Brutus – *et qualis quantusque vir* – chosen to read him before the battle of Pharsalus.[33] Francesco Patrizi and many others repeated with Polybius that the eye is better than the ear as a historical organ.[34] Uberto Folietta in his *De similitudine normae Polybianae* could play with the sophistic question: if Polybius is right in asserting that the true historian tells only the truth, why is it possible to have good stories (such as Homer's account of the Trojan war) which are not entirely true? What is the difference, if any, between *historicus verax* and *historicus verus*?[35] Patrizi was indeed inclined to believe that Polybius had crossed the border between history and philosophy, but had to allow one of the speakers in his *Della Historia Diece Dialoghi*, 1560, to interrupt him: 'E io vorrei ... che tutti gli historici fossero cosí misti di filosofo et d'historico, come si è Polibio.'

One of the reasons why Polybius became so authoritative was that he offered the best alternative to the obsession with Tacitus which was typical of the intellectual climate about 1585, especially in Italy and Spain. In more than one sense, Tacitus had become irresistible. He offered exactly that mixture of Machiavellianism, moralism, epigrammatic acuteness and pathos which the age liked. But the cooler minds turned to Polybius with relief, as he obviously knew more about war and politics and spoke about a better historical period. Justus Lipsius, the greatest student of Tacitus – but never a vulgar 'Tacitista' – was the most exacting interpreter of Polybius as a military historian.

Interest in Polybius as a military historian is noticeable everywhere in the sixteenth century. For instance, Guillaume du Bellay, lieutenant de Roy à Turin, prepared a volume of *Instructions sur le faict de la guerre extraictes des livres de Polybe, Frontin, Vegèce, Cornazan, Machiavel et plusieurs autres bons autheurs* which appeared posthumously in Paris in

1549, if they were his. His concern was the creation of a national militia to replace mercenaries. But in 1594 Lipsius recognized only one real predecessor to his *De militia Romana libri quinque. Commentarius ad Polybium*, namely *La militia Romana di Polibio di Tito Livio e di Dionigi Alicarnaseo* by Francesco Patrizi, 1583. The acknowledgement is significant. Patrizi, as we have seen, was not a blind admirer of Polybius. Even in his *La militia Romana* he shares the reservations expressed by Dionysius of Halicarnassus about Polybius. Yet Patrizi – an ignorant man in comparison with the massive erudition of Lipsius – may truly be described as Lipsius' predecessor because he believed that Polybius could provide a decisive contribution to the improvement of military organization, both in technique and in morale. In his dedication to Alfonso II d'Este Patrizi states that Roman military institutions were the only ones which could cope with the Turks; they would not be essentially affected by the 'nuova inventione della artigliaria'. The mention of the artillery was especially necessary in addressing a duke of Ferrara, since the Estensi had pioneered the use of the new weapon.

Lipsius was not concerned with the rise of national militias. He observes that they are unsuitable for monarchic states and that even a republic like Venice does not use its own citizens as soldiers. But the Turks show that a careful system of recruitment is required: *quid Turca in Ianizaris suis faciat non est ignotum* (ed. 1630, p. 356). The Romans have something to teach about recruitment, too, but it is in battle order and military discipline that they are the best masters. Roman superiority in battle order is clear: *abite Turcae cum Ianizaris vestris, qui imaginem aliquam usurpatis militiae priscae sed falsam* (p. 361). Even the Scythians were better disciplined than modern armies. In the Roman camp *iustitia, castitas, innocentia habitabat, et nusquam violenti aut feroces nisi in hostem erant* (p. 363).

It is not necessary to illustrate here the enormous success of the military commentary on Polybius prepared by Lipsius.[36] Though he published it as a professor in the Catholic University of Louvain, after having run away from the Protestant University of Leiden, his work was used as a military handbook by the Protestants even more than by the Catholics. He was the spiritual and technical guide behind the military reforms of Maurice of Orange, who had been his pupil in Leiden. Wilhelm Ludwig of Nassau was equally an admirer of Lipsius. One of the problems these military reformers had to face was the creation of an educated class of officers who would be able to lead and control their troops. Lipsius provided not only technical principles derived from Polybius, but also moral principles derived from Stoic philosophy. The notion that the Romans of the Republic, having been victorious for so long, held the secrets of military success, was so deep-rooted and widespread that Claudius Salmasius' *De re militari Romanorum*, written originally for Prince Frederick Henry of Orange, was left unpublished on purpose until 1657.[37] Wilhelm Ludwig of Nassau made a thorough study of Polybius' account of the battle of Cannae. He recognized that Perotti's translation of that section of Polybius was unreliable and had another translation made by Volrat von Plessen.[38]

Approved as a pragmatic historian of the highest competence by Bodin, presented to the ruling classes as an authority on war by Lipsius, Polybius was read and studied about 1600 as perhaps never before or after. His difficult and unclassical language was no longer an obstacle to Western readers who had attained new levels of knowledge of Greek and were particularly interested (as were Salmasius and Grotius) in Late Greek. Casaubon never published the monumental commentary he had planned, but his edition and translation of 1609 offered the best guide to interpretation and was a pleasure to the eye. In the introduction he summarized all the contemporary motives for admiring Polybius. He extolled his mastery of the military and diplomatic arts and his ability to understand the causes of events; he maintained that he was a religious man and even praised his style; he compared him advantageously with Thucydides, Xenophon, Sallust, Livy, etc., and finished by preferring him to Tacitus: *quid enim principi, praesertim iuveni, lectione illorum Annalium esse queat pernitiosius?*

Casaubon may well have contributed to the popularity of Polybius in England when he moved to London in 1610. But William Camden needed little encouragement from Casaubon to take Polybius as his mentor for the *Annales rerum Anglicarum et Hibernicarum regnante Elizabetha*, 1615.[39]

The abundant erudite work of the seventeenth century on and around Polybius (such as the edition of the *Excerpta Peiresciana* by H. Valesius, 1634, and the commentary by Jacobus Gronovius, 1670) was supported by this warm feeling for the master of historical pragmatism. In 1615 H. Grotius included Plutarch and Polybius in his plan of studies, but left Thucydides out of it.[40] Gerardus Ioannes Vossius expressed common opinion in making Polybius the central figure of his *Ars historica*, 1623 and in praising him in *De historicis graecis* (2nd ed., 1651): *civilem prudentiam si spectes et scientiam militarem nulli fuerit secundus* (p. 124).

Casaubon's influence is easily recognized in later compilations. For instance, John Dryden composed a 'character' of Polybius which appeared as a preface to the translation of Polybius by Sir H. S[hears] in 1693. Dryden, like Casaubon, is still concerned with the question whether Polybius or Tacitus is the better historian. He has, however, some curious notions of his own, not necessarily inspired by better scholarship. He believes that Constantine the Great collected the 'negotiations' of Polybius as an ambassador. As he assumes Constantine the Great to have been English, he can conclude: 'I congratulate my country, that a prince of our extraction (as was Constantine) has the honour of obliging the Christian World by these remainders of our great historian.'

But if one had to follow seriously the course of Polybius' reputation during the seventeenth century, one would probably have to account for a change of emphasis in his fame. This change ultimately emerged very clearly in England in the early eighteenth century. It was now Polybius' picture of the mixed government which attracted attention. The balance of power in England was compared with the balance of power in Rome. As England was also a state where religion was controlled by the civil power, any reference in Polybius – or indeed in any other writer – to the place of religion in Rome was treated with interest. Even the debate on early parliaments involved Polybius. This makes a very different story, which I hope to tell elsewhere.

I shall conclude by summarizing the story I have been able to put together for today. Polybius was rediscovered in Florence as a historian of the first Punic War by Leonardo Bruni about 1420. Though he had been translated into Latin by the middle of the fifteenth century, his reputation as a historian and as a political thinker does not seem to have been widely diffused. It was in republican Florence, too, that the importance of his Book VI was recognized for the first time by Machiavelli and others at the beginning of the sixteenth century. Even the first philological work on him seems to have been done in Florence, by Politian. The idea of printing the Greek text does not appear to have interested the Italians until it was too late. The publication of Polybius in Germany coincided with the opening of a new stage in Greek studies – and with the new didactic and pragmatic mood of European historiography. Polybius' reputation soared rapidly in the second part of the sixteenth century. His fame was based on his expertise as a military and diplomatic historian. The Dutch republicans took his lessons to heart, though paradoxically the lesson was spelled out by Justus Lipsius after he had preferred Catholicism and monarchy to Protestantism and republic. Finally, Polybius and his Protestant editor, Casaubon, took refuge in England, and the Dutch had a better reason for remaining faithful to both.

Having enjoyed the posthumous company of Casaubon so many times – among his books and manuscripts in Bodley's Library and in the British Museum – I salute his memory from Geneva, where he was a citizen and a professor.

References

1. For general information J. Michaud, *Biographie Universelle*, nouvelle éd. (Paris–Leipzig n.d., 33), pp. 662–73; K. Ziegler in *RE*, s.v. Polybios (XXI, 2, 1952, pp. 1572–8). The bibliography (pp. 179–83) of J. M. Moore, *The Manuscript Tradition of Polybius*, Cambridge, 1965, is here generally presupposed. See also by J. M. Moore, *GRBS*, 12, 1971, pp. 411–50. The introductions by J. Schweighäuser and Th. Büttner-Wobst to their editions are of course indispensable. A summary of the information in P. Pédech, *Polybe, Histoires, Livre I*, Paris, 1969, Introduction; but see the review by J. M. Moore, *Gnomon* 44 (1972), p. 545. Of basic importance P. Burke, 'A Survey of the Popularity of Ancient Historians, 1450–70', *H & T*, 5, 1966, pp. 135–52, whereas A. M. Woodward, 'Greek History at the Renaissance', *JHS*, 63, 1943, pp. 1–14, is of little help for Polybius.

2. B. Rubin, *RE*, s.v. Prokopios (XXIII, i, 1957, cols. 332, 351 and elsewhere); A. Cameron, *Agathias*, Oxford, 1970, p. 147.

3. R. J. H. Jenkins, *DOP*, 8, 1954, pp. 11–30; A. Toynbee, *Constantine Porphyrogenitus and his World*, London, 1973, p. 306.

4. R. Devreesse, *Le fonds grec de la Bibliothèque Vaticane*, Città del Vaticano, 1965, p. 39. In general R..Sabbadini, *Le scoperte dei codici latini e greci ne' secoli XIV e XV*, Firenze, 1905 (reprint, 1967), pp. 43–71.

5. R. Blum, *La Biblioteca della Badia Fiorentina e i codici di Antonio Corbinelli*, Città del Vaticano, 1951, p. 44; L. Martinez, *The Social World of the Florentine Humanists*, London, 1963, pp. 319–20.

6. A. Traversari, *Epist.*, XXIV, 32 (II, 1024, ed. L. Mehus). J. M. Moore, *The Manuscript Tradition of Polybius*, 13, is not quite correct in the interpretation of this letter. Cf. G. Voigt, *Die Wiederbelebung des classischen Altertums*, I, 3, Berlin, 1893, pp. 348–65.

7. J. E. Sandys, *A History of Classical Scholarship*, II, Cambridge, 1908, p. 49.

8. *De ingenuis moribus et liberalibus studiis adulescentiae libellus*, ed. A. Gnesotto, *Atti Accad. Padova*, N.S. 34, 1917–18, p. 121. Cf. the prudent note by E. Garin, *L'educazione umanistica in Italia*, Bari, 1949, p. 78.

9. G. Cammelli, *Manuele Crisolora. I dotti bizantini e le origini dell'umanesimo*, I, Firenze, 1941.

10. Muratori, *RIS*, XIX, p. 920 = Muratori-Carducci, XIX, 3, p. 431 = H. Baron, *Leonardo Bruni Aretino, Humanistisch-philosophische Schriften*, Leipzig, 1928, p. 125 n. Here, p. 122, the Prooemium to *Commentaria primi belli punici* (for its date, p. 167). On p. 104, the preface to Plutarch. The text of the *Commentaria* was printed in Brescia, 1498.

11. *The Crisis of the Early Italian Renaissance* (revised edition, Princeton, 1966 – 1st ed. 1955 to be compared). For further discussion see N. S. Struever, *The Language of History in the Renaissance*, Princeton, 1970, pp. 101–43 and bibliography quoted.

12. H. Baron, *From Petrarch to Leonardo Bruni*, Chicago, 1968, pp. 151–71, 232–63.

13. P. O. Kristeller, *Canadian Historical Review*, 44, 1963, pp. 66–70; S. Bertelli, *RSI*, 76, 1964, pp. 834–6; H. M. Goldbrunner, *Quellen und Forschungen aus Italienischen Archiven* 46, 1966, pp. 478–87.

14. A. Traversari, *Epist.*, VI, 14 (II, 292 Mehus). *Cf.* B. Reynolds, *BiblH&R*, 16, 1954, pp. 108–18.

15. A. La Penna, *Arcadia*, I, 1966, pp. 255–76.

16. The article, originally printed in *La Rivista di Bergamo*, 1925, is reprinted in G. Gervasoni, *Studi e ricerche sui filologi e la filologia classica tra il 700 e l'800 in Italia*, Bergamo, 1929, pp. 16–25, and is mentioned by B. L. Ullman, *Studies in the Italian Renaissance*, Roma, 1955, p. 73 n. *Cf.* in general D. J. Wilcox, *The Development of Florentine Humanist Historiography*, Cambridge, Mass., 1969, pp. 36–7.

17. L. Bruni, *Epist.*, IX, 6 (II, 150–2, ed. L. Mehus).

18. *Commentaria primi belli punici*, Brixiae 1498. P. O. Kristeller tells me that he has found in a MS. of the Biblioteca Nacional of Madrid (MS. 8822 cart., s. XV, 93 fols.) what looks like a Spanish translation of a lost (?) Italian translation of the first book of Polybius by P. C. Decembrio (perhaps based on the Latin translation by L. Bruni).

19. Ed. C. F. Neumann, Frankfurt, 1822; L. W. Hasper, Leipzig, 1861.

20. *Sicconis Polentoni Scriptorum Illustrium Latinae Linguae libri XVIII*, ed. B. L. Ullman, Roma, 1928, Book II, p. 58; Book V, p. 163. S. Timpanaro kindly read for me the corresponding sections of the earlier draft (1426) in the *Cod. Riccardianus* 121, which once belonged to Pietro Crinito. They do not contain any allusion to Polybius, who seems therefore to have come to the notice of Polenton between 1426 and 1437.

21. T. Gasparrini Leporace and E. Mioni, *Cento Codici Bessarionei*, Venezia, 1968, gives the literature (*cf.* p. 127 n. 338).

22. G. Mercati, *Per la cronologia della vita e degli scritti di Niccolò Perotti*, Roma, 1925, p. 144 (correcting R. Cessi, *Giorn. St. Lett. It.*, 60, 1912, p. 77). *Id.*, *Scritti d'Isidoro il Cardinal Ruteno e codici a lui appartenuti*, Roma, 1926, p. 110. On *Vatic. Gr.* 1005 *cf.* also A. Diaz Tejera, *Emerita*, 36, 1968, pp. 121–47, and the art. by J. M. Moore quoted in n. 1, p. 95.

23. G. Mercati, *Per la cronologia della vita e degli scritti di Niccolò Perotti*, 23.

24. H. Baron, *The Crisis of the Early Italian Renaissance*, p. 508, n. 14; *id.*, *From Petrarch to L. Bruni*, p. 153, n. 5. L. Bruni, *Epist.*, VIII, 4 (II, 112 Mehus) may simply have Cic. *Att.*, I, 19, 10 in mind: *quamquam non ἐγχωμιαστικὰ sunt haec sed ἱστορικά quae scribimus*, as suggested by B. L. Ullman, *Studies in the*

Italian Renaissance, p. 331, n. 41. On the allusion to Polybius in G. Manetti's *Oratio funebris* for L. Bruni see the text in H. W. Wittschier, *Giannozzo Manetti. Das Corpus der Orationes*, Köln-Graz 1968, p. 76.

25. C. Dionisotti, *RSI*, 83, 1971, p. 254, with reference to B. Rucellai, *Liber de urbe Roma*, Firenze, 1770, pp. 164–5. *Cf.* F. Gilbert,*JWCI*, 12, 1949, p. 109, n. 1; p. 113, n. 4.

26. IV 9, ed. C. Angeleri, Roma, 1955, p. 131. Demetrius Chalcondylas borrowed Polybius from the library of Lorenzo de' Medici between 1489 and 1491: M. Del Piazzo, *Protocolli del Carteggio di Lorenzo il Magnifico*, Firenze, 1956, p. 448.

27. F. Chabod, *Scritti su Machiavelli*, Torino, 1964, p. 32, with bibl.; G. Sasso, *Giorn. St. Lett. Ital.*, 134, 1957, pp. 482–534; 135, 1958, pp. 215–59; and *Studi su Machiavelli*, Napoli, 1967, pp. 161–280; G. Procacci, *Niccolò Machiavelli*, Torino, 1969.

28. L. A. Burd, *RAL*, 5, 4, 1896, pp. 187–261.

29. On Politian, I. Maïer, *Les Manuscrits d'Ange Politien*, Genève, 1965, pp. 228, 311. For Agricola's study of Polybius in Ferrara, the hypothetical statement by W. H. Woodward, *Studies in Education*, 1906 (reprint 1965), p. 89, becomes a fact in E. Garin, *Ritratti di Umanisti*, Firenze, 1967, p. 73. But Agricola knew Polybius. *Cf.* Ph. Melanchthon, *Opera* XI, Halis Saxonum, 1843, p. 445: *Contexuit igitur Rudolphus eruditissimam epitomem ex Bibliis et Herodoto … ex Thucydide et Xenophonte, de Philippo et Alexandro et successoribus ex Diodoro et Polybio*. On the authorship of this passage on Agricola, F. von Bezold, *R. Agricola*, München, 1884, p. 18.

30. B. Cavalcanti, *Trattati sopra gli ottimi reggimenti delle repubbliche antiche e moderne* (ed. Classici Italiani, Milano, 1805), pp. 55–6; *id., Lettere edite e inedite*, ed. Christina Roaf, Bologna, 1967, especially pp. 91–112 (and Index *s.v.* Polibio). *Cf.* R. von Albertini, *Das florentinische Staatsbewusstsein im Übergang der Republik zum Prinzipat*, Bern, 1955, pp. 172–8. A useful survey for what follows in B. Reynolds, 'Shifting Currents in Historical Criticism', *JHI*, 14, 1953, pp. 471–92. The imposing collection of material in R. Landfester, *Historia Magistra Vitae*, Genève, 1972, to which we refer for further bibl., is too systematic for our purpose. *Cf.* W. L. Gundersheimer, *Studi Francesi*, 42, 1970, pp. 462–7.

31. P. de Nolhac, *La Bibliothèque de Fulvio Orsini*, Paris, 1887, pp. 46–8; but notice the sceptical remarks by T. S. Brown, *AJPh*, 89, 1968, p. 112.

32. *Methodus ad facilem historiarum cognitionem* in *Artis Historicae Penus* I (Basileae 1579), p. 53. *Cf.* G. Cotroneo, *GCFI*, 44, 1965, pp. 504–26. For R. Ascham, *A Report and Discourse … of the affaires and state of Germany*, see *English Works*, ed. W. A. Wright, Cambridge, 1904; reprint 1970, p. 126.

33. *De institutione historiae universae et eius cum iurisprudentia coniunctione*, 1561, in *Artis Historicae Penus* I, pp. 690–1.

34. *Della Historia Diece Dialoghi*, Venezia, 1560, Book II, p. 60, in E. Kessler, *Theoretiker humanistischer Geschichtsschreibung*, München, 1971.

35. Uberti Folietae *De similitudine normae Polybianae* (1574), pp. 106–15, in E. Kessler, *op. cit.* On its importance F. von Bezold, *Aus Mittelalter und Renaissance*, München und Berlin, 1918, p. 374.

36. W. Hahlweg, *Die Heeresreform der Oranier und die Antike*, Berlin, 1941,

and the excellent series of papers by G. Oestreich, now collected in *Geist und Gestalt des frühmodernen Staates*, Berlin, 1969. W. Hahlweg has now published, in *Die Heeresreform der Oranier*, Wiesbaden, 1973, 'Das Kriegsbuch des Grafen Johann von Nassau-Siegen', 1561–1623, which is of exceptional importance for the reputation of Polybius. I owe its knowledge to the generosity of Professor Oestreich.

37. This is stated by G. Oestreich, *Geist und Gestalt*, 68 – without quoting the evidence. For the general background, M. Roberts, *The Military Revolution 1560–1660*, Belfast, 1957, Inaug. Lecture.

38. W. Hahlweg, *Die Heeresreform der Oranier*, 1973, p. 340.

39. H. Trevor-Roper, *Queen Elizabeth's First Historian. W. Camden*, London, 1971, Neale Lecture, p. 21. On Milton, J. A. Bryant, *Phil. Quart.*, 29, 1950, pp. 21–7. Polybius' Latin translation had reached England in the fifteenth century: R. Weiss, *Humanism in England*², Oxford, 1957, p. 152.

40. H. Grotii et aliorum *De omni genere studiorum recte instituendo dissertationes*, Lugduni Batavorum, 1637, p. 11. True enough, Polybius and Plutarch are placed among 'politici'. Grotius avoids giving detailed advice on historians, though he encourages the reader to start with modern historians *ac paulatim deinde in remotiora eniti*. Grotius was convinced that Polybius was the stylistic model of St Luke: *utitur ita saepe Polybius quem sequi amat Lucas* (on *Acts* 17, 18, *Opera omnia theologica* II, Amstelaedami, 1679, 630 b 60). *Cf.* also his note on *Acts*, 11, 26 (II, 609 b 5–6): *Polybius non semel usurpat, scriptor Lucae* [*sic*] *lectus*. [For further details see my J. L. Myres Lecture, *Polybius between the English and the Turks*, Oxford, 1974].

7

Did Fabius Pictor Lie?*

WHAT do we want to know about the origins of Rome? Indeed why
should we want to know anything about them at all? Nobody, except the
specialist, cares very much about the origins of the Greeks or of the
Germans. Even the Nazis were unable to whip up a widespread interest
in German origins. But it seems to be part of our cultural heritage to
want to know the truth about the foundations of Rome, just as we want
to know the truth about the Hebrew exodus from Egypt. The reason is
of course that Jews and Romans had very definite ideas about their own
early history and attributed much importance to them, whereas Greeks
and (ancient) Germans had very confused ideas about their own past and
never set much store by them. Since it was discovered that Jewish
and Roman traditions cannot be accepted at their face value, attempts
to put some other story in their place have never ceased. Such an interest
does not necessarily lead to rational and worthwhile questions – at least
in the case of the Romans (it is more difficult to ask entirely frivolous
questions about the origins of the Hebrew religion). Archaeology has
been expected to confirm or to deny the existence of Romulus and of
Tarquinius Priscus; anthropology and linguistics have been asked to
define the racial composition of the Roman nation. Perhaps not surprisingly, the answers to these questions have been unsatisfactory. We
do not yet know whether there was a Romulus – or an equivalent to
Romulus – and whether the legend of the rape of the Sabine women
reflects an authentic event.

Partly it is just the bad luck of the archaeologists. For the history of a
literate society written documents count more than anything else. But
so far only two semi-intelligible inscriptions in Latin and three *graffiti*
in Etruscan (the latter on vases) have been found in Rome for the period
before 500 B.C. Partly, however, it is really a matter of direct conflict
between the nature of the questions and the nature of the evidence

*The New York Review of Books, 5, 3, 16 September 1965, pp. 19–22, a review
of A. Alföldi, Early Rome and the Latins, 1964.

which is supposed to provide the answers. The excellent systematic exploration of the Forum and of the Palatine and the scattered findings elsewhere have provided information about the tombs, sanctuaries, huts and fortifications of Early Rome and about imports from Etruria and Greece. But all this does not amount to a picture of a society, and even less of a political organization. Unless archaeological methods can be improved beyond recognition, excavations will not uncover the true origins of the distinction between patricians and plebeians. Even less can we expect archaeology to provide us with a military and dynastic history of early Rome to replace the unsatisfactory one given by the literary sources. The duel of the Horatii and Curiatii is not (or not yet) archaeologically falsifiable.

The claims that archaeology has presented us with a new picture of archaic Rome are contradicted by the very fact that archaeologists are now turning more and more to the study of the literary evidence for a necessary integration of their findings. E. Gjerstad, who dedicated the first three volumes of his fundamental *Early Rome* to a systematic collection and analysis of the archaeological evidence, has assigned another two volumes (as yet unpublished) to the literary texts. Indeed, if anything is noticeable in the recent works on early Rome, it is the increased attention paid to the texts as distinct from the monuments. Almost all the work by G. Dumézil on the Indo-European origins of the Roman social system is founded upon texts: so is the recent big book by R. Werner on the beginnings of the Roman Republic. Since questions we are now asking about the origins of Rome were suggested by distrust of the literary tradition, it makes sense to go back to the texts in order to see whether the questions had been properly formulated – and, incidentally, are worth asking.

The great merit of the new book by A. Alföldi of the Institute for Advanced Study at Princeton is that it re-examines the literary sources with the clear purpose of redefining the basic questions: it is a book about fundamentals and confirms the author's characteristic gifts of independent observation and original interpretation of facts. Alföldi thinks that modern historians have underrated the element of deliberate forgery in the Roman historical tradition. As is well known, the first Roman historian was a patrician senator, Fabius Pictor, who wrote his account in Greek at the time of the second Punic War, say about 210–200 B.C. His work is lost, but direct quotations and indirect evidence show that it was very influential and shaped the image of the Roman past for generations to come. As one writing in Greek at a time when

Rome had to counteract Hannibal's propaganda among the Greeks, Fabius is open to suspicions. It is tempting to present him as a Roman agent who tried to make his country respectable in Greek eyes. Alföldi is of course not the first to discover propaganda in Fabius' history, but he is the first to suggest that the whole of Fabius's work was an arbitrary reconstruction of the past of Rome, virtually without any factual foundation, which aimed at embellishing the image of Rome for Greek contemporaries. Actually Alföldi adds a further purpose to Fabius' inventions. A proud member of the Fabian clan would not have missed the opportunity of damaging the reputation of rival clans, such as the Claudii.

Whereas the common notion is that Fabius Pictor and his followers (the so-called annalists) primarily collected and worked upon a pre-existing tradition, Alföldi thinks that the tradition, if it ever existed, was perverted to the point of being annihilated by an arch-master of Roman propaganda – Fabius Pictor. It follows that Alföldi is only mildly interested in defining the nature of the previous Roman historical tradition, if any. He does not discuss at any length the nature and value of the epic banquet songs, pontifical chronicles, magistrate lists, funerary orations, temple records etc., which previous researchers have taken to be the foundations of the historical writing of the Romans about their own past. What matters to Alföldi is that Livy, Dionysius of Halicarnassus, and others who made use of the annals of the Republic were only too often the victims of Fabius' deceptions.

After such a negative criticism, it is not easy for Alföldi to proceed to his own reconstruction of the early history of Rome. Having discarded all he thinks Roman historians derived from Fabius he is hard put to it to find evidence he can trust. But he still believes he has enough in his hands to build a new picture of early Rome. He uses some passages from ancient historians which he takes to be independent of Fabius, some Etruscan monuments, some Latin inscriptions, and above all stray pieces of factual information about the administrative units and the religious ceremonies of the Roman State. Here again his method is not entirely new. Though Mommsen had a different opinion of Fabius Pictor, he, too, believed that religious and legal traditions were better evidence for archaic Roman history than the accounts of the annalists. But Alföldi is entirely original in the way he uses his evidence and in his conclusions. To put these briefly, he believes that for about 150 years before 500 B.C. monarchic Rome was continuously under the control of one or the other Etruscan city. The Tarquinii were only one of the Etruscan dynasties which ruled Rome. Other kings came from Caere, Vulci, Veii, Clusium. One of these forgotten kings Alföldi identifies with Aulus Vibenna, a very dim figure of the heroic period of Rome. Another king he finds in the mysterious Mastarna, who provoked the curiosity of the learned Emperor Claudius (but Claudius thought that Mastarna was the Etruscan name of King Servius Tullius).

In Alföldi's reconstruction Rome is not only a city which exchanges one Etruscan ruler for another: it is also a member of the Latin League. When the Etruscans ceased to rule Rome a few years after 500 B.C. (Alföldi's date), the Romans remained comparatively modest members of the Latin League and fought against neighbouring tribes under federal leadership. Slowly, during the fifth and fourth centuries, the relations between the Latin League and Rome changed. About 350 B.C. what had been one of the many Latin cities finally emerged as the all-powerful ruler and master.

There is a certain disharmony between the two parts of Alföldi's reconstruction – the one stating the subordination of Rome to Etruscan cities and the other asserting the subordination of Rome to the Latin League. One does not see how before 500 B.C. Rome could have been both a city ruled by the Etruscans and a member of a very homogeneous Latin League with its highly developed military organization. Alföldi has certainly made it appear probable that the Latin federal sanctuary of Lavinium was open to Etruscan influences from an early date and, more particularly, received from Etruria the myth of Aeneas. But this is not a proof that the Etruscans controlled the Latin League in the sixth century B.C. and even less an explanation of how a Latin League could remain dynamic under Etruscan control. However, discussion of the disharmonies between the two parts of Alföldi's theory is, at least for me, superfluous, because I believe that, as a whole, both his evaluation of Fabius Pictor and his reconstruction of early Roman history are arbitrary and almost certainly wrong.

Where so little is known, conjectures are inevitable, and we can only admire the boldness and originality of Alföldi's thesis. But all we know of Fabius runs contrary to Alföldi's theory that he invented what later became the accepted tradition about early Rome. I shall only make a few points. Plutarch definitely states that Fabius followed a Greek writer, Diocles of Peparethus, in telling the story of Romulus (this point, so far as I can see, is not mentioned by Alföldi). Pliny the Elder is equally definite in stating that fifty years before Fabius the Sicilian historian Timaeus gave an account of some of the reforms of Servius

Tullius which corresponded to what we find in the Roman sources. Alföldi is compelled to say unconvincingly that Pliny made a mistake and that Timaeus never spoke of Servius Tullius. What is worse, Alföldi attributes to Fabius opinions which he is most unlikely to have expressed. For instance, he thinks that Fabius identified Servius Tullius with Mastarna, whereas it is pretty obvious that neither Fabius nor the other Republican annalists even knew the name of Mastarna: the passage of Dionysius of Halicarnassus III, 65, 6, quoted by Alföldi (p. 215), clearly does not say what Alföldi thinks it says.

If the evaluation of Fabius propounded by Alföldi is without foundation, his consequent reconstruction of early Roman history is prejudiced. A closer examination confirms its weakness. The evidence Alföldi adduces to prove that the Etruscans ruled Rome either is too weak to prove anything or actually proves the contrary. I shall give only one example. Alföldi (p. 209) writes:

Cato the Elder preserves for us the priceless memory of a historical fact in his account of the vintage-festival of the Latins; namely the King of Caere, Mezentius, in the legendary tale Cato reports, is said to have imposed on the Latins the humiliating obligation to deliver to him each year the wine they produced .'. . This story, certainly reflecting Etruscan domination in Latium, unfavorable to national pride, embarrassing for the tendentious misrepresentation of early Latin history in the Annals, is above suspicion . . . The story . . . concerns the whole of Latium, comprising, naturally, Rome.

Now if one looks at the text of Cato – or rather at the texts of those who had read the lost book by Cato (they are all quoted by Alföldi) – it becomes clear that the story told by Cato differed considerably from that told by Alföldi. What Cato said was that the Latins made a vow to Jupiter when they were in danger of being subjected by Mezentius, King of the Etruscans. Having won the war, they fulfilled the promise and made annual offerings of new wine to Jupiter. The point of the story is that the Latins, at least on that occasion, defeated the Etruscans and remained free – whereas Alföldi reaches the opposite conclusion.

The Roman republican tradition implies that Rome was a powerful city in the sixth century B.C. and declined in the fifth century owing to internal struggles and external pressures by aggressive neighbours. Alföldi discards at least the former part of the tradition and replaces it by the picture of a Rome which was insignificant in the sixth century and became increasingly powerful and independent in the fifth century. He has violent words for some of those who believe in 'the great Rome of the Tarquinii'; he calls them 'zealots and opportunists' (p. 319). But the evidence he produces is not convincing – and in a few cases is founded upon plain errors.

With the evidence we have at present it is clearly impossible to reach certainty on the early history of Rome. But with all due appreciation of Alföldi's effort to prove the contrary, his book seems to me to confirm that the Roman historians of the third and second centuries B.C. – and Fabius Pictor *in primis* – knew many authentic facts of the Roman past. No doubt archaeological and epigraphical data have in some points decisively corrected the literary data. But archaeological data seem largely to confirm the picture in the annals of a Rome wealthier and more intellectually adventurous in the sixth than in the fifth century. I cannot understand why Alföldi says that a recent study by E. Paribeni of the import of Greek vases into Rome represents 'a dramatic turn in our appraisal of the historical evolution with which we are concerned' (p. 333) and supports the notion that Rome was at least as rich and independent in the fifth as in the sixth century. The fact is that Paribeni stated that nearly 190 out of 238 sherds found in the Forum belonged to the second part of the sixth century.

What is more difficult to appreciate is the significance of the by now famous discovery of inscriptions, two Etruscan and one Phoenician, made at Santa Severa (ancient Pyrgi), on the Tyrrhenian coast north of Rome in 1964. Alföldi was not, of course, in a position to take them into account in his book. Pyrgi was the harbour of the Etruscan Caere, and the three inscriptions, as far as we can understand them, are dedications by the same King of Caere to the same Carthaginian goddess. The discoverers date the texts in about 500 B.C. If the date is correct, it shows a very close collaboration between one Etruscan city and the Carthaginians more or less at the time in which, according to Polybius, Rome signed her first treaty with Carthage. Alföldi thinks that Polybius' date is impossible and suggests that Polybius was deceived by Fabius Pictor: the treaty should be dated in 348 B.C., which is the date given by other sources (p. 352). It can in any case be easily proved that Fabius Pictor was innocent of any deception about the treaties between Rome and Carthage. But this recent discovery (always assuming that the present dating and the interpretation of the new texts are approximately correct) adds a new presumption in favour of the Polybian date and altogether is not likely to increase confidence in the radical treatment of Roman sources so authoritatively advocated by Alföldi.

At this point a cynic might well remark that it makes little difference whether it is Fabius Pictor or Alföldi who is right, the authentic history of early Rome being anyhow irrecoverable. But there is a difference between the conjecture that emerges from a careful interpretation of the evidence and the conjecture that conflicts with the evidence. Historical studies are more and more committed to the exploration of the remote past where conjectures are unavoidable. Only strict control will prevent the creation (and ultimately the vulgarization) of imaginary history on the grand scale.

8

Pagan and Christian Historiography in the Fourth Century A.D.*[1]

ON 28 October 312 the Christians suddenly and unexpectedly found themselves victorious.[2] The victory was a miracle – though opinions differed as to the nature of the sign vouchsafed to Constantine. The winners became conscious of their victory in a mood of resentment and vengeance. A voice shrill with implacable hatred announced to the world the victory of the Milvian Bridge: Lactantius' *De mortibus persecutorum.*[3] In this horrible pamphlet by the author of *De ira dei* there is something of the violence of the prophets without the redeeming sense of tragedy that inspires Nahum's song for the fall of Nineveh. 'His fury is poured out like fire and the rocks are broken asunder by him. The Lord is good, a strong hold in the day of trouble': this at least has an elementary simplicity which is very remote from the complacent and sophisticated prose of the fourth-century rhetorician. Lactantius was not alone. More soberly, but no less ruthlessly, Eusebius recounted the divine vengeance against those who had persecuted the Church. To us it naturally appears that there is something in common between the Jews who died in defending the old Jerusalem and the Christians who died in building up the new Jerusalem against the same Roman empire. Modern scholars have found it easy to prove that in form and substance the Jewish martyr is the prototype of the Christian martyr. Such scholarly discoveries have little relevance to the realities of the fourth century. The pupils hated their masters, and were hated in their turn. With a cry of joy Eusebius, possibly a man of Jewish descent, retells from Josephus the story of the siege and capture of Jerusalem: thus may perish the enemies of Christ. Perhaps it is no chance that personally neither Lactantius nor Eusebius

*This essay first appeared in A. Momigliano, ed., *The Conflict Between Paganism and Christianity in the Fourth Century*, The Clarendon Press, Oxford, 1963, pp. 79–99.

had suffered much from Diocletian's persecution. Like Tacitus in relation to Domitian, they voiced the resentment of the majority who had survived in fear rather than in physical pain. Eusebius had been near his master Pamphilus who had carried on his work on the Bible in prison while awaiting death.[4]

If there were men who recommended tolerance and peaceful coexistence of Christians and pagans, they were rapidly crowded out. The Christians were ready to take over the Roman empire, as Eusebius made clear in the introduction of the *Praeparatio evangelica* where he emphasizes the correlation between *pax romana* and the Christian message: the thought indeed was not even new. The Christians were also determined to make impossible a return to conditions of inferiority and persecution for the Church. The problems and the conflicts inside the Church which all this implied may be left aside for the moment. The revolution of the fourth century, carrying with it a new historiography, will not be understood if we underrate the determination, almost the fierceness, with which the Christians appreciated and exploited the miracle that had transformed Constantine into a supporter, a protector and later a legislator of the Christian Church.

One fact is eloquent enough. All the pioneer works in the field of Christian historiography are earlier than what we may call their opposite numbers in pagan historiography. *De mortibus persecutorum* was written by Lactantius about 316. Eusebius' *Ecclesiastical History* probably appeared in a first edition about 312.[5] His life of Constantine – the authenticity of which can hardly be doubted – was written not long after 337.[6] Athanasius' life of St Anthony belongs to the years around 360. Among the pagan works none can be dated with absolute certainty before the death of Constantine. The *Historia Augusta* purports to have been written under Diocletian and Constantine, but the majority of modern scholars prefer – rightly or wrongly – a date later than 360.[7] The characteristic trilogy, to which the *Caesares* by Aurelius Victor belong, was put together later than 360.[8] The lives of the Sophists by Eunapius – which are pagan hagiography – were published about 395.[9] Ammianus Marcellinus, too, finished his work about 395.[10] On the whole, the Christians come before the pagans in their creative writing. The Christians attack. The pagans are on the defensive.

Towards the end of the century the situation changed. Theodosius' death precipitated a political crisis, and the barbarians were soon taking advantage of it with invasions on an unprecedented scale. The intervention of the state in theological matters appeared less attractive to people who had witnessed the trials of the Priscillianists and the cruel executions that concluded them. Many Christians became less certain of themselves and went back to paganism. Many pagans became more aggressive and dared to say openly that the new religion was responsible for the collapse of the empire. In the pagan field resignation yielded to fury, and in the Christian field aggressiveness had to be turned into self-defence. This incidentally brought about a revival of pagan historical writing in Greek: pagan Greek historiography had been conspicuously absent from the ideological struggles of the fourth century. It thus becomes clear that the years between 395 and 410 saw new developments in historiography which are beyond the scope of this lecture. Though we shall not disregard them altogether, we shall confine our analysis to the years 312–95. The clear-sighted determination of the Christians, which became suddenly apparent about 312, was the result of centuries of discipline and thought. In times of persecution and of uneasy tolerance the Church had developed its idea of orthodoxy and its conception of the providential economy of history. It emerged victorious to reassert with enhanced authority the unmistakable pattern of divine intervention in history, the ruthless elimination of deviations. The foundations of Christian historiography had been laid long before the time of the Battle of the Milvian Bridge.

We all know the story of the man who went into a London bookshop and asked for a New Testament in Greek. The assistant retired to a back room and after ten minutes came back with a grave look: 'Strange, sir, but Greek seems to be the only language into which the New Testament has not yet been translated.' The story may remind us of two facts. The first is that there was a time in which the New Testament was only available in Greek. The second and more important is that at that time it was as difficult as it is now to find a bookshop with a New, or for that matter an Old, Testament in Greek. About A.D. 180 a man like Galen could walk into a bookshop only to discover that they were selling an unauthorized edition of his own lectures. But though he was interested in the Christians, Galen would hardly have found a Bible. The Bible was no literature for the pagan. Its Greek was not elegant enough. Lactantius noted: '*apud sapientes et doctos et principes huius saeculi scriptura sancta fide care(a)t*' (*Inst.* V, 1, 15). If we find a pagan who had a slight acquaintance with the Bible, such as the anonymous author of *On the Sublime*, we suspect direct Jewish influence: justifiedly so, because the author of the *Sublime* was a student of Caecilius of Calacte, who, to all appearances, was a Jew.[11] Normally the educated pagans of the Roman empire knew nothing about either Jewish or Christian history. If they wanted some information about the Jews, they picked up second-hand distortions such as we read in Tacitus. The consequence was that a direct acquaintance with Jewish or Christian history normally came together with conversion to Judaism or to Christianity. People learnt a new history because they acquired a new religion. Conversion meant literally the discovery of a new history from Adam and Eve to contemporary events.[12]

The new history could not suppress the old. Adam and Eve and what follows had in some way to be presented in a world populated by Deucalion, Cadmus, Romulus and Alexander the Great. This created all sorts of new problems. First, the pagans had to be introduced to the Jewish version of history. Secondly, the Christian historians were expected to silence the objection that Christianity was new, and therefore not respectable. Thirdly, the pagan facts of life had to get into the Jewish–Christian scheme of redemption. It soon became imperative for the Christians to produce a chronology which would satisfy both the needs of elementary teaching and the purposes of higher historical interpretation. The Christian chronographers had to summarize the history which the converts were now supposed to consider their own; they had also to show the antiquity of the Jewish–Christian doctrine, and they had to present a model of providential history. The result was that, unlike pagan chronology, Christian chronology was also a philosophy of history. Unlike pagan elementary teaching, Christian elementary teaching of history could not avoid touching upon the essentials of the destiny of man. The convert, in abandoning paganism, was compelled to enlarge his historical horizon: he was likely to think for the first time in terms of universal history.

The spade-work in Christian chronology was done long before the fourth century.[13] The greatest names involved in this work, Clemens Alexandrinus, Julius Africanus and Hippolytus of Rome, belong to the second and third centuries. They created the frame for the divine administration of the world; they transformed Hellenistic chronography into a Christian science and added the lists of the bishops of the most important sees to the lists of kings and magistrates of the pagan world. They presented history in such a way that the scheme of redemption was easy to perceive. They showed with particular care the priority of the Jews over the pagans – in which point their debt to Jewish apologetic is obvious. They established criteria of orthodoxy by the simple device of introducing lists of bishops who represented the apostolic succession. Calculations about the return of Christ and the ultimate end had never been extraneous to the Church. Since the Apocalypse attributed to St John had established itself as authoritative in the Church, millennial reckonings had multiplied. Universal chronology in the Christian sense was bound to take into account not only the beginning, but also the end; it had either to accept or else to fight the belief in the millennium. Chronology and eschatology were conflated. Both Julius Africanus and Hippolytus were firm believers in the millennium, without, however, believing in its imminence. But the higher purpose of philosophy of history was never separated from the immediate task of informing and edifying the faithful. Hippolytus' introduction to his *Chronicon* is explicit. To quote a sentence from one of its Latin translations (another was incorporated in the Chronographer of 354), it was his purpose to show 'quae divisio et quae perditio facta sit, quo autem modo generatio seminis Israel de patribus in Christo completa sit'.

At the beginning of the fourth century Christian chronology had already passed its creative stage. What Eusebius did was to correct and to improve the work of his predecessors, among whom he relied especially on Julius Africanus.[14] He corrected details which seemed to him wrong even to the extent of reducing the priority of the Biblical heroes over the pagan ones. Moses, a contemporary of Ogyges according to Julius Africanus, was made a contemporary of Kekrops with a loss of 300 years. Eusebius was not afraid of attacking St Paul's guesses about the chronology of the Book of Judges. He freely used Jewish and anti-Christian sources such as Porphyrios. He introduced a reckoning from Abraham which allowed him to avoid the pitfalls of a chronology according to the first chapters of Genesis. He seems to have been the first to use the convenient method of presenting the chronology of the various nations in parallel columns. None of the earlier chronographers seems to have used this scheme, though it has often been attributed to Castor or to Julius Africanus. He made many mistakes, but they do not surprise us any longer. Fifty years ago Eduard Schwartz, to save Eusebius' reputation as a competent chronographer, conjectured that the two extant representatives of the lost original of Eusebius' *Chronicon* – the Latin adaptation by St Jerome and the anonymous Armenian translation – were based on an interpolated text which passed for pure Eusebius. This conjecture is perhaps unnecessary; nor are we certain that the Armenian version is closer to the original than St Jerome's Latin translation. Both versions reflect the inevitable vagaries of Eusebius' mind to whom chronology was something between an exact science and an instrument of propaganda.

But we recognize the shrewd and worldly adviser of the Emperor Constantine in the absence of millenarian dreams. Eusebius, and St Jerome who followed him, had an essential part in discrediting them. Of course, they did not stamp them out. Millenarian reckonings reappear in the *De cursu temporum* which Bishop Hilarian wrote at the end of the fourth century.[15] They also played a part in the thought of Sulpicius Severus about that time.[16] As we have already said, the disasters of the end of the century made a difference to dreams, as they made a difference to the other realities.

Thanks to Eusebius, chronography remained the typical form of Christian instruction in the fourth century. It showed concern with the pattern of history rather than with the detail.

The Christians indeed were not alone in having a problem of historical education. The pagans had their own problem. But we can state immediately the difference between pagans and Christians in the teaching of history. The pagans were not concerned with ultimate values in their elementary teaching. Their main concern was to keep alive a knowledge of the Roman past. After the social and political earthquakes of the third century a new leading class had emerged which clearly had some difficulty in remembering the simple facts of Roman history.[17] This explains why Eutropius and (Rufius?) Festus were both commissioned by the Emperor Valens to prepare a brief summary of Roman history. Eutropius was the first to obey the royal command. But the seventy-seven pages of his Teubner text must have proved too many for Valens. Festus, who followed, restricted himself to about twenty pages. He was not modest, but literal, when he commended his work to the *gloriosissimus princeps* as being even shorter than a summary – a mere enumeration of facts. The new men who, coming from the provincial armies or from Germany, acquired power and wealth, wanted some knowledge of the Roman past. They had to mix with the surviving members of the senatorial aristocracy in which knowledge of Roman history and antiquities was *de rigueur*. The establishment of a new senate in Constantinople, by adding another privileged class, complicated this educational problem. The senators of Constantinople, picked as they were from the municipal upper class of the East, were not likely to be uneducated, but they were not particularly strong either in the Latin language or in Roman history. These people too needed *breviaria*. Eutropius was soon translated into Greek by a friend of Libanius and began his momentous career in the Byzantine world. There can be few other Latin authors able to boast of at least three successive translations into Greek.

112

In their characteristic neutrality, the pagan *breviaria* presented no danger to the Christians. They were so devoid of religious content that they could not give offence. On the contrary, the Christians could easily exploit them for their own purposes. Eutropius was very successful in Constantinople where the aristocracy soon became predominantly Christian. The Christian compiler known as the Chronographer of 354 incorporated in his own work a pagan recapitulation of the history of Rome – the so-called *Chronica urbis Romae*.[18] When St Jerome decided to continue Eusebius' *Chronicon* to 378 he used pagan writers such as Aurelius Victor and Eutropius, not to mention the *Chronica urbis Romae* which he probably knew as a part of the Christian chronography of 354. All this, however, only emphasized the fact that the Christians had no compilation comparable to Eutropius and Festus. If *breviaria* were not needed during the fourth century when the Christians felt very sure of themselves, they appeared less superfluous towards the end of the century when the pagan version of Roman history gained in authority. Sulpicius Severus, who had absorbed pagan culture in Gaul, was the first to realize the deficiency and to fill the gap just about A.D. 400. He combined Christian chronographers and the Bible with *historici mundiales*, the pagan historians. His purpose was still the dual one of the earlier Christian chronography: 'ut et imperitos docerem et litteratos convincerem'. Later, about 417, Orosius followed his example when he was requested by St Augustine to produce a summary of the history of Rome in support of his *Civitas dei*. Orosius gave what from a medieval point of view can be called the final Christian twist to the pagan epitome of Roman history.[19]

*

Epitomes are only on the threshold of history. So far we have considered books which were meant to remind the reader of the events rather than to tell them afresh. But an important fact has already emerged. Whether in the form of chronographies or, later, in the form of *breviaria*, the Christian compilations were explicit in conveying a message: one can doubt whether the majority of the pagan compilations conveyed any message at all. Sulpicius Severus and Orosius fought for a cause, and it is to be remembered that Sulpicius Severus expressed the indignation felt by Ambrosius and Martin of Tours against the appeal to the secular arm in the Priscillianist controversy. Consequently, it was very easy to transform a pagan handbook into a Christian one, but almost impossible to make pagan what had been Christian. Later on we shall consider one possible exception to the rule that the Christians assimilate pagan ideas, while the pagans do not appropriate Christian ones. The rule, however, stands: it is enough to indicate the trend of the century – and, incidentally, to explain why the Christians were so easily victorious. Just because the trend is so clear, we can perhaps conjecturally add yet another case of the easy transformation of pagan historical *breviaria* into Christian ones. All is in doubt about the first part of the *Anonymus Valesianus* – which is a brief life of Constantine under the name of *Origo Constantini imperatoris*. But a fourth-century date seems highly probable; and it also seems clear that the few Christian passages are later interpolations from Orosius. If so, the *Origo Constantini imperatoris* is a beautiful example of a short pagan work which was made Christian by the simple addition of a few passages.[20] The Christians could easily take it over because of the relatively neutral character of the original text. The pagans for their part kept away from Christian explosives.

Christian initative was such that it did not hesitate to appropriate Jewish goods also. Pseudo-Philo's *Liber antiquitatum Biblicarum* was originally a Jewish handbook of Biblical history. It seems to have been written in Hebrew for Jews in the first century A.D., it was later done into Greek, and, to all appearances, in the fourth century, it was changed into a Christian handbook and translated into Latin.[21]

The question then arises whether the Christians became the masters of the field also on the higher level of original historical writing and whether here, too, they confirmed their capacity for assimilating without being assimilated.

If the question were simply to be answered by a yes, it would not be worth asking. The traditional forms of higher historiography did not attract the Christians. They invented new ones. These inventions are the most important contributions made to historiography after the fifth century B.C. and before the sixteenth century A.D. Yet the pagans are allowed by the Christians to remain the masters of traditional historiographical forms. To put it briefly, the Christians invented ecclesiastical history and the biography of the saints, but did not try to Christianize ordinary political history; and they influenced ordinary biography less than we would expect. In the fourth century A.D. there was no serious attempt to provide a Christian version of, say, Thucydides or Tacitus – to mention two writers who were still being seriously studied. A reinterpretation of ordinary military, political or diplomatic history in Christian terms was neither achieved nor even attempted. Lactantius in the *De Mortibus persecutorum* is perhaps the only Christian writer to touch upon social and political events. He does so in a conservative and senatorial spirit which must be embarrassing to those who identify the Christians with the lower middle class, but he never seriously develops his political interpretation: he is not to be compared as an analyst with Ammianus Marcellinus or even with the *Scriptores historiae Augustae*.

The consequence is plain. No real Christian historiography founded upon the political experience of Herodotus, Thucydides, Livy and Tacitus was transmitted to the Middle Ages. This is already apparent in the sixth century when a military and political historian like Procopius was basically pagan in outlook and technique. When in the fifteenth and sixteenth centuries the humanists rediscovered their Herodotus, Thucydides, Livy and Tacitus, they rediscovered something for which there was no plain Christian alternative. It is not for me to say whether an alternative was possible: whether an earlier *Tacitus christianus* would have been less foolish than the post-Reformation one. What I must point out is that the conditions which made Machiavelli and Guicciardini possible originated in the fourth century A.D. The models for political and military history remained irretrievably pagan. In the higher historiography there was nothing comparable with the easy Christianizing of the pagan *breviaria*.

Here again Eusebius was the decisive influence. How much he owed to predecessors, and especially to the shadowy Hegesippus, we shall never know, unless new evidence is discovered.[22] But it is fairly clear that Hegesippus wrote apologetic, not history. Apart from him, there is no other name that can seriously compete with Eusebius' for the invention of ecclesiastical history. He was not vainly boasting when he asserted that he was the 'first to enter on the undertaking, as travellers do on some desolate and untrodden way'.[23]

Eusebius, like any other educated man, knew what proper history was. He knew that it was a rhetorical work with a maximum of invented speeches and a minimum of authentic documents. Since he chose to give plenty of documents and refrained from inventing speeches, he must have intended to produce something different from ordinary history. Did he then intend to produce a preparatory work to history, a ὑπόμνημα? This is hardly credible. First of all, historical ὑπομνήματα were normally confined to contemporary events. Secondly, Eusebius speaks as if he were writing history, and not collecting materials for a future history.

It was Eduard Schwartz who in one of his most whimsical moments suggested that German professors of *Kirchengeschichte* had been the victims of their poor Greek. They had not understood that

'Εκκλησιαστικὴ ἱστορία did not mean *Kirchengeschichte*, but *Materialien zur Kirchengeschichte*. Eduard Schwartz, of course, was fighting his great battle against the isolation of ecclesiastical history in German universities, and we who share his beliefs can hardly blame him for this paradox. But a paradox it was.[24]

Eusebius knew only too well that he was writing a new kind of history. The Christians were a nation in his view. Thus he was writing national history. But his nation had a transcendental origin. Though it had appeared on earth in Augustus' time, it was born in Heaven 'with the first dispensation concerning the Christ himself' (I, 1, 8). Such a nation was not fighting ordinary wars. Its struggles were persecutions and heresies. Behind the Christian nation there was Christ, just as the devil was behind its enemies. The ecclesiastical history was bound to be different from ordinary history because it was a history of the struggle against the devil, who tried to pollute the purity of the Christian Church as guaranteed by the apostolic succession.

Having started to collect his materials during Diocletian's persecutions, Eusebius never forgot his original purpose which was to produce factual evidence about the past and about the character of the persecuted Church. He piled up his evidence of quotations from reputable authorities and records in the form that was natural to any ancient controversialist. As he was dealing with a Church that represented a school of thought there was much he could learn in the matter of presentation from the histories of philosophic schools which he knew well. These dealt with doctrinal controversies, questions of authenticity, successions of *scholarchs*. But he did away with all that was anecdotal and worldly in the pagan biographies of philosophers. This is why we shall never know whether Clemens Alexandrinus was fond of eating green figs and of basking in the sun – which are established points in the biography of Zeno the Stoic. At the same time Eusebius certainly had in mind Jewish–Hellenistic historiography, as exemplified for him and for us by Flavius Josephus. In Josephus he found the emphasis on the past, the apologetic tone, the doctrinal digression, the display (though not so lavish) of documents: above all there was the idea of a nation which is different from ordinary pagan nations. Jewish historiography emphatically underlined the importance of the remote past in comparison with recent times and the importance of cult in comparison with politics.

The suggestion that Eusebius combined the methods of philosophic historiography with the approach of Jewish–Hellenistic historiography has at least the merit of being a guide to the sources of his thought. Yet it is far from accounting for all the main features of his work. There were obvious differences between the history of the Church and that of any other institution. Persecution had been an all-pervading factor of Christianity. Heresy was a new conception which (whatever its origins) had hardly the same importance in any other school of thought, even in Judaism. An account of the Christian Church based on the notion of orthodoxy and on its relations with a persecuting power was bound to be something different from any other historical account. The new type of exposition chosen by Eusebius proved to be adequate to the new type of institution represented by the Christian Church. It was founded upon authority and not upon the free judgement of which the pagan historians were proud. His contemporaries felt that he had made a new start. Continuators, imitators and translators multiplied. Some of them (most particularly Sozomen) tried to be more conventional in their historiographical style, more obedient to rhetorical traditions. None departed from the main structure of Eusebius' creation with its emphasis on the struggle against persecutors and heretics and therefore on the purity and continuity of the doctrinal tradition.

Eusebius introduced a new type of historical exposition which was characterized by the importance attributed to the more remote past, by the central position of doctrinal controversies and by the lavish use of documents.

I am not yet able to answer two questions which are very much on my mind: whether in the Middle Ages there was a school of pure ecclesiastical history from Cassiodorus to Bede, to Adam of Bremen and to John of Salisbury; and whether this school, if any, was characterized by a special interest in documents. What is certain is that from the sixteenth to the eighteenth century ecclesiastical history (especially of the early Church) was treated with a much greater display of erudition, with much more care for minute analysis of the evidence than any other type of history. There is no work in profane history comparable with the Magdeburg Centuriators and with Baronius. Naturally this is the expression of the fiercely controversial character which ecclesiastical history assumed with the Reformation. But we may well wonder whether the ecclesiastical historians of the Renaissance would have entered upon the path of erudition and documentation – and incidentally of illegibility – without the powerful precedent of Eusebius and his immediate pupils. Conversely, we may well wonder whether modern political historiography would ever have changed from rhetoric and pragmatism to footnotes and appendixes without the example of ecclesiastical history. The first man who applied careful scrutiny of the evidence to the history of the Roman empire was Le Nain de Tillemont, who came from ecclesiastical history and worked in both fields. Among the Maurists of St Germain-des-Prés erudition spread from ecclesiastical to profane, even to literary history. Perhaps we have all underestimated the impact of ecclesiastical history on the development of historical method. A new chapter of historiography begins with Eusebius not only because he invented ecclesiastical history, but because he wrote it with a documentation which is utterly different from that of the pagan historians.[25]

Thus we are brought back to our main point. Eusebius made history positively and negatively by creating ecclesiastical history and by leaving political history alone. In a comparable manner another Christian invented the biography of the saints and left the biography of generals and politicians to the pagans. The inventor was Athanasius, whose life of St Anthony was promptly made available in Latin by Euagrius. The complicated pattern of suggestions which lies behind the rise of hagiography – *exitus illustrium virorum*, Jewish legends, lives of philosophers, 'aretalogies', etc. – cannot detain us here. The studies by K. Holl and R. Reitzenstein seem to have established that Athanasius was more directly inspired by the Pythagorean type of the $\theta\epsilon\hat{\imath}os$ $\dot{a}\nu\dot{\eta}\rho$, such as we find in the life of Apollonius of Tyana by Philostratus and in the life of Pythagoras himself by Iamblichus.[26] Athanasius intended to oppose the Christian saint who works his way to God with the help of God to the pagan philosopher who is practically a god himself. By imparting a mortal blow to the ideal of the pagan philosopher, he managed to produce an ideal type which became extremely popular among ordinary Christians. Only small groups of pagans believed that Pythagoras or Diogenes was the best possible man. The great majority of pagans was more interested in Hercules, Achilles and Alexander the Great. But in Christian society the saint was soon recognized as the only perfect type of man. This gives hagiography, as begun by Athanasius, its unique place. It outclassed all other types of biography because all the other types of men became inferior to that of the saint. In comparison, the ordinary biography of kings and politicians became insignificant. One of the most important features of the lives of saints is to give a new dimension to historiography by registering the activity of devils in the plural. It is no exaggeration to say that a mass invasion of devils into historiography preceded and accompanied the mass invasion of barbarians into the Roman empire. A full treatment of 'Devils in historiography' must be reserved for a future course at the Warburg Institute on 'Devils and the Classical Tradition'. But so much can be said here: the devils seem to have respected the classical distinction of literary genres. They established themselves in biography, but made only occasional irruptions into the field of *annales*.

The difficulty of writing a Christian biography of a king as distinct from the life of a saint is already apparent in the life of Constantine by Eusebius, though it was produced perhaps twenty years before the composition of the life of St Anthony by Athanasius. Eusebius had no other choice but to present the life of Constantine as a model of a pious life – παράδειγμα θεοσεβοῦς βίου, as he himself says. The task was certainly not beyond Eusebius' ingenuity, but it flouted anybody's respect for truth. Moreover, it implied neglect of all that counts in a life of a general and a politician: military glory, political success, concern for ordinary human affairs, and the rest of the passions power carries with it. No wonder that this life of Constantine was never a success, had hardly any influence on later biographies, and found some modern scholars ready to deny the Eusebian authorship even at the risk of being contradicted by papyrological evidence. It continued to be easier for a Christian to work on the life of a saint than to write the life of an emperor. We may sympathize with Eginhard when he decided to go back to Suetonius for his life of Charlemagne.

*

We can thus see that a direct conflict between Christians and pagans is not to be expected on the higher level of the historiography of the fourth century. The Christians, with all their aggressiveness, kept to their own new types of history and biography. Eusebius' life of Constantine was an experiment not to be repeated – historiographically a blind alley. The pagans were left to cultivate their own fields. This perhaps reinforced their tendency to avoid any direct discussion with their formidable neighbours in the field of historiography. The opposition to Christianity can be guessed rather than demonstrated in the majority of the pagan students of history. It shows itself in the care with which pagan historians of the past – such as Sallust, Livy and Tacitus – were read and imitated. It is also apparent in the implicit rejection of the most characteristic Christian values, such as humility and poverty. But it seldom takes the form of direct critical remarks. There are two or three sentences in the *Historia Augusta* which sound like a criticism of the Christians. One is the good-humoured remark that in Egypt 'those who worship Serapis are, in fact, Christians and those who call themselves bishops of Christ are in fact devotees of Serapis' (*Firmus*, 8, 2). In the last sentence of Aurelius Victor's *De Caesaribus* there is perhaps a criticism of Constantius II's Christian ministers: '*ut imperatore ipso praeclarius, ita apparitorum plerisque magis atrox nihil*'. But notice with what care the emperor is declared blameless. Finally, there are the well-known criticisms of Ammianus Marcellinus against the Roman clergy and other bishops, such as Bishop George of Alexandria. But here again notice that the same Ammianus praises Christian martyrdom, and respects the blameless life of provincial bishops. The pagans were bound to be prudent – and their mood was altogether that of a generous and fair-minded liberalism. The *Historia Augusta* is by no means the big anti-Christian pamphlet which some scholars have seen in it. On the contrary, the ideal emperor Severus Alexander worships Jesus with Abraham in his private chapel. Ammianus Marcellinus makes an effort to disentangle what is *absoluta* and *simplex religio* and what is *anilis superstitio* in Christianity (XXI, 16, 18). According to him what matters is *virtus*, not paganism or Christianity. As we all know, this attitude is also to be found in Symmachus, in some of the pagan correspondents of St Augustine and in the Panegyricus by Nazarius (IV, 7, 3). Rufius Festus, who was an unbeliever but whose pagan sympathies are shown by the disproportionate amount of space he devotes to Julian, is full of deference towards the Christian God of his master Valens: '*Maneat modo concessa dei nutu et ab amico cui credis et creditus es numine indulta felicitas.*' 'May long last the happiness that was granted to you by the friendly god whom you trust and to whom you are entrusted.' This is a very decent way of saving one's conscience without offending one's master.

The only exception is Eunapius, whose history of the fourth century was so anti-Christian that, according to Photius, it had to be re-edited in a less offensive form. The greater part of this history is lost, but Eunapius' attitude is clear enough from the extant fragments and even more so from his lives of the Sophists, where Julian is the hero and the apology for Neoplatonic paganism is unbridled. If Julian won victories it was because the right gods helped him. We can still read in the margins of the *Codex Laurentianus* of Eunapius' lives of the Sophists the indignant remarks of one of his Byzantine readers. Eunapius clearly meant his lives of the Sophists to compete with the lives of the Christian saints whose cult he despised (*Vit. soph.* 472). But Eunapius reflects the changed mood of the end of the century when even the most optimistic pagan could no longer nurture illusions about Christian tolerance.[27] Furthermore, his particular type of reaction is that of a professor who wrote for

Greek *literati* rather than for the pagan aristocracy of the West. As we observed, the Greek pagans of the East seem to have become vocal only at the end of the century. During the century itself Latin was the main language of pagan historiography.

In the West, among the Latin historians, the resistance to Christianity showed itself in a mixture of silence and condescension; Christianity is rarely mentioned. If it is mentioned, kindness and good humour prevail. What counts is the vast zone of silence, the ambiguity which gives Latin pagan historiography of the fourth century its strange imprint of reticence and mystery. Seldom are historians of historiography faced by works so difficult to date, to analyse in their composite nature and to attribute to a definite background. For the first time we come across historical work done in collaboration – which adds to its elusiveness.

The *Historia Augusta* is the classic example of historiographic mystery. The work purports to have been written by six authors at various moments of the reigns of Diocletian and Constantine. Some at least of the alleged authors claim to have written in collaboration. This very claim of team-work is baffling: cooperative 'Cambridge histories' were not common in antiquity. The writing is sensational and unscrupulous, and the forged documents included in this work serve no obvious purpose. One or two passages may point to a post-Constantinian date either for the whole collection or at least for the passages themselves. But the date and the purpose of the *Scriptores historiae Augustae* remain an unsolved problem.

A less famous, but no less remarkable, mystery is the tripartite corpus under the title *Origo gentis Romanae* – a title which incidentally must be translated as *History of the Roman people*. It includes a history of Roman origins from Saturnus to the murder of Remus, a collection of short biographies from Romulus to Augustus (the so-called *De viris illustribus*), and, finally, short and accomplished biographies of Roman emperors to A.D. 360. The imperial biographies were written by Aurelius Victor whom we know to have been a friend of Julian and a *praefectus urbi* under Theodosius. The other two sections of the trilogy are anonymous: they were written by two different authors, neither of whom can be identical with Aurelius Victor. A fourth man acted as editor and put together the three pamphlets to form the present trilogy. All these people were pagan. I have elsewhere suggested that the editor of the trilogy may have tried to produce a complete pagan history of Rome at the time of the Emperor Julian. But this is a pure guess, though not an unreasonable one, I trust. The compiler himself does not say anything about the precise meaning and date of his compilation. He may have known the Christian Chronographer of 354: he has certainly adopted a compositional scheme which reminds us of the *Chronica urbis Romae* included in the Chronographer of 354. What is extraordinary and, to my mind, important in this trilogy is the absence of any direct allusion to Christianity. The author is pagan: there is no reference to the Christians.

Ammianus Marcellinus is not a mystery in the sense in which the *Historia Augusta* and the tripartite *Origo gentis Romanae* are mysteries.[28] He speaks about himself more than the majority of the ancient historians ever did. His keen eye is constantly on the look-out for individual features. He is a man full of delightful curiosity. Yet what do we ultimately know about Ammianus? He does not even tell us why he, a Greek from Antioch, chose Latin as his literary language. He says very little about the theological controversies of his time and almost nothing about the religious feelings of the people he must have known best. Magic seems to interest him more than theology. Yet theology counted most. He was a soldier. Yet he is apparently not interested in military organization. He has an uncanny ability to describe a character without defining a situation. He never gives himself away. His histories might have for motto his own words: '*quisquis igitur dicta considerat, perpendat etiam cetera quae tacentur*' (XXIX, 3, 1). It is symbolic that the greatest feat of his military career was to escape unnoticed from besieged Amida while the Persians were breaking into the city. He may have become more reticent about religion in the Books XXVI–XXXI which he wrote after 392 when Theodosius hardened against the pagans. But even the earlier books, written as they were in more tolerant years, are not much more explicit. He dislikes the Germans, yet his unwillingness to analyse the causes of the barbarian successes is notorious. He deplores the greed and avarice of some Roman aristocrats, especially of the Anicii who were just then turning to Christianity. But he cannot have had any general objection against the senatorial class among which he had his pagan friends, Praetextatus, Eupraxius and Symmachus. An acute and passionate judge of individuals, he avoids our direct questions and leaves us wondering. His master Tacitus is a paragon of directness by comparison.

If reticence, love of the pagan past, moderation and erudition were the prominent features of these Latin historians, the Christians did not have much to fear from their work. Historians of this kind could please other historians. Ammianus Marcellinus, the *Historia Augusta* and the now lost histories by Nicomachus Flavianus, were read in the sixth century in the circle of Symmachus and Cassiodorus, when there was a revival of interest in Roman history.[29] But Ammianus, the *Historia Augusta*, and Aurelius Victor were never popular for all we know. The fact that at least one of these historical works, the *Historia Augusta*, is guilty of professional dishonesty is not a sign of strength for historiography of this kind. It would be unfair to generalize when so much of the fourth-century historical production is lost. Within the limits of our knowledge we are constantly reminded of the fact that the true pagans of the fourth century found their most profound satisfaction not in writing new history, but in copying existing histories, trying to solve problems of antiquarianism, commenting on Virgil and other classics, reading and writing poetry in a pagan spirit. The real passion was in those who tried to revive the past by direct religious worship, by discussion of ancient customs, by the study of ancient writers. Our instinct is right, I think, when we consider Macrobius, Symmachus, Servius and Donatus more typically pagan than Ammianus Marcellinus. Festus who wrote the historical *breviarium* has sometimes been identified with Festus Avienus, the translator of Aratus. The identification is not to be maintained. The historian Festus was even accused of atheism by Eunapius (p. 481). The poet Festus Avienus, a friend of the Nicomachi Flaviani, was warmly devoted to Jupiter and to the Etruscan goddess Nortia of his native country.[30] When he died, his son wrote on his tomb that Jupiter was opening the skies to him – the son echoing in his lines his father's lines:

> nam Iuppiter aethram
> pandit, Feste, tibi candidus ut venias
> iamque venis (I.L.S. 2944)

This seems to have been the driving spirit of dying paganism in the West. Therefore, St Augustine, who knew where to look for the real enemy, was not worried by contemporary pagan historians in the Latin tongue, such as Ammianus Marcellinus. Greek historians, such as Eunapius, worried him even less because he probably did not know them: his command of Greek was modest. But he was disturbed by the idealization of the Roman past which he found in fourth-century Latin antiquarians, poets and commentators of poets. He saw in them the roots of the new resistance against Christianity which became evident towards the end of the century. He went back to the sources of their antiquarianism, and primarily to Varro, in order to undermine the foundations of their work. He fought the antiquarians, the sentimental and emotional pagans, of his time – not the contemporary historians. The latter might be left to die from natural causes. But the former had to be fought. The result is to be seen in the *De civitate dei*. It is also to be seen in the work of St Augustine's pupil Orosius who was induced by him to write against the readers of Livy, not against the readers of the *Historia Augusta* or of Ammianus. All went according to plan, except that the pagan historians of the fourth century were not really going to die. They were only going to sleep for some centuries. They belonged to that classical tradition in historiography for which ecclesiastical history, whatever its merits, was no substitute. Though we may have learnt to check our references from Eusebius – and this was no small gain – we are still the disciples of Herodotus and Thucydides: we still learn our history of the late empire from Ammianus Marcellinus.[31]

References

---

1. The notes to this lecture are meant to provide no more than an introduction to the recent literature. *Cf.* my later paper in *Riv. St. Ital.*, lxxxi, 1969, pp. 286–303.

2. *Cf.*, however, P. Bruun, 'The Battle of the Milvian Bridge: The Date Reconsidered', *Hermes*, lxxxviii, 1960, pp. 361–70, which puts the battle in 311.

3. The standard commentary is by J. Moreau, *Sources Chrétiennes*, Paris, 1954. *Cf.* W. Nestle, 'Die Legende vom Tode der Gottesverächter', *Arch. f. Religionsw.*, xxxiii, 1936, pp. 246–69, reprinted in *Griechische Studien*, 1948, p. 567. In general J. Stevenson, *Studia Patristica*, i, Berlin, 1957, pp. 661–77. Not convincing S. Rossi, *Giorn. Ital. Filol.*, xiv, 1961, pp. 193–213.

4. The facts are gathered by H. J. Lawlor and J. E. L. Oulton, *Eusebius, The Ecclesiastical History and the Martyrs of Palestine*, translated with introduction and notes, London, 1928; reprint, 1954, ii, p. 332. *Cf.* S. Liebermann, *Ann. Inst. Phil. Hist. Orient.*, vii, 1939–44, pp. 395–446.

5. On the controversial question of the various editions of the *Ecclesiastical History*, with which I do not intend to deal here, see especially E. Schwartz, introduction to his *ed. major*, Berlin, 1909, Volume iii, and article in Pauly–Wissowa, *Realencyclopädie*, s.v. Eusebius (now reprinted in *Griechische Geschichtschreiber*, 1957, pp. 540 ff.); R. Laqueur, *Eusebius als Historiker seiner Zeit*, Berlin and Leipzig, 1929; H. J. Lawlor and J. E. L. Oulton, introduction to their translation, 1928; H. Edmonds, *Zweite Auflagen im Altertum*, Leipzig, 1941, pp. 25–45 (with bibliography).

6. Bibliography until 1956 in B. Altaner, *Patrologie*, 5th ed., Freiburg im Br., 1958, p. 209. Add J. Straub, *Studia Patristica*, i, Berlin, 1957, pp. 679–95.

7. My essay reprinted in *Secondo Contributo alla storia degli studi classici*, Rome, 1960, pp. 105–43, gives the bibliography to which I wish to add

W. Ensslin, *Studi Calderini-Paribeni*, i, 1956, pp. 313–23; J. Straub, *Bonner Jahrbücher*, clv–clvi, 1955–6, pp. 136–55, and more particularly E. M. Štaerman, *Vestnik Drevnej Istorii*, 1957, 1, pp. 233–45, translated in *Bibl. Class. Orient.*, v, 1960, pp. 93–110, and A. I. Dovatur, *V.D.I.* quoted, pp. 245–56. I am not moved by the arguments of J. Schwartz, *Bull. Fac. Lettres Strasbourg*, xl, 1961, pp. 169–76. Further bibl. in *Engl. Hist. Rev.*, lxxxiv, 1969, p. 566, and in the masterly paper by E. J. Bickerman, *Riv. Fil. Class.*, 101, 1973, pp. 25–31.

8. The problem is discussed in my *Secondo Contributo alla storia degli studi classici*, pp. 145–89. A later date is suggested by G. Puccioni, *Studi Ital. Fil. Class.*, xxx, 1958, pp. 207–54, and *Ann. Scuola Normale Pisa*, xxvii, 1958, pp. 211–23.

9. *Cf.* also W. R. Chalmers, *Class. Quart.*, N.S., iii, 1953, pp. 165–70.

10. *Cf.*, however, O. J. Maenchen-Helfen, *A. J. Ph.*, lxxvi, 1955, pp. 384–400.

11. *Cf.* A. Rostagni, *Anonimo–Del Sublime*, Milan, 1947; E. Norden, 'Das Genesiszitat in der Schrift vom Erhabenen', *Abh. Berlin. Akad.*, 1954, p. 1.

12. On the implications of the Christian vision of history see, for instance, L. Tondelli, *Il disegno divino nella storia*, Turin, 1947; O. Cullmann, *Christus und die Zeit*; 2nd ed., Zürich, 1948; W. Kamlah, *Christentum und Geschichtlichkeit*, 2nd ed., Stuttgart, 1951; R. L. P. Milburn, *Early Christian Interpretations of History*, London, 1954; K. Löwith, *Weltgeschichte und Heilgeschehen*, Stuttgart, 1953; C. Schneider, *Geistesgeschichte des antiken Christentums*, Munich, 1956. See also H. Rahner, *Griechische Mythen in christlicher Deutung*, Zürich, 1945, and the studies by S. G. F. Brandon and K. Löwith in *Numen*, ii, 1955.

13. Besides the fundamental H. Gelzer, *Sextus Julius Africanus und die byzant. Chronographie*, Leipzig, 1880–98, I shall only mention A. Hamel, *Kirche bei Hippolyt von Rom*, Gütersloh, 1951; M. Richard, *Mél. Sciences Religieuses*, vii, 1950, p. 237, and viii, 1951, p. 19 (on Hippolytus); B. Kötting, 'Endzeitprognosen zwischen Lactantius und Augustinus', *Hist. Jahrb.*, lxxvii, 1957, pp. 125–39; P. Courcelle, 'Les Exégèses chrétiennes de la quatrième églogue', *Rev. Etud. Anc.*, lix, 1957, pp. 294–319; A.-D. Van Den Brincken, *Studien zur Lateinischen Weltchronistik bis in das Zeitalter Ottos von Freising*, Düsseldorf, 1957; with bibliography.

14. The essential work after E. Schwartz is R. Helm, 'Eusebios' Chronik und ihre Tabellenform', *Abh. Berl. Akad.*, 1923, p. 4. *Cf.* also R. Helm, *Eranos*, xxii, 1924, pp. 1–40, and A. Schöne, *Die Weltchronik des Eusebius in ihrer Bearbeitung durch Hieronymus*, Berlin, 1900, D. S. Wallace-Hadrill, 'The Eusebian Chronicle: the extent and date of composition of its early editions', *J.T.S.*, N.S. vi, 1955, pp. 248–53.

15. The text is edited in C. Frick, *Chronica Minora*, i, 1892.

16. S. Prete, *I chronica di Sulpicio Severo*, Vatican City, 1955.

17. E. Malcovati, 'I Breviari del IV secolo', in *Annali Università Cagliari*, xii, 1942.

18. Mommsen, *Über den Chronographen vom J. 354*, 1850, partially reprinted in *Ges. Schriften*, vii, is still the standard work. Text in Mommsen, *Chronica Minora*, i, 1892.

19. Among the recent literature see K. A. Schöndorf, *Die Geschichtstheologie des Orosius*, Munich, 1952. *Cf.* also J. Straub, 'Christliche Geschichtsapologetik in der Krisis des römischen Reiches', *Historia*, 1, 1950, pp. 52–81.

20. Text and discussion by R. Cessi in his edition of the *Anonymus Valesianus*, *Rer. Ital. Script.*, 1913, but his conclusions are not accepted here. The Groningen dissertation by D. J. A. Westerhuis, 1906, is still very valuable. New edition by J. Moreau, Leipzig, 1961.

21. See the edition by G. Kisch, *Pseudo-Philo's Liber Antiquitatum Biblicarum*, Notre Dame, Indiana, 1949.

22. Among the recent literature see K. Mras, *Anz. Oesterr. Akad.*, 1958, pp. 143–5; W. Telfer, *Harv. Theol. Rev.*, liii, 1960, pp. 143–54.

23. *Cf.*, among many, H. Berkhof, *Die Theologie Eusebius' von Caesarea*, Amsterdam, 1939; idem, *Kirche und Kaiser*, Zürich, 1947; F. E. Cranz, *Harv. Theol. Rev.*, xlv, 1952, pp. 47–66; K. Heussi, *Wissenschaftl. Zeitschr. Univ. Jena*, vii, 1957–8, pp. 89–92; F. Scheidweiler, *Zeitschr. f. d. Neut. Wissenschaft*, xlix, 1958, pp. 123–9; D. S. Wallace-Hadrill, *Eusebius of Caesarea*, London, 1960.

24. 'Über Kirchengeschichte', 1908, in *Gesammelte Schriften*, i, 1938, pp. 110–30.

25. W. Nigg, *Die Kirchengeschichtsschreibung*, Munich, 1934. *Cf.* H. Zimmermann, 'Ecclesia als Objekt der Historiographie', *Sitzungsb. Akad. Wien*, ccxxxv, 1960.

26. *Cf.* R. Reitzenstein, *Sitzungsb. Heidelberg. Akad.*, 1, 1914, n. 8; K. Holl, *Ges. Aufsätze*, ii, 1928, pp. 249–69; K. Heussi, *Ursprung des Mönchtums*, Tübingen, 1936; A.-J. Festugière, *Rev. Et. Grecques*, 1, 1937, pp. 470–94; H. Dörries, *Nachr. Ges. Wiss. Göttingen*, xiv, 1949, pp. 359–410. *Cf.* also the English translation of the life of St Anthony by R. T. Meyer, *Ancient Christian Writers*, x, 1950.

27. The *Vitae sophistarum* are now to be read in the edition by G. Giangrande, Rome, 1956.

28. It will be enough to refer to the two well-known monographs on Ammianus by W. Ensslin, *Klio*, Beiheft, xvi, 1923, and E. A. Thompson, Cambridge, 1947. Full bibliography will be found in C. P. T. Naudé, *Am. M. in die lig van die antieke Geskiedskrywing*, diss., Leiden, 1956. V. S. Sokolov, *Vestnik Drevnej Istorii*, 1959, 4, pp. 43–62. *Cf.* also S. Mazzarino, 'La propaganda senatoriale nel tardo impero', *Doxa*, iv, 1951, pp. 121–48. Idem, 'La democratizzazione della cultura nel Basso Impero', *Rapports XI Congrès Intern. Sciences Historiques*, ii, Stockholm, 1960, pp. 35–54. L. Dillemann, *Syria*, xxxviii, 1961, pp. 87–158.

29. See my *Secondo Contributo alla storia degli studi classici*, 1960, p. 198.

30. *Cf.* A. Garroni, *Bull. Comm. Arch. Com.*, 1915, pp. 123–35.

31. *Cf.* also J. Sirinelli, *Les Vues historiques d'Eusèbe de Césarée durant la période prénicéenne*, thèse, Paris, 1961, and W. Lammers, ed., *Geschichtsdenken und Geschichtsbild im Mittelalter*, Darmstadt, 1961, with bibliography.

9

The Lonely Historian Ammianus Marcellinus*

I

IN the second part of the fourth century the Greek East became economically stronger, militarily safer and religiously more Christian than the Latin West. The rise of Constantinople to the position of a new Rome was the most tangible expression of the new situation; but Antioch was hardly less prestigious. Latin, however, was the language of law and, to a great extent, of administration: it was also the language of the army. Many Greeks felt that they had to learn Latin just because their prospects of a career in the Roman administration had become brighter. In Egypt (and no doubt in other Greek-speaking regions as well) people read the Latin poets and historians for the first time. In Antioch Libanius came to fear the competition of teachers of Latin rhetoric (*Or.*, 2, 44; 58, 21 Förster; *Ep.* 870 Wolf= 951 Förster). Competence in the Latin language was an accomplishment of Greek speakers to be recorded in prose and verse: 'you, replete with the Laws, mixing the Italic muse with the sweet spoken honey of the Attic one'.[1] For the pagan intellectuals of the East, Latin had the additional attraction of being the language of the less Christian part of the Empire. In Rome the aristocrats had the reputation (not always deserved) of remaining faithful to the old gods.[2] They gladly read, translated and imitated Greek works.[3] Yet any careful observer of the contemporary scene would easily have noticed that the position of the pagan Latin writers was becoming increasingly precarious. After the intellectual ascendancy of St John Chrysostom and of the two Gregorii, Latin Christianity began to regain intellectual initiative. The last years of the fourth century were dominated by St Ambrose, St Jerome and St Augustine.[4]

Annali della Scuola Normale Superiore di Pisa, Classe di Lettere e Filosofia, serie III, IV, 4, 1974, pp. 1393–1407. A Hebrew translation of this essay was published as an Introduction to the Hebrew translation of Ammianus by the late Sara Dvoretzky, Bialik Institute, Jerusalem, 1974.

The historian of Latin literature therefore has to insert into a rather complex situation the stark fact that the greatest Latin poet and the greatest Latin historian of the late fourth century were both Oriental pagans whose first language was Greek. The former, Claudianus, was born in Egypt;[5] the latter, Ammianus Marcellinus, came from Syria; both reached fame after emigrating to Italy. Ammianus had been in the élite corps of the *protectores domestici* (15, 5, 22) before settling in Rome about 380. The army was not only Latin in language, but fundamentally indifferent to religious conflicts.[6]

We know very little of Ammianus' life. With the exception of a letter from Libanius to Ammianus of about A.D. 392 (*Ep.* 983 Wolf = 1063 Förster) all we have about him comes from his historical work. Compared to, say, Livy or his own model Tacitus, Ammianus would appear to display an almost indecent readiness to speak about himself. Yet there were limits to what even an unconventional historian could say about himself in the course of his work. Furthermore, the loss of the first part of his History (Books I–XIII) includes the proemium which was the customary place for an author to give some account of the genesis of his work and of the social status of his patrons. In any case, as we shall see, the situation which Ammianus created for himself was not likely to encourage him to produce those items of information – about his education, his authentic feelings during the pagan restoration of Julian and his removal to Rome – which we should like to have.

What he tells us explicitly or implicitly is this. He was born in a respectable family (*Ingenuus*, 19, 8, 6). In 353 he was assigned by the emperor Constantius II to the personal retinue of Ursicinus, *magister equitum* of the East, who was then in Nisibis (14, 9, 1). Four years later, in 357, he was still too young to be promoted to the tribunate (16, 10, 21). We may assume that he was born about 330. In 355 he escorted Ursicinus to the West (15, 5, 24). Involved in the rift between Constantius II and the Caesar Gallus, Ursicinus saved his skin and by implication that of his faithful Ammianus by helping Constantius to get rid of the usurper Silvanus in Gaul. Ursicinus organized the cold-blooded murder of Silvanus, and Ammianus must have collaborated. In Gaul he saw – but hardly spoke with – Julian, the newly appointed Caesar (16, 2, 8). Very soon Ursicinus and Ammianus were sent back to the East, where a Persian attack was expected (16, 10, 21). The unsuccessful war with the Persians provided plenty of adventures and dangers for Ammianus. He was sent by Ursicinus on a mission of espionage (18, 6, 21), for which Ammianus obviously exploited a friendship of earlier days in Syria. He managed to escape from the besieged city of Amida before it fell to the enemy. He admits that in the flight he found it difficult to keep pace with his two lower-born companions (19, 8, 6). He rejoined Ursicinus at Melitene in Lesser Armenia and went safely to Antioch with him: 'Antiochiam revisimus insperati' (19, 8, 12). Not surprisingly, Ursicinus lost his command. What happened to Ammianus we do not know, but three years later we find him following Julian in the new expedition against Persia which ended with Julian's death (23, 5, 7; 24, 1, 5; 25, 3, 1). Ammianus does not say that he was one of the people who listened to Julian's last words (25, 3, 15). He never tries to convey the impression that he was on personal terms with Julian. Nor is he likely to be the *honoratior miles* who advised the postponement of the election of a successor (25, 5, 3). The only personal detail he emphasizes is, again, the retreat to Antioch: 'Antiochiam venimus' (25, 10, 1). Ammianus was in Antioch eight years later in 371 (29, 1, 24), and again in 378 (31, 1, 2). The implication is perhaps that he left the army and lived there. If so, he must have interrupted his residence for travels. His journey to Greece, or more precisely to Mothone in the Peloponnesus, is dated about 365 (26, 10, 15–19: *cf.* Libanius, *Or.*, 18, 392–3). He visited Thrace apparently later, after the battle of Adrianople of 378 (22, 8, 1; 27, 4, 2; 31, 7, 16 'nunc usque').

Curiously, in the extant books he never says that he was a native and citizen of Antioch, though he may have said so in the lost books. We would have had to infer this from the frequency and character of his mentions of Antioch, if it were not clearly stated as a fact by his fellow Antiochene Libanius (*Ep.* 1063 quoted). Libanius also offers the only explicit evidence we have that Ammianus went to live in Rome – perhaps after 378. Here again we might have guessed the state of affairs from his various and, normally, hostile remarks about the present inhabitants of the old capital: especially the two digressions of 14, 6 and 28, 4 presuppose long residence in Rome. There is, however, no sufficient justification for inferring from Ammianus' indignation at the treatment of immigrants to Rome during the famine of 384 (14, 6, 19) that he was one of those thrown out of the city by order of the prefect Symmachus.[7] What in any case Ammianus neither says nor implies is that about 392 he was giving successful readings from his own historical work to Roman audiences. But for Libanius we should never have associated Ammianus with such social events. As the conclusion of the work shows, he wanted to be known simply as 'an ex-soldier and a Greek' (31, 16, 9). Diligence he considered to be characteristic of a Greek historian.

Timagenes, the historian of the Augustan period, was 'et diligentia graecus et lingua' (15, 9, 2). No wonder that in several other passages of his work Ammianus was keen to underline that Greek was his mother tongue (22, 8, 33; 23, 6, 20).

II

The lost part of his histories embraced in thirteen books the period A.D. 96–A.D. 352, whereas the following eighteen books – still extant – contain the story of 25 years, about one book for every 18 months. Arguments have been adduced to eliminate this disproportion. It has been suggested that Ammianus wrote two works which would have been conflated into one by some later editor, just as we know that Tacitus' *Annales* and *Historiae* were united in one work of thirty books (*cf.* St Jerome, *Comm. in Zachariam*, 3, 14 and the subscriptions to individual books in the Cod. Mediceus Secundus).[8] In Ammianus, however, the thirty-one books would represent the second work only, allegedly starting with Constantine. This theory, therefore, solves nothing because it does not explain why the present text of Ammianus in thirty-one books goes, as is explicitly stated, 'a principatu Caesaris Nervae ... adusque Valentis interitum' (31, 16, 9). There is no evidence that Ammianus wrote two different works and that the present books 14–31 are part of the second work. We must accept the fact that the lost books 1–13 told the story from the emperor Nerva onwards. It is better to confess that we do not know how Ammianus distributed his material in the first thirteen books. All we know is that even in the more summary narration of the lost part he indulged in some of his characteristic digressions, because he refers to them in the extant books (22, 15, 1; 27, 8, 4). It was normal for historians to enlarge on recent events, but there was no rule about the space they had to allocate to more remote times. Polybius distinguished sharply between introduction and main narrative of recent events. Livy gradually extended the dimensions of his narrative. Ammianus was probably nearer to Livy than to Polybius. Tacitus' shorter span was no precedent here.

Ammianus seems to have considered book 15 rather than book 14 the beginning of his detailed account. He prefaced it with a methodological declaration which is puzzling in its ambiguity and has not yet been adequately interpreted (15, 1): it was an answer to critics. Another preface indicates that book 26 was the beginning of the last section.

Ammianus seems to imply that there had been an interval before he started to write in book 26 his account of the reigns of Valentinianus and Valens. Now 21, 10, 6, assumes that the historian Aurelius Victor had been the prefect of Rome in 388–9, but 22, 16, 12 was almost certainly written before the Christians destroyed the Serapeum of Alexandria about 391.[9] One can date books 21–22, and probably also 23–25, about the year 390. It is more difficult to date the publication of 26–31. 27, 11, 2–8 attacks the powerful Petronius Probus in a way which clearly implies that he was dead, but all we know is that he died between 389 and 395. 29, 6, 15 has an allusion to Theodosius 'princeps postea perspectissimus' which does not seem to suit a living emperor: one is naturally inclined to take it as having been written after Theodosius' death in 395. On the other hand O. J. Maenchen-Helfen argued that St Jerome derived his information on the Huns from Ammianus.[10] As this information begins to appear in the *Adversus Iovinianum* published in 393, St Jerome would have been able to read Ammianus' book 31 in that year. The verbal similarities between St Jerome and Ammianus are certainly striking (Ammianus, 31, 2, 3 'semicruda cuiusvis pecoris carne vescuntur' is matched by St Jerome, 2, 7 'semicrudis vescuntur carnibus') and cannot be separated from other contacts. It is prudent to leave undecided whether Ammianus ended his work before or after the death of Theodosius.

III

Ammianus had in mind a precise model when he chose to write his history in Latin. He presents himself as a continuator of Tacitus. He begins where Tacitus stops, and his thirty-one books are close enough to the thirty books of the combined edition of Tacitus' *Annales* and *Historiae* which St Jerome knew. He continues Tacitus as the *Historia Augusta* continues Suetonius. In the same vein, the panegyrists of the emperors of the fourth century imitated Pliny's panegyric of Trajan, and Symmachus (or his editor) distributed his correspondence in imitation of Pliny's ten books of letters. The Silver Age authors were coming back into fashion, and though Ammianus seems to disapprove of the new popularity of Juvenal (28, 4, 14) it is evident that he studied him. Claudian may owe more to Virgil than to Lucan, but he is well acquainted with the poetry of the early empire. We are therefore not surprised to hear from Libanius that Ammianus found an approving audience in Rome for his revival of the Tacitean tradition. The self-confidence which is apparent in his style seems to confirm this success.

What we should like to know is *who* were the audience. The rest of the evidence conveys the impression that Ammianus had few and remote, though perhaps powerful, friends and protectors. About 360 Libanius may have introduced him as a young man to friends as 'Ammianus . . . a soldier in appearance, but a Socrates in his deeds' (*Ep.* 234 W. = 233 F.). *If* he is the Ammianus of this letter (which is not certain) there is no sign that their relation between 360 and 390 went beyond mere civilities. Libanius is never mentioned in the extant part of Ammianus' work; and our Ammianus, even in the most optimistic of interpretations, fills a very small space in Libanius' large correspondence. The mere fact that Ammianus moved to Rome seems to indicate that he had severed his roots in Antioch.

In Rome, as far as we can judge from his histories, there were few people he respected; and those he respected, he respected from afar: first of all the great aristocrat Agorius Praetextatus (27, 9, 8; 28, 1, 24), then – in less warm or less bombastic terms – Virius Nicomachus (28, 6, 28), the prefects of the City Eupraxius (27, 6, 14; 28, 1, 25), Hypatius (29, 2, 16) and Aurelius Victor (21, 10, 6). I do not see any reason to doubt that he knew these eminent men personally; this is virtually certain for 'noster Hypatius', an Antiochene by election, if not by birth, who was prefect of Rome in 379. Aurelius Symmachus, prefect of 384, the famine year, is conspicuously absent. Nor can we fill the lacuna by taking Symmachus' letter 9, 110 as being directed to Ammianus. As A. Cameron has definitely shown, in order to identify Ammianus with the anonymous addressee of this letter, one must believe that he was a senator (for which there is no other evidence) and that Symmachus would be so silly as to translate Greek for his benefit.[11] The letter is directed to a historian who was trying eloquence; why should he be Ammianus? It is a poor substitute to have Symmachus' father favourably mentioned by Ammianus (27, 3, 3). There may be an element of prudent adulation in this, as there is certainly adulation in the frequent conventional compliments paid to the father of Theodosius (27, 8, 3; 28, 3, 1; 29, 5, 15, etc., etc.) Strange to say, the only man for whom Ammianus shows real devotion and for whom his eulogy is both constant and sincere is his old patron Ursicinus, an intriguer and a bad general. In mentioning Aurelius Victor, Ammianus qualifies him as a historian. There is, however, no sign that he used or even appreciated Aurelius Victor's summary of imperial history. Victor's booklet was less jejune than other fashionable epitomes of Roman history (such as those by Eutropius and Rufius Festus), but still belonged to that type of 'official' and superficial history against which Ammianus was reacting.

It is even more difficult to explain why Virius Nicomachus is not given credit for his historical work which we know to have been encouraged by Theodosius (Dessau, *ILS*, 2947). A. Alföldi's bizarre notion that Ammianus copied Nicomachus Flavianus in his account of Valentinianus and Valens[12] was disposed of in a few lines by N. H. Baynes.[13] But even the earlier, more sophisticated version of the same thesis by O. Seeck that Nicomachus was the 'Thucydidean' source of Ammianus is refuted by the simple remark that Ammianus had no Thucydidean source.[14] What is evident is that Ammianus was not anxious to tell his readers what his contemporary sources were. As Zosimus did not read Ammianus, the similarities between them on Julian's reign have to be accounted for by a common source. Eunapius or Eunapius' source, Julian's doctor and friend Oribasius, are the most likely candidates for this position.[15] But Ammianus is careful not to mention either, though both were renowned names, Oribasius in particular.

IV

Whatever the reasons, Ammianus himself does his best to give the impression that he is intellectually isolated. He reserves his praise for powerful political men, never for contemporary writers as such. And even the praise of political men is no sign of shared political or (what was almost the same at that time) religious convictions. Ammianus does not belong to a 'party' or 'faction'.

Superficially, there would be some justification in treating him as a representative of the upper stratum of the *curiales*, the hard-pressed governing bodies of the cities. He is certainly very sensitive to any infringement of property rights and to any increase in taxation (16, 5, 13–15). He considers the protection of propertied classes to be one of the first duties of government. He explicitly takes sides with the curiales of Antioch against the Caesar Gallus (14, 7, 2).

Yet the mere fact that Ammianus chose to live in Rome deprives his championship of the *curiales* of any political weight: he is not Libanius. His sympathy for the *curiales* is rather one of the various elements of his conservative outlook, for which concord in the State, lack of greed and corruption, justice, readiness to fight for one's country (15, 12, 3) and simplicity in living (31, 5, 14) are even more important.

What defined a man writing in Latin in Rome was what he thought about Christianity, the Germans and the role of the Roman Senate. About these questions Ammianus was careful not to be drawn. He was quite determined not to make an issue of them. He considered Julian's persecution of the Christians a mistake and could hardly bring himself to mention the prohibition of teaching which he had imposed on Christian grammarians and rhetoricians: 'illud . . . obruendum perenni silentio' (22, 10, 7). The idea of rebuilding the temple of Jerusalem to prove the Christians wrong seemed to him odd (23, 1, 2). It is significant that in order to show that even Julian could talk nonsense he reports a mildly anti-Semitic joke attributed to Marcus Aurelius (22, 5, 5). In the same way he reproaches Julian for indulging in anti-German boasts which proved to be empty (21, 10, 8). Though he is obviously very unsympathetic to Valens' policy of transferring Goths to Thrace (31, 4, 6), he is merciless in denouncing the provocative behaviour of the Roman authorities towards them (31, 4, 9).[16] He even understands the reasons which prompted the rebellion of the Frank Silvanus (15, 5, 32), though he had no compunction in helping his murderer. He never mentions the conflict about the altar of Victoria which represented a challenge to the authority of the Roman Senate and never treats the behaviour of the emperors towards the Senate as a test of the quality of their government. He does not take sides between St Ambrose and Symmachus, between the anti-German Libanius and the pro-German Themistius, and has none of the senatorial nostalgias of the *Scriptores Historiae Augustae*.

Refusal to choose is not equivalent to emotional indifference. Ammianus is openly pagan and admires Julian. He may have no very clear ideas about the *numen* to which he so frequently alludes (14, 11, 24; 15, 8, 9; 19, 1, 4 etc.) or about Adrastia, the goddess of Justice, to which he pays homage in a famous passage (14, 11, 25–26). But he relies on the good old divination of *augures* and *haruspices* (23, 5, 10; 31, 1, 2 etc.); holds the *Libri Sibyllae*, the *Libri Tagetici* and other classics of the *disciplina etrusca* in high respect (23, 1, 7; 17, 10, 2; 23, 5, 13; 25, 2, 7); and finds the cradle of true prophecy in Chaldaea (23, 6, 25). He is disgusted by the disputes of Christian sects (22, 5, 3; 27, 3, 12). Similarly, he has no love for the Germans. If he has to introduce them, animal images come naturally to his mind (26, 5, 7; 31, 8, 9; 31, 15, 2). The fact that he applies the same imagery to Christians (22, 5, 4) and to rebel

Roman troops or provincial tribes (15, 5, 23; 28, 6, 4) only makes the point more evident.

There are at least three reasons why Ammianus refuses to make his emotions the basis for his practical choices. The first reason is quite simply prudence. He is only too aware of the 'pericula . . . veritati saepe contigua' (26, 1, 1). Secondly, he has a genuine respect both for Christianity and for the Germans. Christianity is to him 'religio absoluta, et simplex' (21, 16, 18) which 'nihil nisi iustum suadet et lene' (22, 11, 5). He admires Christian martyrs (22, 11, 10; 27, 7, 5). The Germans are brave (25, 6, 14) and can be devoted to a good general (18, 2, 6). Thirdly, Ammianus does not like unjustified generalizations. He makes a difference between the good (27, 3, 15) and the bad bishop (22, 11, 4; 27, 3, 11), and he defends a bishop accused of having betrayed the Romans (20, 7, 7). In the same way Ammianus denounces bad German officers, but feels free to report that the barbarian Dagalaifus gave the right advice to Valentinian about choosing a colleague: 'if you love your relatives, have your brother; if you love the State, look round for the man to invest with office' (26, 4, 1). The separation between emotions and perception of realities was indispensable to Ammianus, if his conservatism were to have any substance at all. Choice of religion or the admittance of Germans had not been political issues in the old Rome. To yield to anti-Christian or anti-German customs amounted to dereliction of *Roma aeterna*. Contemporary disasters notwithstanding, Ammianus still clung to the notion of the eternity of Rome: 'victura dum erunt homines Roma' (14, 6, 3). Rome was the place where Julian would have deserved to be buried (25, 10, 5).[17] Ammianus never really considered the empire to be in mortal danger (31, 5, 11–17). The continuity of Rome required that the successful defence of the empire, internal justice and peace, and low taxation – not religious conflicts and the recruitment of Germans – should be the true concern of the state.

A position of this kind might easily lead to Utopia or to antiquarianism or both. Indeed there is an undeniable trace of both in Ammianus. He idealizes the past without really knowing it. What he says about ancient Rome is too often derived from literary *exempla*. His bookish attitude is particularly noticeable in his numerous excursuses where too much second-hand knowledge is mixed with personal observations. Ammianus had an altogether exceptional direct knowledge of the empire, the greater part of which he visited: Britain, Spain and Africa west of Egypt were apparently the only three important regions he had never seen. He spoke of course both languages. It is therefore all the more remarkable that so much of his geographical information should be derivative. He gives disproportionate attention to the events of the city of Rome and is deliberately reticent about the new Rome of the East. He is, again deliberately, vague about things he must have known well, such as the Roman provincial administration and the army. He is the opposite of Polybius: he neither claims nor displays any special competence in military matters, though he had been a soldier for many years. His battle scenes are not for the expert; his knowledge of war machines seems to be elementary (23, 4). It was clearly a mistake to attribute to him the contemporary anonymous tract *De rebus bellicis* which is an attempt, however misguided, to use technology for the defence of the empire.

But Ammianus is far too aware of what is at stake to become an opinionated pedant. He has an acute, almost demonic, perception of contemporary realities: one regrets not being able to compare his account of twenty-five years of contemporary history with his narrative of the previous period. It would be illuminating to see whether he changed his method of narration and style when he left the past for the present. What we have is a picture of men and events which in its power of characterization through deformation inevitably reminds us of El Greco. Ammianus exaggerates everything. He may have found it difficult to accommodate his Greek syntactic habits to the Latin language, but his convoluted style is not to be understood as a sum of Graecisms.[18]

He is in the current leading from Tertullian and Apuleius to Sidonius Apollinaris and Ennodius, but with a twist of his own. He gives maximum emphasis to absurdities and follies – to violence and cunning. *Roma aeterna* is the ultimate judge and the ultimate hope. But the extraordinary contortions and complications of his style – which are not incompatible with its self-confidence – indicate how difficult it is for Ammianus to keep control of his world.

Ammianus does not feel safe in his own surroundings. Black magic is not to him an object of intellectual curiosity. He speaks of it as a menace (26, 3, 2; 29, 2, 17 and elsewhere). The fact that emperors encouraged charges of black magic for their own purposes does not make it any less frightful.[19] *Fortuna* and *fatum* are intimation of death (21, 14, 1; 30, 5, 15 etc.).[20] Ammianus, though intellectually in favour of clemency (29, 2, 19), accepts ruthlessness and cruelty as inevitable. We are blandly told that no torture has yet been thought up capable of compelling an Egyptian bandit to reveal his name (22, 16, 23). Brutality and horrors are on display. There is no need here to illustrate in detail Ammianus' love for the grotesque and the horrific to which E. Auerbach dedicated a famous chapter of his *Mimesis*.

Ammianus follows Tacitus in giving pride of place to court intrigues and to wars. But no systematic comparison between the subject matter and the narrative techniques of the two writers is yet available.[21] It would probably show that Ammianus is more sensitive to education and tradition and less so to social status. His factual accuracy must not be taken for granted.[22] He lacks technical competence and aims at literary effects. But few important errors of fact have so far been discovered in his work. Where he reflects contemporary categories of thought or expresses contemporary standards of behaviour, moods and passions, he is, of course, to be trusted unhesitatingly. The authenticity of his accounts of social attitudes is guaranteed by the stylistic elaboration to which they are submitted. This type of distortion is measurable and therefore no source of equivocation. Nobody will take literally the satirical description of the lawyers in the Eastern part of the empire (30, 4, 4): it was probably written for a public lecture in Rome. Even the famous page on the hieratic attitudes of Constantius II during his visit to Rome (16, 10 ff.) has to be appreciated as an imaginative and convincing piece of reconstruction of something Ammianus never witnessed. What is reassuring is that Ammianus never attempts to enter into the minds of dedicated Christians. The neo-Platonic speculations he summarizes (21, 1; 21, 14) still belong to *Roma aeterna*. Beyond *Roma aeterna* Ammianus becomes circumspect.

A Select Bibliography

L. ANGLIVIEL DE LA BEAUMELLE, *Remarques sur l'attitude d'Ammien Marcellin à l'égard du Christianisme*, 'Mélanges W. Seston', Paris, 1974, pp. 15–24.

J. BIDEZ, *La vie de l'Empereur Julien*, Paris, 1930.

K. BRINGMANN, *Ammianus Marcellinus als spätantiker römischer Historiker*, Antike und Abendland, 19, 1973, pp. 44–60.

M. BÜDINGER, *Ammianus Marcellinus und die Eigenart seines Geschichtswerkes. Eine universalhistorische Studie.* In 'Denkschriften der phil.-hist. Klasse der Wiener Akademie der Wiss.', XLIV, Abh. 5, 1896.

P. M. CAMUS, *Ammien Marcellin*, Paris, 1967.

L. DAUTREMER, *Ammien Marcellin. Étude d'histoire littéraire*, Lille, 1899.

A. DEMANDT, *Zeitkritik und Geschichtsbild im Werk Ammians*, Bonn, 1965.

S. DILL, *Roman Society in the Last Century of the Western Empire*, London, 1898.

W. ENSSLIN, *Zur Geschichtsschreibung und Weltanschauung des Ammianus Marcellinus*, Klio Beih. 16, 1923.

H. GÄRTNER, *Einige Überlegungen ... zu Ammians Charakteristik des Kaisers Julian*, Wiesbaden, 1969.

J. GIMAZANE, *Ammien Marcellin. Sa vie et son œuvre*, diss. Bordeaux-Toulouse, 1889.

A. VON GUTSCHMID, *Ammianus Marcellinus*, in 'Kleine Schriften', V, Leipzig, 1894, pp. 567–84.

W. HARTKE, *Römische Kinderkaiser. Eine Strukturanalyse römischen Denkens und Daseins*, Berlin, 1951.

M. HERTZ, *Aulus Gellius und Ammianus Marcellinus*, Hermes, 8, 1874, pp. 257–302.

W. KLEIN, *Studien zu Ammianus Marcellinus*, Klio Beih. 13, 1914.

M. L. W. LAISTNER, *The Greater Roman Historians*, Berkeley, 1947.

S. MAZZARINO, *Il pensiero storico classico*, III, Bari, 1967.

A. MOMIGLIANO, *Pagan and Christian Historiography in the Fourth Century A.D.*, in 'The Conflict between Paganism and Christianity in the Fourth Century', Essays edited by A. Momigliano, Oxford, 1963 (*Cf.* above, pp. 107–26).

TH. MOMMSEN, *Ammians Geographica*, in 'Gesamm. Schriften', VII, Berlin, 1909, pp. 393–429.

CH. P. TH. NAUDÉ, *Ammianus Marcellinus in die lig van die antieke geskiedskrywing*, diss. Leiden, 1956.

R. PACK, *The Roman Digressions of Ammianus Marcellinus*, TAPhA, 1953, pp. 181–9.

G. B. PIGHI, *Studia Ammianea*, Milano, 1935.

Idem, *I discorsi nelle storie di Ammiano Marcellino*, Milano, 1936.

Idem, *Nuovi studi Ammianei*, Milano, 1936.

W. RICHTER, *Die Darstellung der Hunnen bei Ammianus Marcellinus*, Historia, 23, 1974, pp. 343–77.

R. SYME, *Ammianus and the Historia Augusta*, Oxford, 1968.

E. A. THOMPSON, *The Historical Work of Ammianus Marcellinus*, Cambridge, 1947.

Z. V. UDALCOVA, *Mirovozzrenie Ammiana Marcellina*, Vizant. Vremennik, 28, 1968, pp. 38–59.

References

1. I. Ševčenko, 'A Late Antique Epigram', *Synthronon*, Paris, 1968, pp. 29–41 with rich bibliography. *Cf.* A.-J. Festugière, *Antioche païenne et chrétienne*, Paris, 1959, p. 411.

2. H. Bloch in A. Momigliano, *The Conflict between Paganism and Christianity in the Fourth Century*, Oxford, 1963, pp. 193–218, but *cf.* P. Brown, JRS, LI, 1961, pp. 1–11 (= *Religion and Society in the Age of St Augustine*, London, 1972, pp. 161–82).

3. See, for instance, W. Speyer, *Naucellius und sein Kreis*, München, 1959, with the review by W. Schmid, Gnomon, XXXII, 1960, pp. 340–60; *cf.* F. Vittinghoff, HZ, CXCVIII, 1964, pp. 529–74.

4. P. Brown, *The World of Late Antiquity*, London, 1971, pp. 115–23; J. Daniélou–H. Marrou, *Des Origines à Saint Grégoire le Grand*, Paris, 1963, pp. 341–8.

5. A. Cameron, *Claudian*, Oxford, 1970, a book of general importance.

6. A. H. M. Jones in A. Momigliano, *The Conflict* quoted, 23–6.

7. H. P. Kohns, *Versorgungskrisen und Hungerrevolten im spätantiken Rom*, Bonn, 1961, pp. 168–82. The date of Ammianus' journey to Egypt is unknown (17, 4, 6; 22, 15). For other details of his life see 18, 4, 7; 18, 6, 5; 18, 8, 11.

8. H. T. Rowell, *Ammianus Marcellinus, Soldier – Historian of the Late Roman Empire*, Cincinnati (Semple Lectures), 1964; Id., *Mélanges Carcopino*, Paris, 1966, 839–48. On Tacitus, F. Brunhölz, Abh. Marburg Gelehrt. Gesell. 1971, 3, 111–43.

9. J. Schwartz, *La fin du Serapeum d'Alexandrie*, in 'Essays in Honor of C. Bradford Welles', New Haven, 1966, pp. 97–111.

10. AJPh, LXXVI, 1955, pp. 384–99. *Contra* R. Syme, JRS, LVIII, 1968, p. 218; *Ammianus and the Historia Augusta*, Oxford, 1968, pp. 12–24. But see A. Cameron, JRS, LXI, 1971, 259–61.

11. A. Cameron, *The Roman Friends of Ammianus*, JRS, LIV, 1964, pp. 15–28. *Cf.* A. Selem, *A proposito degli amici romani di Ammiano*, Annali Libera Università della Tuscia, III, 1972, pp. 1–50; *Ammiano e la morte di Giuliano*, Rend. Ist. Lombardo, 107, 1973, pp. 1119–35.

12. *A Conflict of Ideas in the Late Roman Empire*, Oxford, 1952.

13. JRS, XLIII, 1953, p. 169.

14. Hermes, XLI, 1906, pp. 481–539, supported by R. Laqueur in *Probleme der Spätantike*, Stuttgart, 1930, pp. 33–6.

15. W. R. Chalmers, CQ, LIV, 1960, pp. 152–60; A. Cameron, *Ib.*, LVI, 1963, pp. 232–6 (also LIX, 1965, pp. 289–98). But *cf.* also L. Dillemann, Syria, XXXVIII, 1961, pp. 87–158; H. Gärtner, Abhandl. Mainz. Akad., 1968, n. 10; C. J. Classen, Museum Africum, I, 1972, pp. 39–47; D. A. Pauw, *Karaktertekening bij Ammianus Marcellinus*, diss. Leiden, 1972.

16. A. Demandt, *Zeitkritik und Geschichtsbild im Werk Ammians*, Bonn, 1965, represents a new departure on Ammianus' attitude towards the Germans.

17. F. Paschoud, *Roma aeterna*, Paris, 1966; M. Fuhrmann, *Die Romidee der Spätantike*, HZ, CCXII, 1968, pp. 529–61. *Cf.* also H. Tränkle, Antike und Abendland, XI, 1962, pp. 21–34.

18. E. Norden, *Antike Kunstprosa*, II, Berlin, 1898, pp. 646–50. The best analysis of Ammianus' style is perhaps H. Hagendahl, *Studia Ammianea*, diss. Uppsala, 1921. For literary allusions, G. B. A. Fletcher, RPh, LXIII, 1937, pp. 377–95. See also in general the excellent essay by J. Vogt, *Ammianus Marcellinus als erzählender Geschichtsschreiber der Spätzeit*, Abhandl. Mainz. Akad., 1963, No. 8 and J. Fontaine, *Ammien Marcellin historien romantique*, Lettres d'Humanité, XXVIII, 1969, pp. 417–35; R. MacMullen, *Some Pictures of A. M.*, Art Bulletin, XLVI, 1964, pp. 435–55.

19. *Cf.* A. A. Barb, in A. Momigliano, *The Conflict between Paganism and*

Christianity, pp. 100–25; H. Funke, Jahrb. Antike und Christ., X, 1967, pp. 145–75.

20. C. P. T. Naudé, *Fortuna in Ammianus Marcellinus*, Acta Classica VII, 1964, pp. 70–88; W. Seyfarth, *Ammianus Marcellinus und das Fatum*, Klio, XLIII–XLV, 1965, pp. 291–306; L. Bonfante Warren, Parola del Passato, 1964, pp. 401–27.

21. *Cf.*, however, Chr. Samberger, *Die Kaiserbiographie in den Res Gestae des Ammianus Marcellinus*, Klio, LI, 1969, pp. 349–483; and above all D. Flach, *Von Tacitus zu Ammian*, Historia, XXI, 1972, pp. 333–50.

22. *Cf.* K. Rosen, *Studien zur Darstellungskunst und Glaubwürdigkeit des Ammianus Marcellinus*, diss. Heidelberg, 1968; but *contra* N. J. E. Austin, *In Support of Ammianus' Veracity*, Historia, XXII, 1973, pp. 331–5. See in the same instalment of Historia the two papers by R. T. Ridley and T. S. Burns respectively on Julian's Persian Expedition and the Battle of Adrianople.

10

Popular Religious Beliefs and the Late Roman Historians *

I

STUDENTS of historiography have become increasingly gloomy in their evaluation of the Greek founding fathers of historiography. All the limits, the shortcomings and the failures of conventional history writing – the *histoire événementielle* of French terminology – have been laid at the door of Thucydides. Herodotus has escaped obloquy, either because he offered a promise of variety, curiosity, humour and sensitiveness which Thucydides spoiled, or because (as Professor Seth Benardete says in a very recent book) 'his foundations are not those of modern historiography'.[1] Thucydides has become the great villain of historiography in so far as he identified history with political and military events. Professor Moses Finley and I may in the past have said some unkind words about Thucydides – so did the late Professor Collingwood. But we are now made to look like mild apologists of Thucydides by Hermann Strasburger. This most penetrating interpreter of ancient historians has treated Thucydides' approach to history as the survival of a prehistoric mode of thinking, for which war was the most important event. According to Strasburger, Thucydides excluded *das Humanum* from history and therefore derived his scale of values from 'prescientific and ultimately precivilized, prehistoric strata of thought'.[2] Strasburger tries to show that some Hellenistic historians, such as Agatharchides and Posidonius, showed more interest in the business of peaceful coexistence than Thucydides ever did, but he is under no illusion about their ultimate success. Thucydides' historical approach prevailed: deviationists were silenced. The Romans inherited from the Greeks a type of historical writing for which war was the central theme. What Thucydides did not know was not history.

Though we may reserve our gloom for nearer relatives in the historio-

Studies in Church History, 8, Cambridge University Press, 1971, pp. 1–18.
[Paper read at the Summer 1970 Conference of the Ecclesiastical History Society.]

graphical family it must be recognized that classical historians did not cover all the field of history in which we are interested. They explored a limited field which corresponds to what we call military and political history, to the almost total exclusion of economic, social and religious phenomena. Furthermore, their interests were centred on contemporary history or on the history of the recent past; and their techniques of research implied a definite preference of direct observation for the study of the present and of oral tradition for the study of the past. When a classical historian ceased to be an independent inquirer about things seen or heard, he tended to become a compiler from previous historians. Research in archives was seldom, and unsystematically, practised by classical historians.

This limitation to political and military history was in itself an attitude towards religion. Religious (and moral) emotions were left out of history, unless they were regarded as having influenced specific military or political events. Even in such cases the historian was unlikely to emphasize direct intervention of the gods in history. Thucydides registered the profanation of the herms in 415 B.C. because it was directly relevant to the history of the Sicilian expedition. He did not mention the trial of Diagoras the atheist, which many of us would date, *pace* Felix Jacoby, in 415 and consider very significant for the religious situation of the time.

Xenophon states that the gods punished the Spartans for having treacherously seized the acropolis of Thebes,[3] but he does not extend his religious interpretation to the whole period of history with which he is dealing. He just hints at the wide implications of Socrates' dissent during the trial of the generals after the battle of the Arginusae.[4] He does not interpret the catastrophe of 404 B.C. as a divine punishment for the miscarriage of justice. If Theopompus relates the political decline of Cotys, king of Thrace, to a vulgar episode of impiety[5] or reports ominous signs about Sicilian tyrants,[6] we are not entitled to generalize his specific allusions to divine intervention in given situations. Timaeus was notoriously accused by Polybius of writing histories 'full of dreams, prodigies, incredible tales and, to put it shortly, craven superstition and womanish love of the marvellous'.[7] What we know of Timaeus, either directly from the fragments of his work or indirectly from the authors who used him as a source, shows that Timaeus attempted no more than an occasional and unsystematic correlation of divine and human affairs in the field of political and military history. Even Livy, in the most religious of his books (Book V on Camillus, Veii and the Gauls), does no more than relate Roman victories and defeats to proper observance of rituals.[8] What meaning Polybius attributed to fortune and Tacitus to fate is a favourite subject for academic disputes, but no one has yet made out a reasonable case for Polybius or Tacitus as religious interpreters of history.[9]

Interventions of gods, miracles and portents, together with other curiosities, were often confined by the historians to digressions and excursuses. Many Greek and Roman historians had some chapters or even books about extraordinary happenings. Theopompus created a model with his excursus on *thaumasia* in Book 10 of his *Philippic Histories*: in it he spoke about Zarathustra and about the Cretan Epimenides who woke up after fifty-seven years of sleep in a cavern. *Thaumasia* grew into a literary genre, as is shown by Pseudo-Aristotle's *Thaumasia*. Much information about religious beliefs and practices was also included by historians in their ethnographic chapters and books. Posidonius provided information in this manner about Celtic and Jewish religious practices. Roman historians, who imitated the Greek technique of excursus, added of their own the registration of *prodigia* which they inherited from the archaic annals of the pontiffs: though we must hasten to add that the relation between the *prodigia* of the pontifical records and the *prodigia* of Livy and his excerptors is by no means simple and clear.

Such isolation of religious phenomena in special compartments amounted to more than a declaration that the historian's real business was elsewhere. The historian with the mind either of a politician or of a general or of a learned man established a distance between himself and the religious practices or miraculous events he described. If he classified them as *thaumasia* he disclaimed responsibility for the truth of what he told: his excursus represented a parenthesis of amusement. If he included religion in a piece of ethnography he automatically placed it outside the world of the educated Greek or Roman: ethnography applied either to barbarians or to backwater Greeks or provincials, according to time and circumstance. Timaeus may have had a superstitious, and Posidonius a religious, mind (a distinction to which we shall soon return), but neither of them presented what he wrote about the beliefs of foreign nations as the truth. The attitude of the historian towards religious beliefs underlined the inherent aristocratic character of history writing. This detachment is equally evident, though in a different form, in Livy's attitude towards the Roman *prodigia*. True enough, he deplored the negligence of those who no longer announced the *prodigia* or reported them in the

Annals.[10] But he made it only too plain that in his concern with prodigies there was an element of literary pose: 'vetustas res scribenti, nescio quo pacto antiquus fit animus'.

A partial exception is represented by writers of biography. The biographer has to register the beliefs and superstitions of his hero, whether they influenced his political and military activity or not. Many biographies dealt with non-political and non-military men. Furthermore, Roman biographical writing seems to have made a special feature of collecting portents about a man in order to bring his exceptional personality into prominence. To judge from what we know of Sulla's and Augustus' autobiographies it was indeed perfectly respectable for a Roman politician to emphasize his own *charisma* by mentioning divine signs and other miracles. It would not be very helpful here to observe that in the ancient theory biography was never quite a part of historiography. What is more important is that the main account of the life of a man was not seriously affected either by the report of his religious beliefs or by the encroachment of the religious beliefs of his biographer. To find in the pagan world the biography of a religious man as such, we must perhaps go to the life of Apollonius of Tyana by Philostratus in the third century after Christ. In any case biography was not likely to reflect popular beliefs except incidentally: the proper subject for biography was by definition a man above the crowd.

Broadly speaking, a historian's approval of a religious belief would be registered in Greek by putting it in the category of *theosebeia* or *eusebeia*, while disapproval would be expressed by the word *deisidaimonia*. The corresponding (though not semantically identical) expressions in Latin would of course be *religio* and *superstitio*. *Deisidaimonia* and *superstitio* applied both to foreign cults and to the religious beliefs and practices of the lower orders. *Deisidaimonia* is the word chosen by Polybius to indicate the religious feelings of the lower classes which the Roman upper class fostered and exploited. Livy applied *superstitio* to the penetration of foreign cults into early Rome[11] or to the excessive trust in *prodigia* at the end of the second Punic war.[12] Tacitus speaks, *inter alia*, of Christianity as *exitiabilis superstitio*[13] and of the *superstitio vana* of the Druids.[14] Modern studies have done more to clarify the notion of *deisidaimonia* in Theophrastus and Plutarch or the earlier meanings of the difficult word *superstitio* than to interpret the actual usage of *deisidaimonia* and *superstitio* in historical texts. Livy, for instance, avoids the word *superstitio* and speaks of *simplices et religiosi homines* about the belief in *prodigia* in 214 B.C., when we would expect the mention of *superstitio*. His prudent usage of *superstitio* in relating the scandal of the Bacchanalia – a *coniuratio* – should be noticed. It would be premature to say that we are at present well-informed about the distinction between *theosebeia* and *deisidaimonia* or between *religio* and *superstitio*. But we are perhaps justified in stating that, before Christianity complicated matters, *deisidaimonia* and *superstitio* were key-words in the evaluation of religious phenomena by Greek and Roman historians.[15]

II

Although historians of the hellenistic period, as Professor Strasburger has shown, were less exclusively interested in politics and war than their masters of the fifth and fourth centuries B.C., a real change in the methods and contents of historical research did not take place until the late Roman empire. Ferdinand Christian Baur taught us 150 years ago that if Herodotus was the father of history, Eusebius was the father of a new history. The notion of ecclesiastical history implied a new importance being attributed to documentary evidence, a true universal scope both in time and in space, and finally a revolutionary change in contents. Religious beliefs and practices replaced military and political events as the central subject of historiography.

Some change of emphasis is, however, also noticeable in those pagan historians who in the fourth century A.D. intended to continue the pagan tradition of history writing. Ammianus Marcellinus continued the narrative of Tacitus; the *Historia Augusta* was modelled on Suetonius' *Twelve Caesars*. Eunapius as a historian continued Dexippus and as a biographer modelled himself on Philostratus' lives of the sophists. In each case greater emphasis was placed on religion and magic.

The *Scriptores Historiae Augustae* are aware of the new value attached to documents in contemporary writing, and where they have no documents they invent them. On the level of frivolity and even of obscenity they produce much information about religious beliefs. They mention *Iudaeorum libri*,[16] *doctissimi mathematicorum*,[17] a golden column inscribed with Egyptian letters.[18] Flavius Vopiscus, one of the alleged six biographers, claims to have received information from his own grandfather about the *omen imperii* of Diocletian.[19] There is nothing new in the fact that emperors should show interest in foreign cults and travel to remote sanctuaries, as the *Historia Augusta* tells us about Septimius Severus.[20] But Hadrian is made to say in a letter that in Egypt those who worship Serapis are Christians, while those who claim to be bishops of Christ are devotees of Serapis.[21] This passage must have been written before the destruction of the Serapeum of Alexandria in A.D. 391. No pagan author after that event could have joked about bishops of Christ being devotees of Serapis.[22] The *Historia Augusta* is certainly written from a pagan point of view under the shadow of Christian victory. According to the *Historia Augusta*, Hadrian wanted to build a temple to Christ but was prevented by those who, having consulted the sacred books, discovered that if Hadrian had done so 'omnes Christianos futuros .. et templa reliqua deserenda' – Christianity would have prevailed.[23] Christian hostility to *libri Sibyllini* is openly mentioned. But it was not yet absurd to consider placing Christ in a pagan pantheon. Jews are looked upon with a certain sympathy and knowledge, and even Samaritans are mentioned.[24] Trebellius Pollio quotes in the life of Claudius Gothicus [25] a legend about Moses who was said to complain about having to die young at the age of 125 – a legend which has some parallels in the Talmud.[26]

The attitude of the *Historia Augusta* towards Christianity would be even more interesting if it were true that its author or authors knew and mocked Christian writers such as St Jerome. As this point is of basic importance for the evaluation of the *Historia Augusta*, I may be allowed to show by a single example why in my opinion, and contrary to present orthodoxy, the matter is still *sub judice*. Professor André Chastagnol, in a brilliant chapter of his newly published *Recherches sur l'Histoire Auguste*,[27] has argued that the *Historia Augusta* knows and ridicules St Jerome's letter to Rufinus about their mutual friend Bonosus:[28] a letter which must have been written about 375. The *Historia Augusta* includes a life of the usurper Bonosus. The identity of name with the holy friend of Rufinus, according to Chastagnol, suggested a certain number of literary tricks to the humorous author of the *Historia Augusta*. One of these tricks would have been to transform Onesimus, the faithful follower of the holy Bonosus, into one of the many imaginary sources of the *Historia Augusta*. Now we happen to know from the *Suda* that a historian by the name of Onesimus lived under Constantine; and it is certain that the *Suda* does not depend on the *Historia Augusta* for this piece of information. It follows that the historian Onesimus was not invented by the *Historia Augusta*. We are in the fortunate and rare position of being able to say that the suggestion that the *Historia Augusta* found the name of Onesimus in St Jerome's letter (where Onesimus has nothing to do with history writing) is disproved by good evidence.

Future researchers may find echoes of Christian Fathers in the *Historia Augusta*, but up to the present, in my submission, the search has not been fruitful.

Even if we suspend judgement on the *Historia Augusta*'s alleged mockery of Christian writers there is enough in this work to make it a first-class document of the reformed paganism of the fourth century. Not once does the word *superstitio* occur in it. Pagan practices of every class and country are registered with sympathy and benevolent irony – unless they happen to offend morality *and* to be supported by emperors hostile to the Senate (as in the case of Heliogabalus). *Sortes Vergilianae* are mentioned,[29] and there is in the life of Probus a strange messianic pacifism which seems to have been introduced to compete with Christian millenarian dreams: 'brevi milites necessarios non futuros'.[30] The sympathy towards Jews and the desire to see Christianity dislodged from its pre-eminence and turned into a syncretistic cult are, as I have said, hardly concealed. While the traditional aristocratic attitude of the Roman historian towards lower-class beliefs and foreign superstitions does not disappear altogether – as is obvious from the life of Heliogabalus – it is fundamentally affected by the new situation. The pagans cannot afford to be divided at a time when the Christians are all out to occupy the key positions in the Roman government. The weakness of the position of the *Historia Augusta* betrays itself in the utopian character of many of its serious statements – and in the triviality of much of the rest.

Ammianus Marcellinus, who is never trivial, does use the word *superstitio*. He uses it very prominently in the passage in which he accuses the emperor Constantius of having corrupted the simple religion of the Christians by encouraging theological disputes: 'Christianam religionem absolutam et simplicem anili superstitione confundens in qua scrutanda perplexius quam componenda gravius, excitavit discidia plurima'.[31] By the second half of the fourth century *superstitio* and *deisidaimonia* were current names for paganism in Christian writers. To quote only the obvious, Lactantius says: 'nimirum religio veri cultus est, superstitio falsi ... sed quia deorum cultores religiosos se putant, cum sint superstitiosi, nec religionem possunt a superstitione discernere nec significantiam nominum exprimere'.[32] The polemical intention of Ammianus is therefore patent: state protection introduced an element of superstition into the Christian religion. Superstition is not the prerogative of the pagans.

No less significant is Ammianus' usage of *superstitio* in his excursus about the Huns. The Huns, according to him, have neither religion nor superstition: 'nullius religionis vel superstitionis reverentia aliquando districti'.[33] What puts the Huns outside the world of human beings is the absence of both religion and superstition. There is a difference between the Huns who have no superstition and the Alani who with barbaric rites worship the naked sword.[34] Ammianus is altogether no longer prepared to draw a sharp distinction between religion and superstition. Pagans and Christians have something of both. A vague monotheist and fatalist himself, he is above all a tolerant man who would like to be surrounded by tolerant men. With all his admiration for Julian, he disapproves of his persecution of the Christians. He even reproaches Julian with being 'superstitiosus magis quam sacrorum legitimus observator'. He praises Valentinian I because 'inter religionum diversitates medius stetit nec quemquam inquietavit'.[35] He believes in magic, astronomy and divination, for the last of which he gives a scientific explanation at some length.[36] He regrets that portents were no longer expiated by public rites.[37] He appreciates the religion of the Egyptians – the cradle of all religions – and the religion of the Persians, in which astrology and divination were prominent.[38] In practice, therefore, Ammianus is open to the amplest appreciation of different cults and tenets, including the cult of the Christian martyrs.[39] Whatever objection he has to Christianity is confined to the intolerance, the feuds, and above all the greed of certain Christian emperors, high civil servants and bishops: he does not generalize about them either. On a different level of intellectual refinement and integrity, Ammianus is not very far from the outlook of the *Historia Augusta*. The difference between religion and superstition is kept alive for polemical purposes only. Within the empire there is no significant distinction between the beliefs of the upper classes and those of the lower classes. What we would normally call superstition, such as readiness to believe in prodigies and magic practices, is quietly incorporated in religion.

A few years later, at the beginning of the fifth century, Eunapius was in a different mood. He belonged to the generation of pagan intellectuals for whom the official prohibition of pagan cults and the destruction of the Serapeum in A.D. 391 were the central experiences. He accused the monks, 'the men clad in black raiments', of having opened the gates of Greece to Alarich in 395.[40] But he, too, within the range of Pagan opinions, practically ignored any distinction between religion and superstition. His philosophers and sophists, quite unlike the sophists pictured by Philostratus, are deeply concerned with the knowledge of the nature of the gods, and consequently with divination and magic. Apollonius of Tyana, as we know, became a model for these men. It was not now infrequent for such philosophers to combine theology, rhetoric and medicine. Two kinds of divination were open to them. As Eunapius explains, one type of divination was given to men for the benefit of medicine, the other derived its dionysiac inspiration from philosophy.[41] There were of course doubts and discussions about the legitimate limits of magic and divination. Prudence had its part. One of these philosophers, Antoninus, 'displayed no tendency to theurgy . . . perhaps he kept a wary eye on the imperial views and policy which were opposed to these practices'.[42] Eusebius of Pergamum warned his pupil Julian, the future emperor, against the impostures of witchcraft. Julian managed to extract from Eusebius the information that he had alluded to Maximus of Ephesus. 'You have shown me the man I was in search of,' exclaimed Julian, and went off to Ephesus to be taught by Maximus.[43] Eunapius himself was present when a hierophant of Eleusis foretold the overthrow of the temples and the ruin of the whole of Greece. He even foresaw that the cult of Eleusis would come to an end during the office of his own successor.[44] Christian sophists were not necessarily excluded from this circle. But when the famous Christian rhetorician Prohaeresius showed his ability to foretell future events it was discreetly assumed that he had stolen his knowledge from the hierophant of Eleusis.

Zosimus must have derived from Eunapius the story that when Alarich approached Athens in A.D. 395 he saw Athena Promachos touring the walls and Achilles dressed as if he were marching against the Trojans to revenge the death of Patroclus.[45] The pagan Olympiodorus, who about 425 continued Eunapius' history, wrote that the removal of an old cult image at Rhegium was followed by a barbarian invasion of Sicily and by eruptions of Etna.[46] In the same way the removal of three silver statues in barbarian clothing from a pagan holy place in Thrace opened the gates of the region to Goths, Huns and Sarmatians.[47] In Zosimus the death of Serena, Stilicho's wife, is connected with a sacrilege she was alleged to have committed against Vesta:[48] this may be derived either from Eunapius or from Olympiodorus. But what Zosimus has to say about the revivals of pagan rituals in Rome during the siege of Alarich almost certainly comes from Olympiodorus. He must be the source of the information that the bishop of Rome, Innocentius, putting the preservation of the city before his religious opinions, consented to this revival.[49] Unfortunately, according to Zosimus, lack of popular support spoilt the experiment. The *Liber prodigiorum* by Iulius Obsequens may well belong, as has recently been suggested, to the same type of pagan apologetics based on verified prodigies.[50]

Pagan historians of the fourth and early fifth centuries give more space to religious events than their predecessors and models, not only because the situation makes this inevitable: they are themselves much more directly involved in the religious controversies. They no longer maintain the traditional distinction between religion and superstition. Pagans needed miracles to neutralize Christian miracles. We have heard much about democratization of culture in the late Roman empire since Santo Mazzarino's important paper at the Stockholm congress of 1960.[51] If there is one operation to which the term democratization can perhaps be applied, it is the removal of the barriers between superstition and religion in the pagan field.

III

The Christians, as we have already mentioned, set up their palisade between religion and superstition to coincide with the frontier between Christianity and Paganism. Within Christendom the dividing line was heresy, not superstition. We need, however, to know much more about the various attitudes of the Christians of the late Roman empire towards miracles, magic, astrology, popular medicine etc. Professor Grant's study on *Miracle and Natural Law in Graeco-Roman and Early Christian Thought* (1952) and the recent Cambridge symposium on miracles[52] are welcome contributions to the understanding of the notion of miracle among those whom Professor Lampe calls 'the more serious Christians'. For a sociology of beliefs in miracles we can expect important results from the research in progress in Paris under the leadership of Professor Michel Meslin. Professor Meslin intends to find out how the Christian notion of miracle and the pagan notion of prodigy competed with and modified each other in a world which daily needed the reassurance of miracles.

It would indeed be impertinent of me to contribute to a debate in which any member of this Society is more competent to speak than I am. But it may be useful briefly to turn our attention to one specific social group in a clearly circumscribed historical situation in order to see how the distinction between upper and lower-class beliefs became meaningless even in highly sophisticated Christian circles. The court of Theodosius II – and especially the enigmatic figure of the Athenian Athenais, who on baptism was renamed Aelia Eudocia – has never ceased to attract attention since Ferdinand Gregorovius wrote his romantic book *Athenaïs, Geschichte einer byzantinischen Kaiserin* (Leipzig, 1882). There is, however, no comprehensive scholarly research on what was one of the most impressive intellectual circles of the ancient world: the court of Constantinople during the long period between 408 and 450 in which Theodosius II reigned and, for the most part, his sister Pulcheria ruled.

To people who a hundred years later looked back on that society the reign of Theodosius II seemed to be the beginning of the decline of Latin as the language of administration and culture in the empire. There was much more than a little truth in this impression of John Lydus[53] because the court of Theodosius II consolidated the eastern part of the empire at the expense of the west. While Gaul, Spain and Africa were invaded by barbarians, and the emperors at Ravenna progressively lost control of the situation, Constantinople kept Persians and Huns at bay and could afford the luxury of being more concerned with religious dissent than with external attack. But it was never the intention of Theodosius II and his advisers to abandon the west to its fate. In the new university of Constantinople there was a place for instruction in Latin as well as in Greek.

For the first time the Christian faith permeated the court in earnest. It was most characteristic of the age that women played a leading rôle in that society. While Pulcheria and her two sisters dictated the rules of behaviour at the court of Constantinople, Galla Placidia shared the government in Ravenna – and Hypatia was savagely murdered in Alexandria. A number of exceptionally cultivated and active Christian women emerged who on the one hand were interested in theological problems and on the other hand kept in close contact with the devotion of the masses. Cyrillus of Alexandria could dedicate some of his theological writings to the queens, that is, to the wife of Theodosius II and to his sisters. But these women entertained, and were entertained by, monks who came from peasant stock and whose command of Greek was dubious. This alone – the predominance of women – represented a bridge between the faith of the intellectuals and the beliefs of ordinary people. Eudocia herself, the daughter of a pagan Athenian philosopher, embraced the new faith in a mood of total acceptance. Very conscious of her Hellenic heritage, as her famous address to the citizens of Antioch showed,[54] she turned her poetic gifts to the metaphrasis of the prophecies of Zacharias and Daniel and to the exposition of the legend of

St Cyprian of Antioch. Little did she suspect that by retelling the legend of the magician who repented and became a Christian – a legend known to Gregory of Nazianzus – she was to become the second chapter of any respectable book on '*die deutsche Faustsage*'.

Eudocia shared with her friend and spiritual guide Melania the younger the taste for theological controversy and the cult of relics. She and Melania were very active in that hunt for relics which was an integral part of the craving for miracles and sanctity and cannot therefore be dismissed as a replacement of the earlier hunt for Greek works of art. Eudocia brought relics of St Stephen to Constantinople. According to a modern interpretation of a doubtful medieval tradition, the church of S. Pietro in Vincoli in Rome owes its name to the gift which Eudocia made to her daughter Eudoxia of one of St Peter's chains. Following the example of Melania, Eudocia chose Jerusalem as her permanent residence when she was compelled to leave the court of Constantinople. Her deviation in the direction of monophysism in those late years of anguish was halted by the intervention of no less a person than Simeon the Stylite.

Eudocia's husband, Theodosius, was even less aware of the distinction between belief and superstition than his wife. Credulity may well be an element of the domestic tragedy which parted for ever two persons who seemed so obviously made to understand each other. The founder of the university of Constantinople, the organizer of the code of laws which takes his name, was known to Sozomenus as someone who spent his nights reading by the light of a specially contrived self-refilling lamp. He read and patronized history, poetry and theology. He copied books with his own hand. One branch of our manuscript tradition of Solinus goes back to the copy made by him.[55] In the fourteenth century a Bible was still shown at Constantinople which Theodosius had copied in lines forming a cross on each page. Our text of Cornelius Nepos probably derives from a copy made for him by Probus.[56] A copy of the Virgilian *cento* by Proba was presented to him.[57] His reputation as a calligrapher reached Mauretania, if we can trust De Rossi's convincing supplements of an African inscription.[58] The contemporary forger of the Apocalypse of Paul tried to exploit Theodosius' name by asserting that Theodosius declared the text as authentic and that he sent a copy of it to the library of Jerusalem.[59] Sozomenus, who knows about the alleged discovery of this Apocalypse and evidently doubts its authenticity, leaves the emperor out.[60] Theodosius acquired and wore the garments of a bishop who had died as a saint. When excluded from communion by an impatient and vulgar monk he refused to eat until the monk was persuaded to revoke the ban. He decided the choice of his own successor by submitting himself to the practice of incubation in the church of St John the Evangelist at Ephesus.

Theodosius tried to the best of his ability to make up his mind about the theological controversies of his time. He had his own soul to think of. But he also had to think of the peace of the realm. He tried to put pressure on theologians, and at least once he used Simeon the Stylite to make Theodoretus less intransigent. But we may suspect that the theologians and monks put at least as much pressure on him. He was not an invariably careful reader of what was submitted to him. We have the story that to teach him a lesson Pulcheria made him sign the sale of his own wife.[61]

In such an intellectual and political climate bishops, lawyers and mere radicals wrote about ecclesiastical history for the same reason which impelled English bishops, bankers and mere radicals to write about Greek history in the thirties and forties of the last century. It was a way of clarifying one's own ideas about the past and of expressing one's own views about the future. For the majority of these ecclesiastical writers of the fifth century it was also a clear attempt to influence the court and particularly the scholarly emperors. Socrates, Sozomenus, Theodoretus (and, we may add, though his work is lost, Philip of Side) were close enough to the centre of the theological spectrum to hope to be heard at court. Sozomenus unblushingly expected a gift from the emperor for his *Ecclesiastical History*. My heart therefore goes out to the Eunomian Philostorgius who had no such hope – indeed no worldly hope. He wrote in an apocalyptic tone about his own time and made it abundantly clear that there was no natural cause for earthquakes. Earthquakes happen by the will of God for the purpose of bringing sinners to repentance: plenty of earthquakes had accompanied the coming of age of Theodosius II.[62] Photius who saved Philostorgius' history from total destruction accused him of attributing miracles to heretics.[63] He was less surprised that Philostorgius, a lover of geography, had such a precise knowledge of the topography of the earthly paradise.[64]

The more orthodox ecclesiastical historians propped up not only theology, but also politics, by miracles. If the manner of Arius' death was taken as proof that his theology was impiou, the death of Valens at the battle of Adrianopolis was interpreted as retribution for his persecution of the orthodox. Two new Dioscuri appeared to Theodosius I before the battle of the Frigidus: one said that he was John the

Evangelist, the other that he was the apostle Philip. According to both Socrates[65] and Theodoretus,[66] God with thunderbolts and lightning burned down the Huns in A.D. 434: the prayers of Theodosius II had been heard.

There is only one step from the stories of miracles and ascetic feats which spice the ecclesiastical histories to the lives of saints which have nothing but miracles and ascetic feats. One of these books came straight to the circle of Theodosius II. Palladius wrote the *Historia Lausiaca* for Lausus, the chamberlain of Theodosius, an admirer and a protector of Melania. Palladius was also interested in non-Christian asceticism and dedicated his *De vita Bragmanorum* to another important man whose name we do not know. It is particularly fortunate that we have the *Religious History* of Theodoretus, because it teaches the vanity of any attempt at separating hagiography from ecclesiastical historiography. Cardinal Newman was naturally puzzled by 'the stupid credulity of so well-read, so intellectual an author'.[67] But Theodoretus lived in the world of the miracles he described. His mother's eyesight had been saved by Peter of Galatia. Peter's girdle functioned as a first-aid box for Theodoretus' family and neighbours. The birth of Theodoretus himself had been due to the prayers of the holy Macedonius. In his youth Theodoretus travelled to visit the Syrian saints whose feats he was later to register. The precise purpose of the *Religious History* cannot be ascertained exactly because we do not know when it was written: the date about A.D. 440 is only an intelligent guess. It is not impossible that Theodoretus was trying to curry favour with the monks who in the past had made his life and that of John of Antioch very difficult.[68] But the essential fact remains that Theodoretus makes no concession to popular tastes. One has to take him literally when he declares that those who believe in the miracles of Moses and Joshua, Elijah and Elisha must also believe in the miracles told by him. The comparison with biblical situations is a constant feature of Theodoretus' stories. Modern researchers are of course free to use these stories either to illustrate the diffusion of certain magical practices or to measure the popularity of the new asceticism. We are glad to know that the holy Macedonius compelled a devil to be a witness for the prosecution in a trial for black magic, or that artisans in Rome had little images of Simeon the Stylite to protect their workshops.[69] To characterize Theodoretus, it is more important to remember that to him the existence of holy nuns was the proof that Christ did not separate virtue into male virtue and female virtue.[70]

As is evident from Theodoretus – and also from Eunapius – biographers of late antiquity included a large number of personal recollections in their work. This lent credibility to the many strange stories they told and at the same time reflected their direct involvement in the experiences they described. The life of Mani which has recently been discovered in a papyrus at Cologne shows that this biographical technique was adopted by the Manichaeans, too. We must now await the publication of the entire text, of which only fragments and a general summary have so far been published in the *Zeitschrift für Papyrologie und Epigraphik*.[71]

Christian intellectuals succeeded where pagan intellectuals had failed for centuries, both in transmitting their theories to the masses and in sharing the beliefs of the masses. Such a delicate balance between the learned and the popular could not be maintained without frequent crises. If some of the crises involved heresy, others represented a temptation by the pagan gods. Hellenism still had its attractions. Even at the court of Theodosius II some pagan literati, such as the poet and historian Olympiodorus, were acceptable. For very good reasons Philostorgius wrote against Porphyry, and Philip of Side against Julian the Apostate. Cyrus of Panopolis, the poet who by a singular distinction combined the position of prefect of the city with that of prefect of the *praetorium* under Theodosius II, was removed from the court on being accused of paganism. It is characteristic of the time that he was relegated to a small town of Phrygia with the rank of a bishop.[72]

The Christian abolition of the internal frontiers between the learned and the vulgar had clear implications. For cultured persons it meant the reception and acceptance of many uncritical, unsophisticated beliefs in miracles, relics and apparitions. For the vulgar and uncultivated it meant appreciation, to the point of fanaticism, of the importance of theological controversies and consequent participation in these struggles. It is probably a modern legend that the factions of the circus, as such, had a share in the religious movements of the fifth and sixth centuries. But anyone who reads in Socrates and Sozomenus the story of the two banishments of John Chrysostom is left in no doubt about the weight and the consequences of mob theology.

My conclusion, as might be expected, is that there is no way of defining a clear separation between an upper-class culture and a lower-class culture in the second half of the fourth century and in the first half of the fifth century. While this applies also to the pagans, it is really a distinctive feature of Christian culture. The pagans are compelled to accept in self-defence a reshaping of their own world. By the end of the fourth century even the most unperceptive pagan rhetorician and philosopher must have been acquainted with saints, miracles and relics.

However divided they were, the Christians were not divided culturally in the upper and lower strata. Their divisions cut across the social pyramid and were influenced by national, doctrinal and institutional factors. It would be very surprising if the Christian historians reasoned differently from the other intellectuals. There is one chapter in Sozomenus which is worth special attention. It is chapter 19 of book VII, in which he reflects on the variety of customs within orthodox Christendom. With almost Herodotean wisdom Sozomenus observes that those who have been brought up in the observance of certain customs would consider it wrong to abandon them. The differences which interest him are due to local tradition. He ignores distinctions, if any, between educated and uneducated Christians. Indeed I do not know of any ecclesiastical historian who condemns a Christian practice simply as being vulgar. Philostorgius condemns the cult of an image representing Constantine as a god:[73] what else could he have done?

Thus my inquest into popular religious beliefs in the late Roman historians ends in reporting that there were no such beliefs. In the fourth and fifth centuries there were of course plenty of beliefs which we historians of the twentieth century would gladly call popular, but the historians of the fourth and fifth centuries never treated any belief as characteristic of the masses and consequently discredited among the élite. Lectures on popular religious beliefs and the late Roman historians should be severely discouraged.

References

1. *Herodotean Inquiries*, The Hague, 1969, p. 2.
2. *Die Wesensbestimmung der Geschichte durch die antike Geschichtsschreibung*, Wiesbaden, 1966, p. 71.
3. *Hellenica*, V, 4, 1.
4. Ibid., I, 7, 15.
5. Theopompus, *Die Fragmente der griechischen Historiker*, ed. F. Jacoby, Berlin, 1926–30, II, B, p. 115, fr. 31.
6. Ibid., fr. 331.

7. Polybius, *Histories*, ed. and trans. W. R. Paton, 6 vols., London, Loeb Library, 1922–7, XII, 24, 5. *Cf.* F. Taeger, *Charisma*, I, Stuttgart, 1957, p. 381.

8. G. Stübler, *Die Religiosität des Livius*, Stuttgart, 1941; W. Liebeschütz, *J[ournal of] R[oman] S[tudies]*, LVII, London, 1967, pp. 45–55.

9. Much information in R. Häussler, *Tacitus und das historische Bewusstsein*, Heidelberg, 1965.

10. Livy, XLIII, 13, 1.

11. Ibid., IV, 30, 9.

12. Ibid., XXIX, 14, 2.

13. *Annals*, XV, 44, 5.

14. *Histories*, IV, 54.

15. P. J. Koets, 'Deisidaimonia' (diss. Utrecht, 1929); H. Fugier, *Recherches sur l'expression du sacré dans la langue latine*, Paris, 1963, p. 172. *Cf.* also the general histories of Greek and Roman religion by M. P. Nilsson and K. Latte.

16. *S[criptores] H[istoriae] A[ugustae]*, ed. D. Magie, 3 vols., London, 1930–2, *Claudius*, II, 4.

17. Ibid.

18. *SHA, Tyranni triginta*, XXII, 13.

19. *SHA, Caracalla*, XIV, 1.

20. *SHA, Severus*, XVII, 3.

21. *SHA, Quadrigae tyrannorum*, VII, 4.

22. For a different opinion, see W. Schmid, *Historia Augusta Colloquium 1964–65*, Bonn, 1965, pp. 153–84.

23. *SHA, Alexander Severus*, XLIII, 7.

24. *SHA, Heliogabalus*, III, 5; XXVIII, 4. *Alexander Severus*, XXIX; XLV, 6; LI, 7. *Gordian*, XXXIV, 2. *Quadrigae tyrannorum*, VII–VIII.

25. *SHA*, Trebellius Pollio, *Divus Claudius*, II, 4.

26. J. Geffcken, 'Religionsgeschichtliches in der Historia Augusta', *Hermes*, LV, Berlin, 1920, p. 294.

27. Bonn, 1970, pp. 69–98.

28. Ep. 3.

29. *SHA, Alexander Severus*, XIV, 5. *Cf.* Y. de Kisch, *Mélanges de l'Ecole Française de Rome*, LXXXII, Rome, 1970, pp. 321–62.

30. *SHA, Probus*, XX, 3; XXII, 4; XXIII, 1.

31. Amm[ianus] Marc[ellinus, *Res Gestae*], ed. C. U. Clark, Berlin, 1910–15, XXI, 16, 18.

32. *Divinae Institutiones*, IV, 28, 11. For editions see *ODCC*.

33. Amm Marc, XXXI, 2, 11.

34. Ibid., XXXI, 2, 23.

35. Ibid., XXV, 4, 17; XXX, 9, 5.

36. Ibid., XXI, 1, 7.

37. Ibid., XIX, 12, 20.

38. Ibid., XXII, 16, 2; XXIII, 6, 32.

39. Ibid., XXVII, 7, 5–6.

40. Eunapius, [*Vitae Sophistarum*], ed. J. F. Boissonade, Paris, Didot edition, 1849, p. 476. Ed. and trans. W. Cave Wright, London, Loeb Library, 1922.

41. Eunapius, p. 499.

42. Ibid., p. 471.

43. Ibid., p. 475.

44. Ibid.

45. Zosimus, [*History of the Roman Empire*], V, 6, 6. For editions see *ODCC*.

46. Photius, *Bibliotheca*, Cod. LXXX, 57b, in *PG*, CIII, 1860, col. 261; ed. and trans. (French) R. Henry (Budé edition), Paris, 1959.

47. Ibid., LXXX, 60*a*, *PG*, CII, 1860, col. 268.

48. Zosimus, V, 38, 2.

49. Ibid., V, 41, 2.

50. It will be enough to refer for these pagan writers to A. Demandt, *Zeitkritik und Geschichtsbild im Werke Ammians*, Bonn, 1965; J. F. Matthews, 'Olympiodorus of Thebes and the History of the West', *JRS*, LX, 1970; W. E. Kaegi, *Byzantium and the Decline of Rome*, Princeton, 1968, pp. 59–145. *Cf.* my characterization in *Rivista Storica Italiana*, LXXXI, Naples, 1969, pp. 286–303.

51. *XIe Congrès International des Sciences Historiques, Rapports*, II, *Antiquité*, Uppsala, 1960, pp. 35–54.

52. C. F. D. Moule (ed.), *Miracles*, London, 1965. *Cf.* M. Meslin, *Le Christianisme dans l'empire romain*, Paris, 1970, p. 168.

53. Johannes Lydus, *De magistratibus*, II, 12; III, 42.

54. Evagrius, *Historia Ecclesiastica*, I, 20, 3–5. The main texts on Eudocia are collected and critically sifted by O. Seeck in *PW*, VI, 1, cols. 906–10. Add *Vita Sanctae Melaniae*, ed. D. Gorce, *Vie de Sainte Mélanie*, Paris, 1962, ch. 58–9, pp. 240–6. For the question of the chains of S. Pietro in Vincoli see E. Caspar, *Geschichte des Papsttums*, I, Tübingen, 1930, p. 421; R. Krautheimer, 'S. Pietro in Vincoli', *Proceedings of the American Philosophical Society*, LXXXIV, Philadelphia, 1941, pp. 353–429; R. Valentini and G. Zucchetti, *Codice topografico della città di Roma*, III (Rome, 1946), p. 42. We have no critical account of Theodosius II. The best anecdotic evidence has been collected by F. Gregorovius, *Athenaïs*, Leipzig, 1882, esp. pp. 95–102. *Cf.* in particular Socrates, [*Historia Ecclesiastica*], VII, 22; Theodoretus, [*Historia Ecclesiastica*], V, 36; Iohannes Malalas, *Chronographia*, XIV; Nicephorus Callistus [(Xanthopoulos), *Historia Ecclesiastica*], XIV, 3 in *PG*, CXLVI, 1865, col. 1063. For editions of all these authors see *ODCC*. See also *Chronicon Paschale*, ed. L. Dindorf, *CSHByz*, 2 vols., Bonn, 1832, pp. 575–90, reprinted in *PG*, XCII, 1865, cols. 9–1160.

55. See, however, H. Walter, *Die 'Collectanea Rerum Memorabilium' des C. Iulius Solinus*, Wiesbaden, 1969, p. xi, n. 6.

56. *Cf.* my paper in *RSI*, LXXXI, 1969, pp. 290–1.

57. *Cf.* the remark by [H.] Dessau, *I[nscriptiones] L[atinae] S[electae]* (repr. Berlin, 1954–5), no. 809.

58. Dessau, *ILS*, no. 802.

59. W. Speyer, *Bücherfunde in der Glaubenswerbung der Antike*, Göttingen, 1970, pp. 60–2.

60. Sozomen, *Historia Ecclesiastica*, ed. J. Bidez and G. C. Hansen, *GCS*, L, Berlin, 1960, VII, 19.

61. The famous story – Theophanes, *sub anno mundi* 5941; Georgius Monachus (Hamartolos), *Chronicon Syntomon*, ed. C. de Boor, 2 vols., Leipzig, Teubner edition, 1904, p. 611; Cedrenus, *Synopsis Historion*, para. 600, *PG*,

CXXI, 1894, col. 654; Iohannes Zonaras, *Epitome of History*, ed. M. Pinder and R. Büttner-Wobst, 3 vols., *CSHByz*, 1841–97, XIII, 23, 44A; Nicephorus Callistus, XIV, 23, col. 1130 – seems to be authentic, but wrongly dated. Its source seems to be Theodorus Lector. *Cf.* G. Gentz, *Die Kirchengeschichte des Nicephorus Callistus*, Berlin, 1966, p. 129, n. 2.

62. Philostorgius, [*Historia Ecclesiastica*], ed. J. Bidez, *GCS*, XXI, Berlin, 1913, XII, 10.

63. Ibid., IX, 1.

64. Ibid., III, 9 ff.

65. Socrates, VII, 43.

66. Theodoretus, V, 373, 3.

67. *Historical Sketches*, II, London, 1876, p. 315.

68. *Cf.* the discussion between P. Peeters, *An. Bol.*, LXI, 1943, p. 29, and M. Richard, *Mélanges de Science Religieuse*, III, Lille, 1946, pp. 147–56. See also H. Bacht, 'Die Rolle des orientalischen Mönchtums', in A. Grillmeier and H. Bacht, *Das Konzil von Chalkedon*, II, Würzburg, 1953, pp. 193–314; A.-J. Festugière, *Antioche Païenne et Chrétienne*, Paris, 1959, pp. 241–401. The identification of the author of the *Vita Bragmanorum* with the author of the *Historia Lausiaca* is made more probable by the important researches of L. Cracco Ruggini, *Athenaeum*, XLIII, Pavia, 1965, pp. 3–80. *Cf.* Palladius, *De gentibus Indiae et Bragmanibus*, ed. W. Berghoff, Meisenheim am Glan, 1967.

69. *PG*, LXXXII, 1864, cols. 1406, 1473.

70. Ibid., col. 1493.

71. V, Bonn, 1970, pp. 97–216.

72. *Cf.* Alan Cameron, *Claudian*, Oxford, 1970, p. 192. Cameron will have more to say on Cyrus in a forthcoming study. The statement by W. E. Kaegi that Cyrus was a pagan seems to be due to a misunderstanding; see W. E. Kaegi, 'The Fifth Century Twilight of Byzantine Paganism', *Classica et Mediaevalia*, XXVII, Copenhagen, 1966, p. 265. Further bibliography for all the questions treated in this paper will be found in Jacques Le Goff, 'Culture cléricale et traditions folkloriques dans la civilisation mérovingienne', *Annales: Economies, Sociétés, Civilisations*, XXII, Paris, 1967, pp. 780–91.

73. Philostorgius, II, 17.

II

Tradition and the Classical Historian*

THE Greek and Latin historians we consider great and exemplary were already considered great and exemplary by ancient readers.[1] They owe their preservation to their reputation; though, of course, not all the historians who were reputable were preserved. The use of certain books in the schools and mere chance played their part in the transmission of texts. What I want to emphasize is that our judgement on the ancient historians of Greece and Rome is in substantial agreement with the ancient canons of judgement. Herodotus, Thucydides, Xenophon and Polybius were already the models for the Greek and Roman historians who were in a position to read them. Similarly, Sallust, Livy and Tacitus were exemplary for their Latin successors. It is a peculiarity of the Greek–Latin culture of the Roman empire that Greek writers seldom used, and even more seldom imitated, Latin writers. Thus, Sallust, Livy and Tacitus did not exercise much influence on the Greek historians of later times, though Plutarch used Sallust and Livy extensively, and Dio Cassius followed the annalistic method of Roman historiography and shows acquaintance with Sallust (XL, 63, 4) and Livy (LXVII, 12, 4). The element of chance or of school selection in survival must be taken into consideration, especially in the cases in which it may distort the physiognomy of an historian. We should know Sallust better if we had his *Histories* (dealing with the period c. 78–67 B.C.) and of course we must never forget that Livy devoted the greater part of his 142 books to near-contemporary history almost all lost to us.

It is evident that all these 'great' historians did in fact tend to write either exclusively or prevalently about facts of the near past. Herodotus wrote about the Persian Wars, an event of the previous generation;

---

*This paper was read at Harvard University as a Loeb Lecture on 24 April 1972 and published in *History and Theory*, 11, 1972, pp. 279–93.

Thucydides wrote the history of the contemporary Peloponnesian War; Xenophon concentrated on the Spartan and Theban hegemonies (404–362 B.C.), which he had witnessed; Polybius started in earnest with the Second Punic War (218 B.C.) and went down to his own time, until *c.* 145 B.C. The same applies to Sallust, Livy, Tacitus (who covered the preceding hundred years), and to Ammianus Marcellinus (who devoted thirteen books to the period A.D. 96–352 and the remaining eighteen to the history of only twenty-six years). The same bias towards near-contemporary events was to be found in other historians of great repute whose works are now lost, except for fragments. Theopompus wrote on the events dominated by his contemporary, Philip II of Macedon; Ephorus dealt with archaic Greek history in ten books, gave another ten books to the fifth century B.C., and reserved approximately ten books to 386–340 B.C.; Timaeus filled the greater part of the thirty-eight books of his history of Western (mainly Sicilian) Greeks with the events of his own time – roughly 340–288 B.C.; Posidonius continued Polybius for the last century from 143 B.C. to his own day, about 70 B.C.

Principles of method were put forward to justify this preference for near-contemporary history. Herodotus emphasized the importance of reporting what one had seen and heard – and gave definite preference to what he had seen. Thucydides made direct experience the first qualification for proper historiography. Polybius, too, emphasized the ability to interview witnesses of events and direct experience (XII, 4c, 3; 25b, 4); he claimed that his own main period of history fell within the lifetime of people who could be cross-questioned (IV, 2, 2).

The Roman historians were perhaps less prone to boast about their ability to witness events or to cross-question witnesses. The most vocal of the Latin historians in this respect is Ammianus Marcellinus, who came from Antioch and never felt quite at home in the Latin society of the West: he delights in giving details in which he was personally involved (XVIII, 6, 11 and 21–3; XIX, 8, 5). But even the most reticent of the Latin historians were in no doubt about the eyewitness methods of a contemporary or near-contemporary historian. It will be sufficient to remind ourselves of how Tacitus questioned his friend Pliny the Younger about events of which Pliny was better informed (Pliny the Younger *Ep.*, VI, 16; VII, 33).

The problem of sources – and the evident advantage of being able to cross-question witnesses or of being oneself the witness – cannot be considered the primary motive for preferring contemporary or recent events as the subject of historiography. Methods had existed since the fifth century B.C. – that is, since the beginning of historiography in Greece – of getting correct information about the remote past. These methods were critical, in the sense that the user, after reflection and study, was satisfied as to their reliability. The first Greek historian, Hecataeus (end of the sixth century), had developed methods of correcting and rationalizing many mythical stories. Herodotus knew how to go about Egypt and other countries and to ask about their antiquities. Even Thucydides used ancient poetry and archaeological and epigraphical evidence to formulate conclusions about the state of archaic Greek society and about specific events of the past. Chronological problems were systematically dealt with by Hippias and Hellanicus at the end of the fifth century. Later, the practice of consulting ancient texts and of criticizing ancient traditions was vigorously pursued by Hellenistic scholars. The Romans themselves – as their antiquarian tradition shows, from Varro in the first century B.C. to Virgil's commentator Servius at the beginning of the fifth century A.D. – knew very well how to collect reliable facts about the past. We shall have to come back to this. The important point here is that the question of the reliability of the evidence about the past cannot have been the determining factor in creating a privileged position for the historians who mainly dealt with recent or contemporary events.

No doubt the historians felt safer in writing near-contemporary history. Some historians, such as Thucydides and Polybius, were hardly able to separate the special importance of contemporary events from the special reliability of contemporary events. Educated readers seem to have agreed with this evaluation of sources and to have regarded the writer of contemporary history as more reliable than the writer about the past. Historians were inclined to commend themselves as reliable witnesses of their own time (for instance, Josephus, *Jewish War*, I, 1; Herodian, I, 1, 3), though according to Lucian, Alexander the Great did not fail to remark that one adulates the living, not the dead (*How to Write History*, 40). But, ultimately, it was the importance of contemporary or near-contemporary events that determined the choice of subject. This importance was adduced by the historians themselves to justify their work. The reliability of the sources, however closely associated with this appreciation of contemporary history, was merely an additional motive. Thucydides and Polybius leave the reader in no doubt about the importance they attribute to the period of history they write about; they see something unique in it, a relevance not possessed by other past events. For Thucydides the Peloponnesian War is the culmination of preceding Greek history, a greater event than anything before. Polybius considers himself the witness of a revolutionary change in the history of mankind: for the first time the various parts of the world coalesced into a whole (I, 3, 4; III, 1, 4; IV, 2, 1). Sallust commends the Jugurthine War as the first episode of the struggle against the Roman nobility. More interestingly, Livy expects his readers to be eager for recent history and excuses himself for detaining them among remote events. Hellenistic and Roman savants were in their own way perfectly respectable. In moments of nostalgia for the past they could even derive glory from their exertions. Varro came near to that. In Late Antiquity antiquarians were in a mood of self-congratulation. Yet they never got the upper hand. The prestige of the interpreter of recent events – of Herodotus, Thucydides, Polybius, Sallust, Tacitus (and Livy, insofar as he was *also* that) – remained unshaken. It was a prestige sanctioned by literary critics and confirmed by the popularity of the works themselves. This means that the interpretation of contemporary or near-contemporary history fulfilled an irreplaceable function in ancient societies from the fifth century B.C. to the late Roman empire: let us say to the sixth century A.D.

While Hecataeus tried his hand at rationalizing ancient stories, it was the Persian War, the epoch-making event of the previous generation, that struck his fellow-Ionian Herodotus. A student and rival of Hecataeus in many respects, Herodotus found his own way by clarifying and explaining the recent past. The Athenians gave him a big prize for it, and he gained the friendship of Sophocles. Herodotus recorded what could easily be forgotten, and furthermore explained what could easily be overlooked: the difference between Persians and Greeks in the matter of institutions and customs, the special contribution of Athens to the victory. Herodotus did not emphasize ancient tradition in telling his story of the Persian Wars. Though connected with old, even mythical, rivalries between Europe and Asia, the war appeared to him a consequence of the Ionian rebellion. The victories of Marathon and Salamis were achievements of the young Athenian democracy. Conscious as he was of the more traditional features of Spartan behaviour in war, he judged the Spartans as less able than the Athenians to defeat the Persians. In any case, the novelty lay in the very victory of the Greeks – and this victory was Herodotus' subject. With all his interest in customs and his sensitivity to religious attitudes, Herodotus firmly chose to take the Persian War as an event that deserved to be remembered in itself – because it was the victory of the Greeks, and by implication of Greek freedom over Persian despotism. He arrived slowly at that decision; we may try to follow his development from a geographer into an historian. In the delimitation of a war as an epoch-making event he had, of course, an illustrious predecessor, Homer. But it was Herodotus' decision to transfer war from epic into history. Thucydides could object to many Herodotean ideas, but not to this decision. He again chose a war – a recent war – as an epoch-making event. He again discarded traditional subjects for something new – new in its causes, the formation of Athenian imperial power; and new in its consequences, the destruction of Athenian imperial power. New perhaps even in its social phenomena, if the plague, the revolutions, and the demagogues had previously not been experienced, as he seems to imply.

After Thucydides no doubt was left that wars represented the most evident factor of change. Xenophon may have thought that the Spartans had lost their hegemony because of their treacherous occupation of the citadel of Thebes. But the gods punished the Spartans through the regular machinery of war: the Spartans were simply defeated by the Thebans. Later the Thebans failed to exploit their victory at Mantinea, because Epaminondas was killed in the battle; and the Greek world was left without a guide, in a state of uncertainty and disorder. Wars were the main subject of Theopompus; and war was the instrument by which Tyche changed the organization of the world, according to Polybius.

Revolutions came next to war as the concern of Greek historians. The model was represented by Thucydides' Book VIII. The historians of the fourth and third centuries B.C. could hardly separate wars from revolutions.

Sallust learned from Thucydides about the importance of war as a sign of change, but there is perhaps altogether less war in Roman historians than in Greek ones. Internal conflicts and constitutional changes commanded the attention of the Latin historians of the late first century B.C. and of the Roman empire. The cumulative effect was, however, the same. The main emphasis of the historians (Livy, Velleius, Tacitus) was on the destruction of the past, on the emergence of new institutions, habits and vices. Tacitus' historical books are entirely pervaded by this sense of change and by resignation to it. It would be interesting to examine why non-ecclesiastical historians were so slow and so reluctant to register the particular change represented by Christianity. Even Ammianus gives a disproportionately small amount of space to it, though he lived under Christian emperors. Whatever the causes of this reluctance may be, the mere existence of Christianity made the historians of the late empire aware of a break in continuity: they know that there is change, even if they are not very eloquent about it.

The 'great' Greek and Latin historians were dominated by the sense of change. In this they accurately reflected the situation of society. Neither the Greeks in general after the sixth century B.C. nor the Romans after the third century B.C. were in any doubt about the magnitude of the changes in their midst. Even when the constitution had not been directly affected, modifications in territories and power had occurred. The historians developed their work in an atmosphere of expectation of change and registered the facts of change. Their task was to indicate profound and comparatively rapid modifications in the condition of the body politic. The very birth of history-writing in the fifth century B.C. can hardly be separated from the victory of democratic institutions in Ionia and Athens, with their demand for change.

All this is very elementary and perhaps trivial. But it carries some important consequences. The Greek and Roman historians were not supposed to be the keepers of tradition. They were not assumed to register events in terms of conformity to, or deviations from, the norm. They were not supposed to succeed each other in a profession supported by the State or by religious institutions, nor were they concerned with keeping change under control. Furthermore, the individual action or event was not to be registered in itself, for the purpose of comparison with the norm, as either praiseworthy or blameworthy; it was to be included in a process of change and evaluated according to the ultimate result of that process. Pericles' policy of defence against Sparta or Fabius Cunctator's tactics against Hannibal were not judged according to an eternal code of conduct, but according to their effects on the war. Taken in its most general features, 'classical' historiography (that is, the historiography which was classical in the eyes of the Greeks and the Romans themselves) was the mirror of change. We can appreciate its difference from other types of historiography. There is nothing in Greece or Rome comparable with the traditionalist approach of an Al-Tabari with his report on the chain of authorities. There is nothing like Chinese official historiography with its minute registration of isolated facts: the history written by civil servants for civil servants, as E. Balázs liked to call it. There is nothing like the *Heimskringla* by Snorri Sturluson, who had old stories written down as told by intelligent people about chieftains who spoke the Danish tongue.

Though Tyche might appeal to a pagan historian, no personal god was ever invoked to explain the course of history. Just as pagan Greece and

Rome had no 'gesta Dei per Graecos' (or 'per Romanos'), so they did not have their Biblical counterpart, the records of a nation in its relation to Yahweh. Ecclesiastical history – the record of the true faith in its fights against heresies and persecutors – was inconceivable in pagan Antiquity. Its appearance meant the beginning of a new era.

History of change in the Greek–Roman world did not, of course, involve a notion of progress, even less a progress *ad infinitum*; nor did it necessarily involve a notion of circular movement. Even Polybius seems to have confined his meditations on cycles to his theory of constitutions: when he came to historical narrative, he forgot cycles. The more limited notion that human affairs made a certain advance in range of knowledge and experience was more likely to be used by the classical historian; at least the majority of the Greek historians seems to have subscribed to it. But there was no obligation for an historian of change to be optimistic about it. Xenophon was sorry about the Spartan defeats. Livy was nostalgic for early Rome. Flavius Josephus (who can be included in a series of pagan historians only with the greatest hesitation) wrote to explain disaster as well as he could. A more detailed account of the attitude of the historian towards his subject matter would involve an evaluation of the treatment of specific institutions and individuals. We cannot, however, expect absolute coherence. Anyone who tries to deduce Thucydides' respect for Nicias (VII, 86, 5) and his contempt for Cleon from his general interpretation of the Peloponnesian War is wasting his time. The Camillus Livy admires in Book V is a very different type of Roman from Cato the Censor, celebrated in Book XXXIX. Tacitus is not entirely consistent in his judgements about the philosophers who opposed the emperors. One interesting feature of this historiography of change is that it leaves the historian free to be a traditionalist at heart. Alternatively, the historian was free to recommend change. But I must admit that I do not know of any extant Greek or Roman historian who positively recommended change. The so-called democratic annalists of the late Roman republic may have done so, but I am not aware of any evidence. If Maecenas' speech in Dio Cassius (Book LII) is a programme for reform, it is written in isolation from the rest of the lengthy work. Philosophers, rather than historians, recommended reforms.

The classical historiography of change, far from being a study of individual cities or states, was concerned with developments involving many states and lands, even several empires. Herodotus included Greeks and barbarians. In the fourth century B.C. Ephorus wrote the history of the Greeks against the background of their neighbours. Polybius considered

Ephorus his predecessor as a universal historian (V, 33). His contemporary Agatharchides wrote universal history in two separate works on Asia and Europe. In the first century B.C. ambitious (and perhaps unprecedented) attempts were made to tell the history of mankind from its origins. Pompey's and Caesar's conquests had given a new meaning to the Stoic idea of the unity of mankind. We know, at least partially, three of these histories, by the Sicilian Diodorus, by Nicolas of Damascus and by the Gallic Trogus Pompeius (the last in a summary compiled by Justin). The best preserved of these universal historians, Diodorus, was not a conspicuous success. He felt compelled to insert into the preface of his *Historical Library* a short compendium of cosmology and anthropology. Whether this piece (Diodorus, I, 7–8) goes back to Democritus or not, it is of no real importance in Diodorus' compilation, who superimposes different histories without achieving (or even claiming) any unity. Quite rightly, Diodorus never obtained the status of a classic in the ancient world. His reputation developed in Byzantine culture, where he served as a model, and as a source of materials, for similar compilations of universal history favoured by the new Christian sense of history. Diodorus certainly missed his opportunity for tackling the problem of the shape of human history as a whole. The other pagan universal historians of Antiquity may not have been much better. Yet the universalistic tendencies of the historiography of change were in themselves a disavowal of any exclusive traditionalism. The variety of mankind in time and space emerged prominently.[2]

We can consequently assess what a historian of this classical type meant by the usefulness of history. There were shades of meaning. The permanent contribution to knowledge which Thucydides claimed for himself is not the same as the training for enduring the changes of fortune in political life which was the aim of Polybius. But what the historian in either case had to offer was a description of changes in the past which would help to recognize the causes and foresee the consequences of similar changes in the future. Polybius repeated with enthusiasm the old saying that 'the beginning is half of the whole' (V, 32, 5). The foundation of this teaching was in the assumption that a comparative study of symptoms was possible. On the other hand, the historian's frequent insistence on the exceptional magnitude and importance of the events he was going to tell implied that he considered that particular change likely to be irreversible. Polybius', Livy's and Appian's declarations on the ascendancy of Rome are good examples. For lesser men there were opportunities for indulging in adulation of winning causes.

Adulation, rather than propaganda, was the insidious tempter of the classical historians. Characteristically, Thucydides avoided committing himself on the subject of irreversibility and put his accent on the rivalry between Sparta and Athens. The lesson history could teach was about how to face change.

*

Since the ancient critics justified their evaluation of historians by a mixture of stylistic arguments and considerations of subject matter, it is difficult to say whether they had a definite preference for historiography as a study of change, as against historiography in support of tradition. Dionysius of Halicarnassus preferred Herodotus to Thucydides because he chose a nobler subject and one more pleasing to the readers (*Letters to Pompeius*, 3), whereas Plutarch's *On the Malice of Herodotus* prefers Thucydides to Herodotus because he is less malicious. However, whether consciously or not, critics were giving their preference to historical subjects describing change.

There was no dearth of history-writing for the sake of recording 'routine' happenings, emphasizing institutional continuity and commending traditional patterns of behaviour to later generations. But such compilers of records and providers of examples from the past soon found themselves in a world in which the historians of change had greater prestige.

Mere recording of certain events did exist in Greece and Rome, though less frequently than we should expect. The annals of the Roman pontiffs are the best-known example. They seem to have been kept going for centuries until at least the end of the second century B.C., and their contents present a famous problem. Cato speaks of these annals as if they confined their records to portents and rituals (Fr. 77 Peter). Cicero (*De Orat.*, II, 13, 52) and Servius (*ad Aeneid.*, I, 373) imply, on the contrary, that they were a chronicle of political and military events. We shall know the truth only when substantial and authentic fragments of these annals are discovered. They may of course have changed their character with time. These Latin annals, put together by the pontiffs, were under the control of the Roman aristocracy, that is, originally of the patricians. When Fabius Pictor decided to write Roman history in Greek at the end of the third century B.C., he clearly broke with the aristocratic and pontifical tradition, though he was a patrician and may well have been a pontiff, too. He still followed (so it seems) the annalistic system of the pontiffs; hence the name of *Annals* for his work. But this does not diminish the revolutionary implications of his decision to prefer the Greek historiography of change to the traditional Latin practice of mere registration of certain events. Timaeus may have been his Greek model. Incidentally, the annalistic method was no novelty to the Greeks. Thucydides in his own way had been an annalist.

It is less certain that in Greece the 'great' historians were preceded by priestly or profane local registrations or chronicles. Dionysius of Halicarnassus (*De Thucydide*, 5) states definitely that priestly and local chronicles preceded the great historiography of Herodotus and Thucydides. A similar line was taken by Wilamowitz in modern times when he assumed that an Athenian priestly chronicle had preceded Attic historiography. F. Jacoby had no difficulty in proving that Wilamowitz was arbitrarily postulating for Athens what he knew to be true for Rome. It has been suggested that Dionysius may have done the same thing for Greece in general. Having lived in Rome at the end of the first century B.C., and being well acquainted with the Roman situation, he might have arbitrarily transferred the Roman model to Greece: first local chronicles, then great historiography. The text of Dionysius is obscure and open to suspicion, since he quotes, and dates as earlier than Thucydides, a writer, Amelesagoras, who was probably a forger of the late fourth century B.C. But Dionysius must have found some support for his opinion in Hellenistic erudition. He was not simply transferring a Roman model to Greece.[3]

Whatever may be behind Dionysius, some cities and sanctuaries had their own chronicles from at least the end of the fifth century B.C. onwards. As the great Greek historiography never confined itself to the events of one city only, city and temple chronicles inevitably became the repository of local pride and antiquarianism. Local chronicles emphasized the individuality of each Greek centre and the continuity of its development: they collected local myths. As such they were traditionalistic, but traditionalism varied in quality and quantity according to place and time. The Attic chroniclers we know wrote best in their private capacity – not as magistrates or priests – and brought their political opinions into their work. They liked antiquarian detail, but they did not ignore change nor did they invariably commend the past as a model. In some cases they projected the present into the past, and made Theseus a democratic king. In other cases the personality of the compiler disappeared behind the prestige of the institution of which he was the recorder. In 99 B.C. the city of Lindos on the island of Rhodes instructed two men, Timachidas and Thersagoras, to compile, under the constant supervision of the secretary of the city, a chronicle of the temple of Athena Lindia: this chronicle was to include a list of the gifts to the temple and of the miraculous interventions of the goddess. The enterprise had learned pretensions: one of the compilers was a scholar, and references to sources were given. But the whole operation was obviously conceived as an impersonal tribute to the continuity and respectability of the sanctuary.[4]

We can hardly underrate the cumulative importance of this 'minor' historiography compiled on behalf of local pride and prejudice. But it was always exposed to the damaging confrontation with the greater historiography. Besides, it developed mainly in the Hellenistic period, when erudition had acquired a place of its own in society. Such erudition flattered local patriotism and conservatism in an age in which the only cultural distinction that really counted was not between individual Greek cities, but between Greeks and non-Greeks. In Rome the mere local chronicle could never entirely reassert itself after Fabius Pictor. The majority of the republican historians paid homage to the national tradition by starting their works with the foundation of Rome, but they modernized the past and gave greater space and emphasis to recent events. One of the few certain things about the *Annales Maximi* is that later historians almost always ignored them. Our fragmentary evidence is not clear, but as far as political historiography is concerned, there was perhaps even less traditionalism in Rome than in Greece. It is a fair guess that the antiquarians and the jurists were the main champions of traditionalism in republican Rome. Greece certainly never produced anything comparable with Varro's *Antiquities*. But the Roman aristocracy had no need of books to know and to defend tradition. The mere appearance of an antiquarian from the Sabine backwater such as Varro was the sign of a crisis.

Traditional patterns of behaviour were also registered and commended in the abundant literature of *exempla*. The Greeks always quoted individual past events as motives for consolidation or inducement to action. The Homeric poems are well acquainted with the technique of paradigmatic story-telling (*Iliad*, V, 381; VI, 128; IX, 524, etc., etc.). Orators used examples. Compilers collected them from historical works and from oral tradition. The Romans, who appreciated *mos maiorum* even more than the Greeks, were paradoxically eager to follow Greek models in quoting examples. But here again we have to reckon with the fact that collections of examples were made especially in times when erudition was valued for itself. Many individual examples were certainly adduced in the hope of encouraging imitation, but elaborate collections of examples were displays of erudition: such is the collection of *Facta et dicta memorabilia* dedicated by Valerius Maximus to Tiberius, which includes both Romans and non-Romans and therefore is not traditionalistic in the strict sense. If the examples were about military stratagems or economic devices (as we have them in Frontinus' and Polyaenus' stratagems or in Pseudo-Aristotle's *Oeconomica*), they might even favour new and unconventional patterns of behaviour in given matters. Similarly, examples could be collected in the interests of the tradition of a philosophic school, as Epictetus did in his *Dissertations*; or they could be produced to glorify the victims of a new political regime in their struggle for the defence of the old order, as C. Fannius and Titinius Capito did when they told the story of the deaths of the victims of Nero and Domitian (Pliny the Younger, *Ep.*, V, 5; VIII, 12). But anecdotes could equally well satisfy curiosity without involving propaganda. The collections of deathbed scenes made by Phainias and by Hermippus in the third century B.C. were not necessarily meant to propagate a creed. Even full biographies varied in their purpose. Pythagoreans no doubt wrote the life of Pythagoras as an example for the adepts of the sect. But we know that Aristoxenus did not spare Plato, Socrates and Aristotle his criticism, though he wrote their lives as an Aristotelian. If anecdotes, sayings and full biographies had their share in consolidating traditionalism, in a political community or in a school, they were a double-edged weapon. Lactantius used the model of the 'deaths of illustrious men' (*exitus illustrium virorum*) to proclaim the defeat of the persecutors of the Church in his *De mortibus persecutorum*. He used a pagan scheme to announce the victory of the Christians (about A.D. 316).[5]

*

It remains for us to define more precisely what we mean by change within the context of Greek and Latin historiography. As I have already implied, the ancient historians were essentially concerned with two types of change: wars and political revolutions. They were not very profound about causes of war and were not helped by the philosophers in grasping the causes of human aggressiveness in war. But they knew how to tell the development of a war and how to describe its consequences. The causes of revolutions they grasped much better, because they were helped by philosophers who had produced a typology of constitutional changes founded on the realities of Greek and Roman life (at least before the empire). In any case, they had gained great skill in narrating the conduct of a revolution: even a biographer like Plutarch displayed a different awareness of realities when he came to tell the stories of Agis and Cleomenes of Sparta. What ancient historians seem to have found difficult to narrate is the slow change in customs and laws in non-revolutionary periods. Unfortunately, we have lost the two major works which intended to give a full account of the social and constitutional changes in Greece and Rome: Dicaearchus' *Life of Greece* (third century B.C.) and Varro's *Life of the Roman People*.[6] In their absence, we can only state that none of the texts available to us gives a satisfactory account of long-term slow changes in law and customs. We have some excellent static descriptions of the Spartan and the Athenian constitutions (Xenophon, Aristotle), but hardly a good account of their modifications through the centuries.

It was the violent, rather than the slow, change that the historian presented to his readers. It was often presented with a note of pessimistic warning about the value of the change (Thucydides, Livy). But even when the result was satisfactory in the eyes of the historian, he does not seem to have indulged in optimism; Herodotus is a very sober narrator of Greek glories. Before Christian writers learned from the Jews how to present the case for the unrelenting true God, the mood of the classical historian was one of caution. There was much to be said for traditionalism and conservatism. Historical literature could help in that direction. But only some, if any, of the 'lower' historians – the antiquarians, the local chroniclers – would unequivocally emphasize this attitude. The overwhelming impression the reader of 'great' historical works would get was, I suspect, that change was inevitable and that the best thing he could do was to brace his heart. It is very doubtful whether the historians taught the Greeks (and the Romans) to feel themselves 'in the grip of the past', as Professor B. A. van Groningen suggested. It is even doubtful whether the historian wanted his readers to understand the present. This is a modern attitude that we must not transfer to the classical historian, who wrote for the generations to come: 'not keeping in view his present audience, but future readers', as Lucian advises (*How to Write History*, 40). The historians did not intend to produce tracts for the times. Immediate help for the present was obviously not excluded, but the historians rather offered help from the past for the future in general. They could do so because the future, however uncertain and different from the past, was not expected to produce unrecognizable situations. It is implicit in the whole attitude of the Greeks and Romans towards history that the variety of events was somehow limited. The limitation was more evident in constitutional changes, as the number of possible constitutional forms was believed to be small. But even in the ordinary activities of war and peace the common assumption was that future events would not be so different from past events as to make experience useless. To the best of my knowledge no classical historian reflected deeply on this point. It was taken for granted. After all, the ordinary Greek and Roman accepted the notion that the oracles could be obscure and useful at the same time. Though the oracles were ambiguous, wise men could perceive their true meaning. The advice of history, too, was vague, but, as Thucydides emphatically suggested, it could be clearer than an oracle (II, 48 compared with 54).

At least in the fifth century B.C., the historians were not alone in treating change as a human problem. Writers of tragedies depicted change or reaction to change. Aeschylus gave an optimistic interpretation of change in the *Persae* and in the trilogy about the murder of Agamemnon. More in general the unity of subject in his trilogies seems to have favoured a presentation of phases of change. Sophocles' heroes, notoriously, were resisting change, fighting against time, and refusing to accept either divine or human interference with their own will. Euripides saw passions as factors of change. I shall not try to compete with Aristotle about the difference between history and tragedy in the matter of change. I shall simply observe that gods have more to do with tragedy than with history.

To acquire and convey his knowledge and wisdom, the historian had to detach himself from the surrounding society. In Greece the 'great' historians were almost invariably exiles or at least expatriates (Herodotus, Thucydides, Xenophon, Theopompus, Callisthenes, Timaeus, Polybius, Posidonius). In Rome the 'senator as historian' was a familiar figure (Fabius Pictor, Sallust, Tacitus, Dio Cassius and others), but these senators had retired from political life. Nobody was under any obligation to listen to what the historian had to say. He was no official figure; history had no definite place in education, and there was no professor of history. For real security against the blows of fortune, the educated man turned to philosophy and the less educated to magic and mystery cults. Yet history was evidently considered to be of some use. After the fifth century B.C. no Greek city or land seems to have been without some kind of historiography and some public for historians. While Sparta may have done without history in the fifth century, it supported Xenophon for part of his life in the fourth century. Later, the Spartans found their man in Dicaearchus and had his *Constitution of*

Sparta read in public once a year. The historian would normally support, or at least presuppose as valid, those aspects of society about which the majority of the Greeks and Romans in their pagan days tended to be conservative: religious practices, family life, private property. At the same time at least the 'best' historians would provide men of action with models of explanation and behaviour for what was felt to be transient in society.

★

I write these pages in homage to the memory of my friend Joseph Levenson, the historian of Confucian China who died prematurely in an accident in 1969. Joe Levenson was not naturally in sympathy with a society like the Graeco–Roman society which, since the fifth century B.C., had accepted limited change as a natural way of living and listened rather casually, but with interest, to the historians as interpreters of change. Levenson's heart was with traditional societies in which historiography was no more and no less than the witness of continuity. As early as 1958 Levenson wrote that historical thinking in China 'was concerned typically not with process but with permanence, with the illustrations of the fixed ideals of the Confucian moral universe. . . . Before the twentieth century to call the Classics history was never construed as a limitation on the Classics but as a philosophical description'.[7] When the Western historical interpretation penetrated into China 'the Classics were not classics any more'.[8]

Had he lived, Joe Levenson would have reinterpreted Judaism – the faith of his fathers, and his own faith – in terms of a recurrent affirmation of life according to traditional patterns. But he was aware that his own understanding of the position of China and of Judaism in regard to Western values was an offshoot of the Greek historical tradition. As the whole of the third volume of his trilogy on China shows, he knew that his traditionalism had to incorporate the conclusions of his historical research conducted according to Western methods. He reduced – I do not know to what extent consciously – his own conflict by developing a highly personal style of historical analysis in which permanent themes prevailed over temporal sequences. I mention here Joe Levenson not only because he was an historian of rare originality, but also because he typifies the difficulty of reasserting tradition within a historiography of change, such as we have inherited from the Greeks.[9]

Appendix

L. H. Jeffery and Anna Morpurgo Davies published in *Kadmos* IX, 1970, No. 2, an inscription, now in the British Museum, from Crete of about 500 B.C. It contains the decree of appointment of a 'scribe and recorder in public affairs both sacred and secular'. This is obviously the first scribe ever appointed by the unnamed community – a city – because the inscription specifies the functions, privileges, and religious duties of the scribe. Ionia produced the first historians about the same time. The text (in which I am disinclined to find an older nucleus, as A. Raubitschek suggests in the same number of *Kadmos*) is full of surprises. The scribe is called $\pi o \iota \nu \iota \kappa a \sigma \tau \acute{a} \varsigma$, that is, in the most likely explanation, the man who writes in Phoenician letters.[10] The scribe is appointed under the explicit condition that his descendants shall be his successors. Even in the East (Assyria, Egypt) the profession of the scribe was only *de facto*, and not always hereditary. The function of the $\pi o \iota \nu \iota \kappa a \sigma \tau \acute{a} \varsigma$ is, of course, primarily to write down the deliberations of the *polis* and its committees. He will register the continuous changes introduced into life by a Greek assembly. As such, like a Greek historian, he will be a witness of change. But as a public officer he will be supposed to register only those changes which were brought about by the deliberations of the people. The historian, being no scribe, no public officer, registered changes of his own choice. He satisfied primarily his own curiosity, not the requirements of a city.

References

1. This paper is connected with other papers of mine which are collected in my *Contributo alla storia degli studi classici*, I–IV, Rome, 1955–69, of which Volume V is forthcoming, and of which a selection is given in *Studies in Historiography*, London, 1966. My main debt is of course to E. Schwartz and F. Jacoby. But I owe much to several papers by H. Strasburger and M. I. Finley. I shall only quote, by the former, *Die Wesensbestimmung der Geschichte durch die antike Geschichtsschreibung*, Wiesbaden, 1966; *cf.* the review by O. Murray, *Class. Rev.*, 18, 1968, pp. 218–21 – and by the latter, 'Myth, Memory, and History', *History and Theory*, 4, 1965, pp. 281–302, and *The Ancestral Constitution*, Cambridge, 1971. Two works of capital importance I have discussed elsewhere: K. von Fritz, *Die griechische Geschichtsschreibung*, I, Berlin, 1967, briefly in *Gnomon*, 44,

1972, pp. 205–7; S. Mazzarino, *Il pensiero storico classico*, I–III, Bari, 1966–7, in *Rivista Storica Italiana*, 79, 1967, pp. 206–19 = *Contributo*, IV, pp. 59–76. My disagreement with two other important books, F. Chatelet, *La Naissance de l'histoire*, Paris, 1962, and Chester G. Starr, *The Awakening of the Greek Historical Spirit*, New York, 1968, will be apparent from what follows. *Cf.* also A. W. Gomme, *The Greek Attitude to Poetry and History*, Berkeley and Los Angeles, 1954; E. Voegelin, *Anamnesis*, Munich, 1966, and the paper by M. Pavan, 'La moderna critica storica e il didascalismo nella storiografia antica,' *Cultura e Scuola*, 18, 1966, pp. 115–25. For an approach to problems of tradition the reader is referred to *Intellectuals and Tradition, Daedalus*, Spring 1972. I should like also to refer for comparison to the illuminating papers by J. Neusner, 'The Religious Uses of History,' *History and Theory*, 5, 1966, pp. 153–71, and by G. Nadel, 'Philosophy of History before Historicism,' *History and Theory*, 3, 1964, pp. 291–315.

For the canon of the historians the main evidence is in Cicero, *De oratore*, II, 13, 55–8; Dionysius of Halicarnassus, *De imitatione* (only partially preserved), 3 (ed. H. Usener and L. Radermacher, *Opuscula*, II, pp. 207–11); Quintilianus, *Instit. Oratoriae*, X, 1, 73–5; Dio Chrysostomus, *Oratio*, XVIII, 9. On modern discussions *cf.* R. Pfeiffer, *History of Classical Scholarship*, Oxford, 1968, p. 206. *Cf.* also L. Radermacher, *Kanon* in Pauly-Wissowa, X, 1919, 1873–8. For the special case of Polybius, who was born too late to be received into the Greek canon, see K. Ziegler, *Polybius*, in Pauly-Wissowa, XXI, 1952, 1572–4.

2. *Cf.* A. B. Breebaart, 'Weltgeschichte als Thema der antiken Geschichtsschreibung,' *Acta Historica Neerlandica*, 1, 1966, pp. 1–19.

3. It will be enough to refer to F. Jacoby, *Atthis*, Oxford, 1949, especially pp. 178–85; K. von Fritz, *Die griechische Geschichtsschreibung*, I, 519; S. Gozzoli, 'Una teoria antica sull'origine della storiografia greca,' *Studi Classici e Orientali*, 19–20, 1970–71, pp. 158–211.

4. *Cf.* R. Laqueur, *Lokalchronik*, in Pauly-Wissowa, XIII, 1926, 1083–1110.

5. Literature in my little book *The Development of Greek Biography*, Cambridge, Mass., 1971. The article by A. Lumpe on 'Exemplum' in *Reallexikon für Antike und Christentum*, 6, 1966, 1229–57 is especially relevant.

6. Fragments of Dicaearchus with commentary by F. Wehrli in *Die Schule des Aristoteles*, I, 2nd ed., Basel, 1967; Varro, *De vita populi romani*, ed. B. Riposati, Milan, 1939.

7. Joseph R. Levenson, *Confucian China and Its Modern Fate*, I, Berkeley and Los Angeles, 1958, pp. 91–2.

8. Ibid., p. 94.

9. On Levenson's vision of history see the very perceptive Foreword by F. E. Wakeman to the posthumous book *Revolution and Cosmopolitanism*, Berkeley, 1971.

10. L. H. Jeffery, *Europa: Festschrift für E. Grumach*, Berlin, 1967, p. 154. But *cf.* P. Chantraine, *Studii Clasice*, 14, 1972, 7–16.

12

Time in Ancient Historiography*[1]

BEFORE I get down to those problems about time that seem to me relevant to ancient historiography, I have to eliminate a series of faulty questions, part of which at least derive from an arbitrary introduction of the notion of eternity into the historian's business; for this conception – even in the form of eternal return – is likely to lead to confusion and errors of various kinds.[2]

'In the beginning God created the heaven and the earth.' To the untutored eye of the non-theological reader this seems to be clear evidence that the priestly author of Genesis I knew that from the beginning of the world events followed each other in a chronological order. (The exact translation of the difficult Hebrew text is irrelevant to our point.) The same priestly author speaks of the first, second, third day, and so forth.

'The wrath do thou sing, o goddess, of Peleus' son, Achilles . . . sing thou thereof from the time when at the first there parted in strife Atreus' son, king of men, and goodly Achilles.' To the untutored eye of the non-philologist this seems to be clear evidence that the author of the first book of the *Iliad* was recalling events of the past with the help of the goddess. At line 70 of the same book past, present and future are mentioned in unmistakable terms. Chalcas, far the best of diviners, knows all three:

ὃς ἤιδη τά τ' ἐόντα τά τ' ἐσσόμενα πρό τ' ἐόντα

But some authoritative theologians in the case of the Bible and some authoritative classical scholars in the case of Homer claim that the ordinary readers are victims of illusions. According to this view the Biblical writers either had no notion of time or had a notion of time that was very different from that which you and I have. As for Homer, we are told that he lived at least two centuries before the Greeks discovered, or perhaps invented, time, as you and I know it.

*

*History and Theory, Beiheft 6, 1966, pp. 1–23.

The theory that the Hebrews either ignored time or had a different idea of time is one of the most important and influential of modern theology. It would take me more than the span of an ordinary article to disentangle all the varieties of this theory. Two presuppositions are easily recognizable in modern treatments of the Hebrew idea of time: one is racial, the other religious. The racial presupposition is that the Semites, being Semites, cannot have the same notion of time as the Indo–Europeans. Nothing anti-semitic is implied in such a statement, at least by the postwar writers. One of the most authoritative supporters of the idea that the Jews and the Aryans have two different notions of time, the Norwegian theologian T. Boman, is very anxious to let it be known that both notions have their merits and that a synthesis of both is desirable;[3] but we are invited to accept the existence of the difference as an elementary fact. As G. von Rad, the eminent professor of Alttestamentliche Theologie in the University of Heidelberg, announces, not without due solemnity: 'Now we are beginning to recognize that what we call "time" Israel experienced differently.' (*Theologie des Alten Testaments*, Volume II, 1961, p. 113.) The same von Rad assures us that one of the few things we know about the ancient Hebrews is that they did not have the notion of absolute time (of 'sheer succession of epochal duration', as A. N. Whitehead would have said). Von Rad's opinion is by no means unusual. In *A Christian Theology of the Old Testament* by G. A. F. Knight (London, 1959), we read (p. 314): 'The Hebrews conceived of time quite differently from us. To the Hebrews time was identical with its substance' – whatever that may mean. As a matter of fact, the notion that there is a difference between the Aryan or Indo–European or Greek idea of time and the Semitic or Hebrew idea is only one aspect of the more general difference which authoritative theologians recognize between Indo–European or Greek thought and Hebrew thought. The whole *Theologisches Wörterbuch zum Neuen Testament* edited by G. Kittel is dominated by the conviction that there is this basic difference. It is in this *Wörterbuch* (article γιγνώσκω) that one of the greatest theologians of our time, R. Bultmann, has maintained that the notion of knowledge is not the same among the Jews as among the Greeks. According to Bultmann, Greek knowledge is founded upon the eye whereas Hebrew knowledge, *da'at*, is founded upon the ear.[4] I mention this because we shall soon see that Boman and von Rad claim that the difference between the Greek and the Hebrew notion of time is really founded upon the difference between the eye and the ear.

The second, religious, presupposition in the current theological analyses of the Hebrew idea of time has something to do, I suspect, with K. Barth. It is certainly part of the double fight by O. Cullmann against the eschatological interpretation of the New Testament on the one side and against the *Entmythologisierung* of the Gospel's account of the Incarnation on the other. Albert Schweitzer and Rudolph Bultmann are the main targets of Cullmann's *Christus und die Zeit*, first published in 1946 (3rd ed., 1962) and soon accepted as a classic.[5] As is well known, Cullmann argues that Jews and Christians conceived time as a series of epoch-making events and that Incarnation is, according to the Christian view of time, the most decisive of these decisive moments. It follows that Schweitzer was wrong in centring early Christianity on the expectation of the end of the world rather than in the Incarnation, whereas Bultmann is proved even more wrong in underrating the historical element (what he calls myth) of the Jewish–Christian idea of salvation. Cullmann found approval in even the most sophisticated German–Jewish philosophers of history, such as K. Löwith in his *Weltgeschichte und Heilsgeschehen*, which was originally written in English as *Meaning in History* (1949). The influence of Cullmann is apparent in J. A. T. Robinson's *In The End, God* (1950) and in John Marsh's well-known *The Fullness of Time* (1952). Marsh's book is an eloquent development of the thesis that Jews and Christians share between them the idea of a realistic time belonging to God and being a function of his purpose.

To confine myself to what I can judge, I am certainly not attracted by the loose terminology which is displayed by our theologians. In some cases they oppose Indo–European to Semitic, in other cases Greek to Hebrew, in others still Greek to Jewish–Christian or to Christian alone. No attempt is made to define times, places, authors. Furthermore, some at least of our theologians have very naïve ideas about the uniformity of Greek thought or the continuity of Hebrew thought. To give only one example, Boman seems to be satisfied that Bergson's theories about time are a revival of the old Biblical ideas of time because Bergson was a Jew. The late A. O. Lovejoy has shown in detail that Bergson develops ideas of German Romantic philosophers.[6] But if we try to discount the obviously silly arguments, the evidence for the alleged difference between the Greek and the Jewish notion of time can be stated under three headings:

(1) As the Hebrew verb includes only *perfectum* and *imperfectum* and has no future tense, the Jews did not possess the linguistic instruments to think historically.

(2) The Hebrew language has no specific word for time. As Marsh says, 'Hebrew cannot translate $\chi\rho\acute{o}\nu os$'; and as von Rad reiterates, 'Für unseren abendländischen Begriff "Zeit" hat das Hebräische überhaupt kein Wort'. Consequently the Jews are allegedly unable to formulate the abstract notion of chronological succession. Von Rad, for instance, argues that, though giving lists both of the kings of Judah and of the kings of Israel, the Biblical writer was unable to see that the time of the kings of Israel is identical with the time of the kings of Judah: 'Jede der beiden Königsreihen behält ihre Zeit' (p. 113). Knight expresses the same idea when he writes: 'Time was identical with the development of the very events that occurred in it. For example the Old Testament offers us such phrases as "Time is rain" (Ezra x, 13). One of the corollaries of this theory would seem to be that whereas the Greek $\chi\rho\acute{o}\nu os$ is not translatable into Hebrew, the Greek $\kappa\alpha\iota\rho\acute{o}s$ is, because it expresses the Hebrew–Christian idea of decisive event. Marsh seems to imply that Hebrew 'eth would translate $\kappa\alpha\iota\rho\acute{o}s$ (p. 25).

(3) The Greeks conceived time as a cycle, whereas the Hebrews and the early Christians conceived it as a progression ad finitum or ad infinitum. Cullmann, H.-C. Puech, and G. Quispel (the latter two in essays in Eranos-Jahrbuch, 1951) express this view in its simplest form.[7] Time is a line to the Jews, a circle to the Greeks. Boman and von Rad, as I have already mentioned, believe that the difference between the Greek idea and the Jewish idea of time is to be related to the more general difference between thought founded upon visual perception and thought founded upon acoustic perception. According to them the Greek idea is spatial, the Jewish idea is rhythmical.[8] Marsh seems to take an intermediate position by describing the Greek view as cyclical, yet denying that the Biblical view can be symbolized either by space or by rhythm in so far as it includes only decisive moments or events. But everyone agrees that the difference between the cyclical view and the progressive view of time is the most important feature distinguishing the Greek from the Hebrew attitude to history.

★

It is perhaps not difficult to show that none of these three main differences between Jewish and Greek thought about time can stand up to close examination. The weakest argument is clearly that of the absence of a distinction between past, present and future in the Hebrew verbal system. The Greek verbal system was classified by Hellenistic philosophers or grammarians.[9] Such classification does not fully correspond even to the realities of the Greek tenses, not to speak of the Indo–European verbal system – which is a much later invention or discovery. The Germans lived happily in the freedom of their forests without a future tense. Nor am I sure that we Italians are invariably displaying fine historical sense in our conversations: *vado oggi* and *vado domani* will create problems to theologians. It would be superfluous pedantry to summarize what anyone can read in an elementary Hebrew syntax about the various devices at the disposal of a writer in Biblical Hebrew when he wants to express the future.[10] But it is perhaps not entirely superfluous to remind ourselves that in ordinary oral or written communication the reference either to past or to future can be left to the understanding or imagination of the recipient. Absence of a verbal or even of a syntactical distinction between past, present and future does not entail inability to distinguish between past, present and future. If it is implied that the absence of a future tense prevented the Jews from developing a proper historical sense, and therefore a historiography, the facts are the best answer. There is a Jewish historiography. But one wonders about the very logic of such an inference. Absence of a clear notion of the future should be a hindrance to thoughts about the Messiah, not about past events. On such premises, it was really for the Jews to have a Herodotus, and for the Greeks to hope in the Messiah.

The second point of our theologians is equally untenable. Biblical Hebrew has of course words for time and eternity. If they are not used in the abstract, almost empty way in which words about time are used in Greek, this is due to a simple reason. The Biblical books (with the exception of Qoheleth, in which Greek influence is likely, though it has never been strictly proved) do not contain meditations about time such as we find in Greek poets and philosophers.[11] Biblical writers speak about time in the concrete way which would have been understandable to the ordinary Greek man, for whom there was a time of the day in which the *agora* was full. It is one thing to say that certain theories about time are to be found in Plato and not in the Bible; it is another thing to say that Hebrew words as such imply a different conception of time. When the first Psalm says that the good man is like the tree that brings forth fruit in its own time, this thought is translatable into any Indo–European language. Can von Rad seriously believe that when the Book of Kings says that 'in the second year of Joash son of Jehoahaz king of Israel reigned Amaziah the son of Joash king of Judah', what was time for the king of Judah was not time for the king of Israel? But further discussion about the Jewish terminology of time is fortunately made superfluous by the recent appearance of Professor James Barr's *Biblical Words for Time*, which should be compulsory reading for any theologian and classical scholar, and I shall say nothing more on this. A simple reflection should have made the theologians pause. The chronological references of the Bible are not more difficult to use than those of Herodotus. They do not need translation into a different system of signs about time to be intelligible to the modern mind.

Finally, there is the third and most publicized difference between the cyclical thinking of the Greeks about time and the non-cyclical, even non-spatial, thinking of Jews and early Christians.[12] This difference has at least the merit of having been stated by St Augustine and of representing an essential part of his argument about time. He warned the Christians against the circular notion of the Greeks: the Christian *recta via* was to him both an image of time and an image of salvation: '*nostram simplicem pietatem, ut cum illis in circuitu ambulemus, de recta via conantur avertere*'. But St Augustine is a valid witness only for himself – or perhaps for those pagan philosophers whom he knew.[13] His dilemma does not necessarily correspond to what ordinary Jews, Greeks and Christians felt in the fifth century A.D. – it is even less valid for what ordinary Jews and Greeks felt about time, say, in the fifth century B.C. We can find many faults with Professor M. Eliade's *Le Mythe de l'Éternel Retour*, but at least he has seen that the cyclical interpretation of time has roots in a religious experience which is manifest in Jews as well as in Greeks – not to speak of other peoples.

The ordinary Jew who every year eats the bread his fathers ate when they left Egypt, or who obeys the ancestral call 'To your tents, O Israel' is likely to know as much about cyclical time and eternal return as a Greek of old – whatever cyclical quality we may attribute to the time experience offered by certain Greek festivals and initiations. The suggestion that the Jews did not use spatial metaphors in connection with time is equally ludicrous. *Qedem* means both *ante* and *olim*, and *ahar* is both *a tergo* and *postea*.[14]

What the Greek philosophers thought about time, I repeat, is another matter. There is no reason to consider Plato's thoughts about time as typical of the ordinary Greek man, even if we ignore the notorious question of the Iranian influence on the Platonic notion of αἰών.[15] Philosophers must be compared with philosophers. In the only case in which comparison is legitimate between a Jewish and a Greek writer the results are paradoxical. 'One generation passeth and another cometh, but the earth abideth for ever.' The nearest analogy in Greek thought is among the Epicureans, who did not admit of eternal returns:

> eadem sunt omnia semper
> ....
> ....eadem tamen omnia restant
> omnia si pergas vivendo vincere saecla
> (Lucretius III, 945)

Yet, as we know from St Augustine, there were Christians who interpreted Qoheleth's notion of time as cyclical (*Civ. Dei* 12, 13).

*

Very few of the theologians so far discussed seem to be aware that while they were making their valiant efforts to define an invariable Jewish view of time as against an invariable Greek view of time, classical scholars were busy demonstrating that the Greeks repeatedly changed their views about time. Hardly noticed when it appeared in 1931 as '*Beilage*' of the *Zeitschrift für Aesthetik*, Hermann Fränkel's paper, 'Die Zeitauffassung in der griechischen Literatur', steadily gained in authority: in recent years its influence among classical scholars has been all-pervasive.[16] To give only a few examples, it has inspired the interpretation of Greek lyrical poetry by M. Treu, *Von Homer zur Lyrik* (1955); the interpretation of Greek syntax by H. and A. Thornton, *Time and Style* (1961); and the interpretation of the origins of Greek historiography by S. Accame, *Gli Albori della Critica* (1962).[17]

H. Fränkel seems to me to be on perfectly safe ground when he says that the emphasis on Chronos as creator, judge, discoverer of truth is to be found first in Solon, Pindar and Aeschylus. Homer has nothing of all that. He is indifferent to exact chronology and in general to temporal sequences. According to Fränkel and his followers, this indicates a change in *Weltanschauung*. This may be so, provided that we include literary conventions and eating habits in the *Weltanschauung*. The epic poem was an after-dinner entertainment which presupposed plenty of heavy food, leisure and taste for the evocation of glorious episodes of the past. There have been civilizations that liked to combine banquets with the contemplation of time, which is too often contemplation of death; but there is no reason to assume that Homer belonged to a civilization of this kind. What I do not know is whether Fränkel ever really implied that Solon, Pindar or Aeschylus progressively discovered what you and I call time. There are some sentences to that effect in his essay, most dangerous of all the final one that only after Aeschylus and tragedy '*wird ein eigentlicher geschichtlicher Sinn möglich*'. But it is only Fränkel's followers, most notably Treu and Accame, who have developed Fränkel's suggestions into a system in which each Greek author makes his contribution to the discovery of time. Accame argued that even the *Odyssey* represents a progress over the *Iliad*: the time of the *Odyssey* is wider than that of the *Iliad*. Others have tried to show that Homer has a qualitative notion of time, which Apollonius Rhodius replaces by a quantitative notion. Virgil, in true Homeric spirit, is claimed to have returned to the qualitative notion.[18]

Little is gained from such speculations. I find it characteristic that none of our critics has been able to find a plausible place for Hesiod in such a development. Hesiod's poems know unlimited time, argue about different ages, have a precise sense of chronological succession according to generations. The history they tell is uncritical history, as Hecataeus of Miletus discovered to his own delight, but history it is. Hesiod even felt the burden of historical destiny: 'would that I were not among the men of the fifth generation, but either had died before, or been born afterwards'. Boman consoles himself by reflecting that 'since Hesiod's father had emigrated from Asia Minor, an Oriental influence is very possible' (p. 124). Hesiod has, of course, ideas in common with Hittite and Hebrew texts, but this only goes to show that it is not possible to treat Greek notions of time as something specifically Greek.[19]

Two conclusions seem to me to emerge from a critical reading of H. Fränkel and his followers:

(1) H. Fränkel has made it impossible once and for all to oppose the Greek to the Jewish idea of time by showing that the attitude to time varied in Greek writers.

(2) It would, however, be unwise to deduce from Fränkel's essay that the Greeks progressively discovered time. There may be a connection between the development of tragedy and the development of historiography in the fifth century. Eduard Meyer was not the first to point out the resemblances between the two friends, Herodotus and Sophocles.[20] But the connection between tragedy and historiography, if any, will have to be sought elsewhere than in the idea of time as such.

*

If one wants to understand something about Greek historians and the real differences between them and Biblical historians, the first precaution is to beware of the cyclical notion of time. Even Greek philosophers were not unanimous about it.[21] Anaxagoras, according to Aristotle, did not hold such a view of time, nor did Epicurus.[22] Aristotle, who made the heavens eternal, attributed limited importance to the succession of Great Years.[23] Greek philosophers were not forced by race or language to have only one view of time. Nor were the historians. Herodotus, Thucydides and of course Polybius have in turn been described as historians with a cyclical view of time. I shall attempt to show that they were not.

We have been told by none other than K. Reinhardt that Herodotus thought in terms of cycles, not of millennia: '*Im Kreislauf realisiert sich die Koinzidenz des Unsichtbaren mit dem Sichtbaren*'[24] (*Vermächtnis der Antike*, 1961, p. 136). We shall not dispute the negative conclusion that Herodotus was not a millenarian, but this does not make him a believer in the idea of eternal returns. Historical cycles in the precise sense of the meaning are unknown to Herodotus. He believes that there are forces operating in history which become visible only at the end of a long chain of events. These forces are usually connected with the intervention of gods in human life. Man must reckon with them, though it is uncertain whether man can really avoid what is ordained. In Herodotus Solon is perhaps the most complete representative of fear of *Hybris* whereas Croesus is the most elaborate exemplification of the operation of super-natural forces in human life. Neither of them supports the notion of cyclical time. There is also in Herodotus the simple notion that men make mistakes and start wars when they should not. But again this conviction has nothing to do with a cyclical interpretation of history, and furthermore represents only one side of Herodotus' appreciation of human events. After all, Herodotus chose to be the historian of the conflict between Greeks and barbarians, though he ridiculed its alleged mythical causes and did not approve of its immediate antecedent, the Ionian rebellion. He attributed to the Persian War a unique, non-cyclical significance, chiefly as a conflict between free men and slaves.

Prima facie there may be more sense in attributing a cyclical view of history to Thucydides, because he wrote with the aim of helping 'whoever shall wish to have a clear view both of the events which have happened and of those which will some day, in all human probability ($\kappa\alpha\tau\grave{\alpha}$ $\tau\grave{o}$ $\dot{\alpha}\nu\theta\rho\acute{\omega}\pi\iota\nu\circ\nu$), happen again in the same or similar way' (I, 22).[25] But here again no eternal return is implied. Thucydides vaguely suggests that there will be in the future events either identical or similar to those he is going to narrate. He does not explain, however, whether the identity or similarity between present and future is meant to extend to the whole of his subject – the Peloponnesian War – or to parts of it, for instance, individual battles or individual deliberations. Let us also consider his two most famous examples of a possible 'return'. He states that he is going to explain the symptoms of the plague of Athens in order that from the study of them 'a person should be best able, having knowledge of it beforehand, to recognize it if it should ever break out again' (II, 48). The plague was a very special event. Though it would not be right to credit Thucydides with a distinction between political and biological events, it would also be unjustified not to suspect in him some awareness of the difference between a plague and a battle. Besides, neither he nor Hippocrates, whose teaching he obviously followed, ever attributed a cyclical cause to plagues in the strict sense of the word, and therefore there is no reason to believe that his description of the plague is part of a cyclical view of history. The other example is in the excursus about revolutions of Book III, 82. Thucydides states that 'the sufferings which revolution entailed upon the cities were many and terrible, such as have occurred and always occur, as long as the nature of mankind remains the same'. But he also immediately limits the value of such a statement by adding: 'though in a severer or milder form, and varying in their symptoms, according to the variety of the particular cases'. A revolution was not so simple and uniform an event as a plague.

*

Supporters of the cyclical view in Greek historiography must really fall back on Polybius. In Book VI he states that men emerged from some sort of primeval cataclysm into monarchy; then they pass from one type of constitution to another only to end where they started: 'until they degenerate again into perfect savages and find once more a master and a monarch'. The cycle is there for anyone to see, and Polybius argues in some detail the single stages of the process. Yet we must not forget that this section of Book VI on constitutions is a big digression. The relation between this digression and the rest of Polybius' work is not easy to grasp, and I venture to believe that Polybius himself would have been embarrassed to explain it.[26] To begin with, it is not clear what is the exact relation between this general theory of the constitutions and the subsequent description of the constitutions of Rome and Carthage. The general theory concerns mankind and seems to imply that all men find themselves at a given moment in the same stage of the same cycle. On the other hand it is quite certain that according to Polybius individual states pass from one constitutional stage to another at different moments. For instance: 'by as much as the power and prosperity of Carthage had been earlier than that of Rome, by so much had Carthage already begun to decline, while Rome was exactly at her prime, as far at least as her system of government was concerned' (VI, 51). Furthermore we have to reckon with the complications brought about by the mixed constitution, which arrests corruption for a long time, if not for ever. But the main consideration is that outside the constitutional chapters, in the rest of his history, Polybius operates as if he did not hold any cyclical view of history. The First and the Second Punic Wars are not treated as repetitions of events which happened in the remote past and will happen again in a distant future. Individual events are judged either according to vague notions, such as fortune, or according to more precise criteria of human wisdom and competence. The Roman supremacy in the Mediterranean provides the historian with a new historical perspective. Just because Fortune made almost all the affairs of the world incline in one direction, it is the historian's task to put before his readers a compendious view of the ways in which Fortune accomplished her purposes. The Roman empire makes it possible to write universal history.

All this is not very coherent and hardly amounts to a comprehensive view of history, but in so far as it expresses a view on the trend of human events and on the forces operating behind them, it has nothing to do with cycles of human existence. Polybius very probably learned about the cycle of the forms of government from some philosopher and liked the idea, but was unable to apply it to his historical narrative (as far as we have it). Polybius the historian of the Punic and Macedonian Wars does not appear to have learnt much from Polybius the student of constitutions. I should like to take Polybius as an instance of the fact that Greek philosophers often thought in terms of cycles, but Greek historians did not. It is useless to argue about whether his successor Posidonius applied the Stoic view of cosmic cycles to historical narrative because we have no precise idea of how Posidonius wrote history at length.[27]

Nor must the so-called organic view of history, such as we can find in Florus, be confused with the notion of cycles.[28] What Florus, and no doubt other historians before and after him, believed is that the history of a state can be divided, like the life of an individual, into periods of childhood, youth, maturity, old age, ending in death. This view is important in so far as it implies a certain fatalism. It may lead to all sorts of biological interpretations of human events, and it can, though it need not, be connected with the theory of eternal returns. In the way in which it is presented by Florus it has no profound implication of any kind. In

Antiquity it was left to poets such as Virgil, to religious seers and to political propagandists to dream of the rejuvenation of the Roman empire. No ancient historian, as far as I can remember, ever wrote the history of a state in terms of births and rebirths. Isolated metaphors do not make historical interpretations.

*

History can be written in innumerable forms, but the Greeks chose a form which was accepted by the Romans and which was unlikely to lend itself to a cyclical view of history. The method of the Greek historians was simple enough, and by comparing it with the approach to history of the Biblical writers we shall perhaps be able to arrive at a more realistic appreciation of the similarities and differences between Greek and Hebrew historians. What Herodotus, the father of history, did was to select a series of events as worthy of being rescued from oblivion. He did not claim to cover all the past. He made a choice, and his choice was founded upon quality. The actions of the Greeks and barbarians he decided to put on record were great and wonderful. But he had also another reason for his choice, though this was less explicit and simple. He told stories which appeared to him sufficiently well established, though he made a further distinction between what he could vouch for himself, having seen it, and what he reported second-hand without necessarily taking responsibility for it. Underlying the entire work of Herodotus is his wish to get the best information he could, to use one of his typical expressions (Book II, 44). In other words, his history is founded upon a selection determined primarily by the intrinsic value of the events and secondarily by the information available. This double criterion of choice is present, in different proportions and with different degrees of awareness, in all the historical works of the Greeks and of the Romans who came after Herodotus until, say, Procopius and Cassiodorus. Each historian is concerned first of all with the importance of what he is going to put on record; in the second place he is concerned with the nature of his evidence and knows more or less clearly that some pieces of evidence are better than others. Indeed, even before Herodotus Hecataeus had chosen to recount the genealogies of the Greeks, not so much because they were obviously important to the Greeks, but also because he was better informed about them than the rest of the Greeks. Few or none of the Greek and Roman historians formulated the two criteria with the severity of Thucydides, who preferred the Peloponnesian War to all that had happened before both because it was more important and because it could be told more reliably. But every historian, more or less, took both criteria into consideration. Hence, according to Thucydides' example, the frequent preference for contemporary history which was obviously important to those who had lived it and which at the same time could be narrated more reliably. Those who told of the past had to sacrifice stories simply because the evidence was not trustworthy. Ephorus jettisoned the period before the return of the Heraclidae, and Livy deplored the unreliability of the traditions on early Rome. Others, like Varro, formulated a distinction between different periods of human history according to the varying reliability of the evidence: Varro called the last period historical because 'res in eo gestae veris historiis continentur' (Censorinus 21). What myth meant to the Greeks before history was invented in the fifth century I do not claim to know, but to the historians myth meant something less well known than an ordinary happening (cf. Herodotus, Book II, 45). Every historian knew with Pindar that men are apt to forget: ἀμνάμονες δὲ βροτοί (Isthm. VII, 13).

The combination of the two criteria of choice – qualitative importance and reliability – did not prevent, even among pagans, the compilation of works which claimed to be universal histories: Trogus Pompeius' Historiae Philippicae was one. But the emphasis was clearly not on repetition and eternal returns, but on the unique value of what was being told: history provided examples, not patterns of future events. Moreover, preference was given to limited series of events. The classical historian, like the classical poet, normally deals with limited time. But the historian, unlike the poet, has to justify his choice of a subject not only by criteria of greatness, but also by those of reliability. The Greek philosopher can deal with unlimited time and can even consider the possibility of different time systems related to the existence of several worlds. The limited amount of available evidence is in itself a cause for the limited extent of historical time in comparison with the unlimited time which the philosopher can contemplate because he needs no evidence. Thus the Greek historian has to find out, to discover the events he wants to preserve. He records, not what everybody knows, but what is in danger of being forgotten or has already been forgotten. History is to the Greeks and consequently to the Romans an operation against Time the all-destroying in order to save the memory of events worth being remembered. The fight against oblivion is fought by searching for the evidence.

Search for the evidence and construction of chronological tables are closely interrelated. The evidence, to be evidence, must somehow be dated. Chronology in its turn must be constructed on evidence. Selection and dating of events are interdependent. But interdependence never amounted to a fusion of historical and chronological research. The Greeks soon decided in the fifth century B.C. – more or less when they began to write history – that written evidence was more useful for the construction of a chronology than for the reconstruction of historical events, such as battles and assembly meetings. The decision was sensible enough when it was first taken. In the fifth century the Greeks possessed many documents mentioning priests, magistrates, victorious athletes, but very few written accounts of battles and assemblies. Later what we call official documents and private papers multiplied, and in the Hellenistic period it would have been perfectly possible to write history as we do now by going into archives or using private letters, memoirs and so on. But the preference for oral tradition and visual observation survived, as is clear from Polybius, even when it was no longer justified by prevailing conditions.[29] The chronological framework was almost invariably supported by written records (lists of eponymous magistrates, priests, etc.). The historical narrative, when presented for the first time and not derived from earlier historians, is more often founded upon oral tradition and personal recollections than on written evidence. Consequently chronological research developed on its own lines. The historian Eunapius in his violent attack against chronographers ('What does chronology contribute to the wisdom of Socrates or to the brilliance of Themistocles?') was probably prompted by his dislike of the Christians who favoured chronography, but he reflected the traditional Greek dichotomy of chronography and history.[30] The *spatium chronographicum* was normally longer than the *spatium historicum*, for the simple reason that professional chronographers were less afraid of 'empty' periods than the historians.[31] But occasionally historians (such as Diodorus) ventured into the fields of primitivism for which chronographers were unable to provide dates.

Chronographers and historians collaborated in the production of synchronisms. Synchronisms had long been known to the historians of Mesopotamia and Israel, but they played a special part in Greek historiography. The wide range of interests and explanations of the Greek historians would never have been possible without synchronisms. They represented the bridges between the stories of different cities, nations and civilizations. The very story of Herodotus hangs upon a chain of synchronisms, which is no less robust for being hardly visible to the casual observer.[32] Later the discovery or invention of synchronisms became almost an art in itself, as if synchronisms were the symbols of hidden relations. Timaeus notoriously indulged in them, though, strangely enough, we do not know what he meant when he stated or rather invented that Rome and Carthage had been founded in the same year. Synchronisms are important as data of historical problems, but are often misleading if used as explanation. The more serious Greek and Roman historians preferred succession to synchronism as a foundation for historical explanations.

It is not easy to formulate generalizations about the ways in which the Greek and Roman historians used chronological succession in causal or teleological explanations.[33] Oracles and dreams would have to be taken into account. The future did not loom large in the works of Greek historians. There was more concern with the future among Roman historians, and it expressed itself in anxiety about the Roman empire. Tacitus' pathos has no Greek equivalent. To the Greeks the more remote past, what was called τὰ παλαιά or *antiquitas*, was a special source of problems and ambiguities. The first Greek historians realized that the chronological limits of what was antiquity to the Greeks did not coincide with the antiquity of other nations. Hecataeus' discovery that his sixteen generations of ancestors cut a poor figure against the 345 generations of Egyptian priests was a sobering experience.[34] In the Hellenistic age the same point was made again and again by the Orientals themselves who had learned how to write history in the Greek way. On the other hand Herodotus was mildly puzzled that the Scythians should consider themselves the youngest nation of the world (Book IV, 5).

It is probably true that to the majority of Greek and Roman historians long duration was in itself a positive quality. Polybius can write in all seriousness: 'I am convinced that little need be said of the Athenian and Theban constitutions: their growth was abnormal, the period of their zenith brief, and the changes they experienced unusually violent. Their glory was a sudden and fortuitous flash, so to speak' (Book VI, 43). There is a difference between admiring what is ancient and appreciating what lasts long. Both feelings normally coexisted. But even if Thucydides admired duration (which is doubtful), he did not admire antiquity.[35] On the other hand Tacitus, the *laudator temporis acti*, never denied himself the pride of belonging to the ruling class of a modern powerful empire. Greek and Latin attitudes towards Antiquity have been much simplified by modern interpreters. This applies also to the notion of progress. Unlimited progress was perhaps not a Greek notion, but unlimited progress is one of those philosophical notions which have seldom been very important to historians. What matters more is that Greek historians recognized a continuous, albeit limited, progress in the sphere of philosophy, science, arts, constitutions rather than in that of ordinary moral and political actions. The first finder, the πρῶτος εὑρετής, was an important figure – often with aristocratic or divine connotations.[36]

This attempt to disentangle the attitudes of Greek historians from those of the philosophers may perhaps be concluded by two remarks. With good cause, historians always ignored the philosophical discussion of whether man can possess only his present, as Aristippus taught (μόνον γὰρ ἔφασκεν ἡμέτερον εἶναι τὸ παρόν).[37] They also ignored the Stoic point of view that the wise man can quietly explore all his past: '*securae et quietae mentis est in omnes vitae suae partes discurrere*'. The '*sine ira et studio*' of Tacitus is something different.

*

If we now go back to the Biblical historians, it will be apparent that differences do exist between them and the Greek and Roman historians as regards time. But the differences are not those suggested by contemporary theologians. The main differences seem to me to be four:

(1) The historical section of the Bible is a continuous narration from the creation of the world to about 400 B.C. In comparison with Christian historians like Eusebius who started from before the creation, this is still a limited time. But in comparison with the ordinary Greek and Roman histories, even universal histories, the Biblical account is unique in its continuity. This remark does not apply to the original independent historical works which are the foundations of the present Bible. There was a time in which Hebrew historians knew how to select special periods.[38] Ultimately the idea of an historical continuum from the creation prevailed. All the other interests, including the interest in non-Hebrew history, were sacrificed to it. A privileged line of events represented and signified the continuous intervention of God in the world he had created: the men who worked along that line received unique importance from the very position in which they found themselves.

(2) Hebrew historians did not use reliability as a criterion for selecting and graduating events even within this continuum. Hebrew historians did not know the distinction between a mythical age and an historical age.[39] They did not think it necessary to explain how they came to know the conversation between Eve and the serpent. Paradoxically, the

Hebrew historians were uncritical not because they did not care about evidence, but because they had good reasons to believe that they had reliable evidence to use. Much of the Biblical account is directly founded upon written records: 'Now the rest of the acts of Solomon, and all that he did, and his wisdom, are they not written in the book of the acts of Solomon?' What had not been written down was yet entrusted to the collective memory of the people of Israel and especially of its priests. Flavius Josephus makes this point vigorously and clearly in one of the most important discussions on historiography left to us by Antiquity. He was quite right in saying that the Jews had better organized public records than the Greeks (*contra Apionem* I, 1). What he did not know was that public records kept by priests need to be looked into very carefully.

(3) The Jew has the religious duty to remember the past. The Greeks and Romans cherished the example of their ancestors and derived inspiration from it. Isocrates and other rhetoricians made this one of the main reasons for writing history. But, as far as I know, no Greek ever heard his gods ordering him to 'remember': 'Thou shalt well remember what the Lord thy God did unto Pharaoh, and unto all Egypt' (*Deuteronomy* vii, 18). Neither perhaps was any Greek god told to remember as Yahweh was: 'Remember Abraham, Isaac and Israel, thy servants' (*Exodus* xxxii, 13). The notion of a Covenant explains this emphasis on memory.[40] The Biblical historian never implied (if I am correct) that he was the first to rediscover the past or to save it from oblivion. He only gave an authoritative version of what everybody was supposed to know, whereas the Greek historian recorded what was in danger of becoming unknown.

(4) The Hebrew historian never claimed to be a prophet. He never said 'The Spirit of the Lord God is upon me.' But the pages of the historical books of the Bible are full of prophets who interpret the events because they know what was, is and will be. The historian by implication subordinates himself to the prophet, he derives his values from him. The relation between the historian and the prophet is the Hebrew counterpart to the Greek relation between historian and philosopher. But, at least since Plato fully formulated the antithesis between time and eternity, there could be no collaboration in Greek thought between history and philosophy as there was in Hebrew thought between history and prophecy.[41]

The four differences which I have mentioned were not much noticed in Antiquity. Jews and Gentiles quarrelled about their respective antiquity and the peculiarities of their national customs. The Gentiles naturally questioned the Jewish claim to be the Chosen People, but do not seem to have found anything illogical in the Jewish notions of evidence, prophecy, archaic history. True enough, the Gentiles did not read the Bible and merely reacted to the hellenized versions of Jewish history the Jews themselves produced. It remains significant, however, that Flavius Josephus could write a Hebrew history which was founded upon the Bible and yet acceptable or at least intelligible to the Greek and Roman readers for whom it was intended.[42]

As far as I know, the Christians were unable to write their history for pagans. From a pagan point of view the Christian claims were far more extravagant than the Jewish ones. The Christians claimed that, though they were the most recent nation, yet they were in fact born with the world, ἀπὸ πρώτης ἀνθρωπογονίας (Eusebius H.E. I, 2, 6). They claimed to be a nation growing not through the process of natural births, but through the process of mystical rebirths. They were expecting – rather soon – a second and final Advent.

The more superficial aspects of this new history were capable of being expressed in the pagan form of chronography. Hence the Christian passion for chronography. But chronology, however subtly handled, was unable to convey the complex and revolutionary implications of the Christian interpretation of history.[43] In the first generations the Gospels filled the need. Later, after a gap which needs explanation, Christian historians created ecclesiastical history to supplement the Gospels. Both the Gospels and the ecclesiastical histories, unlike Josephus' *Jewish Antiquities*, were for the believer, or at least for the potential believer, not for the unbeliever. I have never felt able to accept the view, though authoritatively stated, that Luke wrote his Gospel and the Acts for an ordinary 'Roman official concerned with the public safety and legal procedure'.[44] The Christian accounts offended all the classical notions about Antiquity, memory, evidence. Besides, by the time ecclesiastical history was invented in the fourth century, it had already become too dangerous to discuss Christian claims. Here I rejoin my paper on fourth-century historiography which I read at the Warburg Institute in 1959. We have no pagan discussion of the Christian conception of time and of the connected notion of ecclesiastical history.[45] The modern notion of historical periods selected according to the intrinsic importance of the facts and according to the reliability of the evidence is quite clearly part of our pagan inheritance. Experience seems to show that it can somehow be reconciled with the Jewish idea of a history from the creation of the world. The reconciliation with the Christian notion of a history divided into two by Incarnation is a more difficult problem.

★

Two concluding remarks, though only too obvious, do not seem to be superfluous in the circumstances:

(1) Many students of historiography, and especially the theologically minded among them, appear to assume that there are neat and mutually exclusive views about time: the Jews had one, the Greeks another. To judge from experience, this is not so; and one would suspect that philosophers would have an easier task if it were so. To give a simple instance, two different attitudes towards time have been shown to exist in archaic Greek and Roman law. As L. Gernet has observed ('Le temps dans les formes archaïques du droit', *Journal de Psychologie* 53, 1956, pp. 379–406), in certain cases the judge did not take time into account, in others he admitted the validity of religious or magic practices connected with time. Comparative study of the notion of time in 'primitive' civilizations will increasingly help classical scholars and Biblical theologians to introduce some complexity into their simple ideas of what is Greek and what is Biblical.[46]

(2) Classical and Biblical scholars sometimes give the impression of forgetting that general linguists and anthropologists are still in disagreement among themselves as to whether (or to what extent) language is not merely a 'reproducing instrument for voicing ideas, but rather is itself the shaper of ideas, the programme and guide for the individual's mental activity'.[47]

References

1. This article is based on the text of a lecture delivered at the Warburg Institute in London on 15 May 1963 as one in a series 'Time and Eternity'. The paper develops a few points I made in a review of T. Boman, *Das Hebräische Denken im Vergleich mit dem Griechischen*, 3rd ed., Göttingen, 1959, translated as *Hebrew Thought Compared with Greek*, London, 1960, in *Rivista Storica Italiana*, 74, 1962, pp. 603–7, now reprinted in *Terzo Contributo alla Storia degli Studi Classici*, Rome, 1966, pp. 757–62. Subsequently I was confirmed in my point of view by finding myself in general agreement with J. Barr, *Biblical Words for Time*,

London, 1962, on the Hebrew side and with P. Vidal-Naquet, 'Temps des dieux et temps des hommes', *Revue de l'histoire des religions*, 157, 1960, pp. 55–80, on the Greek side. I specifically refer to these works and more particularly to the bibliography contained in Barr. For further bibliographical information see the important recent volumes by A. Luneau, *L'histoire du Salut chez les Pères de l'Eglise*, Paris, 1964, and S. G. F. Brandon, *History, Time, and Deity*, Manchester, 1965. I quote in the following notes only a fraction of what I have read on this fashionable subject. I give preference to recent works which include references to earlier ones. See in general J. T. Fraser, ed., *The Voices of Time*, New York, 1966.

2. For a brief general history of the idea of time see S. Toulmin and J. Goodfield, *The Discovery of Time*, London, 1965.

3. Racial prejudice is obvious even in the very competent researches by G. Delling, *Das Zeitverständnis des Neuen Testaments*, Gütersloh, 1940, and by J. Leipoldt, *Der Tod bei Griechen und Juden*, Leipzig, 1942.

4. Among the many recent researches on the idea of time in the Old Testament I shall mention only: W. Vollborn, *Studien zum Zeitverständnis des Alten Testaments*, Göttingen, 1951; W. Eichrodt, 'Heilserfahrung und Zeitverständnis im Alten Testament', *Theologische Zeitschrift*, 12, 1956, pp. 103–25; J. Muilenburg, 'The Biblical View of Time', *Harvard Theological Review*, 54, 1961, pp. 225–52 (which can be taken as a popular summary of prevailing views); M. Sekine, 'Erwägungen zur Hebräischen Zeitauffassung', *Supplementum Vetus Testamentum*, 9, 1963, pp. 66–82; B. S. Childs, 'A Study of the Formula "Until this day"', *Journal of Biblical Literature*, 82, 1963, pp. 279–93; N. H. Snaith, 'Time in the Old Testament', in F. F. Bruce, *Promise and Fulfilment*, Edinburgh, 1963, pp. 175–86. Snaith's distinction between 'circular time', 'horizontal time', and 'vertical time' (the last being 'the particular Hebrew contribution' to the idea of time) does not make sense to me.

5. The Italian translation (*Cristo e il tempo*, Bologna, 1964) contains an important introduction by B. Ulianich with bibliography. Cullmann has clarified his position, especially in *Heil als Geschichte*, Tübingen, 1965, which is a reply to R. Bultmann, *History and Eschatology*, Edinburgh, 1957 (the German edition *Geschichte und Eschatologie*, Tübingen, 1958, is slightly different). *Cf.* H. Conzelmann, *Die Mitte der Zeit*, 4th ed., Tübingen, 1962. On the theological scene as a whole *cf.*, for instance, A. Richardson, *History Sacred and Profane*, London, 1964, pp. 125–53, 254–65.

6. A. O. Lovejoy, *The Reason, The Understanding, and Time*, Baltimore, 1961.

7. H.-C. Puech, 'La Gnose et le Temps', *Eranos-Jahrbuch*, 20, 1951, pp. 57–113; G. Quispel, 'Zeit und Geschichte im antiken Christentum', ibid., pp. 115–40 (both translated in *Man and Time, Papers from the Eranos Yearbooks*, London, 1958).

8. The notion of Semitic rhythmical time is also accepted by linguists such as P. Fronzaroli, 'Studi sul lessico comune semitico', *Rendiconti Accademia Nazionale dei Lincei*, VIII, 20, 1965, pp. 142–3, with explicit reference to Boman (and no linguistic argument!).

9. It will be enough to refer to H. Steinthal, *Geschichte der Sprachwissenschaft bei den Griechen und Römern*, 1862–3; 2nd ed., Berlin, 1890–91, I, p. 265; II, p.

267; and to M. Pohlenz, 'Die Begründung der abendländischen Sprachlehre durch die Stoa', *Nachrichten Gesellschaft Göttingen*, 1, 3, 6, 1939, now in *Kl. Schriften*, I, Hildesheim, 1965, pp. 39–87: cf. also Pohlenz's book *Die Stoa*, Göttingen, 1948, I, p. 45. Pohlenz's conclusions are, however, subject to caution. Cf. also H. Weinrich, *Tempus*, Stuttgart, 1964.

10. See for instance M. Cohen, *Le système verbal sémitique et l'expression du temps*, Paris, 1924; C. Brockelmann, *Hebräische Syntax*, Neukirchen, 1956, index s.v. 'Zukunft'. The question is bound up with the whole interpretation of the Semitic and of the Indo–European verbal systems. I can only refer to a few recent works: M. Sekine, 'Das Wesen des althebräischen Verbalausdrucks', *Zeitschr. Alttest. Wiss.*, 58, 1940–41, pp. 133–41; F. Rundgren, *Das althebräische Verbum: Abriss der Aspektlehre*, Uppsala, 1961; G. R. Castellino, *The Akkadian Personal Pronouns and Verbal System in the Light of Semitic and Hamitic*, Leiden, 1962. For Indo–European, J. G. Gonda, *The Character of the Indo-European Moods*, Wiesbaden, 1956, pp. 23–32; L. J. Maclennan, *El problema del aspecto verbal*, Madrid, 1962 (with bibliography). For my remark on German, cf. A. Meillet, *Caractères généraux des langues germaniques*, 5th ed., Paris, 1937, p. 125: 'le germanique ignore toute expression du futur'. Methodologically important E. Benveniste, 'Les relations de temps dans le verbe français', *Problèmes de linguistique générale*, Paris, 1966, pp. 237–50.

11. For a timely word of caution on the Greek influences on *Qoheleth* see R. B. Y. Scott, *Proverbs. Ecclesiastes*, The Anchor Bible, Garden City, N.Y., 1965, p. 197.

12. The list of all those writers (mainly theologians) who in the last twenty years have taken it for granted that the Greeks 'accepted the universal ancient and Oriental view of history as a cycle of endless repetition' (Richardson, *History Sacred and Profane*, 57) would be a very long one. Cf., for instance, R. Niebuhr, *Faith and History*, New York, 1949, p. 17; T. F. Driver, *The Sense of History in Greek and Shakespearean Drama*, New York, 1960, p. 19; F. E. Manuel, *Shapes of Philosophical History*, Stanford, 1965. (P. 7: 'the whole of the surviving corpus of literature inherited from antiquity testifies virtually without contradiction that cyclical theory possessed the Greco–Roman World'.) The notion is accepted but, as one would expect, subtly qualified, by I. Meyerson, 'Le temps, la mémoire, l'histoire', *Journal de Psychologie*, 53, 1956, pp. 333–54, especially 339. One would like to pay tribute to Meyerson and his school for their work on the evolution of the idea of time. Cf. also F. Chatelet, 'Le temps de l'histoire et l'évolution de la fonction historienne', ibid., 53, 1956, pp. 355–78. On the idea of cycle cf. A. Diès, *Le cycle mystique*, Paris, 1909; K. Ziegler, *Menschen- und Weltwerden*, Leipzig, 1913; R. Marchal, 'Le retour éternel', *Archives Philosophiques*, 3, 1925, pp. 55–91; M. Eliade, *Le Mythe de l'Éternel Retour*, Paris, 1949 (English translation: *Cosmos and History*, New York, 1959).

13. It will be enough to refer to some of those French scholars who have contributed so outstandingly to the interpretation of St Augustine: J. Guitton, *Le temps et l'éternité chez Plotin et Saint Augustin*, Paris, 1933, 3rd ed., 1959; H.-I. Marrou, *Ambivalence du temps de l'histoire chez Saint Augustin*, Montreal, 1950; J. Chaix-Ruy, *Saint Augustin, temps et histoire*, Paris, 1956. For elements of cyclical thinking in St Augustine, Luneau, *L'histoire du Salut chez les Pères de*

l'Eglise, pp. 385–407; J. Hubaux, 'Saint Augustin et la crise cyclique', *Augustinus Magister*, 2, 1954, pp. 943–50; E. T. Mommsen, 'St Augustine and the Christian Idea of Progress', *Medieval and Renaissance Studies*, New York, 1959, pp. 265–88. Other bibliography in C. Andresen, ed., *Zum Augustin-Gespräch der Gegenwart*, Darmstadt, 1962, pp. 508–11.

14. So we shall not be surprised if J. Briggs Curtis, 'A Suggested Interpretation of the Biblical Philosophy of History', *Hebrew Union College Annual*, 34, 1963, pp. 115–23, maintains that 'the fundamental notion of history in the Bible is always that history is cyclical'!

15. A. D. Nock, 'A Version of Mandulis Aion', *Harvard Theological Review*, 27, 1934, pp. 79–99; E. Degani, *Aion da Omero ad Aristotele*, Padua, 1961, pp. 107–16, with bibliography. *Cf.* also B. L. van der Waerden, 'Das grosse Jahr und die ewige Wiederkehr', *Hermes*, 80, 1952, pp. 129–55; E. S. Kennedy and B. L. van der Waerden, 'The World-Year of the Persians', *Journal of the American Oriental Society*, 83, 1963, pp. 315–27.

16. Reprinted in *Wege und Formen frühgriechischen Denkens*, Munich, 1960, pp. 1–22.

17. See also by Accame 'La concezione del tempo nell'età omerica e arcaica', *Rivista di Filologia e di istruzione classica*, N.S. 39, 1961, pp. 359–94, and his reply to my criticisms ibid. N.S. 41, 1963, p. 265. *Cf.* M. Treu, 'Griechische Ewigkeitswörter', *Glotta*, 43, 1965, pp. 1–23; B. Hellwig, *Raum und Zeit im homerischen Epos*, Hildesheim, 1964.

18. F. Mehmel, *Virgil und Apollonius Rhodius*, Hamburg, 1940.

19. References on Hesiod and Oriental thought in J.-P. Vernant, *Les origines de la pensée grecque*, Paris, 1962, p. 114. Add U. Bianchi, 'Razza aurea, mito delle cinque razze ed Elisio', *Studi e Materiali Storia Religioni*, 34, 1963, pp. 143–210. For the interpretation of Hesiod see the very stimulating M. Detienne, *Crise agraire et attitude religieuse chez Hésiode*, Brussels, 1963; J.-P. Vernant, *Mythe et pensée chez les grecs*, Paris, 1965, pp. 19–47. (J.-P. Vernant, *Rev. Philologie*, 40, 1966, pp. 247–76.)

20. *Forschungen zur alten Geschichte*, Halle, 1899, II, p. 262.

21. Only a few works can be quoted: A. Levi, *Il concetto di tempo nella filosofia greca*, Milan, 1919; J. F. Callahan, *Four Views of Time in Ancient Philosophy*, Cambridge, Mass., 1948; C. Mugler, *Deux thèmes de la cosmologie grecque: devenir cyclique et pluralité des mondes*, Paris, 1953; R. Mondolfo, *L'infinito nel pensiero dell'antichità classica*, Florence, 1956; C. Diano, *Il concetto della storia nella filosofia dei greci*, Milan, 1954 (from *Grande Antologia Filosofica*, Volume II). I have learned much from R. Schaerer's *L'homme antique et la structure du monde intérieur*, Paris, 1958, and *Le héros, le sage, et l'événement*, Paris, 1964.

22. For the dubious evidence on Anaxagoras, G. S. Kirk and J. E. Raven, *The Presocratic Philosophers*, Cambridge, 1957, p. 390. On Empedocles, U. Hölscher, 'Weltzeiten und Lebenszyklus', *Hermes*, 93, 1965, pp. 7–33.

23. P. F. Conen, *Die Zeittheorie des Aristoteles*, Munich, 1964; A.-H. Chroust, 'Aristotle and the Philosophies of the East', *Review of Metaphysics*, 18, 1965, pp. 572–80. *Cf.* A. Grilli, 'La posizione d'Aristotele, Epicuro e Posidonio nei confronti della storia della civiltà', *Rendiconti Istituto Lombardo*, 86, 1953, pp. 3–44.

24. *Cf.* T. S. Brown, 'The Greek Sense of Time in History as Suggested by Their Accounts of Egypt', *History*, XI, 1962, pp. 257–70; H. Montgomery, *Gedanke und Tat: Zur Erzählungstechnik bei Herodot, Thukydides, Xenophon und Arrian*, Lund, 1965. Herodotus, Book I, 207, 2 must not be misunderstood.

25. J. H. Finley, *Thucydides*, Cambridge, Mass., 1942, p. 83: 'it is clear that he finally adopted a cyclical view of history very much like Plato's'. But see the limitation of this view on p. 292. (K. von Fritz, *Die griechische Geschichtsschreibung*, I, 1967, p. 531.)

26. Much as I admire the recent book by P. Pédech, *La méthode historique de Polybe*, Paris, 1964, I feel that it introduces too much coherence into Polybius' ideas. *Cf.* T. Cole, 'The Sources and Composition of Polybius VI', *Historia*, 13, 1964, pp. 440–85; F. W. Walbank, 'Polybius and the Roman State', *Greek, Roman, and Byzantine Studies*, 5, 1965, pp. 239–60.

27. Recent literature in M. Laffranque, *Poseidonius d'Apamée*, Paris, 1964. Add H. Strasburger, 'Posidonius on Problems of the Roman Empire', *Journal of Roman Studies*, 55, 1965, pp. 40–53, and notice particularly A. D. Nock, 'Posidonius', ibid., 49, 1959, pp. 1–15.

28. C. Tibiletti, 'Il proemio di Floro', *Convivium* N.S. 27, 1959, pp. 339–42; A. Truyol y Serra, 'The Idea of Man and World History from Seneca to Orosius and Saint Isidore of Seville', *Cahiers d'Histoire Mondiale*, 6, 1961, pp. 698–713; R. Häussler, 'Vom Ursprung und Wandel des Lebensaltersvergleiches', *Hermes*, 92, 1964, pp. 313–41; I. Hahn, 'Prooemium und Disposition der Epitome des Florus', *Eirene*, 4, 1965, pp. 21–41; W. Den Boer, 'Florus und die Römische Geschichte', *Mnemosyne*, 18, 1965, pp. 366–87. (P. Jal, *Florus*, I, 1967, p. lxix.)

29. In general, see my *Studies*, ch. 11, 'Historiography on Written Tradition and Historiography on Oral Tradition', pp. 211–20, and especially M. Laffranque, 'La vue et l'ouïe: expérience, observation et utilisation des témoignages à l'époque hellénistique', *Revue Philosophique*, 153, 1963, pp. 75–82; idem, 'L'oeil et l'oreille: Polybe et les problèmes de l'information à l'époque hellénistique', ibid., 155, 1965. Contrast Chinese historiography: 'Il n'y a d'histoire au sens chinois du mot que de ce qui est écrit', J. Gernet, 'Ecrit et histoire en Chine', *Journal de Psychologie*, 56, 1959, pp. 31–40.

30. Eunapius, Fr. 1, K. Müller, ed., *Fragmenta Historicorum Graecorum*, Paris, 1841–70, IV, p. 12. He discusses the performance of his predecessor Dexippus, a pagan.

31. W. von Leyden, 'Spatium Historicum', *Durham University Journal* N.S. 11, 1950, pp. 89–104.

32. H. Strasburger, 'Herodots Zeitrechnung', *Historia*, 5, 1956, pp. 129–61 = W. Marg, ed., *Herodot*, Darmstadt, 1962, pp. 667–725. (*Contra* W. Den Boer, *Mnemosyne*, 4, 21, 1967, pp. 30–60.)

33. It is difficult to find any general treatment of this topic. Much is still to be learned from F. M. Cornford, *From Religion to Philosophy*, London, 1912; now available in reprint, New York, 1957, and from his pupil W. K. C. Guthrie, *In the Beginning*, London, 1957, which contains a chapter on 'Cycles of Existence', pp. 63–79. *Cf.* also B. A. van Groningen, *In the Grip of the Past*, Leiden, 1953; K. von Fritz, 'Der gemeinsame Ursprung der Geschichtsschreibung und der exakten Wissenschaft bei den Griechen', *Philosophia Naturalis*, 2, 1952, pp.

200–23; M. I. Finley, introduction to *Greek Historians*, London, 1959, and F. Chatelet, *La naissance de l'histoire*, Paris, 1962.

34. *Cf.* my essay on Hecataeus, 1931, now reprinted in *Terzo Contributo*, Rome, 1966, pp. 323–33, and bibliography there quoted.

35. He admired the abortive constitution of 411 B.C., VIII, 97, 2.

36. A. Kleingünther, *Protos Euretes*, Leipzig, 1933, *Philologus*, Supplement 26, 1; K. Thraede, 'Das Lob des Erfinders', *Rh. Museum*, 105, 1962, pp. 158–86.

37. Aelianus *var. hist.* 14, 6 = Mullach, *Fr. Phil. Graec.* II, 414.

38. Strong disagreements over the methods of analysis of Hebrew historiography (of which some account is given from the point of view of I. Engnell's school in R. A. Carlson, *David, the Chosen King*, Stockholm, 1964, pp. 9–19) should not, I think, obscure this point. *Cf.*, for instance, the introduction by J. Gray to his commentary on *I and II Kings*, London, 1964; S. Mowinckel, quoted n. 41, and also M. Smith, 'The So-called Biography of David in the Books of Samuel and Kings', *Harvard Theological Review*, 44, 1951, pp. 167–9. See also A. Alt, 'Die Deutung der Weltgeschichte im Alten Testament', *Zeitschrift für Theologie und Kirche*, 56, 1959, pp. 129–37.

39. For this distinction in Greece see the chapter by J.-P. Vernant on 'Aspects mythiques de la mémoire et du temps' in *Mythe et pensée chez les Grecs*, pp. 51–94. *Cf.* R. H. Pfeiffer, 'Facts and Faith in Biblical History', *Journal of Biblical Literature*, 70, 1951, pp. 1–14; R. M. Grant, 'Causation and the Ancient World View', ibid., 83, 1964, pp. 34–41. Other references in G. Fohrer, *Theologische Literaturzeitung*, 89, 1964, p. 488, n. 18. The notion of memory is studied by B. S. Childs, *Memory and Tradition in Israel*, London, 1962. The analysis of the root *zkr* by P. A. H. De Boer, *Gedenken und Gedächtnis in der Welt des Alten Testaments*, Stuttgart, 1962, does not invalidate Child's conclusions. Formulas like Homer, *Iliad*, 15, 375, are something different, but I should gladly like to know more about the memory of Greek gods. There seems to be little about it in books such as J. Rudhardt, *Notions fondamentales de la pensée religieuse . . . dans la Grèce classique*, Geneva, 1958. See now also W. Schottroff, '*Gedenken*' *im alten Orient und im Alten Testament*, Neukirchen, 1964.

40. Bibliography in A. Jaubert, *La notion d'alliance dans le Judaïsme aux abords de l'ère chrétienne*, Paris, 1963.

41. I do not know of any satisfactory study of the relations between prophets and historians in the Bible. For an illuminating paper on the prophet's predicament see E.-J. Bickerman, 'Les deux erreurs du prophète Jonas', *Revue d'histoire et de philosophie religieuses*, 45, 1965, pp. 232–64. Notice, however, A. Weiser, *Glaube und Geschichte im Alten Testament*, Stuttgart, 1931, reprinted Göttingen, 1961; S. Mowinckel, 'Israelite Historiography', *Annals of the Swedish Theological Institute*, 2, 1963, pp. 4–26; G. Fohrer, 'Prophetie und Geschichte', *Theologische Literaturzeitung*, 89, 1964, pp. 481–500, with bibliography; J. Hempel, *Geschichten und Geschichte im Alten Testament*, Gütersloh, 1964; H. W. Wolff, 'Das Geschichtsverständnis der alttestamentlichen Prophetie', *Gesammelte Studien zum Alten Testament*, Munich, 1964, pp. 289–307. (E. Bickerman, *Four Strange Books of the Bible*, New York, 1967.)

42. *Cf.* I. Heinemann, 'Josephus' Method in the Presentation of Jewish Antiquities', *Zion*, 5, 1939–40, pp. 180–203 (in Hebrew); P. Collomp, 'La place

de Josèphe dans la technique de l'historiographie hellénistique' in *Études hist. Faculté Lettres Strasbourg*, III, Paris, 1947, pp. 81–92. There is something to be learned, oddly enough, from G. Bertram, 'Josephus und die abendländische Geschichtsidee' in W. Grundmann, ed., *Germanentum, Christentum, und Judentum*, II, Leipzig, 1942, pp. 41–82, just because it deplores the penetration of Jewish ideas into the Aryan world (*cf.* W. Grundmann, *Die Entjudung des religiösen Lebens als Aufgabe der deutschen Theologie und Kirche*, Weimar, 1939; and for further information K. Meier, *Die deutschen Christen*, Göttingen, 1964). Points in common between Greek and Jewish historiography have been repeatedly emphasized in basic studies by E. Bickerman, for instance in 'La chaîne de la tradition pharisienne', *Revue Biblique*, 59, 1952, pp. 44–54, and *From Ezra to the Last of the Maccabees*, New York, 1962. *Cf.* above, 'Eastern Elements in Post-Exilic Jewish, and Greek, Historiography', pp. 25–35, and M. Noth, *Gesammelte Studien zum Alten Testament*, Munich, 1957, pp. 248–73.

43. J. W. Johnson, 'Chronological Writing: Its Concept and Development', *History and Theory*, II, 1962, pp. 124–45; see also my paper quoted in n. 45.

44. The identification of Theophilus is hopeless for the reasons indicated by F. J. Foakes Jackson and K. Lake, *The Beginnings of Christianity*, II, London, 1922, pp. 505–8. *Cf.* E. Jacquer, *Les Actes des Apôtres*, 2nd ed., Paris, 1926, p. 3 : 'nous ne savons rien sur ce personnage'. H. W. Montefiore, *Josephus and the New Testament*, London, 1962, is not what one would like it to be – a discussion of the two points of view – and is altogether disappointing. K. Löwith, *Weltgeschichte und Heilsgeschehen*, 2nd ed., Stuttgart, 1953, p. 179, has made the remark worth pondering: 'Daraus folgt, dass eine jüdische Theologie der Geschichte möglich und innerlich notwendig ist, während eine christliche Geschichtsphilosophie ein künstliches Gebilde darstellt.' For the opposite point of view *cf.* for instance A.-H. Chroust, 'The Metaphysics of Time and History in Early Christian Thought', *The New Scholasticism*, 19, 1945, pp. 322–52.

45. *Cf.* above, 'Pagan and Christian Historiography in the Fourth Century A.D.', pp. 107–26.

46. French sociologists have a proud record of research on the notions of time and memory, which starts with H. Hubert and M. Mauss, 'La représentation du temps dans la religion et la magie', *Mélanges d'histoire des religions*, Paris, 1909, pp. 189–229, and continues with the great works by M. Halbwachs (who died at Buchenwald on 16 March 1945): *Les cadres sociaux de la mémoire*, Paris, 1925, and 'Mémoire et société', *L'Année Sociologique*, III, 1, 1940–48, pp. 11–177, reprinted under the title *La mémoire collective*, Paris, 1950 – not to speak of the recent developments in I. Meyerson's school, about which see n. 12. *Cf.* also A. I. Hallowell, 'Temporal Orientations in Western Civilization and in a Preliterate Society', *American Anthropologist*, 39, 1937, pp. 647–70; E. E. Evans-Pritchard, *The Nuer*, Oxford, 1940; E. R. Leach, *Rethinking Anthropology*, London, 1961, pp. 124–36; M. Eliade, 'Primordial Memory and Historical Memory', *History of Religions*, 2, 1962, pp. 320 ff.; J. Le Goff, 'Temps de l'Eglise et temps du marchand', *Annales*, 15, 1960, pp. 417–33; J. Pépin, 'Le temps et le mythe', *Les Études Philosophiques*, 17, 1962, pp. 55–68.

I am not here directly concerned with what has become a primary branch in the study of notions of time – the analysis of oral traditions. To mention only one work: J. Vansina, *De la tradition orale*, Tervueren, Belgium, 1961; English translation *Oral Tradition*, London, 1965. For contemporary discussions of the theoretical ambiguities about time, which may perhaps be taken to start with the Göttingen lectures by E. Husserl in 1905, *Zur Phänomenologie des inneren Zeitbewusstseins* (first published by M. Heidegger in 1928), see, among others: R. G. Collingwood, 'Some Perplexities about Time', *Proceedings of the Aristotelian Society*, 26, 1926, pp. 135–50; A. Quinton, 'Spaces and Times', *Philosophy*, 37, 1962, pp. 130–47; G. Kubler, *The Shape of Time*, New Haven, 1962; R. Schaeffler, *Die Struktur der Geschichtszeit*, Frankfurt, 1963; S. Kracauer, 'Time and History', *Zeugnisse Th. W. Adorno*, Frankfurt, 1963, pp. 50–64, reprinted in *History and Theory, Beiheft* 6, 1966; and W. von Leyden, 'History and the Concept of Relative Time', *History and Theory*, II, 1963, pp. 263–85.

47. B. L. Whorf, *Language, Thought, and Reality*, New York, 1956, p. 212. See also H. Hoijer, ed., *Language in Culture*, American Anthropological Association Memoir, No. 79, December 1954, which is entirely devoted to discussing the Sapir-Whorf hypothesis on inferences from linguistic to non-linguistic data. See also M. Cohen, 'Social and Linguistic Structure', *Diogenes*, 15, 1956, pp. 38–47, and his book *Pour une sociologie du langage*, Paris, 1956. J. Barr in *The Semantics of Biblical Language*, Oxford, 1961, p. 294, n. 1, has already observed that the theory of language behind Kittel's *Theologisches Wörterbuch zum Neuen Testament* seems to be that of J. L. Weisgerber, the author of *Deutsches Volk und Deutsche Sprache*, Frankfurt, 1935, *Die geschichtliche Kraft der deutschen Sprache*, 1950, *Die sprachliche Gestaltung der Welt*, 1963, and other works in a similar vein. In Weisgerber, emphasis on 'Muttersprache' and nationalism corresponds to distrust of bilingualism (see for instance *Das Menschheitsgesetz der Sprache*, 2nd ed., Heidelberg, 1964, p. 154). A book like Barr's is needed for classical scholarship. I should like to refer also to Barr, *Old and New in Interpretation*, London, 1966, which appeared when this article was already in proof. R. Häussler, *Tacitus und das historische Bewusstsein*, Heidelberg, 1965, in fact 1966, is another book which appeared too late to be used here. It is devoted to the conflict between cyclical and linear notions of time, and though it contains many perceptive remarks it seems to me to result in confusion worse confounded. *Cf.* my review in *Rivista Storica Italiana*, 78, 1966, pp. 974–6.

13

The First Political Commentary on Tacitus*

ONLY the learning, the wisdom, and the wit of Professor N. H. Baynes could do full justice to the influence of Tacitus on modern political and historical thought. As no ancient historian of our time is so interested in the legacy of Classical Antiquity as Professor Baynes, it has seemed not inappropriate to bring to him from my native Piedmont the following contribution to the history of Tacitus' influence. An earlier chapter of the same history was written in this *Journal* (VI, 196 ff.), by Professor F. J. Haverfield.[1]

I

Pontano, at the end of the fifteenth century, writes: 'Curtium ac Tacitum quasi mutilatas videmus statuas; licetque suspicari potius ac coniicere quam omnino de iis iudicium aliquod absolutum ac certum tradere'.[2] After the *editio princeps* of the first books of the *Annals* (1515), it became evident that Tacitus had a message for contemporaries.[3] As Guicciardini said: 'Insegna molto bene Cornelio Tacito a chi vive sotto a' tiranni il modo di vivere e governarsi prudentemente, così come insegna a' tiranni e' modi di fondare la tirannide'.[4] In 1532 Beatus Rhenanus proclaimed the dethronement of Livy as a *fait accompli*:

> *Unde factum ut praestantium in literis virorum iudicio Livio non sit postponendus Tacitus, quin potius anteferendus: non quod huius floridum ac meditationem et curam olens dicendi genus . . . Livianae dictioni . . . aequari debeat aut praeferri: sed quod singularium rerum narratio, quemadmodum hic non meritam mortem fortiter subierit, quid alius in ius calumniose vocatus dixerit aut fecerit, quam agendum caute cum iis qui solo nutu perdere possunt, quam parce fidendum et iis similia exempla multum conferant ad legentis pectus prudentiae monumentis instruendum.*[5]

Journal of Roman Studies, 37, 1947, pp. 91–100.

The pious Budé,[6] who naturally was hostile to an anti-Christian writer, was outdone by 'impious' Bodin,[7] whose answer remains memorable.[8]

Nevertheless, even contemporaries stated that Tacitus had never been properly understood or appreciated before Justus Lipsius published his text (1st ed., 1574), and commentary (1st ed., 1581). To quote one witness among many:

Sed Iustus Lipsius, ad excitanda ingenia et studia praeclara natus, ita dignitatem pristinam ac splendorem Equiti Romano vindicavit ut nullam impolitiae notam metuat posthac.[9]

It is a fact that the whole of the literature specifically illustrating Tacitus' political thought is later than 1580 and is somewhat influenced by Lipsius. The intrinsic value of Lipsius' contribution to the interpretation of Tacitus is a matter of opinion, but his contribution to the reputation and popularity of Tacitus cannot be exaggerated. Lipsius set 'Tacitismo' in motion inasmuch as nobody declared so frequently, so emphatically, and so authoritatively that Tacitus was 'quasi theatrum hodiernae vitae'.[10] Lipsius first referred to the political importance of Tacitus in the Jena oration of 1572, 'cum inciperet publice interpretari Cornelium Tacitum': his Tiberius was then the Duke of Alba.[11] He insisted on this theme in the various editions of his Tacitus 'saluberrimo et optimo scriptore ad hoc aevum. Aevum calamitosum. Sed ad quod tolerandum multum, me iudice, historia ista faciet: solatio, consilio, exemplo'. He derived from Tacitus the majority of the quotations for his theoretical treatise, the *Politicorum libri sex* (1589), and explained: 'caussa in prudentia viri est, et quia creberrimus sententiis: atque etiam, quia familiaris nobis et offerebat se non vocatus'. In 1605 he was still repeating: 'non est in Graecis aut Latinis, et fidenter dicam non erit, qui prudentiae omnigenae laude huic se comparet'.[12]

There is, however, something to be noted in this connection. Lipsius made it clear in the preface to the first edition of his commentary – dated 'Lugduni Batavorum Kal. Augustis 1580'[13] – that he did not mean to write a political commentary on Tacitus because he thought it useless:

Politica non attigi. Sive enim peritis, sive imperitis, frustra. Illi sponte eligere possunt; hi nec electis recte uti. Et audio iam esse quibus proprie ea cura. Ego quod potui, id feci, nec impedio, si quis in eodem circo curret ad palmam.

This disclaimer was repeated in the following editions and, undoubtedly, always represented his thought.[14] He neither wrote nor encouraged others to write a political commentary on Tacitus: the *Politicorum libri sex* were not this. On the other hand, people were encouraged by Lipsius to study Tacitus from the political point of view.[15] An examination of some relevant facts will easily explain the apparent contradiction. Lipsius' propaganda for Tacitus was obviously not the only element in the field.

II

To begin with, the preface quoted above states that in August 1580 no political commentary on Tacitus was yet available, but something of the sort was in preparation ('audio iam esse . . .'). Lipsius may allude to a work which never materialized, but it is hard to escape the conclusion that he was primarily referring to a book which appeared in Paris more or less at the same time as his commentary: *C. C. Taciti ab excessu divi Augusti Annalium libri quatuor priores, et in hos observationes C. Paschalii,* 1581. This is a political commentary on the first four books of the *Annals* which utilizes Lipsius' edition of 1574,[16] but is not acquainted, as we should expect, with Lipsius' commentary of 1581. The author, Carolus Paschalius (*alias* Charles Paschal, Carlo Pasquale, Pasqual), whose personality we shall presently consider, was then living in France in a circle of learned and influential persons from whom the news might easily reach Lipsius that he was preparing a political commentary on Tacitus.[17] The next political work on Tacitus known to us is the commentary by Annibal Scoto, 'cubicularius intimus' of Pope Sixtus V, which was published in 1589 – too late for the reference in Lipsius' preface of 1580.

But even if Lipsius did not allude to Paschalius, our main conclusion will not be affected; the work by Paschalius must be accepted as the first published political commentary on Tacitus, because Lipsius did not yet know of any in existence in August 1580.

III

Annibale Scoto, who died during the revision of the proofs of his commentary,[18] never mentions Paschalius. Yet it seems certain that he knew him and extended to the whole of the *Annals* and *Histories* the pattern set up by Paschalius for the first four books of the *Annals*. Scoto was sharper in formulation, more abundant in classical quotations, better acquainted with contemporary history (and better trained to use it for flattery). But the similarity of his approach to that of Paschalius cannot be explained in terms of 'Zeitgeist'. First, I shall compare a page from one commentary with the corresponding page from the other commentary. The passage was taken at random and turned out to be *Annals* III, 30, 3 (from 'aetate provecta speciem magis in amicitia principis quam vim tenuit') – 31 (to the end of the chapter). The quotation is long, but may convey an idea of the diluted and pedestrian Machiavellianism of the two commentaries – Machiavellianism reduced to mere prudence.

Paschalius, p. 154

Ex intimis amicis principis alii vim alii speciem in illius amicitia tenent. Vim quidem prudentes, üdem magno et acri ingenio praediti homines, quorum consiliis principes utuntur; speciem ii, quos aut ob insignem nobilitatem et longa familiae decora, a suo latere princeps vix unquam abscedere patitur, illi praesidio, hi ornamento dicuntur esse principi.

Sciant homines esse in fatis ut raro potentiae sint sempiternae.

Satias omnium rerum est, etiam illarum quae hominum opinionibus maximae sunt et amplissimae; atque adeo omnium, cuius modi tandem illae sunt, una excepta virtute.
Etsi id perraro accidit, accidit tamen ut nihil sit reliquum in rebus humanis quod homines cupere possint: adeo suas ipsi spes vicerunt.

Callidi principes ita assuescunt falsa specie quidquid agunt obtegere.
Quae princeps agere decrevit, non omnia simul et uno impetu patrare, sed eo paulatim meditari et quasi aliud agens, sensim coeptare debet, ita qui longam absentiam meditatur, neque id cuiquam palam faciat, neque

Scoto (ed. Frankfort, 1592), p. 225

In amicitia principis alii tenent speciem, alii vim, et raro utramque simul. Sed satius est vim sine specie quam speciem sine vi tenere. Sic infra lib. 16 Ann., etc.

Raro est sempiterna potentia et notent aulici qui ea intemperanter utuntur.

Evenit hoc inter principes et aulicos ut saepe satias capiat illos, cum omnia tribuerunt, aut hos, cum iam reliquum nihil est quod cupiant. Sed nescio an hodie talium aulicorum multi reperiantur.

Princeps non semper quod habet in animo expromit, sed aliud agens, aliud intendit. Sic meditantes longam et continuam absentiam ab urbe, simulant discedere caussa firmandae valetudinis.

se ex hominum conspectu proripiat, sed paulatim se subducat.

Princeps cui est filius iam adultus, specie firmandae valetudinis, aut obtendens alias causas, debet per aliquot dies et menses secedere, eique aliqua reip. munia mandare, ut hoc pacto is paulatim regendae reip. assuescat.

Parvae saepe res ad magna certamina progrediuntur.

Iuniorum est loco maioribus natu decedere. Id nisi fit, senioribus apud senatum queri licet, qui iuventutis irreverentiam gravibus decretis notare et potest et debet. Ratio est apud Arist. lib. I polit. cap. 7 τὸ πρεσβύτερον καὶ τέλειον τοῦ νεωτέρου καὶ ἀτελοῦς ἡγεμονικώτερον *(= Pol. I, 5, 1259 b 4).*

Haec est optima occasio quam principes dant filiis addiscendi artem regendi subditos. Nempe se a negotiis aliquantisper subtrahere ut illi soli munia principatus impleant; et hinc optimi gubernatores subditorum fiant, etc.

Prudentis est nullam rem, etsi parvam, spernere. Nam saepe e parva re materia praebetur apiscendi favoris et odii.

Decet iuvenes cedere loco senioribus, et iuventutis irreverentia gravibus decretis notari debet. Et huc pertinet institutum illud Spartanorum; de quo vide apud Aristotelem in Politica et Plut. in Licurgo [sic].

The last lines of Scoto's passage require some discussion. He adds to his paraphrase of Tacitus: 'et huc pertinet institutum illud Spartanorum de quo vide . . . '. But Aristotle's *Politics* had nothing on the 'institutum illud Spartanorum' – presumably the custom for young people to rise and give a seat to their elders (*cf.* for instance Plut. *Apophth. Lac.* 55, p. 235 D). I cannot help feeling that Scoto took the passage in Aristotle's *Politics* quoted in this connection by Paschalius as referring specifically to Sparta – which it does not – and added from memory a reference to Plut. *Lycurgus*, which is more defensible (*cf.* especially chs. 15 and 17), yet not entirely appropriate.[19]

In other points the similarity between Scoto and Paschalius is much closer, as when both writers complain about the conditions of the legislation of their own times and introduce Justinian *à propos* of *Ann.* III, 25, 1:

Paschalius, p. 149	Scoto, p. 221
Hoc Iustinianus frustra tentavit: cum hodie non tam legibus quam foeda legum laceratione laboremus.	*Cui rei etsi Iustinianus imperator temporibus suis satis providerit, tamen hodie tantus est librorum in hac materia acervus ut vere dici possit quod non minus legibus quam flagitiis laboremus.*

The following passages seem to me decisive for the dependence of Scoto on Paschalius. On *Ann.* III, 34, 2 ('multa duritiae veterum <in> melius et laetius mutata'):

Quae a veteribus duriter ac severe sunt instituta de iis aliquid remitti ac melius laetiusque mutari debent, praecipue si id postulat ratio temporis.

Scoto, p. 229

Multa in dies a duritie veterum melius et laetius mutantur. Idque iure merito fieri solet, cum sic ratio et conditio temporis postulat.

On III, 36, 2 ('neque a diis nisi iustas supplicum preces audiri'):

Paschalius, p. 158

Si quidem nulla re magis deo similes esse nec possunt nec debent quam iustitia.

Scoto, p. 232

Et nulla re alia magis possunt Deo principes similes quam iustitia.

On 1, 41, 3 ('sed nihil aeque flexit quam invidia in Treviros'):

Paschalius, p. 37

Nihil aeque hominum animos perstringit atque invidia: quae non solum est, cum quis ob alius felicitatem livet et marcescit, sed cum quae nobis debentur ea ipsa aliis tribui videmus, quae sane est iustior quam illa prior.

Scoto, p. 60

Vere hoc nomen invidiae tribui debet illi qui ob alterius felicitatem livet et marcescit; non illi qui videt alteri tribui, quae sui ipsius propria sunt. Haec enim in virum bonum cadere potest et non est iniusta, ut prior.

On 1, 42, 1 ('imperium Romanum ceteri exercitus defendent'):

Paschalius, p. 37

Magno principi cautio est adhibenda ne quicquid virium penes se est, id contractum unum in locum simul semperque habeat, etc. Sic. lib. I histor., etc.

Scoto, p. 60

Hinc discant prudentes principes non in unum locum semper habere quidquid ipsi tenent virium, etc. Proinde ut auctor infra lib. I Hist. inquit, etc.

On 1, 43, 4 ('discedite a contactu ac dividite turbidos'):

Paschalius, p. 39

Cum nemo non bonus civis bonusque et obsequens miles haberi velit.

Scoto, p. 63

Cum nemo non existimari velit bonus civis et obsequens miles imperatori suo.

On 1, 47, 1 ('neque se remque publicam in casum dare'):

Paschalius, p. 41	*Scoto, p. 66*
Princeps et respublica eo vinculo sunt adstricti ut nihil alteri separatim accidere possit, quod idem ad alterum non pertineat. Hinc fit, ut nihil sibi princeps utile esse putet quod idem reip. non expediat.	*Ea est principis et Reip. connexio ut nihil uni eorum accidere queat, quod ad alterum non pertineat. Unde princeps nihil debet sibi utile aestimare quod Reip. identidem non conducat.*

IV

The immense Tacitist literature may be roughly divided into three groups:

(1) Political observations and aphorisms written on the margins of the text either in the form of a running commentary or as isolated remarks. These observations are often nothing more than a paraphrase of Tacitus. Thus it is impossible to separate these collections of aphorisms from the anthologies of Tacitean sentences. We can mention among the commentaries, after Paschalius and Scoto, those by Traiano Boccalini (written before 1613, published first in 1677), by Alamos de Barrientos (1614), and by Amelot de la Houssaie (1683 and 1692). Collections of sentences from Tacitus (or of aphorisms inspired by Tacitus) were produced by A. Piccolomini, 1609; G. Frachetta, *Il Seminario dei governi*, 1613; [B. Arias Montano], 1614;[20] F. Frezza, 1616; B. Puccio, 1621,[21] etc., etc.

(2) Lengthy discussions of selected passages from Tacitus, such as the *Discorsi* by Scipione Ammirato (1594); and those by F. Cauriana (1600); the *Osservationi sopra i cinque libri degli Annali* by G. Pagliari del Bosco (1612); the *Discursus aliquot .. non modo iucundi sed et utiles* by Ianus Gruterus (1st ed., 1604; 2nd ed., 1627); the *Discorsi* by V. Malvezzi (1622: translated into English, 1642); the *Considerazioni sopra Cornelio Tacito* by Pio Mutio (1623), etc., etc. The theoretically important *Quaestiones ac discursus in duos primos libros annalium*, by P. A. Canonherius (1609) belong here, although they lose sight of Tacitus. Th. Gordon's commentary also is a belated offshoot (1728) of this type.

(3) Systematic treatises on traditional topics exclusively or almost exclusively composed of sentences from Tacitus, such as A. Gölnitz, *Princeps ex C. Tacito*, 1636; A. S. Freystein, *Consiliarius ex C. Tacito*,

1653; I. Celsus, *Princeps ex C. Tacito*, 1670. The highly significant series of books by that extravagant scholar Cyriacus Lentulus which begins with an *Augustus sive de convertenda in Monarchiam republica iuxta ductum et mentem Taciti*, 1645, comes rather into this than into the former class.

The third group is obviously later and derivative. It systematizes the results of 'Tacitismo' according to pre-existing schemes. It need not detain us. The first group is the earliest. Paschalius was the originator, and it always preserved the form of an aphorism used by him; Guicciardini's *Avvertimenti* had just been published by J. Corbinelli in Paris in 1576.[22]

The literary type of the second group is not dependent on Paschalius. Indeed, it is nothing but the application to Tacitus of the literary methods of Machiavelli as they appear in the *Discorsi sulla Prima Deca*. The chapters of the *Discorsi*, in which Machiavelli discusses three quotations and one pseudo-quotation from Tacitus,[23] and the reply by Guicciardini to his considerations may be called the forerunners of the whole 'Tacitismo'. Another discussion on Machiavellian lines is to be found in a short *discorso* by L. Salviati on the opening words of the *Annals* which was published in 1582.[24] But a full discussion of Tacitus according to the Machiavellian model is not to be found before the *Discorsi* by Scipione Ammirato (1594), when Paschalius and Scoto had already produced their commentaries. The conclusion we come to for the moment is that the Machiavellian type of *discorsi* prepared the way for 'Tacitismo' but was not adopted by the first two fully-fledged Tacitists, Paschalius and Scoto.

V

The immediate success of Paschalius' commentary must have been considerable in France. The commentary was republished in 1600 without the corresponding text of Tacitus under the title *Gnomae seu axiomata politica ex Tacito* – a confirmation that commentary and collection of aphorisms were interchangeable literary forms. The *Gnomae* were again printed as an appendix to a Paris *editio variorum* of Tacitus in 1608.[25] The transformation of the commentary into *axiomata* explains why the reference-books know only of the *Gnomae seu axiomata* of 1600

– not of the original edition of 1581[26] – whereas Toffanin quotes the commentary of 1581 and the *Gnomae* of 1600 as two different works.[27]

But Paschalius had confined his commentary to the first four books of the *Annals* and had referred but briefly to contemporary events. In France itself, his work was later criticized as insufficient. To quote G. Naudé's *Bibliographia politica* (1633), 'Paschalis, denique, tanquam impiger xenagogus, thesauros istius auctoris non quidem effundit, sed virgula tantum ostendit atque subindicat'.[28] Outside France, Scoto replaced him by producing a complete commentary and giving many more references to his own time. Scoto's reputation among contemporaries was not that of a first-class scholar, but his popularity was considerable. His book was reprinted in Frankfort in 1592 and got into the bibliography of Colerus as an authoritative treatise. In 1594 Scipione Ammirato proved that the Machiavellian *discorsi* suited Tacitus better and gained many followers, but Scoto had already found an imitator in the Spaniard Alamos de Barrientos, and also directly influenced later studies on Tacitus.[29]

VI

The fact that Paschalius was the earliest political commentator of Tacitus helps us, perhaps, to a better understanding of the development of the Tacitist movement.

In the period 1515–80 interest in Tacitus, though originating in Italy, tended to spread more especially outside Italy; and, though inspired by politicians, tended to attract lawyers. I leave aside the special German interest in the *Germania* and Arminius. Alciatus and Ferretus, who edited Tacitus, were Roman lawyers: the first an Italian who developed strong French connections, the second an Italian who became to all purposes a Frenchman. Balduinus noted how 'duo aetatis nostrae nobilissimi interpretes iuris, And. Alciatus et Aem. Ferretus, in emendandis atque explicandis Taciti annalibus multum operae posuerint'.[30] Bodin said of Tacitus: 'Nullus profecto historicus magistratui ac iudici utilior'.[31] Towards 1570–80 the two most eminent students of Tacitus were Muretus[32] and Lipsius[33] – neither of them Italian either by birth or by intellectual training. Muretus (incidentally also a student of Roman Law) was interested in Tacitus as a stylist and as the historian of a monarchy; Lipsius took him as a stylist, as the historian of a monarchy, and as a teacher of 'constantia'. Muretus lectured on Tacitus in Rome in 1580-1, and it would be unwise to underrate the importance of these lectures for his Italian listeners: he undoubtedly contributed to the preparation of the atmosphere for the coming 'Tacitismo'. But he had no Italian pupil. His real pupil he had found ten years before in the person of Lipsius. The anti-Ciceronian reaction and the Stoic revival became practically indistinguishable in Lipsius.[34]

From Alciatus (1517) to Lipsius (1574) this movement developed behind a strong barricade of erudition. If one excepts Bodin (and one can doubt whether Bodin has to be excepted), all the people concerned were professional scholars of the severest type. Machiavelli, of course, loomed large. Lipsius did not make much mystery about his sympathies for Machiavelli.[35] But his admiration for Tacitus was not simply Machiavellianism in disguise. It was a learned revision of historical, moral and stylistic values behind the iron gates of erudition.

What had up till then been a discreet movement of learning burst into boisterous publicity in Italy about 1590. It took the form of lengthy books in which the words of Tacitus were isolated from their historical context and were made to serve the purposes of a disguised Machiavellianism. The Tacitist movement, as it was called, spread from Italy over Europe. Tacitist books were written everywhere. Only in England did the interest in Tacitus, such as it was, preserve the more scholarly attitude which Lipsius recommended and Bacon maintained.[36] There are plenty of good and well-known reasons to explain this sudden vulgarization of Tacitus. That it was not superficial is proved, *inter alia*, by its popularity throughout the seventeenth century. But one would expect to find a link somewhere between the prevalently transalpine interest in Tacitus of 1570-80 and the explicit Italian 'Tacitismo' of the nineties. Carolus Paschalius or 'Carlo Pasquale' may well provide it.

VII

Paschalius[37] was born at Cuneo (Piedmont) in 1547 of an aristocratic family. Educated in Geneva as a Calvinist, but later becoming a Catholic, he finally settled in France and accepted various positions in the French civil and diplomatic service. Guy de Pibrac – the refined and brilliant, perhaps too brilliant, chancellor of Marguerite de Valois – was his patron. Pibrac loved the Psalms and Seneca above all writers (as Paschalius himself wrote in a biographical sketch): his *Quatrains*, indeed, repeat many a Stoic idea.[38] This combination of simplified Christianity and simplified Stoicism Paschalius shared. Scaliger, who must have known him personally, expressed the following opinion on him:

Paschal est un gentil personnage, il escrit bien, il a fait de si jolies prières, il a esté nourry à Genève: il est conseiller d'Estat. Je m'esbahis qu'il a quitté l'estat d'Avocat Général à Rouen.[39]

The 'jolies prières' are the *Christianae preces* which went through three editions between 1602 and 1609. Their general religious attitude (so far as my scanty theological knowledge goes) is latitudinarian; the main preoccupation is the religious peace of France.[40] On the other hand, Paschalius' approach to Latin literature is clearly defined in the preface of his commentary on Tacitus where all other Latin (and Greek) writers are subordinated to Seneca and Tacitus:

sine illorum ope [= of the other writers] hos adiri non posse, hos, inquam, gravissimos et sapientissimos vitae moderatores, Senecam et hunc nostrum.

The same intransigent 'Senecan' attitude – which is the clearest proof of Paschalius' connection with the neo-Stoic movement – is defended in the short treatise *De optimo genere elocutionum* (1595).

The rest of Paschalius' activity can only be outlined. A special study of it must be reserved for another occasion. About 1571, when still a Protestant, Paschalius dedicated *De Morte Christi Dialogi Decem* to Lord Burghley.[41] In 1574–5 he apparently followed Guy de Pibrac in the Polish adventure with Henry III.[42] He certainly delivered an oration in Venice when Henry III passed through there on his return from Poland and got 'vingt escus' for the performance.[43] In 1584 he revealed to the government of Geneva the plot organized against the city by François de Gatagurel, seigneur de la Poype.[44] In 1589 he may have come to England on behalf of Henry IV, then in trouble.[45] In 1592 he was 'Conseiller et Avocat Général' at Rouen; between 1604 and 1614 he was French ambassador to the Grisons. He was made 'Conseiller d'État' (year not stated), and died in 1625 as 'Seigneur et vicomte de la Queute' near Abbeville.[46] In the first period of his residence in France he maintained relations with the Piedmontese court. In 1574 he published a Latin speech on the death of the other Marguerite de Valois, the wife of Duke Emanuele Filiberto,[47] and in 1581 he dedicated his Tacitus to Duke Carlo Emanuele I. In 1584 he published his life of Pibrac, in 1586 he translated from Italian into French a eulogy 'della gran Caterina de' Medici reina di Francia',[48] but did not write the eulogy of Elias Vinet, the great editor of Ausonius, which is usually attributed to him.[49] His literary activity became intense only after 1595, when he published his treatise on style mentioned above, a famous book, *De Legato* (1598), which made his reputation as an authority on international law,[50] a *Censura animi ingrati* (1601), a heavy dissertation, *De Coronis* (1610) – a magnified Pauly–Wissowa article – an account of his *Legatio Rhoetica* (1615), a dissertation on *Virtutes et Vitia* (1615).

We must not judge the young author of the commentary on Tacitus (1581) by his later developments. But enough has been said to show that the commentary on Tacitus cannot be dissociated from the Franco-Dutch movement championed by Muretus and Lipsius. He has the same admiration for both Seneca and Tacitus; his very style proves him to be a follower of the 'Attic' reaction (as 'Senecan' style was called). Pibrac obviously influenced him in the same direction; and it is likely that the great French supporter of Christian Stoicism, G. Du Vair, was as well known to him as he was to Pibrac.[51]

On the other hand, it is not indulging in fantasy to say that in 1581 Paschalius was still much of an Italian. The Machiavellian streak is far stronger in his commentary on Tacitus than in any other of his works.[52] He was still in touch with the Piedmontese court – a nest of Machiavellians in action.[53] No doubt he was also well acquainted with those Italians who carried their Machiavellian lore lightly at the court of Henry III and enraged Henri Estienne. It is hardly necessary to recall Davila's picture:

Il re [Henry III] si riduceva ogni giorno dopo pranzo con Baccio del Bene e con Giacopo Corbinelli, Fiorentini, huomini di molte lettere greche e latine da' quali si faceva leggere Polibio, Cornelio Tacito e molto più spesso i Discorsi et il Principe del Machiavelli.[54]

Tacitus is there, and one cannot separate this interest of the court of Henry III in Tacitus from Paschalius' commentary. He had an Italian inheritance and French education. He had legal training and antiquarian doctrine, but also political qualifications. He was conscious of belonging to both Italian and French culture. One can understand that he might set about extracting from Tacitus all those reflections which others were content with reading into Tacitus. Lipsius thought it vulgar to expound Tacitus for the advantage of politicians. About 1588 Montaigne, the friend of Lipsius, said that Tacitus' works were 'une pepiniere de discours ethiques et politiques pour la provision et ornement de ceulx qui tiennent quelque reng au maniement du monde'.[55] But one can hardly imagine Montaigne providing ready-made these 'discours éthiques et politiques'. Paschalius was not the first (and not the last)

Italian to think aloud what other people kept to themselves. Scoto got hold of his observations, preserved (characteristically) the Latin medium and the literary form of his predecessor and cultivated on Italian soil the seed that Paschalius had sown in France. Scipione Ammirato followed and realized to a fuller extent the implications of the movement. Here it is wise to re-read the preface to a Latin translation of Scipione Ammirato published in Frankfort in 1609:

> *Colloquebamur aliquando nonnihil de re litteraria, variosque praesertim de Italicis quibusdam ingeniis, rei politicae plus iusto deditis, sermones serebamus; absurdam rem quibusdam videri aiebat [Christ. Pflugius] civilis facultatis praecepta ab iis viris tradi qui libertatem ne summis quidem labris degustant, cogunturque ad placitum potentiorum, non ad suae normam rationis disserere et de tota republica eas plerumque sententias proferre, quae dominantium rei conducunt magis quam naturae consentiunt.*[56]

VIII

This is not the place to estimate the value of 'Tacitismo' as a whole. Whether we like it or not, it percolated through the political and historical thought of a whole century both because of its Machiavellian and its anti-Machiavellian elements. It roused the opposition of Jesuits and (later) of Free-thinkers. It helped the discussion on Machiavelli when Machiavelli was too dangerous to be dealt with directly. It combined anti-tyrannical sentiments with realistic remarks on modern and ancient tyrants, and finally prepared the way to what has been called the 'red' Tacitus of the French Revolution.

We may rather conclude with a query. Perhaps no political writer of the Counter-reformation was more influential than the Piedmontese Giovanni Botero; and no moment of the life of Botero was more decisive than that year 1585 in which he went to Paris for secret negotiations on behalf of Duke Carlo Emanuele I.[57] In 1582-3, when he wrote *De Regia Sapientia*,[58] Botero apparently did not yet know of Tacitus as a political thinker. In 1589 the preface to the *Ragion di Stato* contained the famous declaration:

> *Nelle corti di re e di prencipi grandi, hor di qua hor di là da monti . . . tra l'altre cose da me osservate mi ha recato somma meraviglia il sentire tutto il dì mentovare Ragione di Stato, e in cotal materia citare hora Nicolò Machiavelli, hora Cornelio Tacito; quello perché dà precetti appartenenti al*

governo e al reggimento de' popoli: questo perché esprime vivamente l'arte usata da Tiberio Cesare e per conseguire e per conservarsi nell'Imperio di Roma. Mi parve poi cosa degna (già che io mi trovava bene spesso tra gente che di sì fatte cose ragionava) ch'io ne sapessi ancor render qualche conto.

Is it impossible that Carlo Pasquale was one of the people 'di là da monti', who introduced Botero to Tacitus?

*Appendix ***

José Ruysschaert, *Juste Lipse et les Annales de Tacite. Une méthode de critique textuelle au XVIe siècle* (Recueil de travaux d'histoire et de philologie, 3e série: fasc. 34). Louvain, Bibliothèque de l'Université, 1949, p. 222.

I

Books that show in detail how humanists worked are few. Now we are offered a contribution of permanent value on Justus Lipsius for which the author must be warmly congratulated. Nobody has ever entertained serious doubts on the merits of Lipsius as an editor of Tacitus. His combination of feeling for style with historical knowledge is still a challenge to any editor of an historical text. Dr Ruysschaert bases his careful analysis of Lipsius' methods as a textual critic on a survey of the changes introduced by him into the text of Tacitus. Having diligently compared all the known editions of the fifteenth and sixteenth centuries he is in a position to establish exactly the paternity of each conjecture (he is not acquainted with Ch. Paschal's edition which I discussed in this *Journal* XXXVII, 1947, p. 91, but I do not expect it would have made any difference in the matter of textual criticism). He shows that Lipsius took the *Gryphiana* of 1542 as the foundation of his text and that he utilized also Beatus Rhenanus' edition of 1544. Contrary to current opinion, Rhenanus' text of 1544 is not a mere reprint of the edition of 1533. R. is able to give back to Rhenanus some emendations attributed to Lipsius by modern editors. It would also seem that Lipsius utilized an otherwise unknown edition of Venice, 1494. Though the facts offered by R.

*Journal of Roman Studies, 39, 1949, pp. 190–2. *Cf.* C. O. Brink, ibid., 41, 1951, pp. 32–51.

on p. 25 are impressive and, as far as I could verify them, correct, the mysterious *Veneta* 1494 deserves further investigation.

Lipsius did not seek access to the *Medicei*. They were first systematically explored by C. Pichena, as Lipsius acknowledged in his last revision of the text of Tacitus issued posthumously in 1607. He worked on three Roman MSS. which R. has identified as *Vat. Lat.* 1863, 1864, and *Neapolitanus* IV C. 21. R. also examined the notes scribbled by Lipsius in the margin of some of his books now in Leyden and compared them with the notes on Tacitus by Muret and Claude Chifflet. Both complained of having been exploited without acknowledgement by Lipsius. The result is not a complete vindication of his honesty. In the case of Chifflet, it is now plain that Lipsius appropriated some of his friend's conjectures. Indeed, certain erasures in the notes written by Lipsius on his copy of the *Gryphiana* 1542 show that an attempt was made to destroy the evidence for the origin of five conjectures. As the question whether Lipsius was truthful or not bears on the problem of the authenticity of his *Oratio* II, which will presently be discussed, I must quote the actual words of Dr Ruysschaert: 'Les singulières ratures de ce volume s'expliquent alors naturellement par le désir de l'humaniste belge de ne pas laisser à la merci d'un ami indiscret les preuves d'un manque d'honnêteté' (p. 151).

These strictures on the character of Lipsius do not affect the substance of his work. Out of more than 1,000 corrections to the edition of 1542 only about a dozen were certainly taken from other scholars in a way which must be called fraudulent. Doubts remain about conjectures in which Muret and Lipsius concur, as Lipsius had access to Muret's notes in Rome, but it is fairly obvious that the coincidence must be fortuitous in the majority of cases. Muret himself, at least in the *Variae Lectiones* XI, I (*Opera*, ed. Ruhnken-Frotscher III, p. 238), was restrained in his claims against Lipsius. The magnitude of the latter's contribution to the improvement of the text of Tacitus is well documented by the complete list of his suggestions provided by R. in an appendix (pp. 172–216). The origin of each emendation (whether a conjecture or the reading of a MS. previously unexploited) is indicated. Where I have checked the list it has proved to be reliable (on p. 24 'l'édition de 1492 conservé a Leyde' seems to stand for 'l'édition de 1542').

II

For the work done by Dr Ruysschaert I have only admiration, but I venture to add that his general conclusions seem to me much less persuasive than his detailed analysis. R. is satisfied that Lipsius learnt little from Muret about editing Tacitus, because Muret did not go back to the manuscripts. He thinks that basically Lipsius applied to Tacitus the methods he had learnt as an undergraduate at Louvain (1563–8), where the example of Petrus Nannius, who had died in 1557, was undoubtedly still influential (see the book on him by A. Polet, Louvain, 1936). Nobody will deny the impact of the teaching of the Collegium Trilingue on Lipsius: Louvain would not have exercised such a permanent fascination on Lipsius' mind if he had not felt that he had got something of great value out of it. From his delightful tribute to the friendships of his undergraduate years in the second book of the *Variae Lectiones* (published in 1569, but written before the Italian journey; and *cf.* also the third book of the *Antiquae Lectiones*, 1575) to the monograph on Louvain of 1605, the emotional appeal of the Alma Mater is obvious in the work of her son. But his autobiographical letter to Joh. Woverius, of 1600 (*Epist. Cent. iii misc.* 87), is not very definite on what he learnt at Louvain. Also his judgement on the classical teaching in *Lovanium, sive opidi et academiae eius descriptio* (p. 99) is somewhat reserved: 'Viros aliquot insignes et professores habuit, inter eos Petrum Nannium, qui alios post se, ut meum iudicium est, reliquit et fortasse relinquet. At nunc iacent ibi omnia et silent.' Johannes Stadius, the commentator on Florus, who apparently was at Louvain about 1566, does not seem to have left any mark on Lipsius. The friendship between him and S. Pighius, the great antiquarian and editor of Valerius Maximus, who though educated at Louvain never professed there, probably developed after Lipsius' return from Italy (the evidence known to me points to a meeting in Vienna in 1572: *cf. Epist. Cent. i misc.* 5 and A. Roersch, *Biogr. Nat. de Belgique* XVII, p. 508; but the matter would repay research). If there is anything remarkable in Lipsius' *Variae Lectiones* written when he was about 20 years old, it is the fact that he was already living within the wide horizon of French and Italian humanism. The two names one meets most frequently are Lambinus and Muretus, but Turnebus is not absent. The very title *Variae Lectiones* recalls Pietro Vettori, and Pietro Vettori he admired and challenged when he wrote: 'P. sane Victorius magnus cum primis vir et de quo illum Ennii proferre merito possim "Multa tenens antiqua sepulta", cum in Graecis et Latinis auctoribus partim castigandis partim interpretandis studiose versatus sit, attamen tot voluminibus variarum lectionum suarum Propertium nunc nostrum semel modo atque id quasi praeteriens nominavit' (p. 133). Also his judgement on Beroaldus senior shows that he was up to date: 'Beroaldus homo, ut illa tempora ferebant, neque indoctus et minime malus' (p. 182). When he went to Rome in 1568 he was well prepared to make friends with Paolo Manuzio, Fulvio Orsini, Muret. He also became personally acquainted with P. Vettori and C. Sigonio (*Epist. Cent. iii misc.* 87). The details of these relations can now be best studied in the article by R. himself 'Le séjour de Juste Lipse à Rome d'après ses Antiquae Lectiones et sa correspondance', *Bull. Inst. Hist. Belge de Rome* 24, 1947–8, pp. 139–92.

The origin of Lipsius' interest in Tacitus cannot be dissociated from his residence in Rome. He arrived in Rome a Ciceronian and departed an admirer of Tacitus and Seneca (though not yet an exclusive one). The change, as M. V. Croll explained long ago, was undoubtedly due to Muret's influence. What Muret could not give to Lipsius was the taste for long-term systematic and many-sided research on a big subject. But some Italians could offer the needed example. Sigonio said that he was tired of simple emendations and aimed at a constructive work on a historical basis: 'Veggio tutto il mondo scrivere Varie Lettioni che non è altro che dir quicquid in buccam, ma continuar una materia senza guida d'alcun antico, et trattarla pienamente et methodicamente, questo reputo opra da Hercole o da Carlo Magno, et non da Carlo Sigonio. Si che non havessi cominciato, vi prometto che non entrerei in questa così difficile impresa' (from a letter of 1567 in P. De Nolhac, 'Pietro Vettori et Carlo Sigonio. Correspondance avec Fulvio Orsini', *Studi e Documenti di Storia e Diritto* X, 1889, p. 142). The method Lipsius followed in his edition is not substantially different from that applied by Manuzio and Vettori to Cicero and by Sigonio to Livy. Combination of search for manuscripts with historical learning and knowledge of style characterizes these scholars. Lipsius shares also the limitation of Manuzio and Sigonio to Latin. That is why P. Vettori, the last of the Grecians of Florence, ultimately meant less to him. See, for instance, what Lipsius says on Manuzio in the third of his *Orationes*.

Whether Lipsius learnt first in Rome to appreciate Tacitus as a guide to political life cannot be decided. But it is worth remembering that in 1572 Tacitus was treated in Rome as a subject to be banished from the teaching in the Sapienza. A letter by Muret to Dupuis, though published by P. De Nolhac, *Mélanges Graux*, 1884, p. 390, is not perhaps as well known as it deserves to be: 'Ie dis aux Cardinaux Sirlet et Alciat ausquels cela touche, que i'aurois enuie de lire Tacitus. Valde dehortati sunt ne id facerem; male eum alicubi loqui de Christianis; male de Iudaeis. denique qu'ils estoient en quelque penser de le prohiber. Multa quidem dixi cur excusatus abirem, sed nihil ab eis extorquere potui. Cela m'a tellement rempli de desdaing que ie voudrois quasi n'avoir iamais touché cest auteur. Neque tamen deterreri possum ne eum amem, ne legam, ne adsidue manibus teram.'

The political implications are so relevant to Lipsius' studies on Tacitus that one is surprised to find them overlooked by R. in his book. He simply follows L. Roersch (art. *Lipse* in *Biographie Nationale de Belgique* XII, p. 243) in doubting that Lipsius ever wrote the *Oratio II, cum inciperet publice interpretari Cornelium Tacitum*. This speech was published after Lipsius' death as one of those delivered in Jena in 1572 (*Orationes Octo*, Darmstadii, 1607, pp. 27–38). If authentic, it would be by far the most important evidence for what Lipsius thought about Tacitus in 1572, two years after having left Italy. The speech presents two difficulties: (1) it is meant to be an introduction to a course on Tacitus, while a letter by Lipsius to Joh. Camerarius of November 1572 mentions lectures on Caesar and Cicero, but not on Tacitus (*Justi Lipsi ad C. Suetoni Tranquilli tres posteriores libros Commentarii. Eiusdem epistolarum praetermissarum decades sex*, Offenbaci 1610, pp. 111–13); (2) it conveys the impression that Lipsius went back to Louvain from Italy before the Duke of Alba entered the Netherlands (1567), while the truth is that Lipsius left for Italy in 1568.

Argument (1) can be appreciated properly only if one reads the text of the relevant paragraph in the letter to Camerarius, which not all students of Lipsius seem to have done: 'De Studiis meis, Commentarios IIX Antiquarum Lectionum habeo in manibus e quibus proxima epistola. Si libenti tibi erit, pauca licebit degustes. Scholia in Cornelium Tacitum ad veteres libros emendatum iam perpolivi, sed his Typographis nihil audeo committere, αἰδέομαι τρῶας. Caesaris Commentarios publice doceo apud eos qui numquam per nebulam nomen elegantioris doctrinae audiverunt. At ego ineptus etiam epistulas ad Atticum adiunxi quae sunt videlicet istorum hominum. Sed mi Camerari ut video et ut res istae fluunt, licebit brevi ut has literas sine rivali amemus.' Lipsius speaks not of his teaching but of his studies. He mentions his lectures on Caesar and Cicero only to round off the picture of his studies and incidentally to let his friend know that his pupils are dunces – a minor pleasure no teacher will ever deny to himself. There is no reason to suppose that Lipsius would necessarily have mentioned that he had given or was giving or intended to give in the near future a course on Tacitus. In the same academic year he also delivered lectures on Roman antiquities (the evidence republished in V. A. Nordman, 'Justus Lipsius als Geschichtsforscher und Geschichtslehrer', *Annales Acad. Fennicae* 28, 1932, p. 35).

The force of argument (2) entirely depends on the idea one forms of Lipsius' truthfulness. The speaker intends to stress the sincerity of his conversion to Protestantism on which the Jena chair depended. Without committing himself to any definite chronological statement (a point already noticed by Nordman, p. 34, n. 2) he tries to give the impression that he saw 'primam lucem Evangelii' in Rome and that the horrors of the Duke of Alba's regime completed his conversion. The true chronology would have shown that Lipsius never contemplated conversion before coming to Jena. Apart from the many accusations launched by Th. Sagittarius in his well-documented but heinous *Lipsius Proteus* (1614) there are at least two cases in which it is difficult to deny that Lipsius intended to deceive. One is the above mentioned deletion of the evidence that he had borrowed conjectures from his friend Chifflet. The other is his denial of having written in 1573 the speech *De Concordia*. This speech was published by his enemies in 1600 after his return to his early faith and is republished in the *Orationes Octo* quoted above. No one who examines the evidence put together by K. Halm in *Sitz. Bayer. Ak.* 1882, vol. II, I ff. ('Ueber die Echtheit der dem Justus Lipsius zugeschriebenen Reden') can escape the conclusion that *De Concordia* was written by Lipsius.

The authenticity of *Oratio* II would be even more certainly proved if we could rely on a contemporary statement by J. M. Meyfart that he saw the autograph of Lipsius (the text reported by F. van der Haeghen, *Bibl. Lipsienne* II, 41, and *cf.* R. Neidhardt, *De Iusti Lipsii Vita Jenensi Orationibusque ab eo habitis*, Progr. Gymnasii Passaviensis, 1893, p. 39). No weight, on the other hand, should be given to the statement, however definite, by Caspar Sagittarius (*Vita et Scripta Iusti Lipsii* in J. G. Meuschenii *Vitae Summorum . . . Virorum* IV, Coburgi, 1741, p. 191) that Lipsius lectured on Tacitus in 1572. It may be a simple inference from the speech. Even without the last mentioned witnesses, the balance of the evidence seems to be clearly in favour of the authenticity of *Oratio* II. What Lipsius has to say on Tacitus in comparison with Livy and Sallust is very important as a signpost to the direction his thought was taking: 'Sed tamen, quod ad Rempublicam et mores nostros attinet, quid afferre Livius potest, praeter bella, exercitus et seditiones tribunitias? Iucundum auribus fateor, sed ego aurium voluptatem cum animi utilitate coniunctam desidero.'

By applying the method of Sigonio, Vettori and Manuzio to the understanding of Tacitus, Lipsius was in fact completing a revolution in historical outlook. Tacitus replaced Livy as the most important Roman historian. Lipsius remained the representative of this new historical outlook for the rest of his life and for long afterwards. He revealed Tacitus to Europe. This statement must be qualified in two ways. First, as I mentioned in my paper in *JRS*, 1947, Lipsius refused to follow the fashion and write a political commentary on Tacitus. Whoever assesses the distinguishing features of Lipsius as a commentator on Tacitus must also remember what Lipsius did not do because this is as important as what he did. He recognized how easy it was to append political remarks to Tacitus – and how difficult it was to interpret him. Secondly, he cared for Seneca, or rather for Stoicism, not less than for Tacitus; and it would make an interesting chapter of his life to explain how he came to care so much for Seneca (R. Kirk, in the introduction to the reprint of Sir John Stradling's translation of *De Constantia*, Rutgers University Press, New Jersey, 1939, is good yet not exhaustive). Tacitus explained to him the misery of contemporary politics, but Stoicism was a faith he jealously preserved throughout the vicissitudes of his life. He was different from the contemporary 'Tacitists' not only because he was more scholarly, but also because he had a positive moral faith. Perhaps even now it is good to remember that the greatest of Tacitus' commentators was also the author of *De Constantia* and *Manuductio ad Stoicam Philosophiam*. One detail is preserved by his biographer, A. Miraeus (*Vita I. L.*, Antverpiae 1609, p. 66): 'Scripserat et Thraseam, siue De Mortis Contemptu, opus philosophicum: quod pro omnium gustu non futurum cum praesensisset iudicio suppressit, calumniam vitare satius ducens, quam deprecari.'

References

1. The research was made possible by the Rockefeller Foundation and the Jowett Copyright Fund. Miss B. Smalley revised the text and Mrs M. I. Henderson has discussed the conclusions with me.

2. *Actius* quoted from *I dialoghi*, ed. Previtera, Florence, 1943, p. 231; also in *Artis Historicae Penus*, Bâle, 1579, p. 587.

3. On Tacitus in the sixteenth and seventeenth centuries, *cf.* especially A. Vannucci, *Della vita e delle opere di Tacito*, Prato, 1848, pp. 68 ff. (reprinted also in his *Studi storici e morali intorno alla letteratura latina*, 2 ed., Florence, 1862); G. Ferrari, *Corso sugli scrittori politici italiani*, Lezione XVIII: *Seconda Scuola dei Solitari – I Tacitisti* (1862: in the reprint, Milano, Monanni, 1929, p. 324); O. Tommasini, *La vita e gli scritti di N. Machiavelli nella loro relazione col Machiavellismo* I, 1883, 27; F. Ramorino, *Cornelio Tacito nella storia della cultura*, Milan, 1898, 36; G. Toffanin, *Machiavelli e il Tacitismo*, Padua, 1921; M. V. Croll, 'Attic Prose in the Seventeenth Century', in *Studies in Philology*, XVIII, 1921, pp. 79–128; Id. 'Lipsius, Montaigne, Bacon', in *Schelling Anniversary Papers*, New York, 1923; Id. 'The Baroque Style in Prose', in *Studies in English Philology in honor of F. Klaeber*, Minneapolis, 1929; B. Croce, *Storia dell'età barocca in Italia*, 1929, p. 82; A. Cherel, *La pensée de Machiavel en France*, 1935; p. 99; A. Momigliano, *Tacitus' political ideas*, ch. III (forthcoming). Toffanin is of the greatest importance, and I am very much indebted to him. But he did not study the 'Tacitist' literature in chronological order and he underestimated the non-Italian 'Tacitists'. Croll is altogether admirable on questions of style – and sees the whole European background.

4. *Scritti politici e ricordi*, ed. R. Palmarocchi, Bari, 1933: *Ricordi*, 2ª serie, n. 18. *Cf.* serie Iª, n. 78, 79, 101.

5. From the preface to his edition of Tacitus (available also in Gronovius, *Taciti Opera*, 1721). Compare A. Alciato's introduction to his edition of Tacitus (1st ed., 1517; 2nd ed., 1519. – I quote from the ed. Bâle, 1544, by Beatus Rhenanus, Alciato, etc.): 'sed et nobis prae Tacito sordescet Livius, cum ille clarorum virorum exemplo plurimis nos praeceptis instructos dimittit, quemadmodum in caput auctorum scelera vertantur, etc.: nisi magis mortalibus prodesse longas prodigiorum narrationes aliquis credat, procurataque a pontificibus portenta, tum fusius explicatos annuos magistratus, quorum nomenclatura vel diem dicendo eximere quis posset'.

6. 'Hominem nefarium Tacitum' ... 'vaecordium omnium scriptorum perditissimus' (*De asse et partibus eius*, Bâle, 1557, liber IV, p. 192 f.).

7. 'Sed quemadmodum Marcellus J. C. meretricem turpiter facere respondit quod sit meretrix, non tamen turpiter accipere, cum sit meretrix; ita quoque impie fecit Tacitus, quod non fuerit Christianus, sed non impie adversus nos scripsit, cum gentili superstitione obligaretur' (*Methodus ad facilem historiarum cognitionem*, 1566, ch. IV, in *Artis Historicae Penus*, 1579, p. 62).

8. Against Bodin, De La Popelinière, *L'histoire des histoires*, 1599, 338. *Cf.* D. Saavedra Fajardo quoted in the next note; N. Stowikowski, *Vindiciae pro Cornelio Tacito*, Cracow, 1638; P. Gaudentius, *De candore politico in Tacitum diatribae xix*, Pisa, 1646; O. Ferrarius, *Pro Cornelio Tacito apologetica*, Padua, 1654.

9. Chr. Colerus, *Epistula de studio politico ordinando* (1601: in the Giessen ed., 1621, 29). Boccalini's *Ragguagli di Parnaso* are the most obvious references. *Cf.*, for instance, L. D'Orléans, *Novae Cogitationes in libros Annalium C. C. Taciti*, Paris, 1622, preface: 'ibat ergo Tacitus aeternum tacendus ... cum

Lipsius vitae reddidit et ornamentis'; D. Saavedra Fajardo, *Republica Literaria,* *obra postuma* (in the Madrid ed., 1735, p. 39). 'Los demàs estuviesen sepultados por muchos años, sin que hiciesen ruido en el Mundo, hasta que un Flamenco [=Lipsius] le diò a conocer a las Nacions; que tambien ha menester valedores la virtud. Pero no sè si fuè en esto mas dañoso al sosiego publico, que el otro inventor de la polvora. Tales son las dotrinas tiranas, i el veneno que se ha sacado desta fuente: por quien dijo Budeo, que era el mas facinoroso de los Escritores'. This passage imitates Boccalini, *Ragguagli di Parnaso* I, 86 (ed. Rua I, p. 314). More on Saavedra and Tacitus in my forthcoming book. [See meanwhile *Athenaeum,* 31, 1953, p. 352.]

10. Preface to the 1st ed. of his Commentary, 1581. Details in *Bibliographie Lipsienne,* Ghent, 1886.

11. *Orationes octo Jenae potissimum habitae e tenebris erutae,* Darmstadt, 1607, *oratio* II, p. 28 ff.

12. Preface to his last edition, Antwerp, 1607.

13. The date is to be found in the 1607 ed.

14. In 1605 he was contemptuous of the many contemporary students of Tacitus: ' ... et multos deinde, quasi muscas, ad odorem bonae famae convolasse et in eodem mustaceo, quod dicitur, lauream quaesivisse'.

15. It is enough to refer to Boccalini's *Ragguagli* I, 86.

16. For instance, Paschalius reads with Lipsius in II, 55, 'occultus rumor incedebat'; in III, 12, 'non principis ulciscar'; in III, 51, 'ante diem <decimum>'. His text, however, is not identical with that of Lipsius. I hope to say more about it elsewhere.

17. Few letters by or to Lipsius of 1580–1 are preserved. Scaliger (on Lipsius and Scaliger, J. Bernays, *Scaliger,* 1855, p. 169), and P. Pithou were already his correspondents. J. Corbinelli was acquainted both with C. Paschalius and Scaliger. The direct correspondence between Corbinelli and Lipsius began, however, only in 1586 (Lipsius, *Ep. Cent.* II, Misc., n. 5). More important is the fact that Paschalius was corresponding with Christopher Plantinus, Lipsius' publisher, in 1581 in order to persuade him to settle in Piedmont (M. Rooses, *Christophe Plantin,* Anvers 1882, p. 318; *cf.* also R. P. Ignace Joseph de Jésus-Maria, *Histoire Ecclésiastique de la Ville d'Abbeville,* Paris, 1646, p. 511).

18. See the epigram in the preface:

> *Dum vigilat Scotus longas ex ordine noctes*
> *ut librum in lucem proferat ipse suum,*
> *mortuus obdormit, qui plus vigilaverat aequo*
> *dumque diem quaerit concidit ante diem, etc.*

19. Mr D. J. Allan of Balliol College, whose advice on this point I gratefully acknowledge, suggested that Scoto might have in mind Plato, *Rep.* IV, 425 B (*cf.* Arist. *Eth. Nic.* IX, 1165 a 28). Another remote possibility is that he was thinking of Arist. *Pol.* VII, 1331 a 40. The interpretation given in the text is perhaps the simplest.

20. The *Aphorismos sacados de la Historia de Publio Cornelio Tacito por el D. Benedicto Aries* [sic] *Montano,* Barcelona, 1614, are *not* by Montano: they are nothing more than an anthology of the *Tacito español* by Alamos de Barrientos.

This will be shown in a forthcoming paper of mine [now published in *Contributo alla storia degli studi classici*, 1955, pp. 61–6].

21. *Sententiae ex Cornelio Tacito selectae*, Venice, 1621, but his earlier work, *L'Idea di Varie Lettere*, Venice, 1612, contains also 'Concetti scelti da Cornelio Tacito da servirsene nelle lettere di ragion di stato'.

22. See V. Luciani, *F. Guicciardini and his European reputation*, New York, 1936, p. 339.

23. See my forthcoming *Tacitus' political ideas* [not yet appeared].

24. L. Salviati, *Discorso sopra le prime parole di Cornelio Tacito Urbem Romam a principio reges habuere* in *Opere* V, 1810, pp. 331–46 (first printed in Dati's translation of Tacitus, Venice, 1582).

25. I have not been able to see the 1600 edition, but the conformity of the 1608 ed. (*C. C. Taciti* and *C. Velleii Paterculi scripta quae extant*, Paris, Chevalier) with the commentary published in 1581, leaves no doubt on the nature of the *Axiomata* of 1600.

26. *Cf.* R. P. Niceron, *Mémoires pour servir à l'histoire des hommes illustres dans la république des lettres*, XVII, 1732, s.v. Ch. Paschal; *Nouvelle Biographie Générale*, s.v.

27. *Machiavelli e il Tacitismo* quoted: bibliography. On p. 146 Toffanin speaks of 'uno dei primi tacitisti italiani, Carlo Paschalis, che non per nulla scriveva a Parigi, dove il suo classicismo si trovava necessariamente a contatto col cristianesimo stoicizzante di Pierre Charron e risentiva gli influssi del mal debellato Calvinismo'. We shall see that there is more than a little truth in these incidental words. But Toffanin, by quoting Charron (*Sagesse* appeared in 1601), confirms that he did not see the chronological significance of Paschalius' pioneer work in 1581. Toffanin underrates also the leading part played by Lipsius.

28. In *H. Grotii et aliorum dissertationes de studiis instituendis*, Amsterdam, 1645.

29. A. Possevinus, *Bibl. selecta qua agitur de ratione studiorum*, 1593, pars II, liber XVI, p. 235, quotes both Paschalius and Scoto. Colerus' *Epistula* quotes only Scoto: 'in Tacitum eleganter et ingeniose Hetrusco sermone Scip. Ammiratus; et quem non aeque admirere Annibal Scotus'.

30. Fr. Balduinus, *De institutione historiae universae et eius cum iurisprudentia coniunctione* in *Artis Historicae Penus*, 1579, p. 676.

31. *Methodus* in *Artis Historicae Penus*, p. 62.

32. On Muretus, Ch. Dejob, *Marc-Antoine Muret*, 1881; M. V. Croll, ' "Attic Prose" in the Seventeenth Century', *Studies in Philology*, XVIII, 1921, p. 79. His notes on Tacitus' *Annals* I–V were posthumously published in 1604.

33. The best writers on Lipsius are M. V. Croll, 'Lipsius, Montaigne, Bacon', *Schelling Anniversary Papers*, pp. 117–50, and V. A. Nordman, 'Justus Lipsius als Geschichtsforscher und Geschichtslehrer', *Annal. Acad. Scient. Fenn.*, XXVIII, 2, 1932. To be consulted also Ch. Nisard, *Le triumvirat littéraire du XVIe siècle*, 1852; P. Amiel, *Un publiciste du XVIe siècle*, 1884; F. Strowski, *Pascal et son temps* I, 1907, p. 18; V. Beonio Brocchieri, 'L'individuo, il diritto e lo stato nella filosofia politica di Giusto Lipsio', *Saggi critici di storia delle dottrine politiche*, Bologna, 1931, pp. 31–94; S. von Dunin Borkowski, S.J., *Spinoza*, IV, 1936, pp. 264–6.

34. *Cf.*, for instance, L. Zanta, *La Renaissance du Stoïcisme au XVIe siècle*,

1914; P. Villey, *Les sources et l'évolution des essais de Montaigne*, 2nd ed., 1933; R. Raduant, *G. du Vair, l'homme et l'orateur*, 1909; J. B. Sabrié, *P. Charron. De l'humanisme au rationalisme*, 1913; H. Busson, *La pensée religieuse française de Charron à Pascal*, 1933; J. Turóczi-Trostler, 'Christlicher Seneca', *Archiv. Philologicum* of Budapest, LXI, 1937, pp. 25–75 made available to me by Professor A. Alföldi.

35. *Politicorum libri sex*. Introduction: 'unius tamen Machiavelli ingenium non contemno, acre, subtile, igneum: et qui utinam Principem suum recta duxisset ad templum illud virtutis et honoris'.

36. M. V. Croll, *o.c.*; F. P. Wilson, *Elizabethan and Jacobean*, 1946, pp. 35 ff.

37. *Cf.* Th. Heyer, *Mém. Soc. d'Hist. et d'Arch. de Genève*, XV, 1865, p. 144; G. Jalla, *Storia della riforma in Piemonte fino alla morte di Emanuele Filiberto*, Florence, 1914, pp. 338 and 381; A. Lombard, *Jean Louis Paschal et les martyrs de Calabre*, Geneva and Bâle, 1881, p. 53; B. Croce, *Vite e avventure di fede e di passione*, 1936, p. 242; A. Pascal, 'La colonia messinese di Ginevra e il suo poeta Giulio Cesare Pascali', *Boll. Soc. Storia Valdese*, April, 1935. These writers help to revise on important points the account by R. P. Ignace Joseph de Jésus-Maria, *Histoire ecclésiastique de la ville d'Abbeville*, 1646, pp. 511 ff., which is the source of J. P. Niceron, *Mémoires pour servir à l'histoire des hommes illustres*, XVII, 1732, and, through Niceron, of later compilations.

38. A. Cabos, *Guy du Faur de Pibrac, un magistrat poète au XVIe siècle* (1529–84), 1922. Notice that Pibrac had been a pupil of Alciato in Pavia. On Pibrac and Ronsard, P. Champion, *Ronsard et son temps*, 1925. Paschalius' life of Pibrac in *Vitae xvii Eruditissimorum Hominum ... olim collectae a Chr. Gryphio*, Breslau, 1739.

39. *Secunda Scaligerana*, Amsterdam, 1740, p. 492 (in the Cologne ed., 1695, p. 301, there is some confusion with P. Paschal).

40. *Cf.* especially the two prayers: LII, *Pro episcopo et pastore ecclesiae*; LIII, *Terminando civili bello gallico et impetrandue paci*.

41. The unpublished MS. of these dialogues is among the Cecil MSS. at Hatfield. It will be discussed elsewhere.

42. This is said by high authority (E. Picot, 'Les Italiens en France au XVIe siècle', *Bull. Italien* III, 1903, pp. 130–1), and is made practically certain by the evidence quoted in the next note, but I have not seen the direct evidence.

43. The evidence collected by P. de Nolhac and A. Solerti, *Il viaggio in Italia di Enrico III re di Francia*, Turin, 1890, p. 252. *Cf. Caroli Paschali Cuneatis ad Henricum III Francorum regem oratio*, Venice, 1574, reprinted in *Composizioni volgari e latine fatte da diversi nella venuta in Venetia di Henrico III re di Francia et di Polonia*, Venice, 1574.

44. A. Lombard, *Jean Louis Paschal*, pp. 100–1; J.-A. Gautier, *Histoire de Genève*, V, 1901, p. 332.

45. Niceron calls him 'ambassadeur extraordinaire'. His ordinary source, Ignace Joseph de Jésus-Maria, speaks more generically of 'seconde légation extraordinaire'. Mr R. B. Wernham, Trinity College, Oxford, who generously consulted for me the proofs and manuscripts of the yet unpublished *Foreign Calendar* for 1589, did not find the name of Paschalius. He was certainly not one of the envoys who negotiated the two loans made by Elizabeth to Henry IV in 1589, but may have been in their suite.

46. Niceron quoted in n. 37.

47. Niceron and Jalla, *o.c.* F. Agostini della Chiesa, *Catalogo de' scrittori piemontesi, savoiardi e nizzardi* (ed. of Carmagnola, 1660), gives the wrong date 1585.

48. *Elogio della gran Caterina de' Medici, reina di Francia, madre del re, fatto in lingua italiana et latina per M. Matteo Zampini et tradotto in francese per M. Carlo Paschali et in spagnuolo per l'illustre signor Girolamo Gondi*, Paris, 1586.

49. The *Elogium Eliae Vineti* in *Ausonii Burdigalensis Opera*, Bordeaux, 1604, and other editions reprinting E. Vinet's commentary is by P. Pascal (or P. de Paschal, often confused with our C. Paschal. *Cf.* P. de Nolhac, *Ronsard et l'Humanisme*, 1921, p. 310. The mistake occurs already in Niceron, p. 242).

50. *Secunda Scaligerana*, quoted p. 492: 'Primus fui qui commendavi librum eius de Legato: est liber praestantissimus, omnia Hotomanus furatus est'. G. Naudé, *Bibliographia politica*, ed. 1645 quoted, p. 54; 'Carolum Paschasium [*sic*] politioris doctrinae luminibus illustrem, ordinis ac methodi perspicuitate clarum, soliditate iudicii maxime praestantem, ac talem in omnibus ut, eo veluti dictante, non Villerius Hottomannus modo, sed, quicumque post ipsum de Legatis scripsere, loquuti sint'. On his discussion with J. Hotman, see provisionally *Biographie Universelle*, nouv. édition, s.d., XXXII, 214, s.v. Charles Paschal.

51. L. Zanta, *La Renaissance du Stoïcisme au XVIe siècle*, pp. 241 ff.

52. *Cf.* his comments on the 'primum facinus novi principatus': 'Non satis est imperium adipisci; sed et aemulus, si quis est, si non continuo amovetur, maximum ab eo periculum est ... Quod siquis clamitat, indignum facinus esse innocentem nec opinantem opprimi, huic oppono verissimum illud Taciti dictum, Annal. lib. 14. Habet aliquid ex iniquo omne magnum exemplum, quod contra singulos utilitate publica rependitur' (p. 8).

53. *Cf.* V. di Tocco, *Ideali d'indipendenza in Italia durante la preponderanza spagnuola*, Messina, 1926.

54. *Historia delle guerre civili di Francia* I (ed. London, 1775), book VI, p. 410. J. Corbinelli went to Poland with Henry III and therefore knew Paschalius very well. He translated Pibrac into Italian for Catherine de' Medici (probably his unsavoury apology for Saint-Bartholomew). *Cf.* R. Calderini de Marchi, *J. Corbinelli et les érudits français*, Milan, 1914, p. 57, n. 2, 59; also P. Rajna, 'J. C. e la Strage di S. Bartolomeo', *Arch. Storico Ital.* XXI, 1898, p. 54. B. Del Bene dedicated a poem to Pibrac. See C. Couderc, 'Les poésies d'un florentin à la cour de France au XVIe siècle', *Giorn. Stor. Lett. Ital.* XVII, 1891, p. 26. He had also close connections with the Piedmontese court. For these Italians, see also P. de Nolhac and A. Solerti, *Giorn. Stor. Lett. Ital.* XVII, 1891, p. 446; L. Clément, *Henri Estienne et son œuvre français*, 1899; P. Soldati, *Giorn. Stor. Lett. Ital.* CX, 1937, p. 120.

55. *Essais*, Livre III, ch. VIII, 'De l'art de conferer'.

56. *Scipioni Ammirati celeberrimi inter neotericos scriptoris dissertationes politicae sive discursus in C. Cornelium Tacitum*, Frankfort, 1609.

57. F. Chabod, *Giovanni Botero*, Rome, 1934, p. 33, n. 5.

58. *Cf.* Paolo Treves, 'Il gesuitismo politico di G. Botero', *Civiltà Moderna*, 1931, p. 543.

14

Perizonius, Niebuhr and the Character of Early Roman Tradition*

'THE famous Ballad theory of Niebuhr of which we seldom hear now except in connection with Macaulay's lays' ... [1] These are the words of Mr Last's tutor – W. Warde Fowler. When he wrote them, in 1912, Warde Fowler was apparently not aware that the ballad theory had been revived a few years before by an Italian historian who was to exercise a deep influence on Mr Last.[2] But the ballad theory involves other names – such as Perizonius, Vico, Niebuhr, Schwegler, Mommsen – which have been ever present in Mr Last's mind and have often recurred in conversation. In more recent years the ballad theory has lost nothing of its prestige in Italy; two pupils of De Sanctis, A. Rostagni[3] and L. Pareti,[4] have made it the cornerstone of their interpretation of archaic Latin literature and historiography. Indeed, the theory has again found favour in England.[5]

A history of this theory has never been written, and therefore its implications have never been properly examined. One can even doubt whether the analysis of the ancient evidence (scanty as it is) has been exhausted. Each section of this paper can claim no more value than that of a hasty sketch of a large territory. But I hope that Mr Last will accept my discussion of a subject that he knows better than anybody else as part of that exchange of ideas between us which has now been going on for twenty-five years and to which I owe more than I can say.

I. THE HISTORY OF A THEORY

One of the consequences of the discovery of America was to confirm classical scholars in the belief that historiography began in poetry.

*Journ. Rom. Studies, 47, 1957, pp. 104–14.

Tacitus had written 'Celebrant carminibus antiquis, quod unum apud illos memoriae et annalium genus est . . .' (*Germ.* 2, 3). Justus Lipsius commented 'Uti apud barbaros fere omnes et rudes litterarum. Nec Hispani aliter comperere apud novos Indos'.[6]

At first sight the Romans seemed not to conform to this pattern. Their authors traced the origins of Latin historiography to the annals of the pontiffs: 'erat historia nihil aliud nisi annalium confectio . . .'. Yet a mistake in the interpretation of the grammarian Diomedes – resulting in an interpolation – provided unexpected inspiration. Diomedes had written: 'epos Latinum primus digne scripsit is qui res Romanorum decem et octo complexus est libris qui et annales inscribuntur . . . vel Romanis' – and, of course, had meant Ennius.[7] But his first modern editors thought that he was alluding to Livius Andronicus, and bravely put Livius into the text: 'Epos Latine primus digne scripsit Livius is qui,' etc.[8] The combined authority of the interpolated Diomedes and of Justus Lipsius was decisive in persuading G. B. Vico that the Romans were no exception to what both the students of the ancient world and the explorers of the new world seemed to expect from a nation in its early stages of development: 'Livio Andronico, il primo scrittor latino, scrisse la *Romanide,* ch'era un poema eroico il quale conteneva gli annali degli antichi romani'.[9]

It will have been noticed, however, that Vico did not adduce the 'banquet songs' to support his opinion that the first Roman historians were poets. It is wrong to say, as some people have done,[10] that Vico was an early supporter of the 'ballad theory'. No doubt he would have welcomed it. But he did not know of it. To the best of my information he never noticed Cicero's references to the 'banquet songs'. Nor did he know that his contemporary, J. Perizonius (1651–1715), who died ten years before the first *Scienza Nuova* was published (in 1725), had written on the subject. Vico was not a very learned man in any case, and his acquaintance with contemporary scholarship was especially inadequate. Epic poems, not banquet songs (hereafter called 'carmina'), were taken by him to be at the origin of Roman (and, of course, of Greek) historiography.

Perizonius accepted the current presupposition that poetry preceded ordinary historiography: indeed, he was impressed by D. Huet's remarks on the great antiquity of Arabic poetry.[11] Nor was he the first to mention the 'carmina'; others (for instance, F. Balduinus) had preceded him. But, as far as I could ascertain, he was the first to introduce the 'carmina' into a concrete discussion on the relation between poetry

and historiography in Rome. Perizonius worked for a 'via media' between the pyrrhonists of his own time and the credulous traditionalists
of any time.[12] He had read La Mothe le Vayer and Bayle and knew that
Cluverius in memorable pages had denied the traditional story of the
origins of Rome; he was also aware that S. Bochart had denied the truth
of the story of Aeneas.[13] Though in sympathy with any rigorous examination of the tradition, he was not prepared to share these doubts. He
admitted an element of truth in the old stories about Aeneas and
Romulus. In his programmatic speech of 1702, *De Fide Historiarum
contra Pyrrhonismum Historicum*, he gave a reasoned account of his
theoretical objections to the fashionable pyrrhonism.[14] But he had
already shown in the *Animadversiones Historicae* of 1685 how he analysed
Roman tradition in practice. There, among other things, he had pointed
to the 'carmina' as a potential source of historical tradition. Like the
Jews, the Greeks, the Spaniards, the Gauls, the Germans and the Arabs,
the Romans celebrated their ancestors in songs that preserved the
memory of old events, though they could obviously not be trusted as
accurate sources for details. It is well to remember that Perizonius'
reference to the 'carmina' is a small part of an argument against the
scepticism of his own century.

Niebuhr was not entirely correct in saying that Perizonius' *Animadversiones* were soon forgotten.[15] Ernesti thought of reprinting them
about 1736,[16] and they were in fact reprinted in 1771. We shall soon
quote other evidence to show that they were read in the eighteenth
century. But Niebuhr may well be right in claiming that nobody attributed importance to Perizonius' theory on the 'carmina' before he
himself had 'rediscovered' it (as we shall see, without at first knowing
that it was a 'rediscovery', not a 'discovery'). The explanation for this
lapse into oblivion is simple. The theory about the 'carmina' was buried
in a few pages (pp. 202–5) of the fat *Animadversiones*, and Perizonius
himself did not attach much importance to it. He never really tried to
explain how such 'carmina' influenced Roman tradition. Later in his
life he produced a detailed defence of the traditional account of the
origins of Rome in which the 'carmina' are never mentioned. He
eliminated the most flagrantly improbable details of the traditional story
and tried to show that the rest was plausible. For instance, he argued
that if Servius Tullius established the 'comitia centuriata', another king
(why not Romulus?) must have originated the 'comitia curiata'. He also
thought that the rediscovery of Numa's books was an argument for the
existence of Numa.[17] If Perizonius himself made no use of his remarks

on the banquet songs one cannot be surprised that other scholars forgot them. In fact, to some extent the whole of the *Animadversiones* was involved in this oblivion. Perizonius was not mentioned during the memorable controversy on the credibility of Roman History that occupied the members of the 'Académie Royale des Inscriptions et Belles Lettres' between 1722 and 1725.[18] Nor was L. De Beaufort acquainted with the *Animadversiones* when he published his *Dissertation sur l'incertitude des cinq premiers siècles de l'histoire romaine* in 1738. De Beaufort was attacked by Chr. Saxius who presented himself as the champion of the moderate critical methods of Perizonius against De Beaufort's excessive scepticism; yet even Saxius barely mentions the 'carmina'.[19] Then De Beaufort, who had been rightly offended by Saxius' suggestion that he had used Perizonius without quoting him, made a minute study of the *Animadversiones* for the second edition of his *Dissertation sur l'incertitude*. The new edition appeared in 1750 and contained a spirited answer to Saxius, but the 'carmina' remained outside the picture.

Thus we come to Niebuhr who in 1811 based his reconstruction of the early Roman tradition on the 'carmina'. He then thought (misinterpreting Cicero) that the Elder Cato had still heard the 'carmina'. Furthermore, he suggested that Cicero complained of their disappearance only because he had not searched enough: the 'carmina' were still surviving in his own time, and Dionysius of Halicarnassus knew at least two of them, on Romulus and Coriolanus. The 'carmina' represented the Roman plebeian tradition while the annals of the pontiffs expressed the patrician point of view. German heroic poetry (the Nibelungen) provided a suitable comparison.

Strange as it may seem, Niebuhr, the great admirer of Dutch scholarship, did not turn his attention to Perizonius until after 1811. In 1808 he had been in Holland for a year on a political mission and had visited, with due reverence, the University of Leiden. We have a precise account of his visit in a letter collected in the *Nachgelassene Schriften nichtphilologischen Inhalts*, and in a moving note in the first edition of his *Römische Geschichte*. Like every visitor to Leiden he was especially attracted by the Senate Room of the University where the portraits of its great masters are hanging to this day. He noticed many portraits but did not mention that of Perizonius.[20] Yet it had been there since about 1737.[21] Indeed, Niebuhr himself candidly admitted in the second edition of his work that he had heard of Perizonius' *Animadversiones* only after he had published the first edition. When and how Niebuhr rediscovered Perizonius I cannot say. But once he had rediscovered him he did not tire of praising him.[22] He even devoted a part of his fees as a teacher in the University of Bonn for a prize essay on Perizonius. The prize was won by G. Kramer about 1828.[23]

Niebuhr's first edition had occasioned a great deal of criticism of the theory of the banquet songs;[24] and Niebuhr considerably modified his position in the second edition. Though he thought that his theory of the 'carmina' was a permanent acquisition for scholarship, he toned down his declaration by allowing that 'die rhythmische Form ist hier Nebensache'.[25] He came very near to conceding that the poetical contents of Roman legends did not necessarily imply poetic form.

All these changes are part of the process whereby Niebuhr enriched his erudition, met his critics, and modified his outlook between the first and the second edition of his *History*.[26] But the essential difference between Perizonius' remarks and Niebuhr's theory about the 'carmina' did not disappear in the second edition. While Perizonius looked upon the 'carmina' as one of the potential channels of information about early Roman history, Niebuhr (though not overlooking that aspect) treated them as the voice of the Roman 'Plebs'. He found in them the explanation of all that he felt to be true about the Roman popular tradition: its richness in details, its poetic character, its value as a mirror of the mind of the heroic peasantry of early Rome. He distrusted the Roman aristocratic sources of the later annalists[27] and took pleasure in legends that, like any popular poetry, had never pretended to be true in a strict sense. Though notoriously impatient of modern Italians, he was ready to believe that the legend of Tarpeia had been transmitted by oral tradition without interruption to the inhabitants of nineteenth-century Rome.[28] He found confirmation even in Herodotus of the phenomenon of poetic tradition preceding and conditioning historiography. In his lectures on Greek history he argued that the poetic element in Herodotus, like that of Livy, was due to poetic sources.[29]

The details of the controversy about Niebuhr's ballad theory need not detain us long. But the following points may be noticed:

(1) Some of those who attacked Niebuhr most determinedly, such as A. W. Schlegel, thought that the Greek elements recognizable in Roman legends excluded their popular and poetic origin.[30]

(2) Some of those who defended Niebuhr, such as Nitzsch, had to admit that the 'carmina' were not of plebeian origin, because the majority of the heroes of the alleged ballads were patricians.[31]

(3) Though it was perhaps A. Schwegler who succeeded best in

criticizing the ballad theory,[32] Mommsen was really the man who made it unpopular for half a century. I am not aware that Mommsen ever expressed an opinion on it, but by implication he rejected it entirely. He accepted Rubino's notion that the Roman tradition was more ancient and reliable on constitutional than on political and military history. He understood much better than Niebuhr the part played by the annalists. He took the legend of Coriolanus as a test case and showed that it was late and influenced by Greek literary tradition – even by Greek etymology.[33] Irrational elements certainly contributed to Mommsen's rejection of the ballad theory. We now know from his correspondence with Wilamowitz how passionately Mommsen disliked Niebuhr's school.[34] And of course he attributed the highest gifts of poetic imagination to Greeks and Germans only.[35] As Niebuhr had admitted that in its present form Coriolanus' legend was later than Fabius',[36] this was not a proper test for the whole ballad theory. There is some truth in Nitzsch's remark that Mommsen never made it clear why he rejected Niebuhr's theory.[37]

(4) De Sanctis revived Niebuhr's theory as a part of his general reaction against Mommsen's treatment of early Roman history.[38] A new interest in Roman poetic imagination – and more generally in the interrelation between poetry and historiography (as can be seen in Croce) – may have contributed to the popularity of Niebuhr among Italian scholars of this century. But general considerations of this kind would have little weight with so cautious a scholar as De Sanctis. He felt that Niebuhr's theory provided the best explanation for the legendary character of early Roman tradition.

It remains for us to turn to the evidence and to decide: (a) whether what we are told about the 'carmina' proves that they existed; (b) whether the 'carmina' provide a satisfactory explanation for the formation of Roman historical tradition.

II. THE EVIDENCE FOR A THEORY

Two sentences by Cicero, referring back to Cato, and one incomplete sentence by Varro quoted by Nonius are really all that matters:

Brutus 19, 75: atque utinam extarent illa carmina, quae multis saeclis ante suam aetatem in epulis esse cantitata a singulis convivis de clarorum virorum laudibus in Originibus scriptum reliquit Cato.

Tuscul. Disp. 4, 2, 3: gravissimus auctor in Originibus dixit Cato morem apud maiores hunc epularum fuisse ut deinceps qui accubarent canerent ad tibiam clarorum virorum laudes atque virtutes.

Varro de Vita Populi Romani II, ap. Non. Marc. p. 77 M = p. 107 L: in conviviis pueri modesti ut cantarent carmina antiqua in quibus laudes erant maiorum et assa voce et cum tibicine.

Cato thought that the poems were sung in turns by adults. Varro seems to say that they were sung by well brought-up children. Valerius Maximus followed Cato;[39] and Horace, picturing these 'carmina' as a family affair, is perhaps nearer to Cato than to Varro.[40]

We do not of course know whether Varro intended to correct Cato or to supplement Cato's information. There have been many attempts to make Varro agree with Cato. The boldest is by N. Pirrone who completed Varro's sentence in this way: '(maiores natu accubantes a ceteris invitabantur, cum aderant quoque) in conviviis pueri', etc.[41] I should not mention this if Pareti had not lent his authority to it.[42] Incomplete sentences must certainly not be treated as if they were complete, but it is even more dangerous to complete them in such a way as to make them agree with what we like to believe. On the other hand, it is too easy to play Varro against Cato and conclude that neither of them had any information about the 'carmina'. According to Dahlmann Cato would have attributed a Greek habit to the early Romans, and Varro would have improved on him by bringing in the children.[43] Dahlmann is a high authority on Varro, but I do not believe that the disagreement between Cato and Varro implies that the 'carmina' never existed. The fact that Aristoxenus and Dicaearchus disagreed about the notion of *skolion* does not imply that the *skolia* never existed.[44] In Greece adult singing at banquets did not exclude children's performances. We have Aristophanes' word for that.[45] As Greek influences had been at work in Rome since the days of the monarchy there is no difficulty in admitting that the Romans – either directly or *via* Etruria – received both styles of convivial performances from the Greeks. To say the least, what the Greek evidence shows is that we cannot play Varro against Cato as if they were mutually exclusive: the more so since we do not know Varro's context. Both Cato and Varro say that the 'carmina' had existed. Better arguments than those propounded so far are required for throwing their evidence overboard.

Cato made it clear that the 'carmina' had disappeared long before his time. They had not yet been rediscovered when Cicero wrote, and there is no serious reason to believe that they were rediscovered after Cicero.

We can begin by eliminating a piece of evidence which, though discredited, comes up again from time to time.

K. O. Müller, who, after all, was under the spell of Niebuhr, accepted a supplement to Festus by Fulvio Orsini that amounted to the fabrication of a 'carmen Saturnium': Festus, p. 162 M. s.v. *Navali Corona* '(Item ali inter quos M.) Atilius bel (lo quod gestum est contra Poenos, ut scrip)tum est in car(mine Saturnio, quod quidem duces ipsi sunt co)nsueti (in tabellis publice ponere in quo no)minabantur (navali corona donati)'. The best criticism of these supplements is in the clean text as one can see it in Lindsay's Teubner edition, p. 156:

. . . . Atilius bel –
. . . . tum est in car –
. . . . onsuetudi –
. . . . minabantur

C. Cichorius may be right in supplementing '(ut a Naevio narra)tum est in car(mine belli Punici), but even that, though more acceptable than Müller's text, should not be taken as a fact.[46]

The two passages of Dionysius of Halicarnassus are a more serious proposition: I, 79, 10 (on Romulus and Remus):

ἀλλ' οἵους ἄν τις ἀξιώσειε τοὺς ἐκ βασιλείου τε φύντας γένους καὶ ἀπὸ δαιμόνων σπορᾶς γενέσθαι νομιζομένους, ὡς ἐν τοῖς πατρίοις ὕμνοις ὑπὸ 'Ρωμαίων ἔτι καὶ νῦν ᾄδεται.

VIII, 62 (on Coriolanus):

οὐ γέγονεν ἐξίτηλος ἡ τοῦ ἀνδρὸς μνήμη, ἀλλ' ᾄδεται καὶ ὑμνεῖται πρὸς πάντων ὡς εὐσεβὴς καὶ δίκαιος ἀνήρ.

The first passage only implies that the twins were mentioned in passing in some religious hymns. No 'lay of Romulus' is necessarily alluded to, but an allusion to a specific 'carmen' is certainly there. The second passage is now usually taken to mean that 'Coriolanus is still celebrated by everybody' – without any allusion to 'carmina'.[47] But this is doubtful. The operative words in the two passages are almost the same. The interpretation of the second passage must at least remain open to doubt. To my mind, the existence of a 'lay of Coriolanus' is neither proved nor excluded by Dionysius' words.

If a poem on Coriolanus was circulating under Augustus, I should like to take it as a piece of archaistic poetry. Cicero's regret that the convivial 'carmina' were lost may have prompted some attempt to revive them.[48] S. Timpanaro showed not long ago that the *Carmen Priami* was probably a post-Ennian (but pre-Varronian) piece of archaistic poetry.[49] The *Laudes Herculis* of *Aen*. VIII are, in a sense, another archaistic piece; in this case Virgil is thinking of the Salii.[50]

There is no reason for maintaining that the 'carmina', if they existed (and I believe they did), disappeared before the end of the fourth century B.C. The end of the fourth century leaves space enough for the 'multa saecula' (=generations) before Cato. If so, the *possibility* must be granted that the 'carmina' influenced the oral historical tradition in the century before it was collected and standardized by the annalists. The possibility also remains open that some Greek historians (say Diocles of Peparethus)[51] and poets (say Callimachus) indirectly came to know the contents of these 'carmina'.[52] Can we go beyond this and decide whether there is positive evidence that the 'carmina' in fact influenced Roman historical tradition?

The great argument in favour of Niebuhr's theory remains the consideration that the Roman historical tradition is singularly rich in figures and episodes that would make good historical ballads. Macaulay can here serve as evidence. However, things are not so simple when one looks at them closely:

(1) Many of these alleged subjects for ballads (the reign of Tarquin the tyrant, the battle of Lake Regillus, Coriolanus, the Fabii and the Cremera battle, Camillus) contain details that are derived from Greek sources. Some of these details (such as that of Castor and Pollux at Lake Regillus) must have come to Rome in pre-hellenistic times.[53] But on the whole one is left with the impression that the majority (Tarquin's poppies, Coriolanus as a suppliant like Themistocles, the Three Hundred Fabii of whom one survived, Camillus' prayer) are the result of a direct acquaintance with Greek literary sources which it would be unwise to place in pre-hellenistic times.

(2) Other features of these legends are hardly compatible with an earlier crystallization in poetic form. The oldest version of the Coriolanus legend, such as was collected by Fabius Pictor, allowed him to die, peacefully if not happily, in old age:[54] this makes it unlikely that the conventional story was handed down in a pre-Catonian ballad. About the Horatii and Curiatii the ancients themselves found it difficult to decide which were the enemies and which the champions of Rome:[55] one would expect a poem to make it clear for ever. The story of Virginia presupposes many legal subtleties that cannot come from a poem.[56]

(3) The very fact that these legends have been described by some as

of patrician origin and by others as of plebeian origin shows that they are neither. Coriolanus, the ferocious patrician, belongs to the gens Marcia – which was plebeian in historic times: this has not yet been explained satisfactorily.[57] Virginia is patrician, but her fiancé is plebeian. The majority of the other 'poetic' stories is not coloured by the political passions that one would naturally attribute to the Romans of the fifth and fourth centuries B.C. This is not decisive, but it makes a date as late as the third century more probable for the present form of the legends.

(4) I know that it may seem 'una pedanteria appena credibile' (to repeat De Sanctis' words) to point out that our sources speak only of 'gesta virorum' as the subject matter of 'carmina', while women prominently figure in our legends. But this is what is stated in our sources, and I do not consider it impossible that in men's banquets the convention was to leave women out. If so Cloelia, Lucretia and Virginia are excluded from the world of the ballads.

(5) If there is a potential hero for our 'carmina' it is M. Atilius Regulus.[58] Unfortunately he is too late for them. The 'carmen Saturnium' on him we have seen to be a modern invention. In his case the 'poetry' of the legend has nothing to do with 'poetic' sources. What is true about him may be true about all the other 'poetic' heroes.

The preceding considerations will perhaps be enough to show that there are difficulties in the view that the so-called poetical episodes of Roman history were the subjects of poems earlier than 300 B.C. Further considerations restrict the importance of the ballad theory in other directions:

(1) Many of these poetical subjects are clearly connected with local traditions, individual monuments, and cult places. The story of the Horatii is connected with the 'tigillum sororium' and the 'sepulcra', the story of Cloelia with the 'statua equestris', that of Lake Regillus with the new cult of Castor and Pollux, that of Coriolanus with the temple of the Fortuna Muliebris.[59] This means that such stories owed their preservation to their connections with visible objects rather than to their literary form.

(2) Roman tradition, as a whole, is neatly divided into two parts: it is non-annalistic about the Monarchy and annalistic about the Republic. The 'poetic' subjects do not prevail in the non-annalistic portion. The kings of Rome (except the first and the last) are perhaps less 'poetic' than is the first century of the Republic. No doubt this has something to do with the fact that the Romans were not too tender with their kings.

240

But the consequence is that 'poetry' and annalistic tradition are closely knitted together. The attempt to separate 'ballads' from 'annals' is bound to be speculative and frivolous. There is no reason to believe that Livy was the first annalist with the soul of a poet. On the other hand, how much less ballad-like certain episodes of Roman history would be if we had only Dionysius to inform us.

III. BEYOND NIEBUHR'S THEORY

There may be something in Niebuhr's theory after all. The 'carmina' (I believe) did exist and did not disappear too soon to influence Roman historical tradition. Some of the 'poetic' episodes of Roman history may come from poetry. But these vague possibilities should not be allow to conceal the fact that this theory no longer serves any real purpose. Perizonius mentioned the 'carmina' to fight historical pyrrhonism. This, I hope, is no longer a living issue. If it were, we should be able to support Perizonius with better arguments. On the other hand, Niebuhr magnified the importance of the 'carmina' because he thought that they were the representatives of the plebeian point of view in a tradition largely dominated by patricians. He idealized the Roman Plebs because he thought that it was so similar to the peasantry of his own Dithmarschen and so different from the French mobs who had made the Revolution and, who, through their antics, were to cause his last illness on a cold December night in 1830.[60] To Niebuhr the 'carmina' were authentic expressions of the political and patriotic passions of archaic Rome. None of us can seriously share this view: the Roman legends, as we have them, are coloured by the somewhat conventional patriotism of the late annalists.[61]

Thus the ballad theory has long ceased to be a real contribution to the understanding of the formation of Roman historiography. Indeed, if kept in the foreground it may conceal a more important aspect of Roman historiography. The annalists, each basing his work on the other, managed to select, combine and unify the traditions of the past with considerable success. A pattern was created, and only a very few of the pieces of information that did not fit into it escaped annihilation. Mastarna was dug out of the Etruscan tradition by an emperor who had among his wives one with Etruscan blood and Etruscan pride.[62] Mastarna had to be identified with Servius Tullius simply because no place had been left for him in the conventional pattern of Roman history.[63] It was perhaps another consequence of the Etruscan studies of the Emperor Claudius that the writers of the early imperial age became aware of a tradition according to which Porsenna had in fact controlled Rome, *pace* Cloelia and Mucius Scaevola. The first treaty between Rome and Carthage was saved by Polybius.[64] A tradition, not necessarily true to fact, that the Gauls occupied the Capitol seems to have been known to Silius Italicus and may go back to Ennius.[65] Theophrastus alone mentions a Roman expedition to Corsica before 300 B.C. Even the 'evocatio' of the gods of Carthage did not survive in the Roman annalistic account: it has to be read in Macrobius who derived it from Serenus Sammonicus.[66]

We can at least learn from the few surviving elements of the non-annalistic tradition how different our image of early Roman history would be if we were in full command of Greek and Etruscan sources about early Rome and of those Roman poets and antiquarians who used unconventional sources for the history of their own city. Mommsen's scepticism about the ballad theory appears on reflection to have been sound. But Mommsen failed to account for the process of selection whereby the annalists built up their national history. He thought that constitutional history was the only authentic history of early Rome. We can now see that the political and military history put together by the annalists is not qualitatively different from their constitutional history. Both contain many elements of truth, but both are the results of a selective arrangement of earlier data. The experience of a century and a half of post-Niebuhrian studies is here to show that more light is to be expected from the comparison of the annalistic tradition with the scanty evidence surviving outside it than from the attempts to isolate the earliest components of the annalistic tradition itself.[67]

References

1. 'The Disappearance of the Earliest Latin Poetry', *CR* 26, 1912, pp. 48–9 = *Roman Essays and Interpretations*, pp. 71–2 (*cf.* pp. 238–40).

2. *Storia dei Romani* I, 1907, pp. 22–5; *cf.* 'La Légende historique des premiers siècles de Rome', *Journal des Savants*, 1909, pp. 126–32, 205–14; 1910, pp. 310–19. De Sanctis was followed by E. Ciaceri, *Le Origini di Roma*, 1937, pp. 47–56 and *passim*. E. Kornemann, *Der Priestercodex in der Regia,*

Tübingen, 1912, p. 7, n. 5, mentioned De Sanctis with contempt for this return to Niebuhr.

3. A. Rostagni, *Storia della Letteratura latina*, 2nd ed., Torino, 1954, I, pp. 38–52, 63–5. This is a very detailed discussion with up-to-date bibliography. Rostagni takes the 'Carmen Priami' and the 'Carmen Nelei' to be banquet songs ('carmi conviviali'): but the 'Carmen Nelei' was probably dramatic, and the 'Carmen Priami' is probably not archaic: see below. C. Barbagallo, *Il problema delle origini di Roma da Vico a noi*, 1926, does not examine the history of the controversy on the ballad theory.

4. L. Pareti, *Storia di Roma*, I, 1952, pp. 4 ff. For a different opinion *cf.* Scevola Mariotti, *Livio Andronico e la traduzione artistica*, Milano, 1952, 32–3. See also *JRS*, 47, 1957, p. 59, for P. Fraccaro's views.

5. C. M. Bowra, *Heroic Poetry*, 1952, pp. 46; 383.

6. I quote from *C. Cornelii Taciti et C. Velleii Paterculi scripta quae extant*, Parisiis, 1608, p. 123. Lipsius of course already combines *Germ.* 2, 3, with *Ann.* 2, 88, 4, 'caniturque adhuc barbaras apud gentes' and Einhardus, *Vita Karoli Magni* 29, 'Item barbara et antiquissima carmina quibus veterum regum actus et bella canebantur, scripsit memoriaeque mandavit'. Lipsius probably derived his information about American 'cantiones' from F. Balduinus, *De historia* lib. 1, in *Artis Historicae Penus*, I, Basileae, 1579, p. 649.

7. *Gramm. Lat.* I, p. 484 Keil.

8. I quote from the Soncino ed. of Pesaro 1511, no page, but the same text also in the Venice ed. 1495. Thence Coelius Rhodiginus, *Lect. Antiq. Libri Triginta*, Basileae, 1542 (quoted by me from the Geneva ed. 1620, col. 324): 'Epica digne omnium primus scripsit Livius qui decem et octo libris Romanorum res gestas perscripsit.' But Rhodiginus did not transcribe the whole passage of Diomedes and therefore cannot be the source of Vico, as has been suggested.

9. *Scienza Nuova Seconda*, ed. Nicolini, 1942, II, 2, p. 5 (vol. I, p. 201, prg. 471). Here Vico refers to the above-quoted passage of Tacitus, *Germania*, and to Lipsius' commentary on it. *Cf.* F. Nicolini, *Commento Storico alla Seconda Scienza Nuova*, I, 1949, p. 192. G. I. Vossius, *De Historicis Latinis* (2nd ed., 1651), p. 6, had noticed the mistake of the editors of Diomedes, but it is typical of Vico's lack of scholarly accuracy that he did not pay attention to Vossius' warning.

10. For instance, L. Pareti, *Storia di Roma*, I, p. 4, 'che buona parte della storia di Roma nei primi secoli sia stata primamente raccolta e formulata dall'epica popolare, è una verità percepita già dal Perizonio (1685) e dal Vico (1710 sgg.)'. *Cf.* also De Sanctis, *Journ. d. Savants* 1909, p. 132.

11. *Animadversiones Historicae*, Amstelaedami, 1685, p. 204: 'De Arabibus similia pene observavit vir Excellentiss. P. Dan. Huetius, quum originem Fabularum Romanensium explicuit'. The reference is to *De Origine Fabularum Romanensium* ex Gallico latine reddidit G. Pyrrho (Hagae Comitis, 1682), p. 13. Perizonius may also have read the following passage in F. Balduinus, *De Historia*, lib. 1, in *Artis Historicae Penus*, I, p. 648: 'Sed iuvat admirari singularem Dei providentiam qua factum est, ut et olim multis modis rerum praeteritarum memoria conservata sit ... Quid dicam, carminibus tantum, quae ediscerentur, et cantionibus quae iactarentur, vulgata diu fuisse, quae postea tandem literis consecrata sunt? Fateor tamen multa esse amissa. Cicero in Bruto: Utinam

(inquit) extarent illa carmina etc.' Balduinus did not think that the 'carmina' had been used by Roman historians (see p. 650). *Cf.* also J. Selden, *Opera* II, Londini, 1726, pp. 969–82 (*Janus Anglorum*, I, 1), and Perizonius' note on Valerius Maximus II, 1, p. 10, ed. A. Torrenius, Leidae, 1726.

12. I do not know of any monograph on Perizonius, who certainly deserves one. See the *Oratio Funebris* by A. Schultingius, Lugduni Bat., 1725, and the *Vita* by E. L. Vriemoet reprinted in the ed. of the *Animadversiones* by Th. Chr. Harles, Altenburgi, 1771: also the *Elogium* in *Actis Eruditorum Lips.*, 1716, pp. 95–6, and the *Vita* by F. G. Westhovius preceding *Orationes*, XII, 1740. Other references in L. Knappert, *Nieuw Nederlandsch Biografisch Woordenboek*, V, 1921, pp. 467–9. Knappert's article does not mention the *Animadversiones*. [H. Smitskamp, *Verslag van de Algemene Vergadering van het Historisch Genootschap*, Utrecht, 1953, pp. 47–68].

13. Cluverius, *Italia Antiqua*, Lugduni Bat., 1624, III, c. 2, pp. 820–55; S. Bochart, *Lettre à M. de Segrais*, 1663, which I read in the Latin translation by J. Schefferus, *De quaestione num Aeneas unquam fuerit in Italia* in appendix to S. Bochart, *Geographia Sacra*, Francofurti, 1674. Cluverius wrote: 'Merum igitur figmentum est quod post Homerum sive poetae sive λογογράφοι ac μυθολόγοι de Aeneae in Italiam adventu regnoque inibi constituto tradiderunt' (p. 834). Also 'Hactenus igitur falsus urbis Romanae conditor Romulus satis remotus est. Quo prostrato nihil est quod aliquis mihi heic amplius proavos eius, certa serie ab Aenea stirpem ducenteis, obtendat' (p. 832). Bochart was attacked by Perizonius' predecessor at Leiden, Th. Ryckius, in his appendix to L. Holstenius, *Notae et Castigationes Postumae in Stephani Byzantini* ΕΘΝΙΚΑ (Lugd. Bat., 1684), pp. 395–467. Later H. Dodwell, *De Veter. Graecorum Romanorumque cyclis*, Oxonii, 1701, pp. 675–80, joined the sceptics with his remarks on the kings of Alba. Dodwell, though a friend and an admirer of Perizonius (with whom he corresponded), was more radical. He did not believe that there had been authentic records of the Alban kings and added 'Caeterum ego tam longe me abesse fateor ut Regum Albanorum tempora certa putem, ut vel Romuli habeam suspecta'. Also J. Gronovius, *Dissert. de origine Romuli*, Lugd. Bat., 1684, expressed doubts on the Romulus legend: he thought that Romulus came from the East. On the historical pyrrhonism of this time see Momigliano, *Contributo alla storia degli studi classici*, 1955, pp. 79 ff. [G. Pflug, *Deutsche Vierteljahrs.* 28, 1954, pp. 447–71; S. Bertelli, *Società*, 1955, pp. 435–56].

14. This very important 'oratio' was reprinted in *Orationes XII*, Lugduni Bat., 1740, pp. 103–54.

15. *Vorträge über römische Geschichte*, 1 (ed. M. Isler, 1846), p. 71, 'Von 1684 an ist eigentlich philologisch für die römische Geschichte so gut wie nichts geschehen' (this N. said in 1828–9, perhaps repeating his lectures of 1826–7).

16. Preface to the *Clavis Ciceroniana*, 1739, 'Perizonii animadversiones ... harum litterarum studiosis valde necessarias putamus'.

17. *Dissert. De Rep. Romana quae agit de Historia Romuli et Romanae Urbis Origine* in *Dissert. Septem*, Lugduni Bat., 1740, pp. 681–714. The date of this dissertation is not known to me, but is certainly later than 1693. It was apparently never printed during Perizonius' lifetime.

18. See *Mém. Acad. Royale Inscriptions*, vols. 4 and 6 (1723 and 1729). An

occasional reference to the 'chants, où l'on célebroit les bienfaits des Dieux, la grandeur de Rome naissante et les belles actions des illustres Romains' is to be found there (*cf. Mém.*, 6, p. 127, and also *Mém.*, 4, p. 389). But they do not go nearer to the 'carmina'. It is perhaps not useless to remind the reader that during this discussion l'Abbé Sallier produced a devastating exposure of the so-called *Parallela minora* attributed to Plutarch. Others had preceded him (see Vossius, *De Historicis Graecis* 112; Perizonius, *Animadversiones*, ch. 1, p. 9) but none was so thorough. Notice also the article 'Tanaquil' in Bayle, *Dictionnaire* (ed. 1697, II, p. 1123) which establishes the debt of seventeenth-century pyrrhonism to L. Valla.

19. Ἐπίκρισις φιλολογική 'sive stricturae in nuperum Franci cuiusdam libellum de incerto historiae Romanorum antiquissimae', *Miscellanea Lipsiensia Nova*, I, 1742, pp. 40–79; II, 1743, pp. 409–495; II, 1743, pp. 670–712 (pp. 671–4 on the *carmina vetusta*); III, 1744, pp. 235–329.

20. *Röm. Gesch.* 1st ed., I, p. 169, n. 8; 4th ed., I, p. 256, n. 660. 'Es giebt ausser Italien und Griechenland für den Philologen keinen heiligeren Ort, als den Saal der Universität zu Leyden'. *Cf. Nachgelassene Schriften*, Hamburg, 1842, p. 141 (the account of the visit to Leiden contained in this book is most significant for Niebuhr's development. See especially p. 133). The first edition of the *Röm. Geschichte* was, as is well known, published in 1811–12 (in two vols.). The second edition of the first volume was published in 1827, the third in 1828. The second volume had a second edition in 1830. A third volume appeared in 1832 after Niebuhr's death. I quote from the so-called 4th ed. of vol. I (1833) and from the so-called 3rd ed. of vol. II (1836), which are reprints.

21. A portrait of Perizonius was painted by K. de Moor and is still hanging in the University Library of Leiden. A copy of it for the Senate Room of the University was made by H. van der Mij, *c*. 1737. I owe this information to Professor W. den Boer, of Leiden.

22. See *Vorträge über Römische Geschichte*, I, p. 71; *Röm. Geschichte* 4th ed., preface and I, 268, with the note 'Dass mir dies unbekannt war als ich zuerst über diesen Gegenstand schrieb, gestehe ich nicht ohne Erröthen; doch wussten es auch wenigstens die nicht, welche mich bestritten'.

23. G. Kramer, *Elogium Jacobi Perizonii* (diss. Berlin, 1828): its origin explained on p. 3. The Elogium is dedicated to Niebuhr, and of course Perizonius *is* the predecessor of Niebuhr (p. 29). It is quoted by J. E. Sandys, *A History of Classical Scholarship* III, 1908, p. 79, n. 2, but is not available either in the British Museum or in the Bodleian. I have used the copy in the Leiden Library. About Niebuhr in Bonn *cf.* F. von Bezold, *Geschichte der Rheinischen Friedrich-Wilhelms-Universität*, 1920, pp. 260–75.

24. Besides A. W. Schlegel, quoted below, n. 30, see W. Wachsmuth, *Die ältere Geschichte des römischen Staates*, Halle, 1819, pp. 19–23. Wachsmuth quite rightly emphasized the differences between Greek and Roman historiography and criticized the attribution of the 'carmina' to the plebeians. Also G. Bernhardy, *Grundriss der römischen Litteratur*, Halle, 1830, p. 71, disagreed with Niebuhr: the disagreement is expanded in later editions, for instance 5th ed., Braunschweig, 1872, pp. 42 and 196. *Cf.* K. Zell, 'Ueber die Volkslieder der alten Römer', *Ferienschriften*, 1829, II, pp. 97–224 (especially pp. 170–200), and W. Corssen *Origines poesis romanae*, Berlin, 1846, pp. 112–24.

25. *Röm. Gesch.* II, 3rd ed., p. 7. Among the points on which Niebuhr changed his mind there is the value of Cato's evidence (I, 4th ed., p. 268). He now recognized that Cato talked about the past. But his description of the 'Lieder' remained substantially the same (*cf.* I, 4th ed., pp. 272–4, with I, 1st ed., p. 178): some were longer ('die [Geschichte] von Romulus bildet für sich eine Epopöe'), some shorter (for instance, about Numa). With L. Tarquinius Priscus a poem started that ended with the battle of Lake Regillus. Niebuhr also thought that Ennius had used these ballads in his poem. In the second edition he tried to establish some connection between the ballads, the 'neniae', and the inscriptions of the Scipiones; this may be disregarded here.

26. A study of the evolution of Niebuhr's critical methods from the first to the second edition of the *Römische Geschichte* has not yet been written. I know that Dr G. Giarrizzo is collecting material for this purpose. Niebuhr's debt to Wolf is clear from the start (*Briefe*, I, p. 31; p. 437 *cf. Lebensnachrichten*, II, p. 7), and Herder (who had written a famous letter to Niebuhr's father, *Werke*, 24, p. 467) is in the background. About 1810 Niebuhr was interested in the Nibelungen (*Briefe*, I, p. 129) and must have read the brothers Grimm's earliest researches. But the rise of German and Romance philology happened between the two editions of the *Römische Geschichte*. *Cf.* on Niebuhr's early phase W. Dilthey, *Gesammelte Schriften*, III, 1927, pp. 269–75; G. Kuentzel, 'Niebuhrs Römische Geschichte und ihr zeitgenoessischer politischer Gehalt', *Festgabe für F. C. Ebrard*, Frankfurt, 1920, pp. 177–90; W. Norvin, 'N. og den historiske kritik', *Scandia*, 4, 1931, pp. 155–70 (pp. 162–7 on the ballad theory); E. Kornemann, *Histor. Zeitschrift*, 145, 1932, pp. 277–300. On the romantic theories of epic poetry *cf.* the bibliography given by I. Siciliano, *Les origines des chansons*, 1951, and by M. Thorp, *The Study of the Nibelungenlied*, 1940. D. Comparetti, *Il Kalevala o la Poesia tradizionale dei Finni*, 1891, is now available in *Poesia e Pensiero del Mondo Antico*, Napoli, 1944, pp. 278–552. See also K. Wais, *Frühe Epik Westeuropas*, 1953.

27. Most typical is his section on 'Die innern Fehden der Patricier' (3rd ed. II, pp. 141–6): 'Von den Fehden unter den Patriciern ist in der Geschichte jede Erwähnung ausgetilgt ... Was die Chroniken ewiger Vergessenheit übergaben, darüber durften die Ritualbücher nicht schweigen'. *Cf.* also II, pp. 188–93, on Sp. Cassius. Niebuhr is not always very kind towards the annalists themselves, e.g. II, p. 281.

28. *Cf. Röm. Gesch.* 3rd ed., I, p. 255 = 4th ed., I, p. 241.

29. What poetic sources Niebuhr ascribed to Herodotus is not always clear. One source was Choerilus (*Vorträge über alte Geschichte* ed. M. Niebuhr, Berlin, 1847, I, p. 387), but others are more vaguely indicated as 'Volkssagen, poetische Sagen' (I, p. 205, indirectly used by Herodotus? pp. 402 ff.). *Cf.* also *Römische Geschichte* 4th ed., I, p. 260, 'bei den Griechen hat noch der Perserkrieg den Charakter freier epischer Dichtung.' Niebuhr repeatedly emphasized the epic character of Livy: *Briefe*, I, p. 318 (1804); *Kleine Schriften* I, 1828, p. 90.

30. *Werke*, XII, pp. 444–512, from *Heidelbergische Jahrbücher*, 1816, pp. 833 ff.; the opinion on the 'carmina', pp. 448, 497. On p. 453: 'Wo Hr. Niebuhr einen Nachhall altitalischer Poesie zu vernehmen glaubt, da spüren wir nichts als griechische und gräcisierende Rhethorik'. Among the supporters of the Greek origin of some Roman traditions there is E. Pais in his 'prima maniera': *Studi*

Storici, 2, 1893, pp. 145–89, 314–57; *Storia di Roma*, I, 1, 1898 (on the 'carmina', pp. 8–10); *Ricerche storiche e geografiche*, Torino, 1908, pp. 306–449. W. Soltau unconvincingly analysed the Roman tradition in terms of Greek substance and Roman form: *Die Anfänge der roemischen Geschichtsschreibung* (1909).

31. K. W. Nitzsch, *Die Römische Annalistik*, Berlin, 1873, p. 249; *cf.* *Historische Zeitschrift*, II, 1864, pp. 1–30; Niebuhr, *Röm. Geschichte*, I, 4th ed., p. 274, had written: 'Wenn die pontificischen Annalen die Geschichte für die Patricier verfälschten, so herrscht in dieser ganzen Dichtung plebejischer Sinn.' On Nitzsch and Niebuhr, H. Merzdorf, *K.W.N. Die methodischen Grundlagen seiner Geschichtsschreibung*, Leipzig, 1913, pp. 4–40, is important.

32. *Römische Geschichte*, I, 1853, pp. 53–73, with a very complete bibliography, and *cf.* H. C. Willenborg, *De Diocle Peparethio ... deque Niebuhrio etc.* (diss. Münster, 1853). *Cf.* G. C. Lewis, *An Inquiry into the Credibility of Early Roman History*, I, London, 1855, pp. 202–42. On the importance of G. C. Lewis see my remarks in *Contributo alla storia degli studi classici*, 1955, pp. 249–62. Among the supporters of Niebuhr there was Friedrich Schlegel, *Geschichte der alten und neuen Literatur*, 1812, Berlin, 1841, pp. 75–8. Later M. A. Krepelka, 'Römische Sagen und Gebräuche', *Philologus*, 37, 1877, pp. 450–3 (the second part of this study does not seem to have appeared). H. Usener's 'Italian myths' have nothing to do with Niebuhr's 'Roman ballads'.

33. *Röm. Forschungen*, II, 1879, pp. 113–52. J. J. Bachofen's attack against it, 1870, in *Die Sage von Tanaquil*, *Gesammelte Werke*, 6, 1951, pp. 380–405 (see also E. Kienzle's Nachwort, p. 455). Bachofen's criticisms are very damaging to Mommsen (especially on the point of the meaning of ἰσοψηφία), but do not contribute anything positive. Mommsen's approach to early Roman history is defined in *Röm. Geschichte*, I (8th ed. 1888), p. 88: 'nur durch Rückschlüsse aus den späteren Institutionen.'

34. Mommsen–Wilamowitz, *Briefwechsel*, 1935, p. 43, 'die Niebuhrsche Wahnkritik'. *Cf. Die römischen Tribus in administrativer Beziehung*, 1844, p. viii. Elsewhere Mommsen was more guarded in his expression about Niebuhr's method. *Cf. Reden und Aufsätze*, 1905, p. 199, and the juvenile utterances in *Juristische Schriften* (*Gesamm. Werke*), III, 1907, pp. 465, 586. The introduction by D. Gerhard to *Die Briefe B. G. Niebuhrs*, I, 1926, pp. lvi–lvii, is still too conventional on this matter. *Cf.* A. Heuss, *Theodor Mommsen und das 19. Jahrhundert*, Kiel, 1956, p. 22, and the important letter from Mommsen published by A. Wucher, *Th. Mommsen*, Göttingen, 1956, pp. 131–2.

35. *Röm. Geschichte*, I, 8th ed., 1888, p. 229. 'Nur die Griechen und die Deutschen besitzen den freiwillig hervorsprudelnden Liederquell.'

36. *Röm. Gesch.*, 1st ed., I, p. 430; 3rd ed., II, p. 273. The analysis of Coriolanus' legend is very different in the two editions. In the first edition Niebuhr emphasizes the peculiarity of the surname Coriolanus and the various versions of his death; in the second edition he makes a determined effort to explain why Coriolanus remained a hero to the Romans (II, p. 271; the whole page is typical of Niebuhr's method). He suggests that Coriolanus gave up the idea of bringing political exiles back to Rome.

37. *Die Römische Annalistik*, p. 249.

38. *Storia dei Romani*, I, p. 22, n. 44, 'il Niebuhr che qui, come altrove, ha segnato la via giusta smarrita poi da' suoi successori.' Among earlier Italian

supporters of Niebuhr, notice R. Bonghi, *Storia di Roma*, II, 1888, pp. 244–8.

39. Valer. Max.: 2, I, 9, 'maiores natu in conviviis ad tibias egregia superiorum opera carmine comprehensa pangebant, quo ad ea imitanda iuventutem alacriorem redderent'. Cato in his *carmen de moribus* had expressed another view about early Roman poetry: 'Poeticae artis honos non erat. Si quis in ea re studebat aut sese ad convivia adplicabat, crassator vocabatur' (Aul. Gell. *N.A.* 11, 2, 5). I admit that the relation between this statement and the other about the banquet songs is not clear to me (perhaps it was not clear to Cato either). It is idle to speculate about Cato's sources, but it is good to remember that Roman jurisprudents were bound to know something about the various kinds of 'carmina'. See below, p. 250, n. 61.

40. *Carm.* 4, 15, 26–32. *Cf.* Quintil. I, 10, 20. It is traditional to assume that both Horace and Quintilian refer to the banquet songs, and I do not want to disagree; but their words are by no means explicit.

41. *Atene e Roma* 4, 1923, pp. 51–4. It is worth recalling Suet., *Aug.* 100, 'canentibus neniam principum liberis utriusque sexus', on which *cf.* H. de la Ville de Mirmont, *Études sur l'ancienne poésie latine* (1903), p. 361.

42. *Storia di Roma* 1, p. 4. *Cf.* also E. Manni, 'Intorno alla questione dei carmi conviviali etc.', *Mondo Classico* 5, 1, 1935, pp. 130–9. But *contra*, B. Riposati, M. Terenti Varronis *De Vita Populi Romani*, Milano, 1939, pp. 187–93.

43. H. Dahlmann, 'Zur Ueberlieferung über die altrömischen Tafellieder', *Abh. Akad. Mainz*, 1950, n. 17, pp. 1192–1202. He is approved by O. Gigon, *Festschrift A. Debrunner*, Bern, 1954, 151 n. *Cf.* W. Kroll, P-W, s.v. 'Nenia', col. 2393; F. Altheim, *Epochen d. röm. Geschichte*, 1, 1934, pp. 223–4. R. Reitzenstein, *Hermes*, 48, 1913, pp. 268–72, tried to eliminate both 'caniturque adhuc barbaras apud gentes' about Arminius (Tac., *Ann.* 2, 88) and Dionys. VIII, 62, about Coriolanus as evidence for 'Heldenlieder'. I am not sure that he has succeeded in either case. On Coriolanus see below. In the case of Tacitus Reitzenstein did not take into account the contrast 'canitur – Graecorum annalibus ignotus' to be compared with 'celebrant carminibus antiquis – quod unum apud illos ... annalium genus est'. As E. Norden said, 'Dass wirkliche Lieder zu verstehen seien, hatte nie bezweifelt werden dürfen' (*Germanische Urgeschichte*, p. 273, n. 3).

44. F. Wehrli, *Dikaiarchos* (*Schule des Aristoteles* 1), fr. 88 and commentary. But see also R. Reitzenstein, *Epigramm und Skolion*, 1893, pp. 3–44; Aly in P-W, s.v. 'Skolion'.

45. *Pax*, 1265 ff.; *Eccles.* 678. *Cf.* also *Nub.* 1365; Plat., *Tim.* 21b. For children eating with their fathers, Plato, *Lach.* 179c; Xenoph., *Symp.* I, 8. I take it that Greek and Etruscan children might sing *assa voce*. Arist., *Eccles.*, 678, is worth quoting καὶ ῥαψωδεῖν ἔσται τοῖς παιδαρίοισιν τοὺς ἀνδρείους ἐν τῷ πολέμῳ. But I do not claim to see clearly the development of the rhapsodos' art. *Cf.* H. Patzer, *Hermes*, 80, 1952, pp. 314–25; H. Koller, *Philologus*, 100, 1956, pp. 159–206. Older bibl. in Aly, P-W, s.v. 'Rhapsodos'.

46. Müller's text is accepted by E. M. Steuart, 'The Earliest Narrative Poetry of Rome', *The Class. Quart.*, 15, 1921, pp. 31–7, and by implication by C. M. Bowra, *Heroic Poetry*, London, 1952, p. 46. Cichorius' conjecture (*Römische Studien*, 1922, pp. 33–6; *cf.* fr. 37 Morel, *Fragmenta poet. Lat. epic. et lyric.*

1927) is rightly considered with some suspicion by S. Mariotti, *Il Bellum Poenicum e l'arte di Nevio*, Roma, 1955, pp. 92–5. As Festus is talking in the same context of M. Terentius Varro as a legate of Pompey in the war against the pirates, it is worth mentioning that P. Atilius was another legate in the same war (Appian., *Mithr.* 95). The allusion, for all that we know, may even be to him. The coincidence is remarkable. I should perhaps mention that F. Altheim (*Geschichte d. Latein. Sprache*, 1951, p. 446) argued that a 'carmen' was the source of Livy 8, 38–39. Apart from other considerations Livy himself rules out this suggestion: 'nec quisquam aequalis temporibus illis scriptor extat' etc.

47. G. Pasquali, *Preistoria della poesia romana*, Firenze, 1936, p. 74, who follows F. Leo, *Gesch. d. Röm. Lit.* I, 1913, p. 19, 'dass der freie Knabengesang alt und ursprünglich ist, der andere, Rundgesang zur Flöte, griechischem oder etruskischem Brauch entspricht'. Niebuhr was already in doubt about the meaning of the passage on Coriolanus (II, 3rd ed., p. 273), *cf.* also H. Stuart Jones, *CAH*, VII, p. 326; E. Bickel, *Geschichte d. römischen Literatur*, 1937, p. 383. [H. T. Rowell's remark *Am. Journ. Phil.*, 78, 1957, p. 422 is interesting, but not decisive for the existence of the 'Carmina'.]

48. This is suggested by A. Rostagni, *Storia*, I, pp. 46–7. *Cf.* also E. Norden, *Die Röm. Literatur* 4th ed., 1952, p. 6. The idea that Dionysius simply copied his source and never knew what he was talking about cannot be disproved, but does not commend itself to me.

49. *Ann. Scuola Normale di Pisa*, 1947, pp. 194–200. Timpanaro follows Leo's suggestion, *Der Saturnische Vers*, 1905, p. 32.

50. Rostagni sees here a banquet song, *Storia*, I, pp. 45, 64. But Virgil clearly implies a carmen sung by the Salii. *Cf.* Diomedes I, p. 476 Keil, 'cum Salios iuniores aequis gressibus circulantes induceret' and Geiger, P-W, s.v. 'Salii', 1878; also E. Norden, *Agnostos Theos* (reprint 1956), p. 153. On the song of Mamurius Veturius (Varro, *LL*, VI, 49; Festus s.v. 'Mamuri Veturi', p. 131 M. = 117 L.), E. Norden, *Aus altrömischen Priesterbüchern*, 1939, p. 231.

51. On Diocles *cf.* my remarks, *JRS*, 33, 1943, p. 102.

52. On Callim., *Dieg.*, V, 25, see R. Pfeiffer, *Callimachus*, I, 110, with the essential correction in II, 114 ('Bellum igitur Etruscum et Horatii Coclitis πήρωσις a Callimacho narrata esse possunt'). Callimachus is enough to show the weak point of J. M. Nap, *Die Römische Republik um das J. 225 v. Chr.*, Leiden, 1935.

53. On F. Altheim's theory – first presented in *Griechische Götter im alten Rom*, 1930, p. 13, *cf. Römische Religionsgeschichte*, Sammlung Göschen, 1956, II, p. 45 – see Wilamowitz, *Glaube d. Hellenen*, II, pp. 329–30, Walde-Hofmann, *Lat. Etym. Wört.* s.v. 'Iuturna'. V. Basanoff, *Evocatio*, 1947, p. 152 ff., agrees with Altheim on many points.

54. See H. Peter, *Hist. Rom. Rell.*, I, 2nd ed., p. 32, fr. 17, from Livy II, 40, 10. *Cf.* the telling passage of Cicero, *Brut.*, 10–11, 41–43. E. Pais, 'Intorno alla genesi della leggenda di Coriolano', *Studi storici*, 3, 1894, pp. 71–91, 263–82, does not improve on Mommsen, but his conjecture that Fabius Pictor may have had something to do with the present form of the tradition of the Fabii at Cremera deserves attention, *Studi Storici*, 3, 1894, pp. 339–52. Pais gave another explanation of the Coriolanus legend in *Storia di Roma* I, 1st ed.,

1898, p. 500. E. Ciaceri, *Le origini di Roma*, pp. 366–9, accepts the tradition on Coriolanus as substantially true. *Cf.* also E. T. Salmon, *CQ*, 24, 1930, pp. 96–101.

55. Livy I, 24, p. 1. *Cf.* Münzer, P-W, s.v. 'Curiatius' and 'Horatius', col. 2322. On G. Dumézil, *Horace et les Curiaces*, 1942, *cf.* H. J. Rose, *JRS*, 37, 1947, p. 185. See also F. Bömer, 'Ahnenkult und Ahnenglaube im alten Rom', *Archiv. f. Religionsw.* Beiheft I, 1943, and G. Dumézil, *Aspects de la fonction guerrière chez les Indo-européens*, 1956, pp. 25–39.

56. *Cf.*, for instance, P. Noailles, *Fas et Ius*, Paris, 1948, pp. 187–221. It is not our business to decide whether Virginia's *Ur-Legende* would fit into a ballad.

57. F. Münzer, P-W, s.v. 'Marcius', col. 1536; W. Schur, ibid., Suppl. V, s.v. 'Marcius' (which replaces his former research in *Hermes*, 59, 1924, pp. 451–3). O. Schönberger, *Hermes*, 83, 1955, pp. 245–8 (following W. Aly, *Livius und Ennius*, 1936, p. 37), tries to establish Livius' debt to Ennius; and Ennius would have imitated *Ilias*, 9, 526 ff.

58. E. Pais' efforts against 'gli argomenti alemanni' and for the authenticity of the story are more patriotic than convincing (*Ricerche sulla storia di Roma*, IV, 1921, pp. 411–37). *Cf.* now F. W. Walbank, *A Historical Commentary on Polybius*, I, 1957, pp. 92–4.

59. It will be enough to refer to the wise remarks by P. Fraccaro, 'La storia romana arcaica', 1952, in *Opuscula*, I, 1956, pp. 1–23, especially 20, see also *JRS*, 1957, pp. 59 ff. An excellent example of analysis of an episode is given by O. Gigon, 'Zur Geschichtsschreibung der römischen Republik', *Festschrift A. Debrunner*, Bern, 1954, pp. 151–77. About the especially difficult case of Tarpeia, see the bibliography in Momigliano, 'Tre figure mitiche', *Pubblicazioni Facoltà Lettere Università Torino*, 1938, pp. 23–8. Later: G. Dumézil, *Tarpeia*, 1947, pp. 249–91; F. Gansiniec, 'Tarpeia', *Acta Soc. Arch. Polon.*, I, 1949; S. Weinstock, *JRS*, 45, 1955, p. 239 [A. La Penna, *Studi Classici e Orientali*, 6, 1957, pp. 112–33; E. Devoto, *Studi Etruschi*, 26, 1958, pp. 3–16].

60. *Lebensnachrichten über B.G. Niebuhr*, III, 1839, p. 299. 'Der letzte politische Vorgang an welchem Niebuhr lebhaften Antheil nahm, war der Process der Minister Carls X, er wurde mittelbare Veranlassung zu seinem Tode'.

61. I have found much of interest in the chapter 'Some remarks on historical truth in ballad poetry', by J. C. H. Steenstrup (trans. by E. G. Cox), in the volume *The Medieval Popular Ballad*, Boston, 1914, pp. 237–51. The author, among other things, remarks that in many Germanic countries heavy penalties were attached to the composition of satirical ballads. He also mentions that in Icelandic legislation there is to be found a provision which forbade the composition of a poem on an individual, even though it contained no satire (two lines, however, were permitted). *Cf.* Hyperides 2 (4) *in Phil.* 3 for Athens. I have often wondered whether the Decemviral legislation may not have had something to do with the decline and end of ballad poetry in Rome. *Cf. JRS*, 32, 1942, p. 122.

On types of ballad poetry *cf.*, for instance, W. M. Hart, *Ballad and Epic*, Boston, 1907; F. E. Bryant, *A History of English Balladry*, Boston, 1913; W. J. Entwistle, *European Balladry*, Oxford, 1939, reprinted 1952; Ph. A. Becker, 'Vom Kurzlied zum Epos', *Zeitschrift f. französ. Sprache und Literatur*, 63,

1940, pp. 299–341, 385–444. W. von Scholz, *Die Ballade*, Berlin, 1942, I have not seen.

62. See J. Heurgon, 'La vocation étruscologique de l'empereur Claude', *C.R. Acad. Inscr.*, 1953, pp. 92–7. This is a very important paper.

63. *Cf.* my remarks in *JRS*, 36, 1946, pp. 198–9, discussing S. Mazzarino, *Dalla monarchia allo stato repubblicano*. Mazzarino is followed by Pareti, *Storia di Roma*, I, p. 312, and by J. Heurgon, *Historia*, 6, 1957, p. 75. They ultimately depend on Niebuhr, *Röm. Gesch.*, II, 1st ed., p. 529. De Sanctis, as is well known, tried to identify Mastarna with Porsenna: *St. dei Romani*, 1, p. 447, but see Fraccaro, *Opuscula*, 1, pp. 13–14. About Porsenna *cf.* Tac., *Hist.*, 3, 72; Pliny, *NH*, 34, 139.

64. On this treaty Perizonius, *Dissertationes*, VII, p. 696; De Beaufort, *Dissertation*, 1st ed., pp. 33–43; 2nd ed., pp. 33–40, should not be forgotten.

65. *Cf.* O. Skutsch, 'The Fall of the Capitol', *JRS*, 43, 1953, pp. 77–8 [*cf.* M. J. McGann, *Class. Quart.*, 51, 1957, pp. 126–8 and J. Wolsky, *Historia*, 5, 1956, p. 44].

66. On Corsica Theophrastus, *Hist. Plant.* 4, 8, 2; *cf.* S. Mazzarino, *Introduzione alle guerre puniche*, Catania, 1947, p. 89; Macrobius III, 9, 6. Sammonicus (early third century A.D.) quoted 'Furii vestustissimi libri' as his source. Wissowa, P-W, s.v. 'evocatio' takes the 'evocatio' of the gods of Carthage to be an invention by Sammonicus, but Horace, *Carm.*, II, 1, 25 ('Iuno et deorum quisquis amicior Afris inulta cesserat impotens'), seems to know it as Ed. Fraenkel once pointed out to me: *cf.* his *Horace*, 1957, p. 237. A conjecture on Furius (L. Furius Philus *cos.* 136?) in M. Hertz, *Fleckeisens Jahrbücher*, 85, 1862, p. 54; *cf.* V. Basanoff, *Evocatio*, 1947, p. 4: Basanoff gives the other bibliography. I am reminded by E. Gabba that the mysterious fragment of republican painting published by D. Mustilli, *Il Museo Mussolini*, 1939, 15, seems to represent events unknown to the literary tradition (*cf.* *CAH*, IX, p. 825).

67. This paper owes much to discussions with Ed. Fraenkel, G. Giarrizzo, O. Skutsch, S. Timpanaro and S. Weinstock. [*Cf.* now A. Rostagni, *Riv. Filologia*, 36, 1958, pp. 100–1 and F. Castagnoli, *Studi Mater. Storia Relig.*, 30, 1959, pp. 109–17.]

15

Vico's *Scienza Nuova:* Roman 'Bestioni' and Roman 'Eroi'*

THE story is by now famous. When at Harvard Gaetano Salvemini was told that a complete English translation of Vico's *Scienza Nuova* was about to appear, his enthusiasm was unbounded: 'L'Inglese è una lingua onesta. Di Vico non rimarrà nulla'. This was the protest by an Italian positivist against the use and abuse of Vico in the Italian idealistic tradition. But Vico has survived even his English translators, as he had survived his idealistic interpreters. One of the few authentically great minds in the field of history, he still eludes his own historians. The first difficulty is to find the exact historical situation in which to place him. In this essay I shall begin by giving a fairly dogmatic statement about what seems to me to be his position in early eighteenth-century Italian thought. Then I shall proceed to illustrate more precisely this position with special reference to the final version of the *Scienza Nuova.* Finally, in my last and longest section, I shall comment on Vico's interpretation of early Roman history. It must be understood that on each point I can offer no more than the impressions of an inveterate reader of those same antiquarian works which had been read by Vico himself.[1]

I

Giambattista Vico's solitude in his day was real enough. It can be compared with Baruch Spinoza's solitude in his own day. Nor would the comparison be an extrinsic one. Spinoza, though, of course, seldom quoted, was never far from Vico's mind. One need not go beyond the first paragraph of the first *Scienza Nuova* (1725) to find this implicit reference to Spinoza: 'we wish there to be a force superior to nature . . .

History and Theory, V, 1, 1966, pp. 3–23.

which is to be found solely in a God who is not that very nature itself'.[2] Ultimately Spinoza provided the model for the *mos geometricus* of the second *Scienza Nuova* (1730).

Spinoza had isolated himself by denying the traditional distinction between sacred and profane history, thereby implying the denial of the truth of both Judaism and Christianity. Vico found himself alone because he tried to re-establish the distinction between Hebrews and Gentiles, at a price which hardly anybody was prepared to pay in the early eighteenth century. The price was to concede to the XII Tables and to Homer the same authority on questions of human origins which the Bible had possessed since the triumph of Christianity.

The very essence of the problem with which Vico was concerned compelled him to part company with his contemporaries who discussed Descartes and Berkeley, Leibniz, Jansenism and the relations between State and Church. For the same reason he progressively lost interest in the problems of erudition which engaged most of the Italian and French scholars of his own time. He contributed nothing to the study of the fashionable Etruscans or of the authenticity of the 'acta martyrum'. The questions which worried him had been formulated one or two generations before in Protestant circles; the whole of his information was superficially anachronistic and intrinsically suspect to Catholic eyes. The prevailing intellectual interests in Italy, as in France, were certainly different from his own. With the trust in reason which came from Descartes and the trust in methodical historical criticism which came from Mabillon, the best French and Italian minds were reasserting in a modernized form a Catholic view of the world. Speculations on the early stages of mankind, on the early migrations of folks and myths, were replaced by archaeological explorations, researches in medieval libraries, exact studies in physics and mathematics. (Even the hypotheses on Etruscans and Pelasgians, which seem to us outrageous, were founded on newly acquired archaeological evidence; indeed this was the time of the first systematic excavations).

But Vico would not have been so isolated if he had simply preferred the problems of one or two generations earlier to those of his own time. After all, his concern with Biblical history was widely shared. Quite evidently many of his Italian contemporaries were thinking, and even writing, about the value of the Bible as a source for facts and doctrines. Like Vico they were aware of the various theories which in continuous succession during the second part of the seventeenth century had questioned the unique position of the Bible in the Christian system of beliefs. Spinoza's works circulated everywhere in Italy, in print or in manuscript, and we may remind ourselves that Giannone inherited a manuscript text of Spinoza's *Ethica* from his teacher Domenico d'Aulisio, a colleague of Vico and the author of *Ragionamenti intorno ai principi della filosofia e teologia degli Assiri*. Spinoza was rightly considered the most extreme and dangerous representative of a type of research which blurred the boundaries of sacred and profane history and often admitted the priority of pagans over Jews in the matter of moral and religious ideas. The works by La Peyrère, Marsham, Spencer, Wits, Huet, against which we shall see Vico battling, were also the best known to his contemporaries. The more we go beyond printed texts into the unprinted dissertations and letters of the early eighteenth century, the better we realize how much time and attention Italian scholars devoted to the question of the relation between sacred and profane history which was at the root of Vico's thought.

This is especially true in the kingdom of Naples, where the twenty-five years of Austrian rule between 1707 and 1734 represented a period of cultural re-orientation in the direction of central Europe and altogether an age of greater freedom. In those years in which Vico was writing and rewriting the *Scienza Nuova*, Antonio Costantino, a friar from Castrovillari, lived in Vienna on the stipend of a poet laureate. About 1730 he composed there a treatise *Philosophia adamito-noetica divina mundana* in which he re-echoed seventeenth-century ideas of a primitive philosophy transmitted impartially by Shem, Ham and Japhet to all the nations of the earth. Moses, Pythagoras and Sanchuniathon independently derived from it. Giannone, who at the time was also in Vienna, read part of Costantino's manuscript and immediately recognized that if Costantino was correct, Christianity was superfluous: 'If the matter should be reduced to this examination, I strongly suspect that the libertine writers especially the English as well as a few Dutch and German ... have won their case'.[3] The allusion to English deists went perhaps beyond Vico's terms of reference. I am not aware that he knew of Toland even indirectly. But the substance of Giannone's criticisms coincided with Vico's preoccupations. The fact that Costantino's treatise and Giannone's criticisms of it remained unpublished and unknown (they have been examined only recently by G. Ricuperati, the young Torinese student of Giannone's manuscripts) does not affect the point that so far Vico was working in a direction shared by others.[4]

To explain what separated Vico from scholars with similar interests we must return to the special kind of dualism he introduced between sacred and profane history. He put all morality and all rationality on the side of sacred history and saw in profane history the development of irrational instincts, truculent imagination, violent injustice – which Providence knew how to guide to its own ends. The question whether Vico's solution was orthodox from the contemporary Catholic point of view is irrelevant because no ecclesiastical authority disputed his orthodoxy. If the doctrinal correctness of some of his arguments was doubted by individual scholars (such as Giovanni Francesco Finetti and Damiano Romano), it was defended by others; this was the ordinary game. What matters is that his theory did not really interest the ordinary Catholic scholar, or the libertine, or the extreme anticurialist. The orthodox, who liked to have his Bible buttressed by pagan learning, soon found out that Vico almost invariably refused to recognize in pagan sources a distorted image of facts told by the Bible. The libertine and the anticurialist, who wanted attacks against papal authority, were bound to discover that Vico accepted papal power *in toto*. While Vico's *Scienza Nuova* passed through ecclesiastical censorship without difficulty, Giannone's *Triregno* remained unpublished for about 150 years. With all the similarities in approach and information to the *Scienza Nuova*, the *Triregno* told only one story; and this was a story which started with a 'civitas terrena', continued with a 'civitas coelestis', and ended with a 'civitas diaboli' – 'Del regno papale.'[5]

Vico attributed too much importance to the Old Testament and too little to the New Testament to be relevant to his Italian contemporaries. But later, in the eighteenth century and early nineteenth century, the origins of each nation became more interesting than the origins of mankind, and the rhythm of barbarism and civilization was taken to be one of the great subjects of historiography. Homer and the XII Tables were acknowledged as two of the most important documents of early times independently of their relation to the Bible. Even the irrational ways of thinking which Vico had recognized as characteristic of archaic paganism became acceptable to an increasing number of scholars. Thus Vico was hailed as their predecessor by those who did not share his concern with a clear separation between profane and sacred history, but who accepted his view of profane history as the true view of history as such. Romantics, anticlericals and pantheists of various gradations were the chief rediscoverers of Vico on the European scene of the early nineteenth century.[6] They turned his novel and original explanation of the old conflict between the sacred and the profane into a pre-Hegelian philosophy of history.

II

The final version of the second *Scienza Nuova*, which appeared in 1744 a few months after Vico's death, is not of course a text to which its author had been able to give last-minute attention. Since about 1740 Vico had only been a shadow of his former self and in the last years, as his biographer tells us, 'no longer did he take pleasure, as he had in the early days of his illness, in the Latin authors read to him by his devoted Gennaro. He would spend the entire day sitting in a corner of his house, not merely calm but silent as well.' But illness is not the explanation for Vico's extraordinary disregard of what his contemporaries were writing. There is very little in the *Scienza Nuova* that could not have been written with the instruments which European erudition had provided before 1700. The few allusions to later works are normally unnecessary and occasionally mere pieces of adulation (such as the reference to the *Iuris Naturalis et gentium Doctrina metaphysica* by Niccolo Concina, a Paduan professor). Vico's boast in 1729 'stabilimmo finalmente da ben vent'anni fa di non leggere più libri' must be very near the truth.[7] There were contributory linguistic factors in this attitude. His inability to read English and French cut Vico off from the original text of many significant contemporary books and put him at the mercy of the summaries which appeared in Italian and Latin journals. But Vico showed equal indifference towards books in Italian – a language which after many hesitations he had decided, and managed, to master: 'Parla con tanta affettazione nella nostra lingua che degenera in un vero seccatore', a visitor from Siena remarked to another Sienese in 1726.[8] For a man who was so desirous of the approval of his contemporaries, so eager to maintain those human contacts of which he felt he was being deprived, ignorance of the contemporary world of learning is doubly significant. There is a letter, a famous letter, by Vico in which this position emerges clearly. In 1725, on receiving the first *Scienza Nuova*, the French Jesuit Edouard de Vitry invited Vico to contribute literary news about Naples and Sicily to the *Mémoires de Trévoux*. Vico answered that he knew nothing about Sicily ('de' letterati di quell'isola qui non si ha affatto contezz' alcuna'). As for Naples, he would only be able to give sad news. The wise men (and by wise men he meant Vico) were satisfied that the literary republic was near its end. The war for the Spanish succession was over, a war to be compared with the Second Punic War or with Alexander's expeditions; yet no king had shown any willingness to pay for the composition of an official history of it in Latin. With kings so insensitive to their own glory and to the preservation of Latin style, could anyone be surprised that the price of Latin books was falling? The library of Giuseppe Valletta, which thirty years before had been worth 30,000 scudi, had now to be sold for 14,000 (Vico himself had valued it). France was not immune from the decline, if the library of Cardinal Dubois had to be dispersed for lack of an *amateur* prepared to buy the whole. In all the sciences exhaustion was noticeable. Descartes had ruined philosophy. Faith in the Latin Vulgate (Vico prudently says 'ragionevole riposo sopra . . . la version vulgata') had destroyed the interest of the Catholic countries in Oriental studies. Roman juris-prudence was cultivated only in Holland – and did not flourish even there. Hence the multiplication of encyclopaedias and dictionaries which reminded Vico of the Byzantine compilations. Hence the luxurious reprints of old books which like 'salse saporose' were meant to make palatable what was no longer fresh. The genius of the century, Vico concluded, was more in the repetition of what was already known than in the mastery of the old in order to discover the new.[9]

*

This manifesto amounted to a declaration of war against the new Cartesian culture and was in keeping with the selection of four old masters – Plato, Tacitus, Bacon, Grotius – as guides towards the *Scienza Nuova*. In practice Vico made little use of Plato and Tacitus: they remained pieces of classical scenery, the one contemplating man as he should be, the other as he is. But he sought his information in the learned books of the sixteenth and seventeenth centuries and derived his problems from them. Thanks to the researches of Benedetto Croce and Fausto Nicolini we are probably better informed about the books read by Vico than about those read by any other Italian writer, Dante included. Even so it remains difficult to separate what Vico read from what he heard about, what he misunderstood because he read from what he misunderstood because he did not read. Vico, as is well known, had an almost infinite capacity for misquotation. One can hardly expect any-thing else from a man who worked in his room surrounded by his eight Neapolitan children as well as frequent visitors. A classic example is provided by his reference in the *Autobiography* to his Jewish friend from Leghorn, Giuseppe Athias, an interesting person who contributed to the diffusion of the first *Scienza Nuova*.[10] Vico says that 'he had formed a friendship with him' in Naples and explains: 'Among the Hebrews of this age, Athias is reputed to be the most learned in the study of the sacred tongue, as is shown by his edition of the Old Testament published in Amsterdam, a work which has won acclaim in the republic of letters'. Unfortunately the edition of the Old Testament alluded to by Vico had been published in Amsterdam by Joseph ben Abraham Athias, quite a different man, two generations earlier in 1661.

What counts, however, is the kind of book with which Vico was acquainted. This is easy enough to establish. When he wrote the *Scienza Nuova*, he was interested in three trends of seventeenth-century erudition. Two of them might be described as resulting from Bacon's New Learning; the third was certainly represented best by Grotius himself. Vico read, or heard of, books about the chronology of ancient history, about the relations between the Jewish–Christian revelation and the wisdom of the Gentiles, and about the earliest evidence for Natural Law. What is more, Vico was well aware that each of the three types of research was closely connected with the others and implied them. To accept the chronological claims of the Egyptians and of the Chinese meant not only to call in question the reliability of traditional biblical chronology, but also to doubt the priority of the Jews over the Gentiles. On the other hand, if it were true that sound religious knowledge (even the belief in the Holy Trinity) was hidden in Egyptian hieroglyphs and other Oriental documents, the unique value of the Bible became automatically questionable. Finally, Vico realized the dangers of attributing a knowledge of the principles of Natural Law to the oldest pagan nations. No doubt it became easy to discover fine moral principles in barbarians if one allegorized their myths and beliefs and attributed a secret wisdom to them. But it became correspondingly more difficult to resist Grotius' claim (the point of Vico's dissent from him) that his system of Natural Law remained true even if God did not exist.

*

Of course the classification of objectionable doctrines is not so neat in the *Scienza Nuova*. My summary runs so counter to Vico's habits that I feel bound to produce a sample of the authentic style of the *Scienza Nuova*. It is taken from those additions to the 1730 edition which remained unpublished until Fausto Nicolini's edition: 'These ideas should, all at once, overturn the system of John Selden, who claims that the natural law of eternal reason had been taught by the Hebrews to the Gentiles, based on the seven precepts bequeathed by God to the sons of Noah; they should overturn the *Faleg* of Samuel Bochart, who maintains that the Sacred tongue had been spread by the Hebrews to the other peoples and then deformed and corrupted in their midst; and, finally, they should overturn the *Dimostrazione evangelica* of Daniel Huet (who follows closely upon the *Faleg* of Bochart, just as the *Faleg* of Bochart follows upon the system of Selden) in which the most learned gentleman attempts to make one believe that the fables are sacred tales altered and corrupted by the Gentiles, and especially by the Greeks'.[11] John Selden, Samuel Bochart and Pierre Daniel Huet are good representatives of the seventeenth-century effort to reduce the differences between Jews and Pagans. They variously tried to show that even before Abraham, or at any rate not long after him, the essential elements of the true religion had been communicated to all the descendants of Noah. It will be noticed that the first of the representatives chosen by Vico was a Puritan, the second was a French Calvinist, and the third was a Catholic bishop of dubious reputation. He was obviously not aware of the far more radical opinions which Toland had opposed to Huet in his *Origines iudaicae sive Strabonis de Moyse et Religione iudaica historia breviter illustrata*, where Moses was transformed into a pantheist 'sive, ut cum recentioribus loquar, Spinosista'.[12]

In his evaluation of the heretical implications of seventeenth-century learning, Vico was certainly taking into account his previous inclination towards some of its tenets. He, too, had once used the notion of secret wisdom and had attributed it to the ancient Italians when in 1710 he had published *De antiquissima Italorum sapientia ex linguae latinae originibus eruenda*. *De antiquissima* was a fiction in the sense that Vico attributed to the ancient Italians a theory of knowledge which was his own, but there is no reason for doubting the genuineness of his belief that such theory was implied in the very structure of the Latin language.

*

It is more difficult to say whether Vico ever accepted integrally Grotius' doctrine of Natural Law. He read Grotius for the first time rather late, in 1713. The *Autobiography* testifies to the enormous impression it made on him. A few years later, about 1717, he was asked to write some notes for a new edition of the *De iure belli* which was being prepared in Naples. Vico himself explains that 'after having covered the first book and half of the second', 'he abandoned the task, reflecting that it was not fitting for a man of Catholic faith to adorn with notes the work of a heretical author'. Fausto Nicolini is probably right in suggesting that the change in the political situation of Naples had something to do with Vico's decision.[13] The appointment of Cardinal von Schrattenbach as viceroy in 1719 started a period of collaboration with the Roman curia. Yet Vico's fears make sense only if his commentary was altogether very favourable to Grotius. Disagreement with Grotius' notion of the workings of Providence in history, such as Vico was to express later in the *Scienza Nuova*, would have been more than sufficient to cover him against accusations of religious laxity. We may surmise that between 1717 and 1719 Vico was not yet in a position to advance decisive objections against Grotius. Finally, we must remember that in his youth, about 1690, Vico had been a friend of the epicureans who were indicted by the Holy Office for their belief that there had been men in the world before Adam. This was the theory of Isaac de La Peyrère (1655), which Vico mentioned in the *Scienza Nuova* as contrary to true religion. The exact impact on Vico of his early association with freethinkers – on which the *Autobiography* is naturally silent – must remain doubtful.[14] But on the whole it seems clear that from the vantage ground of the *Scienza Nuova* Vico criticized views on chronology, on the secret wisdom of the pagans, and on the notion of Natural Law to which he himself had been partial in previous years.

As everyone knows, the *Scienza Nuova* assigned a new meaning to the early traditions of the Gentiles. They were to be taken neither as factual history nor as cryptograms of real knowledge. They were the outcome of undisciplined imagination and as such they were very representative of the society which produced them. They could not claim to compete with the Jewish truth either in the matter of chronology or in points of morality and faith. They were the fancies of brutal giants who even physically were distinguishable from the Jews: indeed only the Jews had been able by proper diet to preserve normal stature. In emphasizing the poetic, irrational, even beastly elements of primitive fantasy, Vico refuted by one stroke the claims of those who preferred Chinese or Egyptian chronology to Biblical chronology, the claims of those who interpreted pagan myths as symbols of Jewish and Christian doctrines, and finally the claims of those who believed early pagan nations to have been ruled by Natural Law. 'Tutte le storie barbare hanno favolosi principi': the accounts the barbarians gave of themselves could not be taken as hard facts. Unlike Newton, who dealt with similar problems, Vico did not have to rely upon complicated chronological calculations to demonstrate the superiority of the Bible over any other historical records. His answer to scholars of dubious orthodoxy was *a fortiori* an answer to Spinoza.

The discovery of the primitive stage of uncontrolled fantasy – which was also the stage of the creation of human languages – was for Vico the answer to all the theological doubts raised by erudition. As the barbarians would not have achieved unaided the transition from imagination to reason, the rule of Providence was consequently reasserted. Providence guided the primitive pagan towards the use of reason and ultimately towards the true understanding of God. The process of development included the formation of a military and intellectual élite, the heroes, who took the lead. The surviving primitive 'bestioni' struggled against the heroes in order to obtain equality. When equality was achieved, Providence further used her own tricks to guide both heroes and 'bestioni' towards monarchy. Relapses into barbarism were of course admitted in such a process. In the early eighteenth century few men, if any, spoke of unlimited, linear progress. As a Christian, Vico accepted the idea of fall; as a humanist, the idea of decline. His theory of the 'ricorsi' was a combination of both, the least surprising feature of the *Scienza Nuova*. But Vico does not seem seriously to have contemplated future dark ages. He seems to have ascribed finality to Catholic monarchies, such as the new kingdom of Naples established by Charles of Bourbon in 1734. There are one or two passages in the second *Scienza Nuova* which seem to envisage an even better political organization – a confederation of aristocratic republics, a sort of *Respublica Christiana*, but the theme is not developed.[15] In any case we would still be in a Christian world untroubled by desires of real social and religious reforms. The discovery of the *Scienza Nuova* gave authentic joy and peace of mind to Vico. As he states in his *Autobiography* 'when he had written this work, enjoying life, liberty and honour, he held himself more fortunate than Socrates'. He was convinced that the *Scienza Nuova* was a powerful support for the Catholic *status quo* against the wrong beliefs of Protestants and atheists.

This was the great paradox of the *Scienza Nuova*. Vico found both his masters and his most dangerous opponents among Protestants and Jews (and the masters were not very distinguishable from the opponents). At the same time he disliked as misguided and dismissed as insignificant most of the Catholic scholars and philosophers of his own time. But he derived his feeling of security from the renewed strength of the Catholic states and the revival of Catholic scholarship. Since the intervention of Bollandists and Maurists, Catholic scholarship had become a match for that of the Protestants. In Italy men like Scipione Maffei and Ludovico Antonio Muratori gained international reputation as Catholic scholars.[16]

The very fact that they had shifted controversy from the Pre-Adamites to the relics of local saints and from the hieroglyphs to the Gothic and Langobard scripts showed their command of the situation. They formulated the new problems. The problems raised by earlier generations were as yet unsolved; they were still being discussed, and were bound to re-emerge in strength with later generations, but they were not the vital questions in the intellectual climate obtaining between 1715 and 1740. Vico relied on this prestige of Catholic scholarship. Yet he ignored its problems and by implication rejected them. In the very way in which he reinterpreted Roman history as part of his argument, he showed the most fantastic disregard of all serious contemporary scholarship.

III

When Vico prepared what was to be the 1744 edition of the *Scienza Nuova*, he attributed equal importance to his Roman and to his Greek example of primitive, heroic civilization. This balance is deceptive in more than one sense.

The section on Homer was greatly expanded in the second *Scienza Nuova*.[17] The 'discoverta del vero Omero', though initiated in the *Diritto Universale* of about 1721, came to fruition only in the *Scienza Nuova Seconda* (1730). The addition of so many pages on Homer in the second *Scienza Nuova* gave new strength to Vico's theory that in the heroic ages men wrote history in the form of epic poetry. Homer was set up as the most conspicuous representative of heroic civilization, medieval French literature offered confirmations in its epic poems, and even the difficult Roman evidence seemed to fall into the pattern. Vico quoted Naevius and Ennius, and followed some wrong-headed editors of the grammarian Diomedes in attributing to Livius Andronicus a poem *Romanis* for which there is no ancient authority.[18] In doing so he broke his own periodization by quoting poets who no longer belonged to the heroic age. But the analogy of Homer gave respectability to this chronological licence. Vico tried to reinforce it further by recognizing 'un'aria di versi eroici' in the *Carmen Saliare* and by quoting some of the preserved lines of the 'carmina triumphalia' which certainly never belonged to the heroic age of Rome.

All this can easily make us forget that even in the second *Scienza Nuova* Vico did not base his interpretation of the Roman heroic age on fragments of epic poetry, but on the fragments of the XII Tables. True enough, already in the first *Scienza Nuova* he had mentioned 'l'aria di verso eroico' of the fragments of the XII Tables (ed. Nicolini, 211). Now he developed the subject. He knew from Cicero that Roman children chanted the XII Tables 'ut carmen necessarium' (*De Leg.* 2.23.59). He tried, therefore, to discover verses in the surviving fragments of the XII Tables. In one of his Pindaric flights he went as far as to say: 'The whole of ancient Roman law was one weighty poem which was performed by the Romans in the forum, and the ancient jurisprudence was an austere form of poetry'.[19] He built up a careful parallelism between Homer and the XII Tables. Both were a collective product, both were couched in 'heroic' language, both summarized various stages of a gradual transition from primitive barbarism to the relative maturity of the heroic age.

Yet this artificial analogy between Homer and the XII Tables can deceive nobody. The fact remains that Vico took law as his chief evidence for Roman archaic civilization, while he chose epic poetry as representative of the Greek heroic age. Furthermore it remains clear that Vico was unable to draw a picture of Greek civilization. He had almost no Greek, and his knowledge of Greek history was below the standards to be expected of a learned man of the eighteenth century. But even if he had been a better Hellenist, there was not much he could have done with two poems for which no historical background had yet been discovered. His theory that Homer was not an individual, but rather Greece itself singing its own heroic history, was one of those profound intuitions to which only later scholars could do justice. Fifty years later, in the age of the encyclopaedic F. A. Wolf, scholars began to possess that knowledge of Greek dialects, institutions, archaeology – and that acquaintance with comparative materials, such as Sanskrit literature – which gradually broke the isolation of the Homeric poems.

★

While archaic Greek history was beyond his reach, Rome was a reality to a man who had confined his linguistic ambitions to Latin and whose training was that of a student of law. He knew the literary sources, the legal texts, and the very language of archaic Rome. He was also acquainted, if only in general terms, with what ten generations of scholars since the fifteenth century had done to determine the position of the plebeians in the Roman State, to interpret the XII Tables in relation to later legislation, and to assess the powers of the Senate under the monarchy and during the early Republic.

The conflict between patricians and plebeians dominated archaic Roman history. It was the elementary datum from which Vico had to start. The patricians naturally filled the role of heroes of the Roman heroic age. They were 'collerici e puntigliosi' like Achilles. Each 'pater familias' ruled his own family despotically and considered himself of divine origin. Collectively the patricians were the priests of the State, filled its Senate and chose the king. The State was therefore aristocratic even if formally the patricians elected a king above themselves. Vico was convinced that Rome had conformed to the rule that men relinquished barbarism through the exertions of an aristocracy, not under the guidance of kings. Effective monarchy, in Rome as elsewhere, was a later stage, the final step of an evolution which went from aristocracy through democracy to monarchy. Vico saw his aristocrats as great colonizers who treated ruthlessly the people they encountered in their migrations. Their representative was 'the famous Gallic Hercules who, with the chains of poetic gold (that is, grain) issuing from his mouth, chains by the ears great multitudes of men and leads them after him whither he will'.[20] (Book II, 560.) The law of the Quirites was the natural law of these conquerors.

The plebeians presented more complex problems to Vico. He took them to be the heirs of the primitive 'bestioni', but was not certain that they really looked like stupid giants. At times one has the impression that in their 'low and cramped quarters' (II, 595), restless and in debt, the Roman plebeians were not perceptibly different from the *lazzaroni* of Naples. Though fond of classical scenery, Vico after all had never visited Rome. It is not quite clear how, according to him, the patricians managed to get their plebeians as clients and servants ('famuli'). But he at least explained that one of the ways was to offer 'asylum' to strangers. 'A plebei, come reputati d'origine bestiale, si permettevano i soli usi della vita e della naturale libertà'. The plebeians were not prepared to endure this treatment forever. They asked for better laws – indeed they asked for laws as such. The patricians believed in 'mores'; the plebeians wanted 'leges'. The impulse to legislate came from the requests of the plebeians. The history of Roman law represented successive attempts by the patricians to placate their subjects. It marked the evolution from aristocracy to democracy. The consequences of the assimilation of the plebeians into Roman society were also to be seen in the Latin language. The plebeians brought into it those words which have 'origini selvagge e contadinesche' – which reminds the modern reader of 'Latin as a language of peasants' according to A. Meillet's teaching.

*

Vico fixed the end of the original regime of clientship for the plebeians in 326 B.C., the date of the *lex Poetelia* which abolished the 'nexum'. He wrongly took the 'nexum' to be identical with the bond of clientship and interpreted its abolition as the act of admission of the plebeians to the full rights of Roman citizenship. It followed that 326 B.C. became in Vico's mind both the date of the entrance of the plebeians into the full rights of citizenship and the date of the transition from aristocracy to democracy in Rome. All the previous events of the internal history of Rome had to be reinterpreted to fit into this scheme – not a mean task. That the *lex Publilia Philonis* 'de patrum auctoritate' of 339 B.C. was thus taken to have transformed the old absolute control of the patrician *patres* over the plebeians into a less binding moral tutorship was a comparatively minor point. The main consequence was that the creation of the *comitia centuriata* had to be transferred from the age of Servius Tullius to a date after 326 B.C. – more precisely to 304 B.C. – because the plebeians, not being Roman citizens, could not have been members of the *comitia centuriata* before 326. If tradition implied that King Servius had enrolled the plebeians in his classes in accordance with his census, it could only mean that the Servian classes had nothing to do with the *comitia centuriata*. In Vico's version of the story, the old king gave the plebeians precarious possession of the land they cultivated in exchange for their paying rent to the patricians and serving in the army: the classes originally determined the military and financial obligations of the plebeians. The census of Servius Tullius appeared to Vico to be 'the first agrarian Law of the world'. It did not satisfy the plebeians for long. They secured a radical improvement of their situation with the XII Tables.

Vico was again unorthodox in his evaluation of the XII Tables. He took the most mysterious clause – on the 'forctes sanates', which nobody understands – to represent a new agrarian law.[21] He persuaded himself that by that law the plebeians obtained full rights to the land they had so far possessed precariously. But this involved the plebeians – or rather Vico – in other difficulties. What benefit would there have been for the plebeians in acquiring 'ius quiritium' on the land, if their marriages were not valid and consequently they were not allowed to transmit their property to their children? Vico's answer was that the plebeians soon realized that they had been cheated by the patricians. With the first death of a plebeian after the enactment of the law on the 'forctes sanates', it became obvious that his relatives were not entitled to inherit the land he had owned. Thus, within four years from the traditional date of the XII Tables, the plebeians forced the patricians to grant full validity to their marriages, which was the prerequisite for the validity of any inheritance. True enough, the ordinary interpretation of the 'lex Canuleia de connubio patrum et plebis' of 445 B.C. was and still is that it abolished the prohibition of marriage between patricians and plebeians. But Vico reinterpreted it to mean that it allowed 'iustae nuptiae' between plebeians.

In such a version of the story there was no place for the decemviral legislation as a whole. Vico had other general reasons for thinking that the law on the 'forctes sanates' was the only one enacted in 451 B.C. As already stated, he stretched the analogy between Homer and the XII Table to imply that the XII Tables were equally the product of a long evolution. This attitude alone would have made it imperative for him to get rid of the ancient tradition that the Romans sent an embassy to Athens to study the local laws before proceeding to formulate the XII Tables. A foreign origin of Roman law was also contrary to Vico's conviction that in the heroic age each nation independently produced its own legislation according to its own needs. Consequently he devoted a whole chapter to a detailed analysis of the tradition of the embassy to Athens, and one is bound to acknowledge that though doubts on this tradition seem already to have been expressed in antiquity, his criticisms were new and remain a masterpiece.

The tale of the embassy was only one of the main links which seemed to connect early Rome with distant Greece; and Vico was anxious to sever them all, without denying that the Romans had received the alphabet from some Greeks. He therefore postulated the existence of an early Greek colony in Latium which communicated the alphabet to the Romans. The same hypothesis also offered an economic explanation of the origin of the names Euander, Hercules, Aeneas and others. Vico was acquainted with the Latin version of Samuel Bochart's dissertation which denied that Aeneas had come to Italy. He accepted Bochart's conclusions but modified them in two points. He construed the legend of the arrival of Aeneas as an invention of the Greek colonists in Latium and conjectured that the Romans came to know it when they conquered and destroyed the colony and transferred its citizens to Roman territory. According to Vico's chronology, this happened before 451 B.C. But it was not until about 280 B.C., at the time of the war against Pyrrhus, that the Romans were sufficiently interested in things Greek to appropriate the legend of their subjects and to transform it into their own national legend. Curiously enough, the idea that the Aeneas legend was nation-alized in Rome only about 280 B.C. was revived in 1943 by J. Perret, unaware of the precedent of Vico. The idea of a Greek colony in Latium as a possible mediator did not occur to Perret. Yet the notion of such a Greek colony was perhaps one of Vico's most realistic guesses. We now know that Cumae performed many of the functions Vico attributed to his unnamed colony, and the part played by Greek emigrants in Etruscan cities, such as Caere, is increasingly realized. There has even been conjecture, supported by respectable archaeological and mytho-logical evidence, of an Achaean or Mycenaean settlement in Latium.

This point, however, is not very important for Vico. What is essential to his argument is that Rome developed its early system of law inde-pendently of the Greeks and that this system was mainly directed to-wards a progressive assimilation of the plebeians – the 'bestioni' – into the city of the patricians – the 'eroi'. The two central events of Roman archaic history were two agrarian laws, one corresponding to the tra-ditional Servian constitution and the other representing the nucleus of the XII Tables.

We are therefore left with a problem which, though hardly noticed by Vico's interpreters, seems to me the most important and difficult in his account of early Roman history. Where did Vico get this extraordinary idea of transforming the Servian constitution and the alleged nucleus of the XII Tables into two agrarian laws? He was well aware of saying something important because he talked of Servius Tullius' Law as the first agrarian law of the world. My researches on the study of Roman agrarian laws in the seventeenth century – and more generally on the interpretation of the Servian constitution and of the XII Tables – have yielded no results. So far I have been unable to discover predecessors to Vico in this theory.[22] Even in the interpretation of the 'forctes sanates' clause, which had already puzzled ancient commentators of the Republican period, he seems to be alone. For all I know, Vico may well be the originator of this unorthodox chapter of archaic Roman history. If it were so, we would have to ask ourselves what inspired Vico. Such bold thinking on agrarian problems, which would not surprise in a Filangieri, is, at least to me, unexpected in Vico. The reform of the feudal institutions was freely discussed in Naples between 1720 and 1740; it has lately been the object of an interesting book by Raffaele

Ajello. But I fail to see any close relation between the attempts to limit
the legal and fiscal privileges of the Neapolitan aristocracy and clergy
and Vico's views about the progressive admission of the plebeians to
full rights of ownership of the land. No doubt G. Giarrizzo is right in
suggesting that Vico's interpretation of early Roman history is influenced
by his identification of Roman 'clientela' with medieval feudalism. But
this was not new and does not explain the introduction, or rather invention, of the two agrarian laws of Servius Tullius and the Decemviri.

*

Not the least difficulty in interpreting Vico is the doubt that we may be
taking him too seriously. The agrarian laws look imposing when we
meet them in the field of Roman history. But what if we meet them
again in a casual interpretation of the myth of Atalanta? According to
Vico, who *more solito* misunderstood his Ovid, it was Atalanta who
threw away the apples of gold, and each apple was an agrarian law.
Perhaps I must produce my evidence to be believed: 'Atalanta, by
throwing away the golden apples, defeats her suitors in the race . . . [the
meaning here is that] Atalanta first concedes to the plebeians the boni-
tary and then the quiritary ownership of the fields while withholding
connubium; just as the Roman patricians [conceded] the first agrarian
law of Servius Tullius and the second agrarian law of the Twelve Tables,
yet retained *connubium* as a prerogative of their own order'. (Book II,
653.) Such is Vico's attempt to extend the notion of agrarian laws to the
heroic age of the Greeks.

*

Beautiful Atalanta and her apples are perhaps not superfluous if we are
to assess the claim that the emphasis on class struggle makes Vico a
Marxist *avant la lettre*. The claim goes back to George Sorel's *Etude sur
Vico* published in the *Devenir Social* of 1896. But it is well known that
Marx himself commended Vico to Lassalle in 1861: 'It surprises me
that you seem not to have read Vico's *New Science* – not for anything
you would have found in it for your special purpose, but for its philosophical conception of the spirit of Roman law in opposition to the legal
Philistines'. Through Antonio Labriola, Paul Lafargue, and Trotsky's
famous quotation on the first page of the *History of the Russian Revolution*, the notion percolated into Edmund Wilson's *To the Finland
Station* and is now the foundation of the very respectable work by

Nicola Badaloni, *Introduzione a G. B. Vico* (1961), the result of twenty years of study on Vico as a forerunner of Marxism.[23]

Vico's interpretation of history certainly relies on class struggle. The heroes are conservative, the plebeians press for change. In so far as Providence decides who is going to make the changes, we may read in Vico some approval of the plebeian moves. Such an unprejudiced historian as Mario Fubini has shown in memorable pages that Vico, the Neapolitan plebeian, was much in sympathy with the Roman plebeians.[24] Yet Providence, in unfolding her plans, guides towards monarchy which abolishes class struggles and gives the aristocrats a chance to retain some power. What Vico calls 'le grandi monarchie ne' loro costumi umanissime' were not likely to enact new agrarian laws. Indeed it is one of the subtleties of Vico to realize that legislation played less important a part during the Roman principate than during the republic. He was reluctant to conceive the transition from democracy to monarchy in terms of legislative steps. He relegated to the world of fable the 'lex Regia', which since Cola di Rienzo had loomed so large in the books of the lawyers and in the fancies of political agitators.

If we look carefully we shall see that class struggles are characteristic of only one stage of Vico's scheme, the heroic period. And the reason why the heroic age anywhere was characterized by class struggle is obviously that its model was to be found in the struggle between Roman patricians and plebeians. With the best will in the world nobody could have eliminated the struggle between patricians and plebeians from the archaic history of Rome.

*

The Marxist interpretation, like any other interpretation, represents only one of the potentialities of Vico's thought. Vico himself seems to have been convinced that in his own time 'bestioni' and 'eroi' had no longer any cause to quarrel. The memory of Masaniello was conveniently fading into the past. There was no disagreement between him and his learned Italian contemporaries on this point. Disagreement, if that is the word, started with Vico's emphasis on Rome. From time to time, it seems, Italians need a rest from Rome – a 'secolo senza Roma' – to help them bear their Roman heritage. Vico's contemporaries were certainly enjoying such a period, with all its implications of municipal and regional pride and of resentment against the Roman curia. If 'etruscomania' was the light side of it – a sort of academic carnival – Giannone's *Istoria civile* represented the other side. Giannone's Neapolitans rather than

Vico's Romans caught the spirit of the age. If we had to add other representative works we should of course mention Maffei's *Verona Illustrata* and Muratori's *Antiquitates Italicae*. On a less provincial horizon Vico was equally unaware of the discussions on the credibility of early Roman history which had started in Holland about 1686 and had been taken up in the French Academy by Pouilly and others about 1722. Vico never analysed the historians of early Rome, though he showed by his criticism of the tradition on the embassy to Athens that he would not have been lacking in technical abilities for such a work. He was altogether indifferent to all the epigraphical, numismatic and archaeological evidence which was the chief interest of his contemporaries. Even his few Neapolitan admirers had to concede that he was not learned enough for his time. In 1766 Tanucci, in retrospect, wrote to Galiani: 'The blessed Vico .. had need of some Vossius, Lipsius, Turnebus, Victorius, Manuzio, Averani, Petavius to act as advisor, to help him fill in – with facts about nations and individuals, and with the reflections of wise men – those lacunae of proofs which lie beneath the arcs of his great leaps'.[25] On the other hand, the only contemporary foreign student of his work, l'Abbé du Bignon, was unable to swallow the 'esprit de système' of the *Scienza Nuova*.[26]

Vico's hour came when the French Revolution showed that an entire generation of 'bestioni' was in existence. Scholars were persuaded to look back, either with nostalgia or in horror, at the unreasonable beginnings of human history. Even so, it was not to be Vico's fate to inspire the new historiography. As Giuseppe Ferrari remarked about 1840, 'Vico finds himself famous just at the moment in which he has no longer anything to teach us'.[27] It was not until Wolf and Niebuhr had done their work, with a thoroughness in research of which Vico had been incapable, that he was recognized as their precursor. Wolf himself later called attention to the similarities between his own doctrines and Vico's, whereas Niebuhr, as far as I know, never mentioned Vico. According to the not always reliable Antonio Ranieri, Giacomo Leopardi vainly tried to provoke Niebuhr into giving his opinion of Vico. There is perhaps more truth in a statement, written by P. Capei while both Leopardi and Niebuhr were alive, that Niebuhr never mentioned Vico to Leopardi. It was J. K. Orelli who in an article in *Schweizerisches Museum* of 1816 first pointed out in public the similarities between Vico and Niebuhr. In the matter of details, the similarities between Vico and Niebuhr were as conspicuous as the differences. Niebuhr, like Vico, thought that the first Roman historians were poets. Like Vico, he meditated intensively on the problem of the 'ager publicus' and saw the plebeian smallholders as the progressive element in Rome. Both Vico and Niebuhr excluded the plebeians from the early *curiae*. On the other hand, Vico never mentioned the heroic banquet songs which, according to Niebuhr, were the carriers of early Roman tradition. (As I have shown elsewhere, modern historians like G. De Sanctis and L. Pareti mistakenly read into Vico certain ideas on popular poetry which Vico never held.) As to the two agrarian laws imagined by Vico, they are very different from the sober delimitation of the notion of 'ager publicus' (formerly identified with the whole of the Roman territory) which is Niebuhr's greatest single contribution to the understanding of archaic Rome.

But on a deeper level Vico and Niebuhr made similar efforts to understand (more intuitively than rationally) the ethos of early Rome and the position of patricians and plebeians in it. Both had the intellectual courage and the originality needed for re-thinking the whole of the Roman tradition. Michelet was right in his famous remark, aimed especially at Niebuhr: 'These illustrious Germans might have remembered that they had all lived in Vico'.

Yet Vico, who had never seen Rome, never made it his business to write about Rome. Instead he started from an intuitive understanding of Rome in his quest to bring Providence back into the process of history. By means fair and foul he evoked the early 'bestioni' because he wanted to be reassured about Providence. In the contemplation of all-pervading Providence he found the divine pleasure which Spinoza found in the contemplation of all-pervading God, *sive natura*. To be more precise, Romulus' 'bestioni' provided Vico with a reassurance against Spinoza and other students of the Bible. Vico was convinced that he had providentially brought Providence back into human actions. Whether Providence shared Vico's view about his own providential rôle is still a point to be decided.

*

A new stage has begun in the study of the *Scienza Nuova* in relation to post-Freudian and post-Wittgensteinian theories on myth and language. Sir Isaiah Berlin's lecture delivered at the Italian Institute in London some years ago is an example of this.[28]

My own contribution to the interpretation of Vico is on more limited ground. Being a student of Rome, my first concern was to try to understand what Vico wrote about Rome. But I hope to have made it clear that Vico's notion of Roman history is a part of his dualistic interpretation of history. According to him the conflict between 'bestioni' and 'eroi' is possible only in profane history. The Jews never produced either 'bestioni' or 'eroi'. Vico's philosophy of history is one of the most serious and profound attempts to reassert a Christian – or, perhaps, Hebrew – dualistic vision of the world on the eve of the age of Enlightenment.

Vico is no longer a simple precursor, but a guide to the understanding of his successors. His position is similar to that of the Dead Sea scrolls in relation to the Gospels. First the Gospels threw light on the Dead Sea scrolls, but now the Dead Sea scrolls are beginning to teach us something about the Gospels. Thanks to Vico it has already become abundantly clear why the Catholic scholars of the early eighteenth century left unsolved the problems of the non-orthodox erudition of the previous century. But we do not yet know, and we shall know only slowly, what Vico can still teach us about the ways of thinking of those later historians and philosophers who never read him.

References

1. The literature on Vico until about 1947 is to be found in the priceless *Bibliografia Vichiana* by B. Croce and F. Nicolini (Naples, 1947–8). The later period until 1958 is well covered by Paolo Rossi in his edition of Vico's *Opere* (Milan, 1959), pp. 41–8. Only some of the later works known to me are mentioned in what follows. Indispensable for the understanding of the *Scienza Nuova* is of course the *Commento storico alla seconda Scienza Nuova* by F. Nicolini, 2 vols. (Rome, 1949–50). Among Nicolini's own works *La religiosità di G. B. Vico* (Bari, 1949) – cf. the discussion by L. Bulferetti in *Annali Facoltà Lettere Cagliari* XIX (1952) with new texts – is essential for the subject of the present paper.

2. 'Desideriamo esservi una forza superiore alla natura ... la quale unicamente è da ritruovarsi in un Dio che non sia essa natura.'

3. 'Se la cosa si vorrà ridurre a questo esame, dubbito forte che gli scrittori libertini e spezialmente gli inglesi e qualche olandese e germano ... non abbiano vinta la loro causa.'

4. *Cf*. G. Ricuperati's paper in *Rivista Storica Italiana*, 1965. See also F. Nicolini, *G. B. Vico e Ferdinando Galiani*, Naples, 1952, p. 66.

5. On the general cultural background, in addition to G. Maugain, E. Garin (*La Filosofia*, Milan, 1947), see B. De Giovanni, *Filosofia e diritto in F. D'Andrea*,

Milan, 1958, and Badaloni's book quoted below. More generally, H. Benedikt, *Das Königreich Neapel unter Kaiser Karl VI.*, Vienna, 1927; R. Colapietra, *Vita pubblica e classi politiche del viceregno napoletano*, Rome, 1961. *Cf.* the bibliography by F. Liotta in the article 'Aulisio, Domenico' in *Dizionario Biografico degli Italiani*, IV, 1962, and P. Piovani, 'Il pensiero filosofico meridionale tra la nuova scienza e la Scienza Nuova', *Atti Accad. Scienze, Lettere ed Arti in Napoli*, LXX, 1959, pp. 77–109.

6. On the special Italian scene – to begin with J. de Maistre (E. Gianturco, 'J. de Maistre and G. B. Vico', Ph.D. thesis, Columbia University, 1937) – it is not surprising to find Vico popular among Catholic romantics. The chief text is N. Tommaseo's book on Vico (on which *Bibliografia Vichiana*, II, p. 600), re-edited by A. Bruers, Turin, 1930. *Cf.* also C. Marini, *G. Vico al cospetto del sec. XIX*, Naples, 1852. On Vico and Hegel see the important remarks by E. De Negri, *Romanische Forschungen*, LXII, 1950, pp. 277–93, based on G. Gentile, *Studi Vichiani* (2nd ed., Florence, 1927), pp. 149–65.

7. F. Nicolini, *La Giovinezza di G. B. Vico*, Bari, 1932, p. 133.

8. F. Nicolini, *Giovinezza*, p. 165. Vico's native language was, of course, the Neapolitan dialect.

9. A convenient text of this letter is, for instance, in *Opere*, ed. P. Rossi, p. 225.

10. See the article by L. Gencarelli in *Diz. Biogr. degli Italiani*, IV, 1962, and supplement this with F. Nicolini, in his edition of the *Autobiografia*, Milan, 1947, pp. 184–90.

11. 'Le quali cose tutte ad un colpo devono rovesciar il sistema di Giovanni Seldeno, il quale pretende il diritto naturale della ragione eterna essere stato dagli ebrei insegnato a' gentili sopra i sette precetti lasciati da Dio a' figliuoli di Noé, devono rovesciare il *Faleg* di Samuello Bocarto, che vuole la lingua Santa essersi propagata dagli ebrei all'altre nazioni e tra queste fossesi difformata e corrotta; e finalmente devono rovesciare la *Dimostrazion evangelica* di Daniello Uezio, che va di seguito al *Faleg* di Bocarto, come il *Faleg* del Bocarto va di seguito al sistema del Seldeno nella quale l'uomo eruditissimo s'industria di dar a credere che le favole siano sagre storie alterate e corrotte da' gentili e sopra tutti da' greci'. *Scienza Nuova Seconda*, ed. F. Nicolini, Bari, 1942, II, 180.

12. It will be enough to mention F. E. Manuel, *The Eighteenth Century Confronts the Gods*, Cambridge, Mass., 1959, pp. 149–67 and his later book *I. Newton, Historian*, Cambridge, Mass., 1963; E. Iversen, *The Myth of Egypt and its Hieroglyphs in European Tradition*, Copenhagen, 1961; M. V.-David, *Le débat sur les écritures et l'hiéroglyphe aux XVIIᵉ et XVIIIᵉ siècles*, Paris, 1965. P. Vernière, *Spinoza et la pensée française avant la révolution*, I–II, Paris, 1954, is essential; we need corresponding research for Italy and other countries. On Vico and Spinoza see R. Sabarini, *Il tempo in G. B. Vico*, Rome–Milan, 1954. As is well known, Vico suppressed in the 1744 edition some offensive remarks against Spinoza contained in the 1730 edition (¶ 1214–27, ed. Nicolini). *Cf.* E. Boscherini Giancotti, *Giorn. Crit. della Filos. Italiana* 3, 17, 1963, pp. 339–62 and bibliography there quoted.

13. 'Vico e Grozio', *Biblion* 1, 1959, fasc. 2. *Cf.* Nicolini's paper on Vico's 'apoliticità' in *Atti Accad. Pontaniana* N.S. 5, 1955, pp. 289–98; 299–317.

14. The whole episode (on which references for instance in A. Corsano, *Umanesimo e religione in G. B. Vico*, Bari, 1935, pp. 17–33) needs further study.

On Vico and Epicurus E. Paci, *Ingens Sylva*, Milan, 1949. See more in general A. Corsano, *Il pensiero religioso italiano dall'umanesimo al giurisdizionalismo*, Bari, 1937, pp. 98–178; G. Spini, *Ricerca dei libertini*, Rome, 1950, pp. 318–26; S. Mastellone, *Critica Storica*, 2, 1963, pp. 451–63.

15. Book V, 1093–4.

16. S. Bertelli, *Erudizione e storia in L. A. Muratori*, Naples, 1960; idem, 'Erudizione e crisi religiosa nella coscienza europea avanti l'opera muratoriana', *Memorie della Deputazione di Storia Patria per le antiche Provincie Modenesi*, 9, 2, 1962.

17. F. Nicolini, 'Sugli studi omerici di G. B. Vico', *Memorie Accad. Lincei*, VIII, 5, 10, 1954.

18. *Cf.* my *Secondo Contributo*, Rome, 1960, p. 70.

19. 'Tutto il diritto romano antico fu un serioso poema che si rappresentava da' Romani nel foro, e l'antica giurisprudenza fu una severa poesia'.

20. Book II, 560. Passages from the *Scienza Nuova* quoted in English are taken from the remarkable translation by T. G. Bergin and M. H. Fisch, Ithaca, 1948, now reprinted in an abridged and revised version with a new important introduction (Anchor Books, Garden City, N.Y., 1961).

21. Notwithstanding F. Nicolini, *Commento storico* II, 220, I am not clear about what edition of the XII Tables Vico used. I have consulted D. Gothofredus' edition (1586), 63; J. Gothofredus in S. Leewius, *De origine et progressu J. C. Romani*, Lugd. Bat., 1671, p. 295; J. V. Gravina, *Origines iuris civilis* Leipzig, 1708, pp. 412–14. *Cf.* M. H. Fisch, *Essays in Political Theory Presented to G. H. Sabine*, Ithaca, 1948, pp. 62–88.

22. Essential help is still provided by M. Lipenius, *Bibliotheca Realis Juridica*, Leipzig, 1757. *Cf.* G. Giarrizzo, *Bullett. Istituto Storico Italiano per il Medio Evo*, 74, 1962, pp. 11–16. The derivation of medieval feudalism from Roman clientela was a well-known sixteenth-century theory (G. Budé, V. Zasius).

23. The references are given by M. H. Fisch and T. G. Bergin, *The Autobiography of G. Vico*, Ithaca, 1963, pp. 104–8. [Originally published 1944.] The notes in this edition (which I have used in my quotations) are a very useful supplement to the *Bibliografia Vichiana. Cf.* also A. M. Iacobelli Isoldi, 'Vico e Marx', *Giornale Critico della Filosofia Italiana*, 30, 1951, pp. 69–102 and 228–53, her book on Vico, Bologna, 1960, and A. Rotondò, *Società*, 11, 1955, pp. 1011–47.

24. *Stile e umanità di G. B. Vico*, Bari, 1946, p. 63.

25. 'Il benedetto Vico ... aveva bisogno di qualche Vossio, Lipsio, Turnebo, Vettori, Manuzio, Averani, Petavio per assessore, onde empiere colli fatti delle nazioni e degli uomini e colli pensieri dei sapienti quelle lacune di prove che rimangono sotto gli archi dei suoi salti'. B. Croce and F. Nicolini, *Bibliografia Vichiana*, I, p. 209 from B. Tanucci, *Lettere a F. Galiani*, ed. Nicolini, Bari, 1914, II, pp. 21–2. *Cf.* R. Cotugno, *La Sorte di G. B. Vico*, Bari, 1914, pp. 195–232.

26. *Histoire critique du gouvernement romain*, Paris, 1765, XXXV. *Cf.* F. Venturi, *L'Antichità svelata e l'idea del progresso in N. A. Boulanger*, Bari, 1947, pp. 149–74.

27. J. Ferrari, *Vico et l'Italie*, Paris, 1841–2, p. 465.

28. 'The Philosophical Ideas of Giambattista Vico', published in *Art and*

Ideas in Eighteenth-Century Italy, Edizioni di Storia e Letteratura, Rome, 1960, pp. 156–233. *Cf.* A. Pagliaro, *Altri saggi di critica semantica*, Messina–Florence, 1961, pp. 297–474, who studies Vico from the point of view of F. De Saussure's general linguistics.

Recent important contributions on Vico include: F. Amerio, *Introduzione allo studio di G. B. Vico*, Turin, 1947; A. R. Caponigri, *Time and Idea: The Theory of History in G. B. Vico*, Chicago, 1953; A. Corsano, *G. B. Vico*, Bari, 1956. Among special studies, F. Lanza, 'Sinossi allegorica della Scienza Nuova', *Contributi dell'Istituto di Filologia Moderna*, Milan, 1961, pp. 99–135; H.-J. Daus, *Selbstverständnis und Menschenbild in den Selbstdarstellungen G. Vicos und P. Giannones*, Geneva, 1962.

There is some useful information in G. Villa, *La filosofia del mito secondo G. B. Vico*, Milan, 1949.

16

Mabillon's Italian Disciples*

I

Two French Benedictine monks of the Congregation of Saint Maur –
Jean Mabillon and Bernard de Montfaucon – stand on the threshold of
the Italian revival of learning in the early eighteenth century. Their
journeys to Italy, and even more their accounts of these journeys, were
momentous. They proved to the Italians the immense superiority of
contemporary French scholarship and indicated the arduous way towards recovery, if recovery there had to be. More specifically, they made
a profound impression on scholars of Northern and Central Italy. The
kingdom of Naples was, politically and culturally, different from the
rest of Italy. It should be treated separately.

II

There was nothing in Italy comparable with the Abbey of Saint Germain
des Prés to which both Mabillon and Montfaucon belonged. There was
perhaps nothing comparable in any part of the world. The Dutch Universities, above all Leiden, were centres of learning. The Dutch scholars
were busy producing those critical editions, commentaries, dissertations
on points of antiquity, which the contemporary world needed and
bought. At Antwerp there were the Bollandists, methodically attending
to their task of studying and publishing the evidence about all the saints:
they were at the height of their reputation with Daniel Papebroch, and
their *Acta Sanctorum* were soon to be condemned by the Spanish
Inquisition. But by the end of the seventeenth century neither the

*A lecture delivered at the Italian Institute, London, in June 1958, and
published only in *Terzo Contributo alla storia degli studi classici e del mondo
antico*, Rome, 1966, pp. 135–52.

Dutch scholars nor the Bollandists could really compete with the Benedictines of Saint Germain des Prés in thoroughness, complexity and
audacity of enterprise. The Maurists published model editions of
Fathers of the Church and other ecclesiastical writers – St Ambrose,
St Augustine, Athanasius, Basilius, Gregorius Nazianzenus, John
Chrysostomus, Gregory the Great, St Anselm, St Bernard; they
systematically explored the libraries of France and other countries; they
studied ecclesiastical history, which meant in fact the whole of the
Roman Empire and of the Middle Ages; they gave rules and established
standards of historical research which nobody had ever seen before.
They combined archaeology with the study of literary texts and documents and were among the founders of medieval iconography. They
methodically extended their work to cover the whole of the history of
France in all its aspects and became the recognized masters of regional
history. The monks were working co-operatively. Their team spirit
became a legend. The healthy and the sick, the young and the old were
made to contribute to the work of the house; and proof-reading was the
most usual occupational therapy. The Abbey functioned as an Academy
where one could meet Ducange, Tillemont, Baluze, the flower of
European scholarship. The leaders were great personalities who were
respected and sought after at the French Court, and whose influence
radiated well beyond France into Catholic and Protestant countries.
Each of their works was suspiciously examined in Rome by the religious
authorities, and almost every one of them provoked controversies in the
Church. But the monks of Saint Germain almost invariably had their
own way. At least until 1713 they never identified themselves with anti-
Jesuits or anti-Jansenists, with extreme Gallicans or extreme Romanists,
though they were rather pro-Jansenist and pro-Gallican. They obviously knew the arts of diplomacy and also knew that they could rely
on the support of the king of France. But basically they trusted their
learning, they wanted 'sincera secernere ab spuriis, certa ab incertis,
ut rebus pie ac sancte gestis sua constet auctoritas', and they sent round
their folios to the glory of the Church.

The older of the two men we have mentioned – Jean Mabillon – was
something more than a great scholar. A peasant's son of meditative
habits, he was invited to join the learned group of Saint Germain des
Prés at the age of 32. For the next 43 years, between 1664 and 1707, he
contributed to the ethos of Saint Maur with his own personality. Dislike
of scholasticism; love for the pagan classics; rigorous, yet pious, criticism of the evidence; an affection for old-established religious practices

and a deep suspicion of any attempt to increase the number of Christian martyrs – all this spread in Saint Germain des Prés from his example. His ingrained respect for established shrines, especially if they belonged to his own order, led him astray in later years, about 1700, when he defended the worship of the Sainte Larme de Vendôme. But in 1685 when he undertook his journey to Italy in the company of Père Michel Germain, he was in the full maturity of his critical genius, in full command of his devotion to truth. He had already published an edition of St Bernard, the first instalments of the monumental work on the saints of his order and the treatise on the proper method of determining the date and authenticity of ancient documents, the *De Re Diplomatica*. Even now, needless to say, these three works remain fundamental. Furthermore Mabillon had already travelled in Germany and Switzerland to explore monastic libraries and had come back from Luxeuil with the discovery of a Merovingian lectionary, a capital document of the Gallican liturgy, of which he made a worthy edition.

The account of the Italian journey that appeared in 1687 under the name of *Iter Italicum* makes fascinating reading even now. The Latin of Mabillon is far from being scholastic. He had a feeling for nature and art. He could describe the waters falling down from the Alpine peaks and the extraordinary ability of the natives in jumping from rock to rock on their mountains. Naples pleased him immensely, though at least one of the local librarians proved to be particularly annoying. He made no secret of his dislike of the devotional habits of the Italians and therefore singled out for praise the conduct of the religious ceremonies in S. Maria Maggiore in Rome. He had no sympathy for dubious relics either. He was suspicious of the Turin Shroud and rather negative about the Pavia claim to preserve the bones of St Augustine. But he had been sent to Italy to collect facts, and facts he did collect, omnivorously. Books, inscriptions, works of art, details of ancient and modern life are duly registered with great economy of words. As one would expect, modern facts are illustrated with learned references, not only to Virgil and Sidonius Apollinaris, but to the Latin Petrarch and to Politian and Muretus. From time to time a pretty anecdote is reported. And at Ravenna where the manuscripts were few and the water was bad, there was the consolation of some good wine sent by the bishop.

Mabillon was not the man to say much about the men he met. He never generalized about the weakness of contemporary Italian scholarship, but it can be inferred from the whole of his report that he never found his match. His companion Père Germain, who combined a little touch of Sancho Panza with the scholar's austerity, was more explicit. In his most interesting letters to French brethren he acknowledged the sympathy and admiration with which Mabillon was being received, but also made it plain that he had a poor opinion of Italian scholars. Père Germain went as far as to say that they could be stirred out of 'dolce far niente' only by jealousy of the French achievements.

Now, two questions of vital importance were raised by Mabillon's journey. Would Italian scholars be receptive to his ideas? And would Mabillon be prepared to intervene directly and to exercise his authority in order to improve Italian scholarly activities?

As to the first point – concerning Italian public opinion – it is certain that already before Mabillon's arrival many people had felt uneasy about the decline of classical and ecclesiastic studies in Italy and realized that the initiative had passed to France and Holland. Something was beginning to be done about the most obvious aspect of this decline: the widespread ignorance of Greek due to the fact that the Jesuits seldom taught it in their schools and that there were very few professors to teach it competently in the Universities. It is well to remember that at the beginning of the eighteenth century Greek was not taught at Padua, Bologna, Turin: the teaching was interrupted for 25 years in Pisa. In Florence, Rome and Naples there were chairs, but the professors were notorious for their incompetence. In Padua, about 1670, the saintly cardinal Gregorio Barbarigo had transformed the local 'Seminario' into a centre of Greek and Latin studies which, especially on the Latin side, was very active throughout the eighteenth century. But not all the people who aimed at better studies were necessarily working in Mabillon's direction. His teaching directly affected medieval and ecclesiastic studies; it was only indirectly relevant to classical antiquities. There was some connection between Mabillon's work and the theological and ecclesiastical disputes provoked by the doctrines of Port Royal. Until further research is done, it would be unwise to attempt any generalization on this subject. It is, however, only too obvious that those Italians who sympathized with the Jansenists and disliked the Jesuits were particularly ready to welcome the work of Mabillon and his brethren.

All would be simple enough if we could say that Mabillon was eager to exploit these sympathies. But the language of the *Iter Italicum* and the tone of Père Germain's letters show that he was suspicious of Italian scholars. Two cases deserve special notice. In Florence there were Magliabechi and Noris. Magliabechi must not be dismissed simply as a book-collector who had a gargantuan appetite for the latest novelty. He was taking full advantage of the relatively liberal atmosphere of the Tuscan regime, and collaborated with the Bollandists and other scholars of advanced views. He is even credited with having helped the early circulation of Baruch Spinoza in Italy. As for Enrico Noris, nobody ever doubted that this friend and protégé of Magliabechi had a sharp mind and was to be reckoned with both in theology and the classics. His controversial *Historia Pelagiana* of 1673, a source of endless discussions, and his model monograph on the *Cenotaphia Pisana* (1681) were there to prove his worth.

Mabillon of course had been in touch with both Magliabechi and Noris long before he came to Italy. He had never had any difficulty in exchanging bibliographical information with Magliabechi, and through Magliabechi he had got to know Noris. But before, during and immediately after his journey to Italy he showed a marked coldness towards Noris which deserves some explanation. Noris dedicated to Mabillon a polemical pamphlet which he published under a false name in 1681. Mabillon was not enthusiastic about this dedication. In the four years that followed, he seems to have communicated with Noris only through Magliabechi. When they actually met in Italy in 1686 they sympathized even less. In a letter to Mabillon Père Estiennot, the Procurator of the congregation of Saint Maur in Rome, accused Noris of having denounced Mabillon's views to the Roman authorities. This incident was not forgotten. It is true that later Mabillon and Noris exchanged kind words. There is for instance in the Bibliothèque Nationale of Paris a letter from Noris to Mabillon of November 1691. Noris had just refused an invitation to settle in Rome when he received Mabillon's treatise on monastic studies. Noris declared that the Papal offer would have made him 'illustrissimus', but Mabillon's gift was making him 'eruditior'. Yet a letter by Mabillon to Magliabechi of December 1696 clearly shows that Mabillon was well aware of Noris' hostility. Even at this later stage Mabillon never sought a close alliance or collaboration with the one great scholar Italy then possessed, a man who meanwhile had confirmed his scholarship by his famous research on Hellenistic chronology, *Annus et Epochae Syro-Macedonum*, 1689. The difference in religious orders – Noris was an Augustinian – may have increased what seems to me essentially a personal mutual distrust. Whatever the explanation may be, it was clear that Mabillon had not chosen Noris as his representative in Italy.

But Mabillon, notwithstanding his implicit pessimism about the Italian situation, had not given up Italy altogether. He had put his trust and his hope in a member of his own order who at that time was almost unknown: Benedetto Bacchini. Here again Père Germain is explicit: 'unum ex illis excipio Benedictum Bacchinum'. Bacchini was the exception. Bacchini, who was born in San Donnino in 1651, had been in touch with Mabillon for some years before the Italian journey. But to judge from the letters I know, it had been a somewhat superficial acquaintance. Mabillon had mainly been instrumental in providing books for Bacchini who was then isolated in Parma. The friendship developed when they met in 1686 and Bacchini accompanied Mabillon on one of his expeditions. When Mabillon wrote his *Iter Italicum*, Bacchini was already a special friend.

III

Unless I am grossly mistaken, what we may perhaps call the *de facto* estrangement between Mabillon and Noris on the one hand and the warm friendship between Mabillon and Bacchini on the other had considerable influence on the development of historical studies in Italy. The publication of the *Museum Italicum*, of which the *Iter Italicum* was a section, made it even more evident that in France more was known about Italian antiquities than in Italy itself. As Dom Germain had foreseen, the traditional rivalry between France and Italy now spurred the Italians to new activity. Many young people were attracted by the new and more rational approach to ecclesiastical history suggested by the French. But after Mabillon's departure this movement had two clearly distinguishable spearheads – on the one side Noris who soon moved to Rome and became a Cardinal, on the other side Bacchini, first in Parma and then in Modena.

When Noris migrated to Rome, his best years were already over. He did less work of his own. But he was by now very influential, and his name was no longer so closely linked with the pro-Jansenist party. His favourite pupil was Francesco Bianchini. Like Noris, Bianchini was born in Verona and ultimately settled in Rome. Even more than Noris he combined mathematical abilities with antiquarian tastes. In fact he was a mathematician and an astronomer in his own right who commanded archaeology and epigraphy and later made an important edition of the *Liber Pontificalis*. In his turn Francesco Bianchini found a close collaborator in his nephew Giuseppe Bianchini, another Veronese. Though Francesco Bianchini did not live in Verona after 1689 and

Giuseppe Bianchini was active there as a Canon of the Cathedral only between 1725 and 1732, their influence, and Noris' influence, was strong in their native city. A generation of clerics grew up in Verona with decided interests in ecclesiastical history and antiquities. Four of them gained international reputations as editors of ecclesiastical texts: Pietro and Gerolamo Ballerini, Domenico Vallarsi and Girolamo da Prato. Gerolamo Ballerini expressed the communal debt to the first master by collecting Noris' works in Verona in 1729. Closely linked with the Roman Curia through Noris and Bianchini, and yet protected by the Republic of Venice, the Veronese group prospered and had leisure for the production of critical editions (for instance of St Jerome and Sulpicius Severus) which, though not comparable with the best of Saint Germain des Prés, were of lasting value.

Bacchini, as the representative of Mabillon's methods and ideals in Italy, had a far less easy life. His very connection with the group of Saint Germain made him a suspect person. The Benedictines of Italy were less independent of Rome than their French brethren. As an Italian correspondent remarked to Montfaucon some years later: 'Chi studia bene non fa altro che subito conseguire il titolo e il carattere di Giansenista.' To us it may be difficult to perceive at first sight the difference between the activities, of, say, Francesco Bianchini and those of Benedetto Bacchini. But the difference did exist. To play safe was never in the ethos of Saint Maur. A partiality for strong civil government, a dislike of superstitious practices and dubious saints, a general critical attitude of mind – and yet a tenacious attachment to the privileges of the Benedictine order – were quite enough to create all sorts of difficulties for a man who tried to live in Modena the life of Saint Germain des Prés.

In that very year 1686, in which he met Mabillon, Bacchini took over the editorship of the *Giornale de' Letterati* with the idea of making it the Italian counterpart of the pro-Jansenist *Journal des Savants*, which just at that time was going through one of its crises. Bacchini was asking for trouble. He carried on under difficulties until 1698 when he was compelled to give up after repeated persecution. The rest of his long life was passed in a characteristic alternation of violent conflicts and peaceful periods of retirement. Appointed a librarian to the Duke of Modena in 1697, he was compelled to retire only two years later. His dissertation of 1703, *De Ecclesiasticae Hierarchiae Originibus*, was attacked, and two cardinals had to come to his rescue. In 1706 he was in Rome to try to secure permission for the publication of what was going to be his masterpiece, the edition of the *Liber Pontificalis* by Agnellus of Ravenna which he had discovered. Thanks to the help of the future Cardinal Tommasi he finally obtained the 'imprimatur', but, significantly enough, he had to overcome the hostility of Francesco Bianchini and to sacrifice one or two points of his thesis. In 1711 he was at last installed as abbot of St Peter in Modena, but in 1713 he quarrelled with the Duke about feudal rights and had to leave the city. Unsettled for eight years, he was given a chair in Bologna in 1721 when he was a dying man. He never occupied it.

With all these difficulties, Bacchini was never a broken man. He never lost the power of inspiring other people. As late as 1713 he was still advising and guiding Scipione Maffei: in 1720, when he went to Santa Giustina in Padua as an invalid, scholars flocked to him. His voice still resounded after his death in the *Lettere polemiche contro il Signor Giacomo Picenino*, which were published in 1738: 'Siamo sinceri seguaci della Verità, alla quale abbiamo sacrificato molte persuasioni de' nostri Padri, esaltando in ciò il vigore della nostra Fede, che non s'appoggia e non ha bisogno d'appoggiarsi a Documenti apocrifi o d'inerte autorità.'

We can easily imagine what Bacchini must have been like in the best years of his life, about 1690–5, when the friendship of Mabillon was a present reality to be proud of; and any book coming from Saint Germain des Prés was a guide and a help. The appearance of the *Iter Italicum* in 1687 was followed by Mabillon's *Traité des études monastiques* in 1691. This impassioned plea for intellectual work and intellectual integrity in religious orders was in fact an appeal to all the Catholic world for higher standards of knowledge and spiritual life. Cicero and the Fathers were implicitly preferred to St Thomas. The treatise involved Mabillon in a long controversy with l'Abbé de la Trappe (Armand de Rancé) who defended the anti-intellectual attitude of his own order. The treatise was later translated into Latin and Italian and made a profound impression everywhere. Bacchini was of course one of the first to praise it in his *Giornale*. It cannot be by chance that just in those years of hope and excitement he persuaded the twenty-year-old Ludovico Antonio Muratori to put ecclesiastical history and the Middle Ages before pagan antiquities and modern Italian literature. Bacchini had produced his greatest pupil. Italy was to have in Muratori the man who could change the face of Italian historical studies.

About 1693–4 Bacchini taught Muratori the first rudiments of palaeography and encouraged him to learn foreign languages. We have some of the letters which Muratori wrote to Bacchini in French, Spanish and

Greek to show his proficiency in these languages. The period of close contact between Muratori and Bacchini was short. The main document of it is a dissertation on the topical subject of the merits of the Greek language, *De Graecae Linguae usu et praestantia*, which Muratori wrote in 1693 and probably modified a year later to recommend himself to Prince Borromeo and to pave his own way to the Ambrosiana. Appointed a librarian of the Ambrosiana in 1695, he returned to Modena in 1700 to succeed Bacchini as a librarian of the Duke. The first two volumes of *Anecdota* with their texts of Paulinus of Nola, the *Fides Bachiarii* etc., had already established him as an independent scholar. But the whole business of his succession to Bacchini remains mysterious. Bacchini had not designated him as his successor. What is certain is that he inherited the hostility of the two Bianchinis towards Bacchini. When about 1704 he conceived the idea of the Repubblica Letteraria, a new ambitious academy, Francesco Bianchini flatly and rudely refused to become its 'arconte depositario'.

IV

At this moment, however, another influence from Saint Germain des Prés was making itself felt directly in Italy. Bernard de Montfaucon arrived in 1698 and remained for three years. His *Diarium Italicum*, the account of his journey, appeared with the customary speed in 1702. Bernard de Montfaucon had not the simple piety, the contemplative peasant nature of Mabillon whom he revered. A quick-witted aristocrat, he had been a soldier before turning monk. His strength was immense. At 85 he could declare that for the last forty years he had worked thirteen to fourteen hours a day without having been interrupted by illness. His memory was equal to his strength. He had a command of Greek and several oriental languages, and the reputation of a living encyclopaedia. By the time he arrived in Italy he had already published what remains to this day the standard edition of St Athanasius and had had an important part in the most famous and most controversial of the editions of St Augustine. This was nothing compared to the work he began to prepare during his journey in Italy and which he published in the next forty years. It will be enough to mention the *Palaeographia graeca* of 1707, the first scientific treatise on Greek manuscripts, the edition of St John Chrysostomus and the fifteen volumes in folio of

L'Antiquité expliquée followed by the five volumes of the first series of the *Monumens de la monarchie françoise.*

The *Diarium Italicum* reflects Montfaucon's prosaic and business-like nature. There is nothing of the excitement and of the poetry with which Mabillon discovered Italy for himself. But he was a man of readier friendships than Mabillon. He attracted many of the men he met in Italy. He saw of course Bacchini and Muratori who opened the Ambrosiana to him. If a few years later Fontanini and Passionei helped Bacchini and took sides with Mabillon in the controversy started by the Jesuit Germon on the value of Mabillon's *De Re Diplomatica,* we may suspect that the impression left behind by Montfaucon was not a secondary cause. Cosimo III of Tuscany, to whom he dedicated the *Diarium,* listened to him and sent Amedeo Banduri, one of the Pisa professors, to learn Greek and the method at Saint Germain des Prés. Banduri liked the place so well that he never came back. In France he became one of the leading Byzantine scholars of the eighteenth century. When in 1709 F. Ficoroni attacked the section of the *Diarium* devoted to the Roman antiquities, Montfaucon found defenders in Italy itself. Vague Jansenist sympathies and liberal aspirations were again on his side. He acquired a friend in Angelo Maria Querini who later, as Bishop and as Cardinal, made Brescia a centre of ecclesiastical studies and of pro-Jansenist thought.

But Montfaucon was not just a second Mabillon. He stood for something of his own. He was the leader of the younger generation of Saint Maur who since 1687 had been turning systematically to Greek studies. If Mabillon compelled the Italians to revise their interests and methods in the study of Latin ecclesiastical writers and of the Latin Middle Ages, Montfaucon introduced new standards in the matter of Greek ecclesiastical writers and of Greek studies more generally. Learned men in Italy were perfectly aware of the importance of what Montfaucon was doing. The name of Montfaucon meant the command of the Greek language, of the Greek Fathers, of Byzantine history. Stories circulated about the humiliations Italian scholars had brought upon themselves by challenging his supreme knowledge of Greek manuscripts. The assimilation of Montfaucon's methods became inevitably the acid test of the Italian ability to compete with the French not only on the Latin, but also on the Greek side. It cannot surprise us that the reception of *Palaeographia Graeca* proved to be much more difficult than the reception of Mabillon's *De Re Diplomatica.* The latter could be grafted upon a wide knowledge of Latin, while the former presupposed a reform of

Greek studies that was still to come. But it is perhaps surprising that the failure to assimilate Montfaucon was complete even among the people who had learnt their Mabillon so well. Few and inconspicuous editions of Greek texts were published. Muratori's *Anecdota Graeca* were among them. But Muratori himself conceded by implication that Greek texts were beyond his powers. His early dissertations *De antiquo iure Metropolitae Mediolanensis in episcopum Ticinensem* (1697) and *Disquisitio de Reliquis, Sanctuaris, oleis miraculorum virtute imbutis* (1698) had been inspired by Mabillon. Later he felt he had learned enough about medieval Latin charters and chronicles to be able to concentrate on medieval Italy and to organize the *Rerum Italicarum Scriptores,* the first volume of which appeared in 1723. Muratori was a pupil of Mabillon, not of Montfaucon.

What is true of Muratori is equally true of Italian culture at large. In the field of University teaching some progress was made. A chair of Greek was established in Turin; another was re-established in Pisa. Other universities, like Padua, at least discussed the establishment of Greek chairs. But the teachers remained incompetent, and the pupils were not forthcoming. In Turin the professor of Greek had no pupil to teach.

V

Mabillon's triumph and Montfaucon's failure were the chief features of the Italian situation in the field of historical studies about 1710. They were not provisional features: even now we can see that Italian scholars move among medieval charters more easily than among Greek manuscripts. Indeed these features were of such long-term importance that we may well leave them aside for a moment and consider some other influences that were at work in Italian scholarship: short-term and secondary influences, yet not negligible.

There was Leibniz whom Muratori had as a partner in his genealogical work on the house of Este. Leibniz as a historian was himself a pupil of the Maurists. What Muratori owed to him specifically is still an open question. Yet anyone who reads the many letters they exchanged between 1708 and 1717 can hardly fail to notice that the discussion with Leibniz trained Muratori to a finer appreciation of scholarly difficulties.

Another influence was that of Dutch erudition. It was subtly pervasive even in a Catholic country owing to the essential texts provided by Holland. The Italians never managed to compete with the Dutch in the field of the edition of Greek and Latin authors. But they learned much from Dutch antiquaries and were greatly impressed by the fact that Dutch scholars were coming down to Italy to study manuscripts and monuments which had not been touched for centuries. Men inclined to free-thinking like Magliabechi had of course ulterior motives in their sympathies for Dutch scholarship. But in 1696 Muratori wrote to Magliabechi to ask the name of 'qualche buon libraro o letterato di Amsterdam o vero di Parigi, co' quali io potessi aver filo in occasione di provveder libri per la Biblioteca, o stamparne de' nuovi o per comunicare molte osservazioni e dubbi eruditi etc.' (*Epistolario* 99). About 1710, a young Dutchman, Hendrik Brenkmann, was sent to study one of the most glorious manuscripts Italy possessed: the *Florentina* of the Pandectae. An object of pride and almost of worship, the *Florentina* had been much less an object of study, at least after Torelli had obtained permission to edit it. All the learned men of Italy became interested in young Brenkmann. H. Newton, the English consul in Tuscany, a great protector of the non-Catholics, took him under his wing. The Academy of Florence made him a member. Antonio Maria Salvini was assigned to him as a supervisor in his work on the manuscript. Giambattista Vico registered with pride in his Autobiography that 'il signor Errico Brenckmann dottissimo giureconsulto olandese' had said a few nice words about his *De studiorum ratione*. Brenkmann was also put in touch with Scipione Maffei, and an exchange of letters in 1711 represents one of the first and most characteristic signs of the part Maffei was to play in matters of erudition.

The contact with the young Dutchman kindled Maffei's imagination. He conceived the idea of organizing a regular import of Dutch books into Italy and saw Verona as the centre of this trade. He went into details about its organization in letters to Cuperus and to Brenkmann. The latter considered these important enough to be copied and transmitted to the greatest of the contemporary Dutch scholars, the Leiden professor Jacobus Perizonius. This explains why in examining Perizonius' papers in Leiden I unexpectedly found myself handling letters of Scipione Maffei. Nothing seems to have come of the project. But Brenkmann may have been inspired by Maffei in his later, more ambitious, plan of a society for the promotion of Italian scholarship. The idea was to help the Italians to publish their works abroad in order to avoid ecclesiastic censorship. In 1712 Maffei (together with Muratori and Bacchini) signed Brenkmann's manifesto. Nothing followed. Curiously enough, for reasons which I cannot quite understand, later in 1721 Brenkmann took up again the idea of his society – this time only with the signatures of French and Dutch scholars. The result was of course the same: nothing happened.

VI

With Maffei we may well return to our main theme and approach our conclusion. In 1711 Maffei was no longer exactly young. He was born in Verona in 1675 and since his early youth he had been keenly devoted to poetry and literary criticism. Like Muratori, he had grown up with the young Arcadia, had admired Lemène and studied Maggi. A group of his letters to Magliabechi of the years 1695–9 which I have recently discovered in the Biblioteca Nazionale of Florence gives a precise idea of his early interests. He tries to obtain as yet unpublished poems by Lemène, discusses the problem of why the Italians had no tragedy comparable with that of the French, takes an interest in the project of an edition of Monsignor Della Casa. Until 1707 there is hardly an indication that Maffei would devote the rest of his life to erudition. But he had probably known Montfaucon in Rome in 1699, and in 1707 was already a professed admirer of Bacchini. Besides, his native Verona was full of inducements to antiquarian studies. The Anfiteatro and the Porta de' Borsari were there for anyone to see. Noris and Bianchini were of course well known to him, but when he had to choose, he chose Bacchini and Montfaucon, not Noris and Bianchini. Personal reasons may have played their part. Maffei had no reputation of a saint in his own city, and his brother was a general in the Imperial service. For many years he sought patrons and allies quite outside his native surroundings. His collaboration with the Ballerinis and Vallarsi belongs to the last stage of his life when he slowly turned from his early sympathies for the French Benedictines and perhaps the Jansenists to an alliance with the French Jesuits and to the ambition of competing with the Benedictines in their own fields.

In 1711, when he met Brenkmann, Maffei was firmly on Bacchini's side. In that same year he was induced by a young German theologian, Christopher Pfaff, to explore the manuscripts of the derelict Royal Library of Turin. This was in the spirit of Saint Germain de Prés, and Bacchini must have helped to piece together the report on the texts found in the library. Later Bacchini helped Maffei in questioning the authenticity of a text of Irenaeus which Pfaff professed to have discovered in the library of Turin. In the year 1712 the close connection between Maffei and the French Benedictines was secretly confirmed. Maffei prepared an attack against the Equestrian Order of St George, which claimed to have been created by the Emperor Constantine and was an ally of the Jesuits. We now know that the attack had been planned in agreement with Montfaucon and that Querini served as liaison. Montfaucon had the pamphlet printed in Paris. It was condemned by the Pope and gave Maffei no end of trouble for some years.

In the same year, 1712, Maffei contributed to the discovery of the manuscripts of the Biblioteca Capitolare of Verona. The story of the rediscovery has been told many times, and I do not propose to tell it again. But we may well pause to consider the state of affairs laid bare by this discovery. The Library of the Cathedral of Verona had been one of the best provided in the Middle Ages. It gave the early humanists some of their most important manuscripts and incidentally saved the poetry of Catullus for the world. The manuscripts apparently disappeared towards the end of the sixteenth century and were certainly missing when Mabillon inquired after them in 1685. Nobody had ever looked into the top of a big cupboard until Monsignor Carinelli, goaded by Scipione Maffei, thought of it one October morning in 1712. The cry of triumph of Maffei was doubly justified. The recovery, though partial, of these manuscripts represented the last great discovery of manuscripts made in Italy and perhaps in Western Europe: it was an exceptional contribution to the knowledge of the early Middle Ages. At the same time Maffei knew that with the help of Bacchini and with the wise utilization of the methods of Mabillon he was in a position to exploit the discovery. As always, he was far too sanguine in his projects.

He tended to forget that in his habits of life he was no monk, and that in any case the monks of Saint Germain des Prés worked co-operatively. Nevertheless, by 1715 Maffei had already reached conclusions that revolutionized the history of Latin palaeography and went beyond Mabillon's classification of medieval scripts. In another field, Latin epigraphy, he conceived the idea of a corpus of inscriptions which, if realized, would have had some of the qualities of Mommsen's *Corpus*. He recognized the need for checking the copies against the original text of each stone. While Bacchini had assimilated Mabillon's methods and Muratori was applying them on a very large scale (though without much refinement), Maffei was the first Italian to correct Mabillon on essential points and to elaborate a critical method that can be described as personal.

Mabillon was corrected. But Montfaucon remained inaccessible even to Maffei: the acquisition of Greek was a problem that worried Maffei throughout his life. He tried to consolidate his own knowledge of Greek, first by giving hospitality to a learned Englishman, then by keeping the Greek Panagioti in his house. He tried to establish the public teaching of Greek in Verona and formulated projects of University reforms for Padua and Turin in which the teaching of Greek was duly considered. But Maffei's amateurish efforts failed. Panagioti abandoned his house in wrath and went to Brescia. Maffei never managed either to acquire or to spread a real mastery of Greek. Like the best men of his generation, he remained a pupil of Mabillon. He never became a pupil of Montfaucon.

VII

There was something in the general trend of Italian studies in the early eighteenth century inevitably giving priority to Latin studies. But even Latin studies were pursued only within certain limits. Neither the Noris group nor the Bacchini group was ever concerned with the great ages of Roman history except in order to clarify points of antiquarian interest or problems directly relevant to later Italian history. They were mainly concerned with medieval history. If a distinction has to be made, it is that the younger generation (Muratori, Maffei) had a great interest in municipal affairs, while the older generation (Noris, Bacchini, Bianchini) was more exclusively ecclesiastic. But the older and the younger equally preferred the medieval to the classical, the Christian to the pagan, the local antiquity to the Roman monuments of general importance. They read local inscriptions and medieval chronicles with greater love and deeper insight than they read Cicero, Virgil and Boethius. This was of course the result of Mabillon's teaching, but implied also the realization, however obscurely formulated, that modern Italy was primarily the heir of the Middle Ages. The fact had finally to be faced. Each Italian city had a history in which the Romans played only one part: German feudal lords, and Christian bishops were no less relevant. As Muratori said: 'quasiche l'Italia nostra madre non sia stata, e non sia sempre la stessa, tanto sotto i Romani padroni del mondo, quanto sotto i Longobardi, Franchi, Germani'.

By 1720 the powerful revival of interest in the Latin past of Italy and in its medieval developments had resulted in a loss of interest in the general European aspects of Roman civilization. The strength of Italian medieval studies resulted in a weakness of Italian classicism. This must be kept in mind if we want to explain why towards 1723 the Italian revival of learning took a turn which only superficially can be called unexpected. The Italians began to develop an extraordinary interest in the Etruscans and other pre-Roman civilizations of Italy – and at the same time began the archaeological exploration of their own soil. This was simply carrying municipal history further back to its origins, the pre-Roman stage. The Italian cities and regions discovered a new source of glory in a period in which Rome was not yet the exclusive ruler. The age of the Etruscans and of the Pelasgians was the counterpart of the age of Goths and Langobards. The positive result was the discovery of the Etruscan necropoleis, of Herculaneum, Pompeii and Velleia, the new examination of the foundations of Italian civilization. The negative aspect was a further divorce from the sources of classicism, a rather unhealthy concentration on texts (such as the Etruscan) which nobody could understand and on historical periods where fancies were easier than sober interpretations of facts. True enough, this was not an isolated phenomenon: the countries which did not have enough Etruscans to play about with resorted to the Druids or to other equivalents. The Italian development had international roots which have not yet been sufficiently investigated. But in Italy serious research suffered more than elsewhere. While Italian medievalists were beginning to be respected in the wider world, Italian classical studies were unilaterally diverted towards a half-mythical past that discredited them. Throughout the eighteenth century the history of Roman civilization itself was left to non-Italians. Montesquieu, Middleton, Ferguson and Gibbon reinterpreted Roman history, while the Italians were discussing the mutual relations of Pelasgians and Etruscans. In its turn the absence of a serious interest in the European aspects of Roman civilization further weakened the efforts to recover the link with Greece. The failure of Montfaucon to interest the Italians in Greek manuscripts was made worse by the perverse passion for the Etruscans. When the rest of Europe began to go back from the Greek Fathers to Classical Greece, Italy hardly contributed to the journey. A new approach to Homer and Plato was found in England and in Germany. Winckelmann paradoxically discovered Greek art in Italy, but not for the Italians. I am unable to mention even one important edition or commentary of a

Greek classical text made by an Italian in the eighteenth century.

While Mabillon triumphed in Italy and medieval studies there were consolidated to the admiration of foreigners, Italian classical studies took a turn of their own which carried them further into isolation. Fear of Jansenism may also have been a further factor in slowing down relations with foreign scholarship. In 1713 and afterwards the Congregation of Saint Maur showed definite hostility towards the Bull *Unigenitus* promulgated by Clement XI. Both Maffei and Muratori slowly re-established cordial relations with the Jesuits. Cardinal Querini (a die-hard pro-Jansenist) remained fairly isolated in Brescia. When about 1735 Maffei finally broke with his former friends of Saint Germain des Prés, historical studies had already become municipal, for better or for worse, in Northern and Central Italy. Naples, as I said, was the exception. Naples was not municipal. There Pietro Giannone could write a *Storia civile* completely intelligible to the rest of Europe; there Giambattista Vico could write a *Scienza Nuova* completely unintelligible to the rest of Europe. Neither knew Greek.

17

Introduction to the Griechische Kulturgeschichte by Jacob Burckhardt*

'*Mir als Geschichtsdozenten ist ein ganz*
merkwürdiges Phänomen klargeworden:
die plötzliche Entwertung aller blossen
"Ereignisse" der Vergangenheit.'
Burckhardt to F. von Preen, 1870

AN inspired teacher with a natural aptitude for collecting together his researches and reflections and presenting them clearly and calmly, Burckhardt was able, as were few other historians, to express his ideas in courses of lectures. This is particularly true of the *Griechische Kulturgeschichte*, a course of lectures given repeatedly between 1872 and 1885, which he had already started to think about shortly after 1860. Although he prepared it and even partly drafted it for future publication, he never considered it ready for the press, and in the end, in about 1880, he decided finally to abandon his attempt to turn it into a book. Whatever the reasons for this decision, the reader must remember that he has before him an unfinished work, indeed a course of lectures never approved by the author for publication.[1]

Inevitably most courses of lectures aim at more than one end. In the case of the *Griechische Kulturgeschichte* it is easy to distinguish two tendencies. Burckhardt intended to offer his listeners a course in Greek history and antiquities that would be more satisfactory in method than those he had himself attended as a young man. At the same time he was communicating certain reflections on the nature of Greek civilization – reflections clearly connected with the course of lectures on the 'study of History' which he gave three times (in 1868–9, 1870–71, and 1872–3)

---

*This essay was written in 1955 as an introduction to the Italian translation of the *Griechische Kulturgeschichte*, Sansoni, Florence, 1955. We omit the 'Appendice critico-bibliografica' reprinted in *Secondo Contributo*, 1960, pp. 293–8.

and which were later published posthumously with the title *Welt-geschichtliche Betrachtungen.*

*

As we know from the letter quoted in the introduction by the editor J. Oeri, Burckhardt decided in 1868 to arrange his course on Greek culture in systematic, not chronological, order. He was not alone in these years in preferring the descriptive approach in historiography to the evolutionary scheme. In 1871 Mommsen published the first volume of his *Römisches Staatsrecht,* possibly the greatest descriptive work of modern historiography. Mommsen never really returned to evolutionary historiography: even the fifth volume of the *History of Rome,* which came out subsequently in 1885, is structurally descriptive and systematic.

Chronological order and systematic order have alternated in historical works since the fifth century B.C. At least from Varro onwards the two methods of arrangement have corresponded to two kinds of historiography, the one concerned with describing institutions and customs, the other with narrating events: the *Antiquitates* in systematic order went side by side with the *Annales* and *Historiae* in chronological order. But in the eighteenth century antiquarian research fell into disrepute with the majority of philosophically trained historians, and in the nineteenth century this disrepute was combined with a feeling of doubt as to whether such research could rightfully exist alongside narrative history. In the century of evolution it was easy to observe that even institutions and customs undergo evolution and should be studied in chronological order. Without wishing to simplify a complex situation, it is perhaps legitimate to assert that about 1870 antiquarianism was at best admitted as an inferior form of historiography.[2]

It is to some degree surprising that just at that time Mommsen and Burckhardt should have had recourse to the systematic form typical of the study of antiquities. Both believed it necessary for their interpretations, and from different points of view they hoped for greater advantages from it than from the chronological form. Naturally neither intended to relapse into the antiquarian genre as such. While the traditional *Antiquitates* described all aspects of ancient life without attempting to look into their meaning, Burckhardt aimed at describing the Greek spirit as it emerged from an analysis of the institutions and forms of life in Greece. Furthermore, though systematic, he did not aim to review every aspect of Greek life: as is well known, he always claimed the right to a subjective choice of interesting details.

In the introduction to the course Burckhardt himself explains the advantages he attributes to his own method. Historiography in chronological order blurs the essential with the particular, the permanent with the changing, the typical with the accidental; furthermore it must inevitably involve endless discussion of the authenticity and chronological sequence of documents. In a *Kulturgeschichte* in systematic order a document stands on its own, as evidence of a state of mind, quite apart from the objective truth of the facts attested in it and its exact chronological position. The return to the systematic form therefore has the virtue not only of making possible an understanding of the spirit of the Greek world, but also of dispelling the doubts introduced by historical criticism concerning the value of the ancient sources.

Similarly Mommsen's aim was to describe the essential principles of the Roman state, the lasting ones, without losing himself in details; and in the coherence of his description, echoing the organic unity of the Roman state, he found the best remedy against the proliferation of conjectures. While Burckhardt was establishing a correlation between the systematic form and the presence of the Greek spirit, Mommsen was justifying the same form by adducing the organic nature of the state. Both wanted to avoid the consequences of the destructive criticism at which the successors of Niebuhr excelled. In short, in both of them a descriptive and systematic historiography reaffirmed its right to exist – a type of historiography which was in danger, since it offended the evolutionary principle so widely accepted in the nineteenth century. The new antiquarianism of the nineteenth century, like that of the seventeenth and eighteenth centuries, was an answer to Pyrrhonism; but unlike the earlier antiquarianism it claimed to be able to penetrate beyond phenomena into the spirit of a people and the structure of a political organization. It was a study of antiquity revised in accordance with romantic notions of national character and the organic State, which in its turn paved the way for the sociological investigation of the ancient world introduced by Max Weber.

But the notion of the Greek spirit (like that of a political organization) is not in fact so simple and definite as to justify the abandoning of chronological order with no further discussion. And the solution of taking the evidence on its own, out of time, is at best only a partial reply to sceptical criticism. It is still necessary to decide if the historian is lying or mistaken about himself or things which happen during his lifetime. The method of *Kulturgeschichte* favoured by Burckhardt might make it possible to avoid the problem of whether Herodotus was well-informed about Gyges, but it does not free one from the task of deciding whether his picture of contemporary society corresponds to the facts or whether it is the product of his imagination. There is clearly a difference between a description of customs based on Herodotus or Tacitus and one based on unreliable writers such as Ctesias or the *Scriptores Historiae Augustae*. However, Burckhardt did not want completely to eliminate chronological order, and, like some earlier antiquarians and archaeologists – including Winckelmann and K. O. Müller – and later Mommsen, he arrived at a rather cloudy compromise between systematic order and chronological order. For example, in the last volume he discussed the evolution of Greek man; but the types and characteristics were at least partly the same as those he had described in the preceding volumes without reference to their chronological context.[3]

In abandoning chronological order Burckhardt laid himself open to the accusation immediately levelled against him by Wilamowitz, E. Meyer and J. Beloch of lacking critical sense in the examination of evidence.[4] The accusation was all the more easily made in that, unlike Mommsen, Burckhardt did not keep abreast of the progress made in classical studies after his youth (let us say, roughly speaking, after 1850) and for this reason often appeared out of date in the matter of details. But more serious still was his uncritical acceptance of the notion of the Greek spirit, even though this had been traditional in German historiography from Winckelmann onwards and was therefore far less irritating to Burckhardt's critics, who took no account of the fact that one of his reasons for adopting an a-temporal form was that it corresponded to an a-temporal Greek spirit. There is clearly no way of deciding *a priori* if those who understood one another by talking or writing one of the many varieties of the language we call Greek had mental habits and characteristics in common which could be designated a Greek 'spirit' or 'character'. Only a piece of research extending over the centuries and the various regions of the Greek world could establish whether Homer and Tzetzes, the Arcadian peasant of the fourth century B.C. and the Alexandrian intellectual of the sixth century A.D., reveal common mental characteristics, or whether on the other hand what is called the Greek spirit was the sum of intellectual qualities restricted to a Greek-speaking group found in a particular chronological, geographical and social situation. Burckhardt and his predecessors were wrong not because they admitted the existence of the Greek spirit, but because they presupposed it. Far from justifying a non-chronological exposition, the question of the Greek spirit demands research in strictly chronological order. Even some more recent works inspired by Burckhardt or written in this same non-chronological order (such as *Der hellenische Mensch* by M. Pohlenz and *Die Götter Griechenlands* by W. F. Otto) arbitrarily extend observations and reflections which are or could be true only of a limited section of the Greek-speaking peoples: their margin of error is directly proportional to the extension of the generalization. The question of the existence of the Greek spirit is open, because it has not yet been critically approached.

In so far as he offered a systematic description of the Greek spirit, Burckhardt satisfied a deeply felt need of the whole of nineteenth-century German culture. It is certain that he was strongly influenced by Boeckh; he not only attended Boeckh's lectures on Greek antiquities in 1839–40, but also probably knew of his plan (which was never realized) for a *Culturgeschichte* of the Greeks with the title *Hellen*.[5]

The section on the Greeks in Hegel's *History of Philosophy* was also a *Griechische Kulturgeschichte* in embryo. But the fact that Burckhardt was the first to present an extensive analysis of the Greek spirit shows that although the idea had been in the air for a century it was difficult to realize: it required a breadth of reading and a constructive ability that are rarely found. In this sense the *Kulturgeschichte* of Burckhardt is a monument to the Romantic spirit he had absorbed before 1848; a monument if not actually anachronistic, at least certainly created when the main German historians of the Greek world could no longer fail to see its defects.

*

There is, however, another aspect in which Burckhardt shows himself to be far more original, though here too it is possible to sense traces of Boeckh's teaching. The publication in 1905 of the *Weltgeschichtliche Betrachtungen* revealed the thorough revision of values undertaken by Burckhardt in the years preceding and following the foundation of the German empire. The letters of this period (particularly those to F. von Preen), the text of certain lectures and the recollections of his pupils confirm that Burckhardt not only cut himself off from Bismarck's Germany, but showed a greater appreciation of Catholicism and modified his own ideas on the Middle Ages and Counter-Reformation. Religion appeared to him, at least in some cases, as a bulwark of the individual against the State: one such case was naturally the resistance of the Catholics in the *Kulturkampf*.

The *Weltgeschichtliche Betrachtungen* attempted to unravel the thread of an historical process in which democracy kills liberalism, the national State strangles the small regional and civic units, and the desire for power grows in inverse proportion to education in truth and beauty. But his pessimism in the face of the immediate future was tempered by his radical pessimism about all human history, since Burckhardt recognized that the historical forces regulating the present had also operated in the past, from which everything beautiful, good and true in the world had come. Though the State and religion could devitalize culture, culture would not exist without religion and the State. Precisely because he had no illusions about the cost of culture, Burckhardt was ready to recognize the conditions upon which culture depended. The analysis does not end in relativism. Two decisive chapters discuss historic 'greatness' and the question of what constitutes a favourable outcome (*Glück*) in history. The first, while it makes concessions to the relativity of points of view, reaffirms the possibility of an objective judgement on the greatness of individuals. The second calls for the replacement of the approximative and optimistic notion of the providential by that of the evil which cannot be eliminated from history: the only consolation is knowledge.

Burckhardt saw that Greek civilization had experienced the same conflicts that were to be found in modern civilization – those between material power and spiritual culture, between masses and individuals, between religious subjection (and inspiration) and humanistic independence. He developed a sharp eye for the failings of the Greek world; but an awareness of the fragility of every culture also sharpened his perception of the greatness and variety of Greek culture. A tenderness, a warmth, a new intimacy in the contemplation of the Greek miracle were combined with a merciless analysis of those forces with which and against which Greek culture developed. Realism and pessimism colour Burckhardt's exposition: it is possible to recognize the roots of both of these in Boeckh's teaching at Berlin.[6] Burckhardt established a new solidarity between Greek culture and modern culture on the basis of their common difficulties and common conflicts. He explicitly repudiated the interpretation diffused by Schiller and later by E. Curtius of the Greek world as a serene and beautiful world, undisturbed by anxieties about what lay beyond.[7] Less explicitly, Burckhardt also opposed the interpretation of G. Grote and the other radicals for whom Greek democracy and sophistics were the height of Greek civilization.

In both these points (as in his scant respect for the *viri eruditissimi*) Burckhardt naturally agreed with Nietzsche. In those years of friendship between 1869 and 1872, Burckhardt and his young colleague must have said more to one another than has been documented. But the letters that Nietzsche, who was less reticent than Burckhardt, wrote to Rohde are sufficient proof that fellow-feeling never actually amounted to collaboration. Nietzsche and Burckhardt, though encouraging and possibly inspiring one another, proceeded independently. There are few traces of Nietzsche in Burckhardt's work. Even the chapter on tragedy bears his mark only slightly. Dionysiac elation, let alone rebellion against morality, attracted Burckhardt little, being as he was cautious by nature and by now over fifty years old.[8]

Burckhardt turned to the Greeks because they too derived a basically pessimistic conclusion about life from their own conflicts. His most telling pages concern Greek pessimism, and of these the ones dealing with the propensity to suicide, which are also particularly fully documented, are especially striking: the most carefully drawn figure, almost a self-portrait, is that of the pagan ascetic Diogenes the Cynic, *der heitere Pessimist*. Burckhardt was fully aware of the debt which Greek art and poetry owed to religion, but at the same time he believed that Greek religion was more a matter of imagination than moral energy. It was not in the myths, but in the pessimism of their ethics and their praxis that Burckhardt saw and loved the essential seriousness of the Greeks; and here his Calvinist heritage came to the fore. It is pointless to speculate on what would have been his reaction to the new trend which was started in the studies on Greek religion by E. Rohde and the Scandinavian school, if he had ever known about it. Burckhardt knew only the interpretation of Greek religion as the religion of an artistic people and accepted it as an indication that the moral strength of the Greek people was to be sought elsewhere.

Burckhardt appreciated Greek myth as an immediate apprehension and purification of reality, as a fruit of beauty; but believed that there was a tension between myth and the precepts of morality and reason. Among the Greeks pessimism was the complement of the mythical imagination; it sustained their moral life and made possible the co-existence of imagination and rational effort. Greek pessimism was therefore liberating and creative; it expressed itself in terms of knowledge and beauty and was thus inseparable from the Greek vocation for dispassionate contemplation. Prepared for death, the Greeks were also prepared for life. Unafflicted by a priestly religion, they could easily transform religious experience into a source of aesthetic pleasure. They had in fact to struggle not against the Church, but against the State.

The basic conflict of the Greek world was between State and culture, not between religion and culture.

Burckhardt's antipathy to democracy explodes in the famous chapter in which the paradoxical thesis is expounded that the Greek culture of the fifth century was the product not of a golden age but of the resistance of the spirit to an age of iron. On the other hand admiration for Greek aristocracies led him to the definition of the agonistic, individualistic phase of Greek culture which, even if exaggerated by later scholars, is one of Burckhardt's genuine discoveries.[9] In the world of archaic Greece the historian of the Renaissance found himself at home once more. He is not really praising the aristocratic state, but an aristocracy which lives according to its own rules of honour and its own artistic tastes. There is therefore no contradiction if subsequently he extends his sympathy to the a-political individual of the Hellenistic period. Other extremely powerful passages examine the position of sculptors, painters and architects in a society which equated art with manual labour, but for this very reason left it undisturbed, while it tended to exert control over poetry, philosophy and science.

Chiefly concerned with religion, State and culture, Burckhardt's exposition leaves out of account, for instance, law, finances, the art of war, education, family life, friendship and love. Comparison with Boeckh's *Encyclopedia* and K. F. Hermann's *Lehrbuch der griechischen Antiquitäten* is instructive in connection with these limitations.

But the fact remains that much of the *Griechische Kulturgeschichte* was written not to analyse the conflicts of Greek civilization, but to provide a systematic treatment of Greek art, politics, religion and poetry. To express the conflicts between religion, State and culture, a representation of Greek civilization in movement would have been necessary, yet the antiquarian treatment is static. The result is uneven. The two tendencies hamper one another, and certain of the author's prejudices and shortcomings become more evident because of the work's lack of proportions. For example, the one-sidedness of the judgement on Greek democracy would be less offensive if Burckhardt had not taken upon himself the task of describing Greek democracy.

*

Although it was badly received on publication by historians and philologists, Burckhardt's book soon gained the favour of German philosophers and aesthetes.[10] The prestige of the work grew between the two world wars.[11] Burckhardt became fashionable in Germany because he was anti-democratic, pessimistic, sophisticated and wise, and because many of his judgements could easily be translated into the sociological language current at the time. The specialists themselves ended by accepting the judgement of the educated public and were won over to admiration for Burckhardt. Some of his ideas, such as those of Greek pessimism and of the competitive spirit, became common property. But it would be inaccurate to say that Burckhardt had a deep effect on Greek studies between 1919 and 1939. Burckhardt moved in an area of problems concerning the conflicts between State, culture and religion which were of little interest to the German classical philologists locked in the blind alley of the third humanism. The warning of the *Weltgeschichtliche Betrachtungen* was as little heeded as that of F. Meinecke's *Idee der Staatsräson*. Burckhardt had rather the negative effect of causing many philologists to persist in the uncritical acceptance of the postulate of the Greek spirit.

Anyone wanting to develop Burckhardt's ideas must have a clear knowledge of the difficulties inherent in his thought. His *Kultur-geschichte* belongs to two historical periods. As an analysis of the Greek spirit it is rooted in German Romanticism and inherits the laziness with regard to chronology, as well as a certain indifference to source criticism, of some representatives of German Romantic thought (Creuzer, Schelling, Hegel). As an examination of the complex and contradictory roots of Greek culture it is an anti-Romantic and revolutionary book, comparable with Nietzsche's *Die Geburt der Tragödie*, but, although sharing many of its prejudices, far more realistic and sincerely humane. Burckhardt's novelty lies in the intense, pessimistic concern with the position of a free culture *vis-à-vis* politics and religion. His *Griechische Kulturgeschichte* should therefore bear fruit in historians of a liberal turn of mind who read it together with Grote's *History of Greece* and are able to benefit from the pessimism combined with awareness of the good things of life which is the distinctive characteristic of Burckhardt.

References

1. The material on the origins of *Griechische Kulturgeschichte* is quoted by F. Stähelin in the introduction to the new edition in *Gesamtausgabe*, Volume 8, p. xvi. Here one should note particularly the letter to O. Ribbeck of 10 July 1864: 'Ich bin doch einigermassen infiziert von jener Idee, welche einst beim Bier in der Wirtschaft gegenüber vom badischen Bahnhof zur Sprache kam: einmal auf meine kuriose und wildgewachsene Manier das Hellenentum zu durchstreifen und zu sehen, was da herauskommt, freilich gewiss nicht für ein Buch, sondern für einen akademischen Kurs "Vom Geist der Griechen".' (*Briefe*, ed. Kaphan, 1935, p. 282). But one should also bear in mind what Burckhardt wrote to H. Schreiber in October 1842 (Kaphan, 65; *Briefe*, Vollst. Ausg., ed. M. Burckhardt, I, 218): 'Ist es nicht ein Jammer, dass nach drei Jahrhunderten einer tyrannisch behaupteten klassischen Bildung doch noch immer keine vernünftige Geschichte Griechenlands existiert?' And to G. Kinkel in February 1843 (Kaphan, p. 72; M. Burckhardt, I, p. 234): 'Die Philologie beweist ihren geistigen Bankerott immer mehr dadurch, dass sie noch nicht eine gute Darstellung des Altertums hervorgebracht hat.—Niebuhr ist bloss zum Studieren;—zum Lesen scheusslich. Ueber Griechenland existiert noch nichts; Ottfried Müller hatte bloss gelehrte Zwecke. Man wird noch den Triumph erleben, dass die erste lesbare alte Geschichte ohne Zutun der Philologen ans Tageslicht treten wird.—Die Philologie ist jetzt nur noch eine Wissenschaft zweiten Ranges, so grosse Airs sie sich auch gibt . . .'

2. *Cf.* my *Contributo alla storia degli studi classici*, pp. 95, 395, and elsewhere. G. von Below, *Die deutsche Geschichtschreibung*, 2nd ed., Munich, 1924, p. 71, rightly says of Burckhardt 'Man möchte ihn fast mehr einen Antiquar nennen . . . als einen Historiker'.

3. It should be noted that Burckhardt valued Greek historiography (and especially Herodotus) because it was true as far as the typical was concerned, even if it was mistaken about the individual.

4. Wilamowitz, *Griechische Tragödien*, II, 1899, p. 7: '. . . würde ich es für feige halten, wenn ich es hier nicht aussprüche, dass die Griechische Kulturgeschichte von J.B. . . . für die Wissenschaft nicht existiert . . . dass dies Buch weder von griechischer Religion noch vom griechischen Staate zu sagen weiss, was Gehör verdiente, einfach, weil es ignoriert, was die Wissenschaft der letzten fünfzig Jahre an Urkunden, Thatsachen, Methoden und Gesichtspunkten gewonnen hat. Das Griechentum Burckhardts hat ebensowenig existiert wie das der klassicistischen Ästhetik gegen das er vor fünfzig Jahren mit Recht polemisiert haben mag'. Another negative judgement by Wilamowitz in this same tone in *Kleine Schriften*, V, 2, 185, from *Deutsche Literaturz.*, 1899, col. 15. For an opinion of Mommsen ('Diese Griechen hat es nie gegeben'), see H. Wölfflin, *Gedanken zur Kunstgeschichte*, 2nd ed., 1941, p. 135. For E. Meyer, see *Geschichte des Altertums*, III, 1901, p. 291, in a passage (IV, p. 273, in H. E. Stier's edition) which also attacks Ranke's *World History*. For J. Beloch, Gercke-Norden, *Einleitung in die Altertumsw.*, 2nd ed., III, 1914, p. 150;

Griech. Geschichte, 2nd ed., I, 2, 1926, p. 18. The anonymous review in *Liter. Centralbl.*, 1899, pp. 197–8, is worth bearing in mind: 'die Zeugnisse versteht er gar nicht zu benutzen. Ohne es selbst zu wissen und zu ahnen (das ist das Allerschlimmste) ist er ihnen gegenüber einfach hülflos'. With a different orientation and therefore more appreciative, A. Holm, *Berl. Phil. Woch.*, 1899, pp. 686–95, 717–24; J. Kaerst, *Die Geschichte des Altertums im Zusammenhange der allgemeinen Entwicklung der modernen historischen Forschung*, 1902, now in *Universalgeschichte*, ed. J. Vogt, Stuttgart, 1930, pp. 58–60, and *Geschichte des hellenistischen Zeitalters*, I, 1st ed., 1901, p. v (missing from the *Geschichte des Hellenismus*, 1927). But for an immediate recognition of Burckhardt's position in Greek historical studies *cf.* above all the vigorous pages of R. Pöhlmann, *Griechische Geschichte im neunzehnten Jahrhundert*, Munich, 1902, pp. 18–23, reprinted in *Aus Altertum und Gegenwart*, II, Munich, 1911, pp. 297–301.

5. *Cf. Allgem. Deutsche Biogr.*, s.v. A. Boeckh, p. 774 (the idea of the *Hellen* goes back to 1810). Apart from the first volume of Kaegi's biography, *cf.* also his 'Jacob Burckhardt und seine Berliner Lehrer', *Schweizer Beiträge zur allgemeinen Geschichte*, 7, 1949, pp. 101–16.

6. Thanks to Burckhardt, A. Boeckh's saying in *Staatshaushaltung der Athener*, 3rd ed., I, p. 710, has become famous: 'Die Hellenen waren im Glanze der Kunst und in der Blüthe der Freiheit unglücklicher als die Meisten glauben'. A mine of information on this interpretation and in general on all Burckhardt's predecessors can be found in G. Billeter, *Die Anschauungen vom Wesen des Griechentums*, Leipzig and Berlin, 1911.

7. C. Neumann, *Jacob Burckhardt*, Munich, 1927, p. 175, has rightly noted that Burckhardt engaged in implicit controversy with Curtius in attributing little importance to the Persian Wars and in defining the trophies of Delphi as a document of hatred between the Greeks.

8. The facts are examined with exemplary intelligence by K. Löwith, *Jacob Burckhardt*, Lucerne, 1936, pp. 11–61.

9. *Cf.* V. Ehrenberg, 'Das Agonale' in *Ost und West*, Prague, 1935, pp. 63–96, which has the essential bibliography.

10. A history of Burckhardt's reputation up to 1935 is traced (not in chronological order) by E. Colmi, *Wandlungen in der Auffassung von J.B.*, diss., Köln, Emsdetten, 1936.

11. This is reflected in discussions of the history of Greek culture. *Cf.* for instance W. Otto, *Kulturgeschichte des Altertums*, Munich, 1925, pp. 89–91; the preface by T. von Scheffer to *Die Kultur der Griechen*, Phaidon-Verlag, 1935; E. Howald, *Kultur der Antike*, 1938, 2nd revised ed., Zürich, 1948, p. 11, with the criticism of W. Otto, 'Antike Kulturgeschichte', *Sitzungsb. Bayer. Akad.*, No. 6, 1940. More recently B. Knauss, *Staat und Mensch in Hellas*, Berlin, 1940, and W. Kranz, *Die Kultur der Griechen*, Leipzig, 1943. Here it may be as well to bear in mind two of the most independent assessments of the German third humanism: R. Pfeiffer, *Die griechische Dichtung und die griechische Kultur*, Munich, 1932, and K. Reinhardt, 'Die klassische Philologie und das Klassische' in *Von Werken und Formen*, Godesberg, 1948, pp. 419–57. On post-war works A. Heuss, 'Kulturgeschichte des Altertums', *Archiv f. Kultur.*, 36, 1954, pp. 78–95.

18

J. G. Droysen
Between Greeks and Jews*

IF asked what we mean by Hellenism, we should probably answer that we mean the historical period which goes from the death of Alexander the Great (323 B.C.) to the death of Cleopatra in 30 B.C. Egypt was the last important survivor of the political system which had developed as a consequence both of the victories of Alexander and of his premature death. With the absorption of Egypt into the Roman empire, that political system came to an end. Even today, however, there is considerable disagreement among historians as to what the word Hellenism is intended to signify. Hellenism suggests to us more the idea of a civilization than the idea of a mere political system. When used to indicate a civilization, the word Hellenism is seldom confined to the chronologies and spatial limits within which we use it to indicate a political system. We often speak of Hellenism in the Roman empire to indicate the cultural tradition of the Greek-speaking part of the Roman empire: we even incline to extend the Hellenistic tradition into the Byzantine empire. On the other hand, the word Hellenism is often associated with the cultures of Carthage and Rome – not to speak of southern Italy and Sicily – which were never part of the empire of Alexander.

As a rule terminological ambiguities should never detain a scholar for long. We all know what a waste of time the word Renaissance has represented. But at the root of this particular terminological ambiguity there are the ambiguities of the *Geschichte des Hellenismus* by Johann Gustav Droysen, one of the greatest historians of any time.[1] It was J. G. Droysen who introduced the word Hellenism to designate the civilization of the Greek-speaking world after Alexander. He himself was not very clear about the chronological limits he intended to give to this word. There are passages of his work in which it is applied to the whole

*History and Theory, 9, 1970, pp. 139–53.

period before the Arab invasion of Egypt and Syria, whereas more frequently he calls Hellenism the period between Alexander and Jesus, which roughly corresponds to our usage.[2] But what matters to us is that Droysen himself never reached clarity about the main characteristics of the period he set out to explore. I do not intend to return here to those aspects of Droysen's thought which are best known.[3] The problem with which I shall be dealing here is new, at least to the best of my knowledge.[4]

A tradition which goes back to antiquity makes the decline of Greece coincide with the death of Alexander the Great – or rather with the death of Demosthenes. This is a deserved tribute to the role of Athens in Greek civilization. In literary terms it means classicism. To quote Plutarch only, both Demosthenes and Cicero ended their lives as soon as their countrymen ceased to be free (*Demosthenes* 3). Such a tradition, however, does not account for the poor reputation of Egypt and Syria and Pergamum as political, social, and cultural organizations of the third and second centuries B.C. Here two factors played their part: one is ancient, the other modern. One factor was the contempt in which the Romans held their Greek-speaking enemies after they had reduced them to impotence in the first part of the second century B.C. – a contempt which was shared by influential Greek observers such as Polybius. The other factor is the paucity of the literary evidence about the third century B.C. The literary fragments of the third and second centuries B.C. seemed to confirm by their very nature the impression of decline and fall. After Theocritus, Callimachus and Apollonius Rhodius, there seemed to be a desert in Greek literature of the third and second centuries B.C. – except for epigrams. No historian or philosopher of the third century B.C. has come down to us in a complete text. True enough, the loss of third- and second-century Greek literature happened in the Middle Ages and has nothing to do with the conditions of the period between the death of Alexander and Roman rule in the East. But it is difficult to resist the first impression that there is something wrong with an age which has left an insufficient account of itself. When Droysen wrote his doctoral dissertation *De Lagidarum regno Ptolemaeo VI Philometore rege* in 1831, it was still necessary for him to apologize for dealing with an age which '*propter sterilitatem suam atque languorem negligi, a Romanarum rerum scriptoribus despici, a Christianarum deformari defamarique solet*'.[5]

As we all know, it was precisely J. G. Droysen who first decided to explore thoroughly the Greek-speaking world in the centuries after

Alexander. Alexandrian literature had been put on the map by a famous essay by C. Gottlob Heyne, *De genio saeculi Ptolemaeorum*, in 1763.[6] Later on, the discovery of the Armenian Eusebius was to inspire a fundamental essay on the political and dynastic events of the third century B.C. by Niebuhr (1819). Inscriptions and papyri were attracting increasing attention. Champollion's decipherment of Egyptian hieroglyphics naturally added interest to those Greek inscriptions of Egypt from which his discovery had started. In France an epigraphist of genius, Jean Antoine Letronne, showed what one could do with these inscriptions in his *Recherches pour servir à l'histoire de l'Égypte sous la domination des Grecs et des Romains* (1823). Droysen learned all these things from his teacher Boeckh at the University of Berlin. From Boeckh he also learned to reflect on the differences between Classical civilization and Christian civilization. Boeckh returned regularly to the subject in his lectures on *Encyclopädie und Methodologie der Philologischen Wissenschaften* which he gave twenty-six times between 1809 and 1865. He did not, however, offer any precise suggestion about the process of transition from the pagan to the Christian world. The theologians and philosophers of Berlin University were much readier to produce ideas on this question of the transition. Droysen listened to several of them: the theologian August Neander, Eduard Gans, the pupil of Hegel, and Hegel himself. Hegel had offered one solution in his *Philosophie der Weltgeschichte*. This solution was to find in Roman civilization, and more precisely in the Roman state, the preparatory stage for the development of the Christian idea. Droysen meditated on Hegel and accepted his basic presupposition that history moves forward by thesis, antithesis and synthesis. But Boeckh saved him from *a priori* speculations about the course of history and very probably also directed his attention towards the Greek-speaking states of the post-Alexandrian era.

Whatever the precise origins of his ideas may be, they matured very rapidly. In December 1833, two years after his rather crude dissertation, Droysen published his *Geschichte Alexanders des Grossen*, 584 pages thick, in which his idea of Hellenism is clearly formulated.

The word itself, Hellenism, already existed in scholarly terminology.[7] It was originally taken over from Acts of the Apostles vi, 1, where Ἑλληνισταί are opposed to Ἑβραῖοι. Scaliger spread the notion of Ἑλληνισταί as Jewish speakers using Greek in the synagogue service: Ἑλληνισταί *Iudaei graecis Bibliis in Synagogis utentes* (*in Eusebium*, ed. Lugd. Bat. 1606, 124 b). The existence of a special Greek dialect for these Jewish speakers in Greek was hotly debated in the seventeenth century. Salmasius denied it in a discussion with D. Heinsius and wrote one of his most famous polemical pamphlets, or rather books, on this subject: *Funus linguae hellenisticae* (1643).[8]

The notion of *lingua hellenistica* to indicate the Greek of the Old and New Testaments survived Salmasius. Later, in the eighteenth century, the word *Hellenismus* was extended to cover the way of thinking of those Jews who spoke Greek. Herder used *Hellenismus* repeatedly in that sense.[9] Closer to Droysen, J. Matter, a French scholar who was under the influence of German scholarship, wrote in 1820: '*Les études auxquelles se livrèrent les Juifs en Égypte produisèrent cette manière de penser et d'écrire qu'on désigne sous le nom d'Hellénisme*' (*Essai historique sur l'école d'Alexandrie*, Volume I, 203). The originality of Droysen was to take Hellenism to mean, not specifically the way of thinking of Jews under the influence of Greek language and thought, but generally the language and way of thinking of all the populations which had been conquered by Alexander and subjected to Greek influence. In other words, he used the word Hellenism to indicate the intermediary and transitional period between classical Greece and Christianity. As we shall see later, the Jews interested Droysen much less than the Egyptians, the Babylonians, the Syrians. Hellenism was to Droysen essentially that stage in the evolution of paganism which led from classical Greece to Christianity – not via Judaism, but via other Oriental religions. It was a stage in the evolution of paganism which resulted from the contact between Orientals and Greeks in the empire created by Alexander and subdivided by his successors. So conceived, Hellenism had two aspects. It was a cultural movement which produced a new synthesis of Oriental and Greek ideas. It was also a political development which resulted in the constitution of a system of states in which Oriental natives were governed by a Graeco–Macedonian aristocracy.

Droysen was perhaps never fully aware that the notion of Hellenism he propounded had two very different aspects – the political and the cultural – and that there was a problem in relating one aspect to the other. This was not a serious difficulty in the initial stage of his work, when he wrote the history of Alexander. In the original plan the volume on Alexander was meant to be only the necessary introduction to the history of Hellenism proper. The question of the relation between political history and cultural (and religious) history was bound to become serious, indeed decisive, when he entered the specific field of Hellenism.

In a sense he never gave an answer to the question. Droysen devoted the only two volumes of the *Geschichte des Hellenismus* which he was actually to write (one published in 1836, the other in 1843) to the political history of the period 323–221 B.C. The volumes he had intended to write on the period from 221 to Augustus and on the cultural history from Alexander to the Arabs were never written, and we do not know what Droysen meant to put into them. After 1843 he devoted more than forty years of his scholarly activity to the history of Prussia, on which he became the highest authority: *Vorlesungen über das Zeitalter der Freiheitskriege* (first ed. Kiel, 1846); *Das Leben des Grafen Yorck von Wartenburg* (Leipzig, 1851); *Geschichte der preussischen Politik* (Leipzig, 1855–85). One might have thought that he had forgotten his former field of study. But in 1877–8 he surprised everyone by providing a revised, fully up-to-date edition of his work on Hellenism. One of the new features of the new edition was that the volume on Alexander was now explicitly the first part of the *Geschichte des Hellenismus* instead of being an introductory volume. Readers are advised to remember that *Geschichte des Hellenismus*, Volume I of the first edition has become *Geschichte des Hellenismus*, Volume II in the second edition. It is this new edition, which was translated into French by A. Bouché-Leclercq, that started the great revival of studies in the political and institutional history of the Hellenistic period in the last decades of the nineteenth century and in the early twentieth century. Like the first edition, the renewed *Geschichte des Hellenismus* contained a programme of cultural and religious history, but was in fact exclusively an examination of the political history of the period 323–221 B.C. We are therefore faced with the following paradox. Droysen set out to write a history of the transition from paganism to Christianity and never changed his mind on this. Though in the second edition of 1877–8 he modified the text of some of his programmatic declarations of the first edition, he never departed from his original interpretation of Hellenism as the period of three centuries in which Greeks and Orientals met and made Christianity possible. On the other hand, Droysen never wrote about these cultural developments. He never went beyond programmatic declarations on them. What he really achieved was a political history of one century – a political history which became a classic as soon as it was published. We may sharpen the paradox by a further remark. If there was an historian Droysen disliked, it was his contemporary Ranke.[10] Ranke represented for Droysen the very image of the detached historian, of the '*Quellenforscher*', who does not take sides and prefers mild diplomacy to battles of ideas doubled by battles of swords. Yet what we have of the history of

Hellenism closely resembles the masterpiece of Ranke's youth, *Geschichten der romanischen und germanischen Völker* (1824). Both works are histories of relations between states belonging to the same civilization.

Droysen's paradox used to be explained in a simple way. Droysen started as a Hegelian historian of ideas, but soon turned to political history. He discovered that what mattered in Hellenism was the power of the Macedonian army. Macedon being the Prussia of antiquity, he was consistent in proceeding from Macedon to Prussia. The history of Hellenism was a *praeparatio evangelica* to the history of Prussia. I am of course making this explanation simpler than it is. Ultimately it goes back to Droysen himself. In his *Antrittsrede* to the Berlin Academy in 1867 he said that he had interrupted his *History of Hellenism* because his appointment as a professor in Kiel (1840) had made him more acutely aware of the political problems of Germany. Kiel was 'in the border zones, already imperilled, of German life' (*'in den schon gefährdeten Grenzgebieten deutschen Lebens'*).[11] In its two most sophisticated versions, provided by historians such as F. Meinecke and F. Gilbert, this explanation takes into account Droysen's profound concern with the Christian faith.[12] Yet even in these subtlest versions such an interpretation leaves out something.

★

Droysen worked for twelve full years on the history of Hellenism before turning to modern history (and not just to the history of Prussia), and in these twelve years he never lost sight of his aim of making Christianity intelligible in historical terms. He was then, and remained afterward, an unorthodox Lutheran. Religion mattered to him. He always felt that Providence had been at work in sending Alexander and in making East and West meet in the kingdoms of his successors. The statements to this effect are many in the *History of Hellenism* and in the *Correspondence*. In the last chapter of the final volume of the *History of Hellenism* (1843) he says solemnly: 'Truly history has now created the body for the Holy Spirit of the New Revelation and of the New Covenant. Around it congregates the community of the Believers, the Church of Christ.'[13]

The most striking document of this religious attitude is the so-called *Theologie der Geschichte*, an open letter to his friend J. Olshausen. It was originally meant as an introduction to the 1843 volume of the *Geschichte des Hellenismus* (Volume II). Droysen must, however, have felt that this was more a profession of faith than an historical essay, and he published it separately in a few copies for private circulation. The paper became generally accessible only after Droysen's death when it was included in the *Kleine Schriften zur Alten Geschichte* in 1893. The title of *Theologie der Geschichte* is to be found in the reprint by E. Rothacker (1925), not in the *Kleine Schriften*. Droysen here stated his belief of how Providence worked in the obscure and despised centuries he called Hellenism.

It is therefore remarkable that in the same decade 1833–43 Droysen showed far more interest in the classical than in the post-classical literature and religion of the Greeks. Though the importance of Droysen's work on Aeschylus and Aristophanes is acknowledged, the implications of it for his attitude towards Hellenism have not yet been sufficiently considered. In 1832 Droysen published his translation of Aeschylus, which contributed much to the interpretation of the poet in literary and historical terms. But epoch-making was the translation of Aristophanes in three volumes which appeared in 1835, 1837 and 1838 respectively. Nobody had previously understood Aristophanes so well in relation to Athenian social and political life. The care which Droysen put into this work is shown by his paper 'Des Aristophanes Vögel und die Hermokopiden' which appeared in *Rheinisches Museum* 1835–6[14] and has since remained the standard work on the scandal of the desecration of the Herms in 415 B.C. In later years Droysen returned to Aeschylean problems under the influence of F. G. Welcker, whose admirer and correspondent he was. He wrote papers on the questions of the Trilogy in 1841 and 1844, with further contributions to the political interpretation of Aeschylus' *Persae*.[15] In 1842 he published a revised edition of his translation of Aeschylus.

As is evident from many of his remarks on Aeschylus and Aristophanes, Droysen intended to contribute to contemporary artistic life. He considered it important to make Athenian classical poetry accessible to the German public. The first volume of his translation was dedicated to Felix Mendelssohn-Bartholdy, the composer, and to Albert Gustav Heydemann, a fellow student; the third volume was dedicated to Eduard Bendemann, the painter. His appreciation of Aristophanes was enhanced by his personal acquaintance with Heine. The performance of the *Antigone* in Berlin in 1842, with Mendelssohn's music, was an occasion for a literary manifesto by Droysen on the situation of the contemporary theatre.[16] It is unnecessary here to expatiate on the well-known friendship and collaboration between Droysen and Mendelssohn.[17] It was Droysen's ambition and pride to provide his friend with words for his music. The revival of Greek classical art was the aim of this collaboration, at least as Droysen saw it.

Droysen was aware of the roots of Athenian art in Athenian society. Just as he was abandoning the classical world for modern politics in 1847 he produced a paper on 'Die attische Communalverfassung',[18] which for almost thirty years remained his last substantial contribution to classical studies. It was a searching and original analysis of the political life of the Attic villages in the archaic and the classical age. In Droysen's interpretation, Solon and Clisthenes allowed freedom in religious, patrimonial and administrative matters to the villages of Attica. They created a characteristic balance between the Athenian *polis* and its individual components which eliminated any rivalry '*zwischen Staat und Commune*' and contributed much to the liberty of the Athenian citizens. No doubt Droysen had in mind contemporary problems of the Prussian state in speaking of the balance '*zwischen Staat und Commune*', but he also felt that there was some connection between the varied and free life of Attica and the varied and free poetry of Athens. His perception of such a connection was never very clear, but it was certainly more definite than anything he ever thought about the relations between Hellenistic institutions and Hellenistic culture.

The surprising fact is that while he was working on Hellenistic political history Droysen did not concurrently study Hellenistic poetry, philosophy and religion, as we should have expected. He was reading, translating, interpreting, popularizing Attic literature, and clearly considered it the centre of his emotional life. While he was intellectually convinced that Providence had guided mankind along the path of Hellenism in order to produce Christianity, he found the pagan literature of pre-Hellenistic Athens far more satisfying. He claimed that Hellenism interested him as a Christian. But he recommended Aeschylus and Aristophanes to his contemporaries. In other words, literary classicism kept him away from Hellenistic culture, though culture, including religion, was supposed to be the principal object of his study of Hellenism.

*

Nor was classicism the only obstacle in Droysen's attempt to explain Christianity historically. He had started his work on Hellenism on the assumption that the rise of Christianity could be explained by the situation of the pagan world in the Hellenistic age. He was no theologian and knew little of Judaism. What he knew had apparently convinced him that Christianity was nearer to Greek paganism than to Judaism. One of the theses he offered for discussion at the oral examination for his doctorate in 1831 was: '*a doctrina Christiana Graecorum quam Iudaeorum religio propius abest*'.[19] Of course, theses offered for discussion at an examination need not be stated on oath. Sophistry is part of the game. But Droysen's point of view, at least in the first two volumes of his Hellenistic work (1833 and 1836), is in agreement with this doctoral thesis. When he speaks of Christianity, the emphasis is invariably on the encounter of Greeks and non-Jewish Orientals: Jews are left out.

The appearance of the *Life of Jesus* by D. Strauss in 1835–6 shocked Droysen as it shocked many others. But there was nothing in the work of Strauss which caused him to change his mind about his interpretation of Hellenism. What Droysen felt after reading Strauss (and later Bruno Bauer) was an increased distrust of Hegel's methods, if they could lead to such blasphemous conclusions.[20] There was, however, other research in progress which Droysen was bound to examine with greater care in relation to his own studies. In the early 1830s a remarkable upsurge of interest in Philo and in Alexandrian Judaism in general was noticeable in Germany. The purpose of this research was to ascertain whether Philo had influenced St Paul and altogether contributed to the development of Christianity. It will be enough here to mention two books which are still worth consulting today: A. Gfrörer, *Philo und die alexandrinische Theosophie* (1831) and A. F. Dähne, *Geschichtliche Darstellung der jüdisch-alexandrinischen Religionsphilosophie* (1834). This new research added to the importance of a relatively older book by one of Droysen's teachers: the *Genetische Entwickelung der vornehmsten gnostischen Systeme* by A. Neander, which had appeared in 1818. Neander had propounded a distinction between Jewish and anti-Jewish Gnostics and had indicated the relevance of Jewish Gnostics (among whom he included Philo) to the origins of Christianity. The topical interest of Neander's book was recognized by F. C. Baur who developed Neander's thesis in his book *Die christliche Gnosis* (1835) to the point of connecting Schleiermacher with anti-Jewish Gnosis and Hegel with Jewish or pro-Jewish Gnosis.[21]

The whole of Baur's research in those years underlined the significance of Jewish–Greek contacts for the origins of Christianity. Baur believed that the Essenes had been influenced by the Pythagoreans and that in their turn the Essenes had influenced early Christianity (*Apollonius von Tyana und Christus*, 1832). The interpretation of St Paul, with which Baur's name is connected for ever, implied that Pauline doctrines were an internal development of Judaism in the direction of the Graeco–Roman world. The fact that Baur had turned from Schleier-macher to Hegel in his research on the Christian origins may not have been a point in his favour with a disillusioned Hegelian like Droysen. But Droysen was too good a scholar to remain indifferent to all the serious research which was going on around him on the relations between Judaism and Christianity. The notion of Gnosis, which Neander and Baur had forcibly made a contemporary issue, competed with his own notion of Hellenism. Gnosis indicated a combination of Jewish and Greek factors in the origins of Christianity, whereas Hellenism implied a purely pagan approach to Christianity.

There are signs that Droysen reconsidered his position in the years between 1837 and 1843, while he was writing his third volume on Hellenism. In 1838 he published a very important review of G. Bern-hardy's *Grundriss der griechischen Litteratur*, Volume I, in which he formulated a distinction between the learned and the popular literature of Hellenism.[22] He took the popular (*volksthümliche*) literature to include the expressions of non-Greek people writing in Greek – such as Philo and the Septuaginta translation of the Old Testament. He recognized that it was a mistake on the part of classical scholars to leave such a literature in the hands of theologians. It is therefore not surprising that in the last chapter of the *History of Hellenism*, Volume II (1843) Judaism is mentioned for the first time as an important factor in the origins of Christianity. The mention is cursory, but Droysen is aware that he is saying something new.[23] A few months later, in a letter to F. G. Welcker of 12 September 1843, we find Droysen talking about the Sibylline oracles and the Hellenistic books of the Old Testament. He expresses his intention of extending his reading to the vast mass of Apocrypha.[24]

To sum up, at least from 1838 onward Droysen became more inter-ested in Judaism. He included Jewish books in the popular literature of which he intended to make a special study. He was not indifferent to the mounting research on Alexandrian Judaism, on the Essenes and on Paulinism. He seemed to be preparing himself for the next volume of the *History of Hellenism*. Yet nothing happened. He must have soon inter-rupted his readings. He never expressed any articulate opinion on what he had already read.

Once again we are faced with the question: why did he not pursue this obviously fruitful line? Once again, no easy answer will do. What Droysen envisaged in his study of Oriental texts was in many ways premature. A glance at R. Reitzenstein's *Poimandres*, which appeared in 1904 and can be said to have been written in Droysen's spirit, is enough to show how much of the evidence was still unknown in 1843. Inscriptions, papyri, Egyptian texts, even literary texts, such as Hippolytus' *Philosophoumena*, were later additions to knowledge. Yet what was available in 1843 was more than sufficient for spade work. Droysen did not suspend his work for lack of evidence.

The classicism of his literary tastes may have helped to delay his research on Jewish texts, but does not explain why he interrupted his work on them once he had started it. In 1838 Droysen had satisfied himself that new research on Jewish texts was necessary – and possible. The reasons for his unwillingness to pursue it, if it can be explained at all, must be sought elsewhere. Increasing involvement in the German national problem is certainly part of the story. But it is also true that Droysen had reached the point in his exploration of Hellenism at which he had to decide whether to include or exclude Judaism. The inclusion would have meant a radical revision of the original conception; it would have involved him in the difficult exegetic problems raised by the Tübingen theologians; and it would have touched intimate recesses of his personal life. The last aspect deserves special attention.

*

As a student and young teacher in Berlin, this son of a Lutheran pastor found his friends and his first wife in a circle of highly educated Jewish converts to Protestantism. He dedicated his book on Alexander to Gottlieb Friedlaender, who was the grandson of David Friedlaender, the champion of Jewish emancipation. He married Marie Mendheim, the sister of Gottlieb Friedlaender's wife. Marie Mendheim was the daughter of a Jewish bookseller who apparently changed his name Mendel to Mendheim when a convert. Her mother belonged to the Friedlaender family. Droysen's other two closest friends, F. Mendelssohn and E. Bendemann, were both of Jewish origin. Heine and Gans belonged to the same society. It is interesting to note that G. Bernhardy, whose history of Greek literature Droysen discussed from the point of view of religious history, was himself a convert from Judaism. Less near, but influential, was another convert, August Neander, born David Mendel – at that time perhaps the most eminent and respected Lutheran theologian. Some of these converts thought hard about Judaism before and after their conversion. Neander made a thorough study of Philo. Both Gans and Heine had belonged before conversion to the *Verein für*

Cultur und Wissenschaft der Juden. Gans had presided over it. This was a society for the study and reform of Judaism, and it was deeply under the influence of Hegelian ideas. For a while Hegelianism and Judaism had seemed to be reciprocally compatible: an attitude which perhaps explains why Baur had classified Hegelian philosophy as Gnosticism of the Jewish variety.[25] Readers of Heine are in no need to be told that all his work, even after conversion, was a continuous *confessio iudaica* – as indeed it has been called. I am less clear about the religious ideas of Felix Mendelssohn and Gottlieb Friedlaender, but both are said to have combined deep Christian beliefs with devotion to the memories of their respective Jewish grandfathers. Conversion was taken seriously, but did not mean oblivion of the Jewish ancestry and tradition. Yet surrounding society asked these men and women to behave as if they had no Jewish past, and in general they complied with this requirement. Heine had greater freedom because he was in exile in Paris. Silence on Judaism was the official line. Droysen seems to have conformed absolutely to this convention in his relations with his friends of Jewish origin. His letters to Gottlieb Friedlaender, Mendelssohn and Bendemann, as far as I remember, never touch upon Jewish subjects. Even the marriage to Marie Mendheim must have happened under this unwritten law. Gustav Droysen, himself an historian, who left a good unfinished biography of his father Johann Gustav, never mentions the circumstance that his mother was Jewish. The taboo was deeply ingrained, and I wonder whether it did not affect Droysen as an historian. He had started from the notion that Christianity can be explained with little reference to Judaism. He had perhaps come to realize the weakness of such an exclusive approach. The work of the Tübingen school had indeed shown that it was difficult to talk seriously about the origins of Christianity without a prolonged study of the Jewish background. Droysen did some work on Jewish texts, but he never brought himself to face the whole problem of the relation between Judaism and Christianity. It was the problem which at a personal level had deeply concerned his best friends, his wife and his relatives – and it was going to affect his own children. He must have known that his friends were thinking about it in their silences. He remained silent, too. The *History of Hellenism* was never finished.

*

To write chapters of the history of historiography with reference to social taboos about allegedly unpleasant subjects is a dangerous task – and I do not claim to be on safe ground. But certain consequences for the concept of Hellenism must now be considered.

As we have seen, Droysen claimed that Hellenism was an avenue (or rather *the* avenue) to Christianity, but he himself studied it as a political phenomenon. His two approaches – one programmatic and the other effective – conditioned the research of the next generations. Hellenism, as a religious phenomenon, attracted the minds of many great scholars at the end of the nineteenth century: Usener, Cumont, Reitzenstein are the most distinguished. They were mainly interested in the interplay of Oriental and Greek beliefs: syncretism was their guiding notion. Reitzenstein undoubtedly cherished the hope of explaining the origins of Christianity in Hellenistic terms. His hope seemed to come near fulfilment when the Mandaean texts attracted his attention. It was his thesis that these were documents of a pre-Christian faith connected with St John the Baptist. As we all know, the Mandaean question proved to be more intractable than Reitzenstein had anticipated.[26] But other documents, such as the Egyptian Gnostic texts, too late for Reitzenstein to use, have raised analogous hopes in more recent researchers.

Meanwhile great progress was also being made in the study of Hellenism inside Judaism. E. Bickerman's recent work, *Four Strange Books of the Bible* (1968), is perhaps the most striking product of this trend of research, of which the volume by Martin Hengel, *Judentum und Hellenismus* (1969), provides an up-to-date summary in 692 pages.

Even the proto-monks of Qumran have not remained immune from the suspicion of Hellenistic influences: their *Manual of Discipline* has been compared with the rules of Hellenistic religious associations. However, to start from Hellenism in the interpretation of Christianity does not necessarily mean to end with Hellenism. A great specialist of Hellenistic religious movements, A. D. Nock, indicated the points in which Christianity appeared to him original: conversion was one. So much for the religious side of Droysen's approach to Hellenism.

On the other side Droysen inspired research on political history and political institutions. Such research was helped by the discovery of new epigraphical and papyrological material. The more one knew about Hellenistic institutions, especially of Egypt, the stronger the temptation became of presenting Hellenism as a bourgeois, capitalistic civilization. The bureaucratic apparatus, the growth of urban centres, the realism in art, the banks, the international traffic, the development of science and technology reminded the historians of conditions in France and Germany in the middle of the nineteenth century. U. Wilcken, K. J. Beloch, U.

Wilamowitz, J. Kaerst and later of course M. Rostovtzeff, described the modern features of the Hellenistic world. The new papyri of Menander and Herodas confirmed this impression of a bourgeois culture. Even the combination of superstitition and of technological progress seemed to fit into the bourgeois pattern. The major departure from Droysen was in the new insistence on the purely Greek character of Hellenistic civilization, at least in its creative phase. In that vigorous survey of Hellenistic history which is the first volume of *Hellenistische Dichtung in der Zeit des Kallimachos* (1924), Wilamowitz presented Hellenistic culture as the imperialistic achievement of Greek conquerors. The continuity between Greek and Hellenistic civilizations was also the main theme of Kaerst's fine work. W. W. Tarn indeed saw his Graeco-Macedonians as precocious Englishmen and Scotsmen settling on colonial land. He idealized the Greek kingdoms of Bactria and India as the predecessors of the British Raj. Even the very recent *Kulturgeschichte des Hellenismus* by the theologian Carl Schneider (1967-9) is imperialist and racist.[27] Nobody saw any basic contradiction between the image of Hellenistic man in need of religious salvation and the image of the Hellenistic state providing the comforts of life for a capitalist society. The two directions indicated by Droysen appeared after all to be not incompatible with each other, especially after some rectifications by his successors.

It is, however, doubtful whether this harmony is likely to last. Decolonization and Marxism have in recent years contributed to a shift in attention towards the poorer natives and the slaves, while a reassessment of the intellectual achievements of Hellenistic thinkers, scientists and scholars is now in progress. The suspicion is growing that the benefits gained by science from state protection were short-lived and fraught with evil consequences.[28] At the same time pre-Christian Judaea, which produced the scepticism of Ecclesiastes, the revolution of the Maccabees, and the monasticism of Qumran within a period of perhaps seventy to eighty years, is once again forcing itself on the attention of scholars not exactly as a Hellenized country. But it is too early to be sure that the dual interpretation Droysen encouraged both by his word and by his silence is now on the wane.

References

1. On Droysen, in addition to the works quoted below in the text and in the notes, see especially O. Hintze, *Allgemeine Deutsche Biographie*, 48, 1904, pp. 82–114, reprinted in *Gesammelte Abhandlungen*, II, 2nd ed., Göttingen, 1964, pp. 453–99 (*cf.* also the later [1930] paper reprinted there, pp. 500–18); and G. Droysen, *J. G. Droysen*, I, Leipzig and Berlin, 1910. Hintze and G. Droysen speak about Droysen's political activity (the latter only up to 1848); R. Hübner, 'J. G. Droysens Vorlesungen über Politik', *Zeitschrift für Politik*, 10, 1917, pp. 325–76; H. Astholz, *Das Problem 'Geschichte' untersucht bei J. G. Droysen*, Berlin, 1933; J. Wach, *Das Verstehen*, III, Tübingen, 1933; H. Diwald, *Das historische Erkennen*, Leiden, 1955, pp. 50–76; W. Hock, *Liberales Denken im Zeitalter der Paulskirche. Droysen und die Frankfurter Mitte*, Münster, 1957; P. Hünermann, *Der Durchbruch geschichtlichen Denkens im 19. Jahrhundert*, Freiburg, 1967, pp. 49–132. Among the general histories of historiography G. von Below, *Die deutsche Geschichtschreibung*, 2nd ed., Munich and Berlin, 1924, pp. 49–50, is still best on Droysen. A criticism of Droysen from the point of view of Holy Roman Empire ideology is made in H. von Srbik, *Geist und Geschichte vom deutschen Humanismus bis zur Gegenwart*, I, Salzburg, 1950, pp. 367–77. *Cf.* also, G. G. Iggers, *The German Conception of History*, Middletown, Conn., 1968, pp. 104–19.

2. *Cf. Geschichte der Nachfolger Alexanders*, Hamburg, 1936, Vorrede, pp. xv–xvi, which seems to include, at least on the literary side, even Byzantine history in the notion of Hellenism.

3. My *Contributo alla storia degli studi classici*, Rome, 1955, pp. 165–93, 263–73, with bibliography, contains two papers which I wrote in 1933 and 1934 devoted to these aspects of Droysen.

4. I have been led to reconsider the notion of Hellenism in Droysen by the appearance of a remarkable book on him by Benedetto Bravo, an Italian who teaches in Poland: *Philologie, histoire, philosophie de l'histoire. Étude sur J. G. Droysen, historien de l'antiquité*, Warsaw, 1968. Some observations which I formulated in a review of Bravo's book in *Rivista Storica Italiana* in 1969 were the starting point for an article of mine in *Saeculum*, 'Hellenismus und Gnosis', in the *Festschrift J. Vogt*, 1970.

5. Now in *Kleine Schriften zur Alten Geschichte*, II, Leipzig, 1894, p. 351.

6. *Opuscula*, I, Göttingen, 1785, pp. 76–134.

7. See the history of the term in the deservedly famous essay by R. Laqueur, *Hellenismus*, Giessen, 1925. St John Chrysostom gave an interpretation of the term which must have inspired Scaliger, in Homily XIV on the Acts: *Opera*, IX, Paris, 1837, p. 129.

8. *Cf.* D. Heinsius, *Aristarchus Sacer* in *Sacrarum Exercitationum ad Novum Testamentum libri XX*, Lugduni Bat., 1639, p. 653, p. 668, and elsewhere. The story of this dispute deserves further research.

9. R. Pfeiffer, *Philologische Wochenschrift*, 46, 1926, pp. 961–6; Momigliano,

Contributo, p. 183 n. 58; R. Pfeiffer, *Ausgewählte Schriften*, Munich, 1960, p. 151. In 1926 Pfeiffer showed that Herder even included other Oriental nations in his notion of Hellenism.

10. *Cf.* J. G. Droysen, *Briefwechsel*, I, ed. R. Hübner, Berlin and Leipzig, 1929, p. 119 (letter to F. Perthes, 8 February 1837), where Droysen quotes the motto 'Das wahre Faktum steht nicht in den Quellen'. Note the significant episode in O. Hintze, *Allg. Deutsche Biogr.*, 48, p. 98, and in general G. Birtsch, *Die Nation als sittliche Idee. Der Nationalstaatsbegriff in Geschichtsschreibung und politischer Gedankenwelt J. G. Droysens*, Cologne, 1964.

11. *Historik*, ed. R. Hübner, Munich and Berlin, 1937, pp. 425–8. *Cf.* O. Hintze, *Allg. Deutsche Biogr.*, 48, p. 88; G. von Below, *Die deutsche Geschichtschreibung*, p. 48; T. Schieder, *Neue Deutsche Biographie* 4, 1959, p. 135.

12. F. Meinecke, *Historische Zeitschrift*, 141, 1930, pp. 249–87, reprinted in *Schaffender Spiegel*, Stuttgart, 1948, pp. 146–210, and *Zur Geschichte der Geschichtsschreibung*, 1968, pp. 125–67; F. Gilbert, *J. G. Droysen und die preussisch-deutsche Frage*, Munich and Berlin, 1931. *Cf.* also K. Jordan, *Archiv für Kulturgeschichte*, 49, 1967, pp. 262–96, and J. Rüsen, *Begriffene Geschichte. Genesis und Begründung der Geschichtstheorie J. G. Droysens*, Paderborn, 1969, pp. 28–49.

13. *Geschichte der Bildung des hellenistischen Staatensystemes*, 1843, p. 584.

14. *Kleine Schriften*, II, pp. 1–61.

15. *Kleine Schriften*, II, pp. 75–145.

16. *Kleine Schriften*, II, pp. 146–81.

17. C. Wehmer, *Ein tief gegründet Herz. Der Briefwechsel Felix Mendelssohn-Bartholdys mit Johann Gustav Droysen*, Heidelberg, 1959, adds nothing to the material in the *Briefwechsel*, ed. Hübner.

18. *Kleine Schriften*, I, pp. 328–85.

19. *Kleine Schriften*, II, p. 431.

20. *Briefwechsel*, I, pp. 103, 118.

21. This question deserves re-examination. *Cf.* H. Jonas, *Gnosis und spätantiker Geist*, I, 3rd ed., Göttingen, 1964; S. Wagner, *Die Essener in der wissenschaftlichen Diskussion*, Berlin, 1960; F. Parente, *La Parola del Passato*, 95, 1964, pp. 81–124; P. C. Hodgson, *The Formation of Historical Theology: A Study of F. C. Baur*, New York, 1966.

22. *Kleine Schriften*, II, p. 74.

23. *Geschichte der Bildung des hellenistischen Staatensystemes*, p. 581.

24. *Briefwechsel*, II, p. 253. Droysen's failure in his Hellenistic project may be taken either as a contribution to, or as a symptom of, the decline in the importance of ancient history which is evident in German universities after 1840: cf. J. Engel, *Historische Zeitschrift*, 189, 1959, p. 346.

25. Hans Liebeschütz, *Das Judentum im deutschen Geschichtsbild von Hegel bis Max Weber*, Tübingen, 1967, on Droysen pp. 86–90; M. A. Meyer, *The Origins of the Modern Jew. Jewish Identity and European Culture in Germany, 1749–1824*, Detroit, 1967. On the political side H. Fischer, *Judentum, Staat und Heer in Preussen im frühen 19. Jahrhundert*, Tübingen, 1968. *Cf.* also the introduction by K. Wilhelm to the selected papers on *Wissenschaft des Judentums im deutschen Sprachbereich*, 2 vols., Tübingen, 1967.

26. *Cf*. K. Rudolph, *Die Mandäer*, Göttingen, 1960, for a summary of the question.

27. *Cf*. the important review by O. Murray, *Classical Review*, 19, 1969, pp. 69–72, with further bibliography on Hellenism.

28. Claire Préaux, 'Réflexions sur l'entité hellénistique', *Chronique d'Égypte*, 40, 1965, pp. 129–39, and in general all the historical research by this author, beginning with *L'Économie royale des Lagides*, Brussels, 1939; S. K. Eddy, *The King is Dead*, Lincoln, Nebraska, 1961. *Cf*. for new points of view R. Pfeiffer, *Ausgewählte Schriften*, pp. 148–58; R. Lévêque, *Le Monde hellénistique*, Paris, 1969. The standard political history of the Hellenistic age is now E. Will, *Histoire politique du monde hellénistique*, 2 vols., Nancy, 1966–7. Louis Robert occupies a place apart through the invaluable contributions to our knowledge of all aspects of Hellenism provided by his work on inscriptions: see especially his series *Hellenica*, Paris, 1941 ff.

19

The Ancient City of Fustel de Coulanges*

To E. J. Bickerman
'sodali fusteliali'

W HEN one talks of the ancient city as a society within which institutions operate and ideas circulate, the first modern historian whose name comes to mind is Fustel de Coulanges. We think of him above all because in the very title *Cité antique* he defined his dependence upon and his distance from the greatest ancient interpreter of the city, Aristotle. Like Aristotle, and through the influence of Aristotle, Fustel places the city at the centre of his interpretation; but it is the ancient city, not the city as such and not even specifically the Greek city.

Furthermore, with Fustel we can now see the characteristic beginnings of French historiography of the ancient world in the elements that distinguish it from the German historiography of the ancient world on which my generation in Italy was still reared. When we were young we were naturally aware that it was French and Belgian scholars such as H. Francotte and G. Glotz who were describing the Greek city. Indeed in the first pages of his admirable *Cité grecque* of 1928 Glotz referred to Aristotle and Fustel as his two predecessors. But I am afraid that we did not make a clear distinction between these works and the so-called *Staatskunde* of the German scholars, as exemplified, after A. Boeckh, in the fundamental *Griechische Staatskunde* by G. Busolt and H. Swoboda (1920–26) or, on a lesser scale, in the successive contributions by B. Keil and V. Ehrenberg respectively to the second and third editions of the *Einleitung in die Altertumswissenschaft* of Gercke and Norden. We did not clearly understand the origins of the psychological and ethnological interests, the *'perpetuelles contaminations d'idées et de coutumes'* which were characteristic of Glotz's books. While the German treatises dis-

★Rivista Storica Italiana, 87, 1970, pp. 81–98.

tinguished between public law and private law, Glotz conflated them: he saw in the *polis* a patriarchal society. Following Francotte (1856–1918) whose studies of the *polis* had been accompanied by works on the industry and finances of the Greek cities, Glotz arrived at the *Cité grecque* after his well-known thesis on the *Solidarité de la famille dans le droit criminel en Grèce* (1904) and a volume on *Le travail dans la Grèce ancienne* (1920). L. Gernet, several years his junior, combined a whole series of basic papers and textual commentaries on purely juridical problems with a study on economic history, *L'approvisionnement d'Athènes en blé au Ve et au IVe siecle* (in *Mélanges d'histoire ancienne*, ed. G. Bloch, 1909, pp. 269–391), with a thesis of an ethical-legal nature, *Recherches sur le développement de la pensée juridique et morale en Grèce* (1917), and lastly with a religious history of Greece, *Le génie grec dans la religion* (1932), in collaboration with André Boulanger.

Today there is no doubt about the origins of this complex interest in Greek society, seen variously in its economic, intellectual, legal and religious aspects. Born in 1862, Glotz was a student at the École Normale in the years in which it was dominated by Fustel. The Belgian Francotte passed from the study of the Encyclopedists (1880) to the study of Greek law and economy (*c.* 1890) under the influence of the problems formulated in France. Gernet began to work under Paul Girard, the author of a volume on *L'Éducation athénienne au Ve et au IVe siècle av. J.C.* (2nd ed., 1891). Girard was a pupil of Fustel and a biographer of Fustel's biographer, Paul Guiraud (1908). In Guiraud, who wrote his biography of Fustel in 1896, the economic aspect of the school of Fustel is particularly marked: *La propriété foncière en Grèce jusqu'à la conquête romaine* (1893) and *La main-d'oeuvre industrielle dans l'ancienne Grèce* (1900).

The other main characteristic can equally clearly be traced back to Fustel: the comparative method. It is enough to open the introductory pages of Glotz's *Solidarité de la famille* to see that he is caught up in a discussion between jurists on the respective merits of the comparative method and the historical method. By Glotz's time this discussion was circulating throughout Europe. It entered Italy, for instance, with the translation by P. Bonfante and C. Longo (1906) of the *Grundriss der ethnologischen Jurisprudenz* by A. H. Post (1894–5). But it originated with H. S. Maine's *Ancient Law* (1861) in England, and the *Cité antique* by Fustel in France (1864); and it is well known that Fustel was writing without knowing Maine. In France the first application of the comparative method in the study of ancient law was by Fustel. The French jurists' awareness of the value of the comparative method was subsequently enriched by the particular theorization of this method on the part of a pupil of Fustel who followed a path of his own: Emile Durkheim.[1] Already in Glotz, and more noticeably in Gernet,[2] Fustel's influence was inseparable from that of Durkheim, at least in the sense that Durkheim interpreted and generalized Fustel's system of observation of social facts. Anyone wanting to assess the more recent developments of this French school must devote at least as much attention to Durkheim's re-elaboration and generalization as to the original inspiration of Fustel. In Gernet, who died in 1961, and was the general secretary of the *Année Sociologique* in the last years of his life, the direct legacy of Fustel, treasured in the École Normale and the Sorbonne, is possibly of less importance than the new spirit of research that he found in the company of his sociologist friends Robert Hertz, killed in the First World War, Marcel Mauss and Marcel Granet (to whose *Études sociologiques sur la Chine* he wrote a preface in 1953).

I have especially the Italian situation in mind in emphasizing this complication of Durkheim's intervention in giving a new meaning – more rigorous and also broader – to Fustel. In Italy there has been an attempt to present *La Cité antique* as a work that should be assimilated into our culture. And it is typical of the intelligence of Giorgio Pasquali that it should have been he, apparently so remote from French culture, who noted Fustel's absence from our midst and who pointed out his importance.[3]

But Pasquali's introduction to the Italian translation of the *Cité antique* by G. Perrotta (1924) was inevitably affected by the bias of its author, who believed on the one hand that Fustel had never read either Niebuhr or Mommsen, and on the other hand that he had 'found successors only in Germany in Rohde, and in the Scandinavian countries in Wide and Nilsson' (pp. v–vi).

We shall have more to say about the systematic neglect of modern historians that Fustel displayed in the *Cité antique*. The assertion that Fustel found his successors outside France, and that he should be seen so to speak as a part of a German–Scandinavian tradition of the history of religion, is certainly misleading. If the name of Glotz were not enough, that of Durkheim with all that it entails would be sufficient to refute this interpretation. Moreover, the extent of Fustel's influence on Rohde should not be exaggerated. Nothing could be further from the truth than the assertion in the *Enciclopedia Italiana* that he was 'a fully conscious' successor of Fustel. In two notes to his *Psyche* (4th ed., 1907, Volume I, p. 166, n. 2; p. 253, n. 2) Rohde accepted Fustel's postulate that the state is more recent than the family, and showed sympathy for the idea of the worship of ancestors preceding other cults, but refused to follow Fustel into the world of prehistory. *La Cité antique* was translated into German only in 1907, and as we see from the review by L. Wenger in the *Deutsche Literaturzeitung*, 1907, col. 1733-7 and 1797-1801, and from an observation by B. Keil in *Einleitung in die Altertumswissenschaft* III, 2nd ed., 1923, p. 429, it was never very widely read and had even less authority. V. Ehrenberg repeatedly defined it as '*sachlich wie methodisch phantastisch, aber bedeutende Konzeption mit zum Teil tiefer Erkenntnis der religiösen und sippengebundenen Kräfte des Staates*' (most recently *Der Staat der Griechen*, 1965, p. 305), which is incidentally an intrinsically contradictory judgement. Not only does Fustel fit rightfully into the French sociological tradition – as is borne out by the dedication to him of Durkheim's Latin thesis on Montesquieu – but he contributed to this tradition by establishing the connection between economic structure and religious beliefs. More particularly, Fustel saw in the worship of the dead the first justification of private property.

*

The relatively short life of Numa-Denis Fustel de Coulanges (1830-89) is divided, as far as intellectual activity is concerned, between the two decades of the Second Empire and the other two of the still shaky Third Republic.[4] Educated at the École Normale, where he studied under V. Duruy, A. Cheruel and J.-D. Guigniaut, but found sustenance in Descartes, Guizot and Tocqueville, Fustel took his doctorate in 1858 with a French thesis on *Polybe ou la Grèce conquise* and a Latin thesis on *Quid Vestae cultus in institutis veterum privatis publicisque valuerit*. The first thesis already contained the substance of the conclusions of the *Cité antique*, while the second, within the limits we shall shortly indicate, foreshadowed its beginning. Only six years elapsed between the thesis and the publication of the *Cité antique*, written at Strasbourg when he was already a professor. Before his doctorate, as a pupil at the French School at Athens, Fustel had explored Chios between 1853 and 1855 and had written a *Mémoire sur l'île de Chios* which appeared in 1856 and was republished by Camille Jullian, pupil and editor of Fustel, in *Questions historiques* (1893): this was a history of the island of Chios from its origins to the nineteenth century.

A basically conservative and religious interpretation of political life, such as that contained in the *Cité antique*, naturally made Fustel *persona grata* at the court of Napoleon III. He was appointed, on Duruy's recommendation, to give history lectures at the École Normale in Paris in February 1870 and immediately invited to give a special course to the Empress Eugénie and her suite. Clearly it was remembered that Ranke had lectured for Maximilian II of Bavaria in 1854. The lectures were published only in 1930 by P. Fabre with the title *Leçons à l'Impératrice sur les origines de la civilisation française.*

When the Second Empire fell, Fustel became the upholder of the French character of Alsace against Theodor Mommsen and defended it with a remarkable clarity of ideas about the principle of nationality (*Questions historiques*, 1893, pp. 506–12). These and other pages by Fustel could still be reprinted during the First World War as being of real relevance.[5]

In 1872 he was writing the manifesto of the new French historiography, as he wanted it to be after the disaster of 1870. The German victory had been made possible partly by the difference in the attitude of historians in the two countries. German scholars were united in celebrating Germany, while the French had given themselves over to diatribes against France's past, particularly against the pre-1789 regime. 'In France scholarship is liberal, in Germany it is patriotic.' 'True patriotism is not love of one's native soil, it is love of the past, respect for the generations who have gone before us.' In other words, Fustel was asking for respect for pre-revolutionary France, for the *ancien régime*, as a sign of French patriotic unity after the defeat. He did not want an imitation of patriotic German scholarship. He hankered after the scholarship '*si calme, si simple, si haute de nos Bénédictins, de notre Académie des Inscriptions, des Beaufort, Fréret*' – themselves products of the *ancien régime*. But if it was necessary for France, he was ready to encourage a militant historiography around '*les frontières de notre conscience nationale et les abords de notre patriotisme*' (*Questions historiques,* 1893, pp. 3–16).

This anti-German ideology was echoed by the general tendency of the work already outlined in the lectures at Strasbourg, but actually written in Paris, on the *Histoire des institutions politiques de l'ancienne France,* of which the first volume came out in 1875. Re-written and largely posthumous, the definitive edition appeared in six volumes, edited and completed by C. Jullian, between 1891 and 1893. Fustel aimed at separating the history of France from its Germanic roots. As he wrote in 1877: 'I have talked neither of the spirit of freedom of the Frankish warriors, nor of elective kingship, nor of national assemblies, nor of popular juries, nor of the confiscation of the lands of the conquered, nor of the allodia distributed to the conquerors. I have sought for all this in the documents and I have not found it. On the other hand some definite facts are to be found there: for instance the preservation of the right to landed property without any modification; the continuity of the administrative regime, at least in its outward forms, particularly the persistence of the same social distinctions, and the existence of an aristocracy to which many Germans certainly belonged, but which was not exclusively German.' (*Histoire des institutions politiques de l'ancienne France*, Volume II, *L'invasion germanique*, 1891, pp. xi–xii.) Fustel gave new significance to the eighteenth-century polemic of J. B. Dubois and H. de Boulainvilliers and came to the defence of Dubois' theory that the roots of modern France lay in the Roman world, not in the Germanic one. As he says in another passage: 'It is indisputable that the link between Rome and Gaul was not broken at the will of the Gauls, but by the Germans. We shall see again in the course of our studies that the Gallic population preserved all it could of what was Roman and was intent on remaining Roman, as far as was possible' (*Histoire des institutions politiques de l'ancienne France*, Volume I, *La Gaule Romaine*, 1891, p. 96).

This thesis included a defence of the antiquity of private property among the Gauls, which resumed a basic idea of the *Cité antique* and was further reinforced in the essay of 1889 on *Le problème des origines de la propriété foncière* (*Questions historiques*, pp. 19–117).

Although he was sometimes suspected of Bonapartism, Fustel continued to prosper after 1870. In 1875 he obtained a teaching post in Ancient History at the Sorbonne; in 1880 he became director of the École Normale and remained there for three years. He found the ideal position in the Chair of Mediaeval History at the Sorbonne created specially for him in 1878. He also outlined a plan (*c.* 1872?) for the reform of the Constitution of the Republic, and declined an invitation from Thiers to become the official historian of the defeat. One may well acknowledge that his political position was genuinely uncertain. His defence of the *ancien régime*, his hostility towards German intellectuals and his vague religious sense endeared him to the Right: later on he became the favourite of Maurras and Daudet.[6]

But the men of the Right never managed to convince their adversaries, even after Fustel's death, that he was entirely theirs. The harshest attack, from H. d'Arbois de Jubainville, in *Deux manières d'écrire l'histoire* (1896), was primarily the attack of a *chartiste* against a *normalien* –

diplomatics and palaeography versus literary and legal sources; Mabillon versus Condorcet and Taine. There was a certain irony in setting Mabillon against Fustel, who about 1870 had looked upon Mabillon as one of the glories of French historiography. But the truth is that in France there was never an open revolt against Fustel. Not even the bias of Marc Bloch and Lucien Febvre for Michelet really signified opposition to Fustel. Bloch, whose father was one of Fustel's most eminent pupils, felt able to take part without any qualms in the celebrations for the centenary of his birth in 1930.[7] With the foundation of the *Annales* in 1929 and the appearance of *Les caractères originaux de l'histoire rurale française* in 1931 the centenary in fact coincided with the start of a new phase of French historiography.

★

Let us now return to the two theses of 1858 and the *Cité antique* which grew out of them. Paul Guiraud tells us that Fustel defended his theories 'with extraordinary asperity and that on several occasions he treated his examiners somewhat roughly'. They nonetheless praised Fustel's theses unreservedly, particularly because, as they said, they really were theses (*Questions historiques*, p. vii n. 2). The short book on Polybius aimed at clarifying a single but important point. Polybius, for Fustel, offered the explanation of why Greece willingly yielded to Rome: 'he is frankly on the side of the conquerors, one feels that he is happy to see Greece obey' (*Questions historiques*, p. 121). Why was this? Polybius' patriotism could not be doubted. But in Greece civil war was hampering civil life: a war of aristocracy against democracy, or rather of rich and poor. Revolutions there were not political, but social. The redistribution of wealth in a more legitimate way was not a part of the revolutionary programme. The winners despoiled the losers; and city alliances reflected these opposing movements. For this reason the citizen became estranged from the city, became a mercenary, sold himself, allowed himself to be corrupted. Polybius 'rose above the petty interests which divided his fellow-citizens' (p. 140). He was an exemplary man, like Philopoemen, and a moderate. Like all moderates he began as impartial and ended by desiring foreign domination. When he arrived in Rome he was won over by the Romans and especially by their aristocracy. He understood that if the Romans had conquered the empire, it was because they deserved it (p. 194). In reality, concludes Fustel, there was more to Roman domination than the renewal of the life of the city. There was the disappearance of the political regime in the precise sense of a regime of independent and sovereign cities. The virtues of the cities had been great: they had taught a taste for freedom and had contributed to the progress of literature and the arts. But now the cities were no longer enough for the needs of men's souls. 'Those principles of exclusion and hatred against the foreigner and against the inhabitant of the neighbouring city, the blinkered patriotism which generated so many wars and covered the land with ruins, began to sicken men. Relations had become too general, minds understood one another too well, philosophy and the arts had made too much progress for society not to change shape' (p. 208). The internal struggles of the Greek cities, which provoked or facilitated foreign intervention, are therefore for Fustel a mysterious means by which it became possible for the peoples to come together. Note the exact phrase: '*les mêmes luttes . . . ont été le moyen mystérieux par lequel les peuples ont réussi à s'unir*' (p. 209).

It seems that Fustel never believed in God: he had himself buried as a Catholic as a token of respect towards his ancestral faith, not out of personal conviction. When he was accused by a critic of the *Cité antique* of being a reactionary romantic, he protested and declared himself a rationalist. He made it quite clear in his reply to C. Morel in the *Revue Critique* of 1866 (pp. 373 ff.) that he was in agreement with his critic about the human origin of the religion of the ancients and about the absence of individual freedom in the ancient world. Even more precisely, in an important letter of 7 April 1868 to another of his critics, Louis Ménard, Fustel stated: 'You are more pagan than I; I am not more Christian than you' (E. Champion, *Les idées politiques et religieuses de F.d.C.*, 1903, pp. 18 ff.). Yet his reply is not entirely unequivocal. Atheistic Catholicism has a long history in France, which may have ended with the condemnation of the *Action Française* in 1926.[8]

For Fustel it was providential that Rome should have intervened to save the Greeks from themselves. By saving Greece the Romans substituted a new principle for that of city government – and protected private property from the dangers of frequent alternating revolutions. Polybius 'renounced independence at first out of fear of democracy, then out of admiration for Rome' (p. 207). He recognized in Rome the defence of private property and the end of the ancient city. The Roman cosmopolis was later to become the Christian cosmopolis. In 1858, the year of Orsini's assassination attempt and the eve of the Italian War, the Second Empire complacently presented itself as a revival of the imperial idea, of order, hegemony and defence of property.[9]

Contrasted implicitly with Tacitus (and the antithesis has a long history), Polybius was interpreted by Fustel with discernment and a basic fidelity to the conditions of the second century B.C., but also with some rather obvious interpolations due to nineteenth-century ideologies.

Fustel had therefore isolated in Polybius, the truest historian of Rome, the final phase of the ancient city, and more exactly of the Greek city. Its beginning, as we have already said, was outlined in the other thesis. Vesta, the goddess of the hearth, represented the nucleus of the domestic and family religion which was, according to Fustel, the first phase of civilized development in all Aryan peoples. However, the notion that the principle of private property was derived from domestic religion – which is essential in the *Cité antique* – is absent from the thesis on Vesta.

'The religion of the sacred fire dates from the distant and dim epoch when there were yet no Greeks, no Italians, no Hindus; when there were only Aryans' (*The Ancient City*, Doubleday Anchor Books, New York, p. 29). The *Cité antique* would have been inconceivable without the arrival of the Aryans on the scene of ancient history. The Celts and the Slavs entered Fustel's mental horizon later on. As far as I know, he concerned himself with them only after 1875 – mainly in connection with the problems of property. In the *Cité antique* only the Indians figure alongside the Greeks and Romans. His information on the Indians is based on readings of the Vedas and the laws of Manu in translation, and probably on E.-L. Burnouf, *Essai sur le Véda* (1863).

Fustel therefore believed that he had arrived at the origins of human society and that he was giving an explanation of the institution of property which on the one hand refuted the notion of a primitive communism and on the other precluded any superficial parallel between the Graeco–Roman city and modern society. Fearful of the revolutionary intoxication which had identified the ancient heroes with the protagonists of the Terror, Fustel deepened the gulf which separates our conflicts from the ancient ones and made it virtually unbridgeable: 'The ideas which the moderns have had of Greece and Rome have often been in their way. Having imperfectly observed the institutions of the ancient city, men have dreamed of reviving them among us. They have deceived themselves about the liberty of the ancients, and on this very account liberty among the moderns has been put in peril' (*The Ancient City*, p. 11). The contrast between ancient and modern freedom, already formulated by B. Constant, is here taken up not to be developed, but to lead back to the religious principles of ancient organization. It will be observed that the Bible and Jewish history are left *a priori* out of consideration. Whether or not this was simply a matter of prudence,

Fustel is addressing himself, as an Aryan, to Aryans. Salomon Reinach of course, realized this immediately (*Manuel de Philologie Classique*, 2nd ed., 1883, p. 222, n. 1). What characterized Aryan society, according to Fustel, was the cult of the dead, who were considered divine. But the worship of the dead was closely connected with the worship of the hearth, with the cult of Agni, Vesta and other hearth deities. Ancestors lived, like Lares, in the hearth. The hearth was therefore the symbol of the cult of the dead, who reposed near the hearth itself. Fire was lit there to honour the ancestors, and the fire itself in some way kept them alive or at least represented their still watchful souls (p. 27).

The worship of the dead had its effects. Religion was centred not in a temple, but in the house and in the tomb, which (Fustel adds rather inconsequently) was near the house, in an adjoining field. Every family had to possess both the hearth and the tomb with the field containing it in perpetuity, because without this permanent possession the worship of the dead was not possible. It was not the laws which protected private property, but religion. The limits of the inviolable domain were the Termini, themselves treated as gods. The worship of the dead, the family and property had a single origin; they were three indissolubly inter-connected concepts. For this reason property was in origin inalienable (p. 71). One cannot sell one's own ancestors. 'Found property on the right of labour, and man may dispose of it. Found it on religion, and he can no longer do this; a tie stronger than the will of man binds the land to him' (p. 70). It also follows that dispossession would be impossible; and that property would not be individual, but of the family. The son inherits from the father, because he is responsible for worship. The daughter does not inherit because she is not qualified to worship. The son is *heres necessarius*: there is no need for a will. 'The property is immovable, like the hearth, and the tomb to which it is attached' (p. 74). But in order that the unity of the family be maintained, it is necessary that the first-born son should be the sole heir and, so to speak, should watch over the indivisibility of the patrimony (p. 85). Fustel points to traces of this law of primogeniture in India and in Greece: in Rome he himself admits that he could not find them, but postulates them (p. 84).

According to Fustel, the true family, the original family, is what the Greeks call *genos*, and the Romans *gens*, i.e. all the descendants of a common ancestor through the male line. The family of Latin terminology (*pater familias* etc.) is therefore the product of a later development with the separation of the various branches of the *gens*. But the later family tends to retain the essential characteristics of the organization of the *gens* in the authority of the *pater familias* and the laws of inheritance. In Rome the connection between *familia* and *gens* was kept up by personal nomenclature, as well as being at the basis of the right of *agnati* and *gentiles* to inherit.[10]

A characteristic of the original *gens*, and consequently of the family, was that it included not only the physical descendants of a common ancestor, but also the slaves. If a slave was later freed, he became part of the *gens* or family as a client. Furthermore the *gens*, according to Fustel, had nothing above it: it was a state run by the *pater*, in which the *liberi* were the aristocracy and the clients were the lower orders, to be distinguished from the *plebs*. Each *gens* had its worship, its territory and its egoistic ethics, devoid of charity towards anyone who was outside it.

Through a religious development, the cause of which is apparently not discussed by Fustel, it became possible for several *gentes* to join together in a common worship; this gave rise in Greece to the *phratria*, in Rome to the *curia*, with a leader, *phylobasileus* in Greece, *curio* in Rome. The new worship could not be that of ancestors. Instead, it addressed itself to nature. Evidently Fustel considered it probable that certain nature gods had already been recognized within the *gens* before the setting up of the *curiae* and corresponding Greek institutions (p. 120). But the very recognition of a new type of divinity, no longer linked to the family and ancestors, encouraged the association of the various *gentes* into *curiae*, as it subsequently encouraged the association of the various *curiae* into tribes, and of the tribes into cities.

There is no point here in repeating in detail what can easily be read with enjoyment in the original. It should simply be emphasized that the city was constructed on the model of the *gens*: it was based on a common religion, it was limited by inviolable territory; it honoured the founder as its head, almost an ancestor; it contained in particular an altar to Vesta; it periodically confirmed its unity with sacred banquets for the citizens; it assigned to the king absolute powers, on the religious basis of the *pater familias*; it excluded the foreigner, as the *gens* excluded anyone who did not belong to it. Since the city incorporated the *gens* and was modelled on it, it naturally recognized the right of family property.

But gradually the city favoured the dissolution of the *gens* into families, facilitated the disappearance of the right of primogeniture and undermined clientship. Those who did not have citizenship and in Rome were called plebeians gradually managed to get themselves admitted into the city and to obtain the right to convene for religious ceremonies.[11] In

Rome at the time of Servius Tullius the plebeians were admitted into local tribes and, according to Fustel, became responsible for celebrating sacrifices and festivals (*compitalia, paganalia*), which became their religion: '*le plébéien eut une religion*'.

Fustel gives a schematic account of this process of dissolution of the primitive city based on the *gens*. He speaks of a first revolution in which power was removed from the king, and of a second revolution in which the *gens* broke up into families, the right of primogeniture disappeared or was weakened and the clients were freed. The third revolution was that of the plebeians' entry into citizenship. With the fourth revolution democracy was attained, as well as a humanization of the law, by now the product of assemblies. Fustel continues:

> When the series of revolutions had produced an equality among men, and there was no longer occasion to fight for principles and rights, men began to make war for interests. . . . . As men departed from the ancient system, a poor class began to grow up. Before, when every man belonged to a *gens* and had his patron, extreme poverty was almost unknown. A man was supported by his chief. . . . Inequality of wealth is inevitable in every society which does not wish to remain in the patriarchal state or in that of the tribe. The democracy did not suppress poverty, but, on the contrary, rendered it more perceptible. Equality of political rights made the inequality of conditions appear still more plainly (pp. 336-7).

The right of property was no longer respected because the religious sanction was lacking: 'the religion of property has disappeared', 'men no longer saw the superior principle that consecrates the right of property' (p. 338).

We are back at the situation described in the thesis on Polybius: Roman intervention. But what was merely implicit in the thesis on Polybius becomes explicit in the last pages of the *Cité antique*. Christianity arrives to combine the reform of the organization of the state with a new element. Fustel says: 'Christianity is the first religion that did not claim to be the source of law. It occupied itself with the duties of men, not with their interests' (p. 395). According to Fustel, Christianity therefore made possible the transformation in the right of property, based no longer on religion, but on labour (p. 396).

From Fustel's point of view it is an ambiguous conclusion. It is not clear if this new basis of the right of property represents progress or retrogression for Fustel, if it affords the same guarantees of stability as the religious conception of property had ensured for the ancient city in its golden period. In his reply to C. Morel in the *Revue Critique* of

1866, Fustel defended his right not to take up a position on contemporary problems in a book devoted to ancient civilization.

The ambiguity of the conclusion accorded well with the situation of Fustel, who then and later found himself torn between attachment to a religion in which he did not believe and a nostalgic admiration for a primitive society which had worshipped its own ancestors and had made them the guarantee of private property.

*

Something about the composition of the *Cité antique* is revealed to us by two letters from Fustel published by L. Halkin in *Mélanges Bidez*, Volume I, 1934, pp. 465–74. A German scholar who for a long time had been Professor of Law at Liège and had now retired to Stuttgart, L. A. Warnkoenig, had said that he would be willing to review the *Cité antique* in a German periodical. He did in fact publish a long and admiring review in *Jahrbücher der deutschen Rechtswissenschaft* 11, 1865, pp. 81–94. Fustel thought it expedient to explain to him the method he had used in writing the book. He stated without false modesty that 'his type of mind was such that he could not be content with details'. His method had been the comparative one. By comparing the Rig-Veda with Euripides, the laws of Manu with the Twelve Tables or Isaeus and Lysias, he had arrived at the conclusion of a remote community of beliefs and institutions among Indians, Greeks and Italic peoples. He had not troubled to read what the moderns had written. Indeed he had imposed upon himself the principle of not reading them, and in particular of not reading the works of Mommsen, until he had almost finished his book. He insists on this independence from modern authors also in the reply to Morel, where the books of Becker and Marquardt are specified among those not read. It is nonetheless clear that these claims only go to demonstrate that Fustel was fully informed about contemporary historical research and made a distinction, for instance, between Marquardt and Mommsen. If the *Cité antique* is haughtily devoid of references to modern authors while revealing an enviable familiarity with classical texts, one must deduce from this not simple ignorance, but intentional disregard: the same disregard that led Hegel to ignore Niebuhr's critical method and that made Bachofen (with certain exceptions) indifferent to Mommsen's methods. The attitude they have in common is one which repudiates modern criticism of the sources in order to preserve the sources' data. In his inaugural lecture at Strasbourg in 1862 Fustel declared: 'I then resolved to have no masters on

Greece other than the Greeks themselves, nor on Rome than the Romans.' Even more explicitly, in fragments published after his death: 'I would rather be mistaken in the manner of Livy than that of Niebuhr; and in the manner of Gregory of Tours than that of Mr Sohm.' And he added more generally about his adversaries: 'They put themselves up as critics because they have no critical spirit' (*Revue Synthèse Hist.* 2, 1901, pp. 249–50, 257–8). Later, in writing, or rather in rewriting the *Histoire des Institutions politiques de l'ancienne France*, Fustel confessed with regret that he had had to yield to the new fashion of presenting all the scholarly material (*Histoire*, I, *La Gaule Romaine*, 1891, p. iv n.).

The history which he brought to the attention of his readers was therefore composed of four main elements:

(1) the development of the organization of the state from *gens* to city through *curia* and tribe;

(2) the parallelism of Indian, Greek and Roman institutions;

(3) the evolution of religion from the worship of ancestors to the gods of nature;

(4) the prehistoric origin of private property safeguarded throughout the whole evolution of the ancient world by religion, and more precisely by ancestor worship. At the margins of the ancient city Christianity appeared, and brought to an end the security of private property founded on religion. A new epoch began in which labour became the justification for private property.

Fustel's critics are naturally free to stress one or other of the four main principles of his *Cité antique* as the most important and significant. Hitherto critics, particularly in Germany, have seen Fustel as the theoretician of ancestor worship and of the *gens* as the predecessor of the State. To me there seems little doubt that anyone who surveys the development of the studies on ancient history over the last century will emphasize the link between the history of private property and the history of ancient religion. Not only does this question play a part in post-Marxist interest in the problem of the origin of property (in its relations with religion); it is also important for the specific reason that the new social history of the ancient world was born in France through the reconsideration of Fustel, converting his theories into sociological categories (Durkheim), extending his analysis to other civilizations (Egypt, China), and above all keeping religion at the centre of socio-economic life.[12]

Appendix 1

FUSTEL AND DURKHEIM. I do not know of any detailed studies on the relationship between the thought of Fustel de Coulanges and Durkheim, but the literature on Durkheim is only partly known to me: I have followed the bibliographies in the books of T. Parsons, *The Structure of Social Action*, 1937, H. Alpert, 1939, K. H. Wolff, ed., 1960, R. A. Nisbet, 1965, on Durkheim and, also by Nisbet, *The Sociological Tradition*, 1966; *cf.* R. Aron, *Les étapes de la pensée sociologique*, 1967 (and S. Lukes, *Emile Durkheim: His Life and Works*, Allen Lane, 1973).

There is no doubt about Fustel's influence on Durkheim. The dedication '*Memoriae Fustel de Coulanges*' of Durkheim's thesis on Montesquieu (*Quid Secundatus politicae scientiae instituendae contulerit*, Burdigalae, 1892) is more than an act of formal homage. The link between Montesquieu and Fustel was in everyone's mind during those years (*cf.* A. Sorel, *Mém. Ac. Sc. Mor.*, 18, 1894, p. 229). To Fustel Durkheim owed above all his sociological interest (*cf. Année Sociol.*, I, 1896–7, pp. i–vii): Fustel had said 'History is the science of social facts, that is to say sociology itself.' There was, however, a certain distance between Durkheim and Fustel. In his youth Durkheim showed himself to be sympathetic towards socialism (*cf.* for instance M. Mauss, *Oeuvres*, III, 1969, p. 505), concerned himself with the problem of the division of labour, which was alien to Fustel, and stressed the interdependence of division of labour and the evolution of property. In fact it is in *De la division du travail social*, 1893, that Durkheim's well-known criticism of Fustel occurs: 'M. Fustel de Coulanges has discovered that the primitive organization of societies was based on the family and that, furthermore, the formation of the primitive family had religion as its base. However, he has taken the cause for the effect. After putting forward the religious idea, without deriving it from anything, he deduced from it the social arrangements that he observed, whereas on the contrary it is the latter which explain the power and nature of the religious idea' (I, VI, 1, 6th edition, 1932, p. 154). But Durkheim's socialist sympathies paled with the years, though his group of pupils largely retained socialist sympathies. The orientation of his researches altered accordingly. About 1911 Georges Davy could write in his *E. Durkheim*, p. 44: 'he began to study religious phenomena only after having written the *Division* and the *Règles* and it was this new study which revealed to him the importance of the ideal factors'.[13]

In the *Leçons de Sociologie*, published posthumously in 1950, which apparently date back to 1898–1900, Durkheim turns back to Fustel's idea that property has a religious basis, but criticizes the connection with the cult of the dead and replaces it with the new concept of collective religious representation. This position is substantially the same as that of M. Mauss in 1906 (*Oeuvres*, II, pp. 139–42).

In the *Formes élémentaires de la vie religieuse*, 1912, religion creates the social system. Although the most elementary form of religio-social awareness, totemism, is certainly not identical with ancestor worship, which Fustel considers the elementary form, for Durkheim individual souls are originally the reincarnation of the souls of ancestors and in point of fact are 'of the same substance as the totemic principle' (II, 8, 2, ed. 1912, p. 355).

The most interesting difference for our purposes between the Durkheim of the *Formes élémentaires* and his master in the *Cité antique* is the former's uncertainty about the relation of religion to economic life. While Fustel resolutely derived private property from religion, Durkheim has a note in his conclusion to *Formes* (p. 598, n. 2) in which he declares that some connection exists between ideas of economic value and ideas of religious value, but that it has not yet been studied. The very nature of Australian societies, with which Durkheim was primarily concerned in *Formes*, made the study of property in relation to religion difficult; but from the book as a whole it is evident that Durkheim had lost interest in the problems of the origin of property that were central to *De la division* (this point does not seem to me to emerge from G. Aimard, *Durkheim et la science économique*, 1962).

Another important difference between Fustel and Durkheim is in the implicit religious experience which underlies their conceptions. For Fustel, born a Catholic, the idea of individual immortality was essential: it was at the root of his ancestor worship. For Durkheim, of a rabbinical family and originally destined to become a rabbi, individual immortality counted for rather less than the collective sense of the community preserving itself and laying down laws throughout the centuries. It is interesting that Australian totemic society should have been Judaized by Durkheim and should have come to resemble one of those small communities, no longer agitated by waves of mysticism or Messianic fervour, that Durkheim, born in 1858, must have known in the Alsace-Lorraine of his precocious and earnest childhood.

Appendix 2

THE ARYAN IDEA IN FUSTEL. The notion of Aryan unity is already quite clear in the dissertation of 1858 *Quid Vestae cultus in institutis veterum privatis publicisque valuerit* dedicated to J.-D. Guigniaut, the expounder and biographer of Creuzer. We read on p. 2: '*Nempe Persarum, Scytharum, Graecorum ac Romanorum ut idem fuit genus, ita communis religio. In ultima antiquitate et in ultimis Asiae regionibus ortus est apud homines cultus Vestae.*' An unpublished piece of evidence for this conviction of Fustel's is found in the *Cours d'histoire grecque* at the École Normale of 1876–7: the notes on this course taken by E. Groussard are in manuscript in the library of this school, and I owe the permission to read them to the librarian (P. Petitmengin). In stressing the importance of the Aryan origin of the Greeks, Fustel claimed: 'Let us now compare the customs, the institutions and the beliefs that we have just expounded with the customs, the institutions and the beliefs of the Semitic peoples. The whole is completely different: we find no relationship from any point of view; it is an absolutely different world from our own.' Even more significant is the fact that Fustel should make an exception: the law of property. He finds among the Semites, and in particular among the Jews, the 'instinctive conception of family property' (*Nouvelles Recherches*, p. 30). As A. Sorel observed (*Mém. Ac. Sciences Morales*, 18, 1894, p. 215), the question of the origin of property 'became a positive obsession with M. Fustel'.[14]

References

1. See Appendix 1.
2. Cf. *Hommage à Louis Gernet*, Paris, 1966, with essays by G. Davy, J.-P. Vernant and others. A selected bibliography of L. Gernet is also appended to *Anthropologie de la Grèce antique*, 1968. On Gernet and the school of Durkheim cf. S. C. Humphreys, *History and Theory*, 10, 1971, pp. 172–96.
3. The *Cité antique* was translated into Italian a second time in the same years by G. E. Calapaj (Laterza, Bari, 1925). The most interesting German review of the original publication of 1864 is possibly that by F. Liebrecht, *Götting. Gel. Anz.*, 1865, pp. 841–80.
4. An excellent bibliography on Fustel is given by Jane Herrick, *The Historical Thought of Fustel de Coulanges*, Catholic University of America, Washington,

1954 (a thesis supervised by F. Engel-Janosi). Apart from the biography by P. Guiraud, 1896, it is sufficient to mention: J. Simon and A. Sorel, *Mém. Ac. Sciences Morales et Politiques*, 18, 1894, pp. 33–72, 185–230; G. Monod, *Portraits et Souvenirs*, 1897, pp. 135–54; E. Jenks, 'Fustel de Coulanges as a Historian', *Engl. Hist. Rev.*, 12, 1897, pp. 209–24; C. Jullian, 'Le Cinquantenaire de la Cité antique', *Revue de Paris*, 23, 1916, pp. 852–65; H. Leclercq, Cabrol, *Dict. d'archéol. chrét.*, V, 1923, pp. 2717–32; J. M. Tourneur-Aumont, *Fustel de Coulanges*, 1931; G. Dodu, *Rev. Ét. Hist.*, 100, 1933, pp. 41–66; H. de Gérin-Ricard, *L'Histoire des institutions politiques de Fustel de Coulanges*,1936 (Gérin-Ricard is the co-author with L. Truc of a *Histoire de l'Action Française*, 1949). A *Catalogue des livres composant la bibliothèque de feu M. Fustel de Coulanges* was published in Paris in 1890. *Cf.* also A. Grenier, *Camille Jullian*, 1944, pp. 117–49; *Lettres de C. Jullian à H. d'Arbois de Jubainville*, Nancy, 1951, pp. 12–13.

5. *Questions contemporaines*, Paris, 1916. For a similar rebirth of interest in Fustel in Italy after the Second World War *cf.* the preface by F. Martinazzoli to his translation of Fustel's *Polybe*, Laterza, Bari, 1947.

6. *Cf.* C. Maurras, *La bagarre de Fustel*, Paris, 1928 ('Cahiers d'Occident', II, 1). The book by H. de Gérin-Ricard quoted above is, on a higher level, of the same tendency. So also is A. Bellesort, *Les intellectuels et l'avènement de la Troisième République (1871–1875)*, Paris, 1931, pp. 189–217 (and, now, S. Wilson, 'Fustel de Coulanges and L'Action Française', *Journ. Hist. Ideas*, 34, 1973, pp. 123–34).

7. M. Bloch, *L'Alsace Française*, 19, 1930, pp. 206–9 (not seen by me). *Cf. Mélanges Historiques*, I, 1963, pp. 100–106.

8. H. Stuart Hughes, *The Obstructed Path*, New York, 1966, pp. 66–7, and bibliography mentioned.

9. *Cf.* my essay on Caesarism in *Secondo Contributo*, 1960, pp. 273–82, and more generally P. Stadler, *Geschichtschreibung und historisches Denken in Frankreich, 1789–1871*, Zürich, 1958, pp. 249 ff.

10. I have not yet managed to ascertain what influence Fustel's ideas on the *gens* have had on scholars of Roman law (e.g. Bonfante). The impression I have gained from running through the vast material collected and elaborated by L. Capogrossi Colognesi, *La struttura della proprietà e la formazione dei Iura Praediorum nell'età repubblicana*, I, Milan, 1969, is that H. S. Maine is better known than Fustel (*cf.* particularly pp. 79–80). One exception is V. Arangio-Ruiz, *Le genti e la città*, Messina, 1914, reprinted in *Scritti giuridici raccolti per il centenario della casa editrice Jovene*, Naples, 1954, pp. 109–58. Incidentally, in his thesis on Vesta of 1858 Fustel still accepts that the family preceded the *gens*.

11. *Cf.* also *Questions historiques*, 1893, pp. 411–52 (a piece which dates from the years 1867–8, published posthumously by C. Jullian). For Athens the article *Attica Respublica* by Fustel in Daremberg-Saglio, *Diction. des Antiquités*, I, 1877, emphasizes the development from *genos* to the city and confirms the central importance attributed to the problem of private property. According to Fustel the non-nobles were admitted into the land-owning classes by Solon – an interpretation already rejected in the same *Dict. des Antiquités* by C. Lécrivain, s.v. *Eupatrides*. For private property in Sparta, Fustel, *Nouvelles recherches*, 1891, pp. 54 ff. For property among the Germans, *Recherches sur quelques*

problèmes d'histoire, 1885, pp. 319–56. *Cf.* R. Schlatter, *Private Property, the History of an Idea*, London, 1951, pp. 266–7.

12. A study of Fustel's alterations to the successive editions of the *Cité antique* has not yet been undertaken, as far as I know. The corrections made to the 2nd ed. of 1866 and the 6th ed. of 1875 should be particularly important. I have not been able to study the 1st ed. A comparison I made between the 2nd ed. of 1866 (Hachette) and the 7th ed., 1878, seems to indicate only one substantial addition to the text after 1866: in Part III there is a new Chapter XVI, 'Les confédérations, les colonies,' with the result that the original Chapter XVI became Chapter XVII. But several other points in the text were altered (for instance the penultimate paragraph of I, 1) and there is much new source material in the notes. The change of title in II, 10, 4, and III, 7, 3, does not imply any alteration in the text. My French quotations are from the 18th ed., 1903. The exposition in the *Cité antique* should be complemented by the articles in *Diction. des Antiquités: Attica Respublica* already quoted; *Epula* (II, 1, pp. 736–8); *Lacedaemoniorum Respublica* (III, 2, pp. 886–900); *Regnum* (IV, 2, pp. 821–7); *Romanorum Respublica* (IV, 2, pp. 878–91).

13. *Cf.* also G. Davy, *Sociologues d'hier et d'aujourd'hui*, 2nd ed., Paris, 1950, pp. 79–122. Of course the discovery of the classificatory systems of kinship also stands between Fustel and Durkheim. *Cf.* for instance U. Bianchi, *Storia della Etnologia*, Rome, 1965, pp. 79, 112.

14. *Cf.* T. C. Barker, *Aryan Civilization . . . based on the work of De Coulanges*, 1871. For the considerable coincidences in E.-L. Burnouf, *Essai sur le Véda*, 1863, with Fustel, *cf.* p. 183: 'In the eyes of the Vedic Aryans the role of the Ancestors is fused, at least in some measure, with that of the gods.' On pp. 441–69 Burnouf stresses the opposition between Semites (Jews) and Aryans (Indians).

20

Reconsidering B. Croce
(1866–1952)*

To the memory of Eugenio Colorni

I HAVE found myself wondering how Croce would have taken his own centenary. After all he came rather near it. Croce was entirely without vanity, but cared for anniversaries and was a prudent administrator of his own reputation. Honours and ceremonies he considered part of that reality which nobody can presume to escape. But he always tried to turn anniversaries into opportunities for useful work. When he was fifty he wrote his autobiography; when he was sixty he concluded forty years of studies on the Italian Seicento with his *Storia dell'età barocca* (it appeared in 1929). When he was seventy the few friends Fascism had left him published in his honour a reprint of Baumgarten's *Aesthetica*; but he added a quite characteristic celebration of his own: he wrote the book on *La Poesia* which was by implication the most searching criticism both of Baumgarten's *Aesthetica* and of his own previous *Estetica*. When he was eighty he founded an institute for historical studies in his own house in Naples and gave himself a last lease of creative life in the company of the gifted young historians who were just emerging from the ruins of Fascism. I suspect that, faced by his own centenary, Croce would have got up two hours earlier than usual, as he is said to have done when he became a minister in the Giolitti cabinet (1920) and wanted to have a little time for his private work. He would have gone through ceremonies and interviews with that mixture of impatience and old-fashioned courtesy which was his own – and at the end of the year he would have produced the only useful book inspired by his own centenary.

*

*A memorial lecture delivered at Durham University in May 1966 and published in the *Durham University Journal* in December of the same year.

To say that Croce remains something of an enigma even to those who knew him personally may seem a paradox. He wrote perhaps more than any other writer of the twentieth century. The eighty-odd volumes of his works in the characteristic Laterza edition are full of personal recollections and anecdotes.[1] We have his autobiography,[2] the recollections of his eldest daughter[3] and of some of his intimate friends – to begin with, Fausto Nicolini.[4] Though his correspondence with Giovanni Gentile is still unpublished, for perfectly valid reasons – those who have seen it speak of it as a document of great importance – the correspondence with K. Vossler is available.[5] There are enough other letters both by Croce and his correspondents (for instance Georges Sorel[6] and Antonio Labriola[7]) to give an idea of Croce's relations with his contemporaries. I single out for its interest the publication of some letters by Croce to Emilio Cecchi which comment on Cecchi's articles about Croce.[8] The autobiographical and biographical evidence about him is as plentiful as one can wish for any contemporary. Yet the basic riddle of Croce's personality is perhaps only increased by the abundance, ease and elegance of his writing – and by the observations of his friends.

Part of the difficulty in understanding Croce lies in the variety of the historical situations in which he operated during his very long life. At least six periods can be distinguished in his own activity, and each of them corresponds to a well-defined period in the history of modern Italy. The apprenticeship years ended in 1900, when Italy was shaken by the murder of King Umberto. The creative years of collaboration with Giovanni Gentile, the years in which he wrote all his systematic philosophy, ended approximately with the war in Libya (1911). In the Libyan War and even more in the First World War Croce found himself isolated and he deeply modified his ideas. In the post-war years 1919–24 he collaborated for all practical purposes with Christian democrats, nationalists and Fascists – even if he maintained his distance from them in theory. Then for nineteen years (1925–43) he was not only the moral leader of Italian Anti-Fascism, but also the constant term of reference for all the intellectual activities of the Fascists themselves. Finally in the last decade of his life the old thinker had to realize that the new generations were going their own way; but it would be rash to infer that his influence became negligible or his own writing merely repetitive.

In comparison with the majority of Italian intellectuals, Croce grew up slowly. He published his first original considerations on 'La storia ridotta sotto il concetto generale dell'arte' when he was twenty-seven and he took another nine years to develop his theory in the *Estetica* of 1902. For about eighteen years between 1882 and 1900 he devoted the greater part of his time to the local history of Naples (where he had B. Capasso as a guide) and to literary criticism (where F. De Sanctis was his model). A contemporary described Croce as he appeared in 1891: '*Questo giovane imberbe, che ha tutte le apparenze di un fanciullo e che rivolgendovi la parola ha nello sguardo l'espressione più sincera della sua naturale timidità, questo lavoratore silenzioso e taciturno, che la fortuna fece nascere molto ricco . . .*'[9] For a few years between 1895 and 1900 Croce also intensively studied in an original manner the economic and social ideas of Karl Marx and made himself the editor of the writings on historical materialism by his former teacher Antonio Labriola. The combination of pure erudition and Marxism was unusual: even Labriola was suspicious. As a matter of fact, Croce remained outside the circles of both academic *érudits* and militant socialists. Italian culture was then a culture of professors. Poets were professors too. One of the points which distinguished Croce and D'Annunzio from the surrounding world was that neither had cared to get a university degree and both maintained an ambivalent attitude towards academic respectability. On the other hand, Croce's friendship with Labriola and Georges Sorel was that of a thinker with thinkers. The study of Marx was of permanent importance for Croce: he learnt from it that legal systems reflect an economic and social order and that political history is a struggle for power. Marx – rather than Francesco De Sanctis – led Croce to the rediscovery of Hegel and Machiavelli and perhaps even of the Neapolitan Vico. But Croce had no intention or desire to subvert the social order to which he owed his affluence and consequently his freedom to study what he liked; even less did he care to overthrow the moral order he instinctively recognized as his own, though he had abandoned the religious beliefs which had created it.[10]

In 1900 he gave up the study of economics and much to the disgust of Labriola he concentrated his reflections on the nature of beauty and on the relations between poetry and ordinary language.[11] De Sanctis had first proposed these problems for his attention many years before, but now he made a careful study of Vico and mastered the rest of the relevant literature. By claiming to be the continuator of Vico and De Sanctis he gave retrospectively a new meaning to all the time he had spent studying Neapolitan history and could feel that he was the restorer of a native tradition of philosophic thought.

Outside Naples, however, the appearance of Croce's *Estetica* had a different meaning. By 1902 D'Annunzio was replacing Carducci as the fashionable poet for younger Italians. His appeal was a mixture of well-digested sensuality and half-digested Nietzsche. In later years Croce was right in reminding his younger readers that his own generation had been *carducciana*, not *dannunziana*: Carducci remained to the end his favourite modern poet. Croce was not the man to indulge in aesthetic refinements: if anything is obvious from his work as a literary critic in the decade 1900–1910 it is the unadventurous, even provincial, character of his taste. The fact, however, remains that Croce came out of his isolation, found followers and admirers – and was soon recognized as an intellectual power to be reckoned with – when he offered to the Italians a philosophy which proclaimed the centrality and amorality of art. Many followed Croce because they thought that Croce had left Marx for D'Annunzio. As Marx was commonly taken to be a democrat, and Croce showed no sympathy for democracy, it was inferred that Croce was for the advent of the Superman.

Croce started his own journal, *La Critica*, in the same year 1903 in which Enrico Corradini began to publish *Il Regno*, and Papini and Prezzolini set up their *Leonardo*. In the following year G. A. Borgese began to print *Hermes*. The four journals were closely associated. Borgese, then a protégé of Croce, was both a full-blown follower of D'Annunzio and a nationalist. The *Regno* – a nursery of the future Fascist intelligentsia from L. Federzoni to R. Forges Davanzati – was committed to the same anti-positivistic, anti-democratic creed. Papini and Prezzolini, though less predictable, joined forces in attacking the conventional ideas of academic circles.[12]

The contrast between Croce and his younger allies was certainly marked, so marked as to become almost symbolic of the differences between two generations. Croce, as we have observed, was by nature slow in forming his opinions and correspondingly slow in changing them. All the noise around him never distracted him from his rigid routine of scholarly work which, supported as it was by an exceptional memory, made him one of the greatest *érudits* of any time. In 1906 he began to make a daily list of his reading in order to check whether he had wasted time. The companion he had chosen for his work in *La Critica*, Giovanni Gentile, though younger by nine years, shared his scholarly habits and discipline. With the help of Gentile, Croce transformed a small southern publishing house – Laterza of Bari – into the most important in Italy and dictated its editorial policy. The younger intellectuals, born between 1880 and 1890, had exactly the opposite characteristics. Precocity and lack of method were the norm. A few were of rare intellectual distinction. These died young. Carlo Michelstaedter, an original, perhaps a great, philosopher, committed suicide at twenty-three.[13] Renato Serra, the literary critic, was killed at thirty in the war he had chosen to fight after a searching self-examination.[14] Others – most conspicuously Borgese, Papini and Prezzolini – were self-appointed geniuses, quick to learn and even quicker to forget. Papini and Prezzolini, with their hotch-potch of pragmatism, Bergsonianism and mysticism à la Novalis, considered themselves capable of doing the things which Croce was too much of a bourgeois to attempt. In 1905 Prezzolini could write to Papini in all seriousness: '*La nostra amicizia . . . potrà durare ora che tu sai e che io so che* non posso diventare Dio?' In their uneasy alliance with Croce there was a great deal of cold calculation: '*Di quell'uomo bisogna essere in ogni modo alleati,*' Papini wrote to Prezzolini in 1907. But they were in good faith when they took Croce's message as an invitation to revolt. Croce's first *Logica*, which appeared in 1905 as a continuation of the *Estetica*, seemed even more to encourage contempt for natural sciences and intolerance of errors.[15]

The confusion and equivocations which ensued were not all on the side of the young. Croce deluded himself in hoping for a quick intellectual revolution of national, or perhaps international, importance. The equivocation extended to what in a way was the most pleasant and solid aspect of *La Critica* – the steady collaboration between Croce and Gentile. If Croce loved poetry and history and correspondingly distrusted metaphysics, Gentile was a born metaphysician and, like many other metaphysicians, kept a nice balance between mysticism and rhetoric. Both Croce and Gentile must have known from the start how different they were, but they were friends and they thought that they complemented each other. They compromised: Croce perhaps more than Gentile. Croce accepted many Hegelian assumptions which were really more appropriate to Gentile. Under the influence of Gentile he came to identify history and philosophy in plain contradiction to the structure of his own system and involved himself in insuperable difficulties.[16] Gentile consented to cooperate in a routine of reviewing books and writing short monographic articles which were probably outside his real interests and often remained superficial.

Time slowly dissolved some of these alliances. When the third volume of Croce's philosophic system, the *Filosofia della pratica*, appeared in 1909, it ended on an austere note of religious resignation which was not calculated to please the followers of D'Annunzio and Barrès. The first big quarrels coincided with the colonial war of 1911–12, which was the first success of the Italian nationalists. Borgese used Croce's book on Vico, which had just appeared (1911), as an occasion for a frontal attack.[17] Papini abandoned in wrath the journal *La Voce* which, since its inception in 1908, had supported Croce.[18] Prezzolini himself, who remained for a while the editor of *La Voce* after Papini's departure, gave increasing space to those pupils of Gentile who, with varying degrees of condescension, treated Croce as 'superseded' – *superato*. The opinion that Croce was out of touch with the new generation was often repeated. On the eve of the First World War, in February 1914, Giuseppe De Robertis defined Francesco De Sanctis and Croce as obstacles to be overcome; '*e c'è tra i giovani qualcuno ardimentoso e adatto al compito*'.[19] One of the young men he had in mind, Renato Serra, echoed him: '*D'Annunzio e Croce cominciano oggi a essere messi da parte.*'[20] Curiously enough, these young people were to follow D'Annunzio against Croce a few months later. '*Giovinezza, giovinezza*' was repeated only too frequently in those years, though not yet with musical accompaniment.

*

The First World War left Croce in marked isolation. What Croce disliked was not really the war – he was no pacifist – but the rhetoric which accompanied it. He hated the idealization of war and imperialism. He knew the difference between search for truth and propaganda and despised those who mistook the latter for the former. He never changed his attitude on this point – which explains his later hostility towards the Fascist regime. He defined the World War as the war of 'historical materialism'; the definition has stuck.[21] In this isolation he re-examined himself and explored new fields. He studied the great European poetry of Dante, Ariosto, Shakespeare and Corneille and found a congenial spirit in the greatest poet of the enemy country – Goethe. This study led him to revise his judgement about the nature of poetry and to emphasize its inherent morality: he even saw in it an equivalent to religious experience (1917). At the same time he studied the great historians of the past and reflected on historical method. Though he had previously claimed that all is history, the historical work he had so far done had been confined to episodes of Neapolitan history. He had educated a new generation of literary critics which included Tommaso Parodi, Renato Serra, Eugenio Donadoni, Attilio Momigliano, Luigi Russo; but he had hardly influenced historians. The only historian of considerable merit who had so far contributed to *La Critica*, Gioacchino Volpe, was in basic disagreement with him. The other leading historian of the time, Gaetano Salvemini, never disguised his total lack of sympathy for Croce's philosophical opinions. The situation was changed by the appearance of the *Teoria e storia della storiografia* in 1915, and of the *Storia della storiografia italiana nel secolo decimonono* in 1918. Croce began to interest young historians in his ideas and prepared himself for that kind of '*storia etico-politica*' he exemplified in *Storia del regno di Napoli* (1924); *Storia d'Italia dal 1871 al 1915* (1928); *Storia dell'età barocca in Italia* (1929); *Storia d'Europa nel secolo decimonono* (1932). But between the new theory and the new practice of historiography Fascism intervened.

In the first years after the Great War Croce's ambiguous position on the contemporary Italian scene had merely been confirmed. Old Italian socialists owed traditional allegiance to the positivist philosophy of Roberto Ardigò. But the younger Marxists of the post-war period were ready to start from Croce who himself had started from Marx. Still during the war, in 1917, Antonio Gramsci declared Croce '*il più grande pensatore dell'Europa in questo momento*'. After the war, another of the young leaders of the left, Piero Gobetti, emphatically repeated that whoever was against Croce was against moral integrity.[22] Croce liked Gobetti and did not dislike Gramsci, but personally became a steady supporter of, and contributor to, the nationalist journal *Politica*.[23] He approved, as a senator and as a minister, of Giolitti's implicit support of Fascism. While in 1915 he had refused to accept the *coup d'état* which led to the declaration of war, in 1922 he sympathized with the Fascists. He went on voting for Mussolini in the Senate even after Matteotti's murder. A problem which only the publication of their correspondence will solve is the political influence of Gentile on Croce in the years between 1919 and 1924. They had continued to collaborate during the war though Gentile was much more favourable to it than Croce. After the war it became apparent that philosophically their ways would part. Gentile started a philosophical journal of his own in 1920, and his pupils were more than ever convinced that Croce was *superato*. But paradoxically Croce and Gentile became much closer to each other in political matters. Under Gentile's influence Croce, as a minister of education in 1920, introduced religious instruction – that is, the Catholic catechism – into the State elementary schools.[24] The appointment of Gentile as a minister in the first Mussolini cabinet was commonly interpreted as a sign of Croce's willingness to collaborate with the new regime. In 1923–4 Croce supported Gentile's reform of education against all the attacks by liberals and socialists.

It is difficult now to realize how suddenly the situation changed in Italy in 1925. After Mussolini's speech of 3 January 1925, no illusion was possible as to the character of the new regime. In a matter of months, Amendola and Gobetti had been beaten to death, Salvemini had to run for his life, Gramsci was sent to a slow death in gaol. In April 1925 Gentile discredited himself with his '*Manifesto degli intellettuali fascisti*', and Croce became almost overnight the leader of the anti-Fascist intelligentsia by drafting the answer to it.[25] The change resulted from the new situation: it was also the sign that Mussolini had really managed to kill, gaol or banish the majority of his active opponents. The very success of Mussolini's political dictatorship made Croce the virtual dictator of Italian culture. The most obvious feature of the Fascist regime was that it discouraged intelligent men from doing research. G. Gentile, G. Volpe, G. Q. Giglioli, F. Ercole, P. De Francisci and so many other leading scholars remained under Fascism the intelligent men they had always been, but they no longer entered a library to discover something new. There was also plenty of intelligence among the young men who led the new 'corporativist' movement, but they never learned enough economics to face a Cambridge economist – or even old-fashioned Einaudi. Croce went on studying, discovering new facts – even forgotten poets – and writing books full of learning. Some of these books were extremely relevant to the political situation. Such were not only the histories of Italy and Europe, but also the biographies of Italian heretics who looked so much like Anti-Fascists of previous ages. Other books, such as *Poesia popolare e poesia d'arte* and *La Poesia*, kept alive peculiar interests of his own and modified his former theories on the relation between poetry and literature. With Croce as an example, the habit of studying became almost an anti-Fascist habit. Croce himself was fond of saying that Papini and Prezzolini had been much more intelligent than he, but had done nothing good because they had not worked hard enough. Only members of religious orders or the professed Catholics who had their centre in the Università del Sacro Cuore in Milan competed in studious habits with Croce's group.[26] Though the philosophic disputes of the time were mainly between Neo-Thomists and pupils of Gentile (the so-called *attualisti*), we may well wonder whether the most serious intellectual conflicts did not pass above the heads of Gentile, Volpe, Bottai and were really between the Catholics and Croce's group. The school of Gentile was going to pieces. Some of his pupils returned to traditional Catholicism, others became crypto-Communists, or pragmatists or even open racialists. The two most authoritative –

Adolfo Omodeo and Guido de Ruggiero – went over to Croce and contributed to *La Critica*. Gentile himself remained more important as an organizer and patron than as a thinker.

Croce's activity during the Fascist regime was clearly conditioned by certain unwritten rules. He was allowed by Mussolini to go on with *La Critica*, provided that no direct political attack on the Fascist government was published. Mussolini, who read Croce's books and articles with attention, found it convenient to keep alive an anti-Communist, anti-clerical and, after 1933, anti-Nazi journal. Some of these unwritten rules suited Croce's temperament perfectly well, others of course less well. Indefatigable as he was in introducing new and old foreign books to his Italian readers, he naturally chose those which best conformed to his conservative taste. We must recognize that the selection had its negative effects in a situation of virtual monopoly. This situation was made even more static by the circumstance that any criticism of Croce automatically became support for Fascism. When in 1937 Giorgio Pasquali, the great classical scholar, made some intrinsically harmless remarks on Croce's opinions about Greek and Latin writers, we knew it was the price Pasquali – a former Anti-Fascist – had to pay to become an Accademico d'Italia.[27]

The liberalism Croce now put before his readers was that of Constant, Guizot and Cavour; his economic thought never went beyond Henri De Man; his literary sympathies went as far as G. M. Hopkins – and that was already a remarkable discovery.[28] Of Wittgenstein, Freud, Husserl, neo-Marxism, American sociology we were to hear little; and what we heard was not encouraging. Perhaps one should add in fairness to Croce that Guido de Ruggiero, who was mainly responsible for these subjects in *La Critica*, was singularly narrow in his taste. Even the contemporary foreign historians to whom we were introduced look very odd now. That old-fashioned book, H. A. L. Fisher's *History of Europe*, because it was translated under Croce's auspices, was impounded by the police. Croce saw himself as a Thrasea Paetus or a Boëthius in a time of tyranny and barbarism. He expected the end of Fascism to come not from the hands of men, but from mysterious Providence. Though what the Fascists and even more the Nazis had done compelled him to admit that certain historical periods represent an authentic regress, his resigned attitude towards the world remained the same. His notion of history as the history of liberty was essentially fatalistic: it relied on Providence.[29]

Thus Croce was not able to indicate a way out of Fascism. If he had been, Mussolini would not have allowed him to speak. But the liberty Croce spoke about there was not just a philosophic notion. It was the liberty our fathers had won for themselves in the revolutions and on the battlefields of the Risorgimento. Croce represented a constant reproach to Fascism, a constant reminder of what we had lost – freedom and honesty of thought, especially in matters of religion, of social questions and of foreign policy, tolerance, representative government, fair trials, respect for other nations and consequently self-respect. He spoke for Italian civilization, and his speech was the more moving because he might so easily have become a Fascist. He was the living link with the Risorgimento.[30] When Nazism came to add its own brutality, his protests became more radical, his famous jokes bitter. His remark that the word 'Aryan' was in danger of becoming synonymous with imbecile has not been forgotten.[31] By its very nature the precise importance of Croce in the years 1925–39 is very difficult to assess, but anyone who lived in Italy in those years will probably agree that Croce prevented Fascism from becoming a respectable ideology in the eyes of educated Italians. The active Anti-Fascism of those years is inseparable from Croce's teaching.

I was not in Italy when the Second World War broke out, but in retrospect it seems clear that about 1940 Croce must have lost his position of moral leader of the anti-Fascist intelligentsia. The fact that philosophers now turned to existentialism and to phenomenology under the guidance of N. Abbagnano and especially of A. Banfi is perhaps not very significant. Italian professional philosophers were never much under Croce's spell. But existentialism percolated among the young; it affected literary taste. Even in the traditional preserves of Crocean orthodoxy – literary criticism and political historiography – one heard new voices. Gianfranco Contini turned to linguistic and stylistic analysis, Delio Cantimori, more significantly, to the Jacobins.

With the end of the war and the re-establishment of freedom of speech (which meant return to the free circulation of ideas on an international level), the obsolete and reactionary aspects of Croce's attitude to life inevitably came to the forefront. In 1949, the posthumous publication of Gramsci's notes on Croce produced results which Gramsci had certainly not foreseen and probably had not wanted. His acute epigrammatic remarks on Croce's attitudes – his *ateismo da signori*, his *papato laico* – circulated widely, while it was less noticed that Gramsci's basic indifference to natural sciences, anthropology, even economics, was a direct result of Croce's teaching.[32] The dominating preoccupation of

Croce's last years – which was to fight Communism – formalized the opposition between Croce and Marx. Croce himself seemed to encourage his pupil Carlo Antoni to present a new version of his own philosophy in which the principle of dialectic opposition – hitherto the most obvious connection between Croce and Marx – was carefully deleted.[33]

What is surprising is not that Croce found himself so distant from men who were fifty or sixty years younger than himself. What is surprising is that he still maintained contact with them, especially through the historical Institute he had established in Naples. Indeed his influence on professional historians remained stronger than his influence on literary critics. The director of the Naples Institute, Federico Chabod, wrote on Crocean lines the most important historical book of the post-war years – the prolegomena to a history of Italian foreign policy after 1870. Even more surprisingly Croce developed ideas on the elementary conditions of spiritual life – what he called *vitalità* – which interested the Italian existentialists and seemed to introduce a new meaning into his old distinction between economics and ethics.[34] When he died at eighty-seven he left the impression that he had not yet said all he wanted to say.

*

Nobody can foresee whether Croce's philosophy will be a point of departure for future philosophers. It has few followers in Italy at the moment; and perhaps none abroad. Collingwood had already ceased to be a disciple of Croce before his premature death. In Germany and Austria the men who were in constant debate with Croce – Karl Vossler, Friedrich Meinecke and Julius von Schlosser – have left no successor.[35] What one can take for granted is that scholars will have to use the facts collected by Croce even if they do not like his ideas. Croce the scholar will be indispensable for a long time to come even to those who care little for Croce the philosopher. In the matter of Neapolitan history, of Italian literature and history in general, and perhaps also of the history of aesthetic theories, Croce provides an immense amount of instruction. Oddly enough, nobody has yet attempted to place Croce's historical books within the history of modern historiography. It is easy to indicate Guizot's *Histoire de la civilisation en Europe* as the model for the *Storia d'Europa*; and the *Storia dell'età barocca* belongs to the tradition of German *Kulturgeschichte*. But the *Storia del regno di Napoli* and the *Storia d'Italia* are more difficult to classify and may well represent an original departure from the traditional type of national history. All these books were certainly new in Italy. They exercised an enormous influence which extended to mature historians like Gaetano De Sanctis and Luigi Salvatorelli, and gave Croce even in Fascist eyes the position of the greatest contemporary Italian historian. The notion that every history is contemporary history and therefore that books on the past serve to clarify problems of the present; the emphasis on the relations between politics and ethics; the sympathy with intellectual *élites* who find themselves in opposition to both the rulers and the masses were for a time typical of Italian history writing. Even now any debate on the history of Italy is bound to start with an examination of Croce's theses.[36]

But if we want to understand our own time, we shall certainly need to understand more clearly the meaning of Croce's philosophy as a whole. A great deal of good work has been done in Italy and abroad to analyse and criticize single aspects of Croce's thought – such as his ideas on art, his attitude to politics, his conception of history and even his notions of religion and of nature. But only H. Stuart Hughes, to my knowledge, has attempted to relate the whole of Croce's philosophy to what he called the 'reconstruction of European social thought 1890–1930'. In Hughes' book (*Consciousness and Society*, 1958) Croce takes his place among those who, from Freud to Max Weber and Bergson, came to the conclusion that the former conceptions of a rational reality were insufficient. This is true enough. I wonder, however, whether there is not also a homelier aspect of Croce's attitude towards the world.

The philosophic system Croce built between 1900 and 1909 was in itself such as to put him automatically outside the mainstream of modern science. Nothing of the kind, to my knowledge, happened to Freud, Max Weber and Bergson. By identifying language and poetry Croce lost contact with modern linguistic research – and never managed to re-establish it later.[37] By denying the character of true knowledge to natural sciences and mathematics, he offered strange support to those Italians who mistook Guglielmo Marconi – a good technician, but no scientist – for a new Galileo Galilei.

Croce's intellectual world was limited to literature (poetry) and history. We can now see what connected literature and history so closely in his mind. Both 'represented' individual facts, 'expressed' individual situations. Beyond individual situations Croce saw nothing but mystery. It cannot be emphasized enough that Croce never believed that the human mind can understand the whole of reality.[38] Mystery surrounds Man. We cannot even talk of ourselves as personalities, as individuals – each with his own destiny. Each of us in each moment finds himself as a fraction of the Whole in a position he cannot change. We can understand the circumstances of the present, if we have the intelligence to look at the past. But historical intelligence is not something we can be sure of acquiring. It comes as an act of Grace. If Croce thinks that any error of judgement is to be attributed to a moral failure, he does not mean that by proper care and attention each of us can avoid mistakes. He means that if Providence does not put us in the right frame of mind, we shall never find the truth. Nothing is evil simply because we have not the means to judge what is evil. If we had, we should have solved the riddle of the universe once and for all. Ludovico Antonio Muratori and the idiot he took as companion on his walks are, according to Croce, equally necessary to the harmony of the universe: we cannot assign different values to either of them.[39] Unconditional acceptance of what is given characterizes also Croce's distinction between politics and ethics. If human behaviour has proved throughout the centuries to be different in political affairs from private affairs, there is nothing we can do about it. We can only recognize the existence of a double morality – Machiavellianism in politics, Kantian duty in private life.

Grace, Providence, Humility are not words Croce uses rhetorically or analogically. They exactly define his attitude to life – which is one of acceptance of mystery and weakness.[40] One must read his *Filosofia della pratica* and even more his *Frammenti di etica* which were the results of his meditations during the crucial years 1915–20. They are the essential texts for the understanding of Croce's view of the world. They explain why Croce, rather late, about 1906, found little difficulty in accepting Hegel's notion that what is real is rational, with the consequence that evil does not exist. In Croce's interpretation '*la positività del reale*' meant that you and I have to take what is given, do the best we can and never ask questions about ultimate meaning.

A personal God, in any interpretation of the word, was excluded from this world. The mystery was absolute mystery just because there was no personal God behind it. Those who put Croce's works on the *Index librorum prohibitorum* knew perfectly well what they were doing. But we may well ask whether such an interpretation of the position of man in the world does not represent, at least partially, a modernized, atheistic version of the Catholic education Croce had received. I am not speaking of Catholicism 1966 – not even of the *ratio studiorum* Padre Gemelli, a medical doctor and an experimental psychologist, established in the Catholic University of Milan about 1922. In the *Contributo alla critica di me stesso* Croce described rapidly, but perceptively, what was the education in the boarding school to which he had been sent as a child:

357

'*collegio cattolico, non gesuitico in verità, anzi di onesta educazione morale e religiosa senza superstizione e senza fanatismi*'. He was grateful for that education. There was nothing new in Croce's article of 1942 '*Perchè non possiamo non dirci cristiani*'.[41] It was silly to interpret it as a sign of conversion; but it was also unimaginative to take it as a political programme for an alliance between Liberals and Christian Democrats against Communists. Croce uses in it the language he had repeatedly used in his *Frammenti di etica*: '*Siate di buona fede e otterrete la fede buona*'. Perhaps this explains also why Croce preferred Vico to all other philosophers. It was not only *Lokalpatriotismus*. Vico put Providence in the centre of his interpretation of history, but seldom mentioned Jesus Christ or the Incarnation.

The note of mystery and resignation in Croce's philosophy was reflected well in Croce's personal modesty, punctilious discipline, fear of moral weakness. '*Non a torto la Chiesa considera l'errore quale suggestione della volontà cattiva.*'[42] On the other hand, the same attitude left him no illusion about the possibility of avoiding violence, punishment, economic inequality and physical pain. The world to him was beyond human control.

I do not know whether Croce was personally satisfied with a theory which precluded any ultimate truth and any decisive modification of the human condition. His Goethean serenity was achieved at the price of a hard discipline – and he disliked too searching personal questions. But Croce was well aware that his contemporaries had not his Goethean temperament, and he treated them with that mixture of severity and sympathy, sheer amusement and curiosity, condescension and wholehearted solidarity, which was his fascination and his personal mystery.[43]

References

1. The three most useful bibliographical guides are E. Cione, *Bibliografia crociana*, Milan, 1956, which lists not only Croce's works, but also works on Croce (pp. 305–438); F. Nicolini, *L'*'*editio ne varietur*' *delle opere di B.C.*, Naples, 1960, with unpublished documents; S. Borsari, *L'opera di Benedetto Croce*, Naples, 1964, which adds much new information. Croce himself published an introduction to his own work under the name of his secretary Giovanni Castellano (*B.C.; il filosofo—il critico—lo storico*) in 1924, 2nd ed., Bari, 1936,

which has a bibliography. *L'opera filosofica, storica e letteraria di B.C.*, Bari, 1942, is mainly a selection of papers on C.

The best guide to Italian philosophy in the period 1900–1943 is provided by E. Garin, *Cronache di filosofia italiana*, Bari, 1955, supplemented for the period 1945–50 by his essay in *La Cultura italiana tra '800 e '900*, Bari, 1962, pp. 211–351: this essay has been incorporated in the 3rd edition of the *Cronache*, Bari, 1966. See also E. Garin, *Storia della filosofia italiana*, III, Turin, 1966, pp. 1261–1350. Garin is presupposed throughout my paper. See also C. Antoni and R. Mattioli, ed., *Cinquant'anni di vita intellettuale italiana (1896–1946)*, Naples, 1950. G. N. Orsini, *B.C. Philosopher of Art and Literary Critic*, Southern Illinois University Press, 1961, is indispensable: he gives the necessary references to works by Croce or on Croce in English. I shall only add S. Hughes, 'The Evaluation of Sociology in Croce's Theory of History', in W. J. Cahnman and A. Boskoff, *Sociology and History*, New York, 1964, pp. 128–40. Among recent Italian works I mention: M. Abbate, *La filosofia di B.C. e la crisi della società italiana*, 2nd ed., Turin, 1966; A. Bausola, *Filosofia e storia nel pensiero crociano*, Milan, 1965; A. Caracciolo, *L'estetica e la religione di B.C.*, Arona, 1958; R. Franchini, *Croce interprete di Hegel*, Naples, 1964; idem, *La teoria della storia di B. Croce*, Naples, 1966. The little book by A. Guzzo, *Croce e Gentile*, Lugano, 1953, includes personal impressions.

2. *Contributo alla critica di me stesso*, Naples, 1918 (it was written in 1915), later included in *Etica e politica*, Bari, 1931, pp. 363–411: R. G. Collingwood's translation with a preface by J. A. Smith, Oxford, 1927. It is important to see what C. writes about himself in *Storia d'Italia dal 1871 al 1915*, 1st ed., 1928, especially pp. 245–63. Parts of his diaries for the period September 1943–June 1944 are published in *Scritti e discorsi politici (1943–1947)*, I, Bari, 1963, pp. 171–344. The *Nuove pagine sparse*, I–II, Naples, 1949, are especially full of autobiographical recollections. (Earlier importants drafts of the *Contributo* have now been published: B.C., *Memorie della mia vita*, Naples, 1966.)

3. Elena Croce, *Ricordi familiari*, Florence, 2nd ed., 1962 (notice pp. 35–6 on the religious education of Croce's daughters); idem, *L'infanzia dorata*, Milan, 1966. *Cf.* also D. Marra, *Conversazioni con B.C. su alcuni libri della sua biblioteca*, Milan, 1952 (D. Marra was C.'s librarian from 1945).

4. *B. Croce*, Turin, 1962.

5. *Carteggio Croce–Vossler (1899–1949)*, Bari, 1951. (*Cf.* now B.C., *Epistolario*, I–II, Naples, 1967–9 and the first volume of the letters by G. Gentile to C., Florence, 1973.)

6. The letters by G. Sorel were published partially in *La Critica*, 25, 1927, and following years.

7. *Cf.* the appendix to A. Labriola, *La concezione materialistica della storia*, Bari, 1938, pp. 267–312, to be found also in *Materialismo storico ed economia marxistica*, 6th ed., Bari, 1941, pp. 265–306.

8. E. Cecchi, *Ricordi crociani*, Milan and Naples, 1965, pp. 73–100. Among the interesting letters so far published notice those to R. Serra (in A. Grilli, *Tempo di Serra*, Florence, 1961) and to G. Amendola (in E. Amendola Kühn, *Vita con G. Amendola*, Florence, 1960).

9. This description by the historian F. Nitti is quoted by M. Corsi, *Le origini del pensiero di B.C.*, Florence, 1951, p. 182. Croce himself evaluated 'La vita

letteraria a Napoli dal 1860 al 1900' in *La Critica*, 8, 1910, pp. 241–62 = *La letteratura della Nuova Italia*, IV, pp. 293–319.

10. On all this it will be enough to refer to E. Agazzi, *Il giovane C. e il marxismo*, Turin, 1962, and to the introduction by E. Garin to A. Labriola, *La concezione materialistica della storia*, Bari, 1965: both give bibliography. E. Santerelli, *La revisione del marxismo in Italia*, Milan, 1964, pp. 29–80, is a partisan evaluation with few new facts.

11. The first version of the *Estetica*, 1900, is conveniently available (together with the first version of the *Logica*) in A. Attisani, *La prima forma della Estetica e della Logica*, Messina, 1924.

12. There is a very valuable anthology of these periodicals by D. Frigessi, *La cultura italiana del '900 attraverso le riviste, Leonardo, Hermes, Il Regno*, Turin, 1960, with an important introduction. *Cf.* also M. Puppo, *Croce e D'Annunzio e altri saggi*, Florence, 1964.

13. His *Opere* (the most important of which is *La persuasione e la rettorica*) were collected by G. Chiavacci, Florence, 1958: notice on p. 661 an opinion on Croce (written about 1908).

14. *Cf.* R. Serra, *Scritti*, II, Florence, 1938, pp. 265–71: 'Il Croce di Prezzo-lini'; idem, *Le lettere*, Rome, 1914, pp. 39–47, 139–44; idem, *Esame di coscienza d'un letterato*, Milan, 1915 = *Scritti*, I, pp. 395–6, *cf.* pp. 444–5. E. Garin, 'Serra e Croce', *Belfagor*, 21, 1966, pp. 1–14.

15. G. Papini–G. Prezzolini, *Storia di un'amicizia*, Florence, 1966, pp. 72, 136. See also Papini's review of Croce's first *Logica* in *Leonardo*, 1905, 3, 115 (D. Frigessi, *La cultura italiana* etc., p. 255). In general G. Prezzolini. *Il tempo della Voce*, Milan and Florence, 1960 (with several letters by Croce).

16. The identification of history (historiography) and philosophy was first formulated in the second *Logica*, 1909. For Croce's evolution on this point see for instance C. Antoni, in *Cinquant'anni di vita intellettuale italiana* quoted I, pp. 68–77 (where bibliography).

17. Borgese's article, published in *La Stampa*, Turin, 10 April 1911, pro-voked C.'s reply in *La Critica*, 9, 1911, pp. 223–9 (*Pagine sparse*, I, 1943, pp. 329–38). Hence Borgese's attack, 'Vico, Croce e i giovani', *Cultura Con-temporanea*, 5 April 1912, pp. 110–73, reprinted in *La vita e il libro*, III, Turin, 323–402.

18. See G. Prezzolini, *B.C.*, Naples, 1909.

19. *La Voce*, 6, No. 4, 28 February 1914, 10–33 at p. 28, partly republished in the anthology of *La Voce*, ed. G. Ferrata, S. Giovanni Valdarno, 1961, pp. 447–59 (at p. 458).

20. *Le lettere*, 1914, 30.

21. *Cf. Storia d'Italia*, 1st ed., Bari, 1928, p. 345. In general *L'Italia dal 1914 al 1918. Pagine sulla guerra*, 3rd ed., Bari, 1950.

22. *Cf. 2000 pagine di Gramsci*, I, Milan, 1964, p. 19; *Le riviste di Piero Gobetti*, a cura di L. Basso e L. Anderlini, 1961, p. 87 (from *Energie nuove*, 1918).

23. On this episode L. Salvatorelli, in F. Flora, ed., *B. Croce*, Milan, 1953, pp. 397–416.

24. *Cf. Cultura e vita morale*, 3rd ed., 1955, pp. 253–9 (a defence of religious education in elementary schools written in 1923). A. Omodeo had written in

1914: 'Il mito cristiano rinverdirà nell'atto in cui il padre si profonda nell'animo miticizzante del figlio' (*La Voce*, 6, No. 14, 28 July 1914). Prezzolini (ibid.) had answered: 'Caro Omodeo, che l'idealismo difenda il valore preparatorio del grado religioso sta bene; ma che difenda per l'appunto il valore preparatorio del cattolicesimo di Papa Pio X non mi pare nè giusto nè opportuno.' See also F. Nicolini, *Il Croce minore*, Milan and Naples, 1963, pp. 47–9, for interesting declarations by C.

25. The text in *Pagine sparse*, II, Naples, 1943, pp. 380–83. For Croce's point of view after Matteotti's murder in 1924, ibid., pp. 376–9. New evidence in G. Levi Della Vida, *Fantasmi ritrovati*, Venice, 1966, pp. 167–209. *Cf.* D. Mack Smith, *The Cambridge Journal*, 3, 1949, pp. 343–56; C. McArthur Destler, *Journ. Mod. History*, 24, 1952, pp. 382–90; G. Salvemini, *Il Ponte*, 10, November 1954, p. 1728.

26. Catholic philosophers, as is well known, varied in their reactions to Croce. E. Chiocchetti, *La filosofia di B.C.*, 1st ed., Florence, 1915; 3rd ed., Milan, 1924, approves of the greater part of C.'s philosophy. F. Olgiati, *B.C. e lo storicismo*, Milan, 1953, is an invective. Further literature in G. Mastroianni quoted in footnote 35.

27. G. Pasquali, 'Croce e le letterature classiche', *Leonardo*, 8, 1937, pp. 45–50. See Croce's reply, *Pagine sparse*, III, Naples, 1943, pp. 170–73.

28. On G. M. Hopkins, *Poesia antica e moderna*, 2nd ed., Bari, 1943, pp. 421–46 (written in 1936).

29. Even in 1938 (*La storia come pensiero e come azione*, pp. 47–9) C.'s notion of liberty was ambiguous: liberty is both ubiquitous and aristocratic – independent of political régimes. See the interesting personal recollections by E. Chichiarelli, 'Il limite della mia lezione crociana', *Riv. Studi Crociani*, 1, 1964, pp. 482–98. Perhaps the most important analysis of Croce's liberalism is in N. Bobbio, *Politica e cultura*, Turin, 1955. See also N. Valeri, *Da Giolitti a Mussolini*, Florence, 1956, pp. 197–212 and E. Agazzi, 'B.C. e l'avvento del fascismo', *Riv. Storica del Socialismo*, 9, 1966, pp. 76–103.

30. It would be worth examining in what sense and to what extent there was a group of 'Crociani' in Italy between 1925 and 1940. The situation, of course varied not only according to years, but according to places: the Turin Crociani were different from those of Naples. The personality of two young Turin Crociani – L. Ginzburg and A. Mautino (the former died in gaol as a victim of Nazi-Fascism) – emerges clearly from the posthumous publication of their writings: L. Ginzburg, *Scritti*, with an introduction by N. Bobbio, Turin, 1964; A. Mautino, *La formazione della filosofia politica di B.C., con uno studio sull'autore e la tradizione culturale torinese da Gobetti alla Resistenza di G. Solari*, 3rd ed., Bari, 1953. See more in general G. Luti, *Cronache letterarie tra le due guerre, 1920–1940*, Bari, 1966.

31. *Pagine sparse*, III, Naples, 1943, p. 138: 'per questa via, la parola "ario" finirà a prendere il significato d' "imbecille" '. Croce's help to persecuted Jews, both Italian and foreign, was unlimited. *Cf.* E. Cione, *B. Croce e il pensiero contemporaneo*, Milan, 1963, pp. 121 and 578 (the first edition of this book, under the title *Croce*, appeared in Milan, 1944: the author, a former pupil of Croce, became bitterly hostile to him).

32. A. Gramsci, *Il materialismo storico e la filosofia di B. Croce*, Turin, 1948 (these notes must have been written about 1932), pp. 247, 250. *Cf.* also his notes on *Gli intellettuali e la organizzazione della cultura*, Turin, 1949, where there are typical judgements inspired by Croce, for instance p. 140: 'la grandezza del Machiavelli consiste nell'aver distinto la politica dall'etica'.

33. See C. Antoni, *Commento a Croce*, Venice, 1955, where the author puts together earlier papers: for Croce's approval see the preface.

34. *Cf. Filosofia e storiografia*, Bari, 1949, pp. 217–23 (1947) and the whole volume *Indagini su Hegel e schiarimenti filosofici*, Bari, 1952, and especially pp. 29–45 (1951). For existentialist criticism, *cf.* E. Paci, *Esistenzialismo e storicismo*, Milan, 1950. See also A. Bruno, *La crisi dell' idealismo nell' ultimo Croce*, Bari, 1964.

35. The Neapolitan group of 'Crociani' now has its own journal, the *Rivista di Studi Crociani*, 1964 ff. *Cf.* G. Mastroianni, 'La polemica sul C. negli studi contemporanei', *Società*, 14, 1958, pp. 711–37. I am not sure that J. W. Meiland, *Scepticism and Historical Knowledge*, New York, 1965, can be described as a book by a pupil of Croce. On C. and Meinecke, W. Hofer, *Geschichtschreibung und Weltanschauung*, Munich, 1950, pp. 389–403. On C. and Collingwood, Croce, *Nuove pagine sparse*, I, Naples, 1948, pp. 25–39 (1946). Collingwood's early essays on C. are now collected in *Essays on the Philosophy of History*, Austin, Texas, 1965.

36. The most important essay on Croce as a historian is by F. Chabod, *Riv. Storica Ital.*, 64, 1952, pp. 473–530. *Cf.* A. R. Caponigri, *History and Liberty, the Historical Writings of B. Croce*, London, 1955; F. Gaeta, *Riv. Studi Crociani*, I, 1964, pp. 153–67; W. Mager, *Benedetto Croces literarisches und politisches Interesse an der Geschichte*, Graz, 1965. On the *Storia d'Italia*, V. de Caprariis in F. Flora, ed., *B.C.*, quoted, pp. 291–301. On Chabod's interpretation of C., G. Sasso, *Interpretazioni crociane* (a collective volume), Bari, 1965, pp. 221–304 (interesting also for other points). See now also E. Ragionieri, *Belfagor*, 21, 1966, pp. 125–49 and K.-E. Lönne, *B.C. als Kritiker seiner Zeit*, Tübingen, 1967.

37. See C.'s paper of 1941 in *Discorsi di varia filosofia*, I, Bari, 1945, pp. 235–50, and also *Letture di poeti*, Bari, 1950, pp. 247–58. A useful collection of evidence in S. Cavaciuti, *La teoria linguistica di B. Croce*, Milan, 1959; *cf.* T. De Mauro, *Giorn. Crit. della Filos. Ital.* N.S. 8, 1954, pp. 376–91, and *Introduzione alla semantica*, Bari, 2nd ed., 1966. But I should like to mention especially the little volume by E. Colorni (to whom the present paper is dedicated), *L'estetica di B.C.*, Milan, 1932. Colorni died in 1944 as a victim of Fascism.

38. This was particularly well emphasized by F. Flora, *Croce*, Milan, 1927, p. 129. Croce's later work is no departure from this basic attitude. An important analysis of Croce's ideas on history in P. Rossi, *Storia e storicismo nella filosofia contemporanea*, Milan, 1960, pp. 287–330, with which I fundamentally agree. Perhaps less rewarding: D. Faucci, *Storicismo e metafisica nel pensiero crociano*, Florence, 1950; F. Albeggiani, *Lo storicismo di B.C.*, 'Atti Accad. Palermo' 4, 13, 2, 1953; R. Raggiunti, *La conoscenza storica. Analisi della logica crociana*, Florence, 1955. Among foreign critics it will be enough to mention two classics: M. Mandelbaum, *The Problem of Historical Knowledge*, New York, 1938; H.-I. Marrou, *De la connaissance historique*, Paris, 1954.

39. This example is given by Croce, *Frammenti di etica* in *Etica e politica*, Bari, 1931, p. 57.

40. See for instance his characteristic letter to K. Vossler on the war as 'azione divina', *Carteggio Croce–Vossler*, pp. 206–7: 'Come sai bene, le lotte degli Stati, le guerre, sono *azioni divine*. Noi, individui, dobbiamo accettarle e sottometterci. Ma sottomettere la nostra attività pratica e non quella teoretica' (1919).

41. It is reprinted in *Discorsi di varia filosofia*, I, Bari, 1945, pp. 11–23. *Cf.* *La religione di B. Croce*, Bari, 1964; A. Bausola, *Etica e politica nel pensiero di B.C.*, Milan, 1966.

42. 'L'indole immorale dell'errore e la critica scientifica e letteraria', 1906, *Cultura e vita morale*, 3rd ed., Naples, 1955, pp. 88–94 at p. 89. Croce lived to regret his earlier (1909) eulogy of the Inquisition in *Filosofia della pratica*, 3rd ed., Bari, 1923, p. 43.

43. (Among the innumerable publications inspired by the centenary, notice: *Terzo Programma*, 2, 1966, pp. 1–130 (various authors); E. Paratore, *Il Croce e le lettere classiche*, Rome, 1967; G. Contini, 'L'influenza culturale di B. Croce', *L'Approdo Letterario*, 12, 1966, pp. 3–32; V. E. Alfieri, *Pedagogia crociana*, Naples, 1967; U. Benedetti, *Benedetto Croce e il Fascismo*, Rome, 1967; G. Sasso, *La Cultura*, 5, 1967, pp. 44–69, and above all the survey by V. Stella, *Giornale di metafisica*, 22, 1967, pp. 643–711.)

21

Historicism Revisited*

I

I REALLY have revisited Historicism. In 10–12 June 1974 I was one of
the participants in a conference on Historicism organized by the editors
of *History and Theory* at the Warburg Institute in London. The papers
were excellent, and the level of the discussion was very high. But when
after the conference I tried to formulate for my own use what I had
learnt from it, I found myself writing an introductory paper for a future
conference in which the participants would be kind enough to discuss
the rather old-fashioned points of view on which I want to be either
reassured or refuted. As there is something to be said for not having
conferences in accordance with one's own wishes, I publish my paper
as the lesser evil.[1]

II

It is of course old-fashioned to say that the historian always starts from
facts, but I do not know what else I could say. A historian may register
the mere existence of a fact: for instance the date of an event. Or he
may ask questions about that fact: questions which incidentally may
very soon lead him to make a distinction between fact and evidence. It
is very difficult to define what sorts of facts are the characteristic concern
of the historian; and it is equally difficult to define what precisely is
the concern of the historian in his facts. But to judge from the historians
we respect – from Herodotus and Thucydides to Eduard Meyer and
Marc Bloch – four features would seem to characterize the historian's
work: (1) a general interest in past human deeds; (2) pleasure in

Mededelingen der Koninklijke Nederlandse Akademie van Wetenschappen,
Afd. Letterkunde, N.R. 37, 3, 1974, pp. 63–70.

discovering *new* facts about the human past; (3) awareness that the information we have about the human past raises problems which affect the credibility of the information itself and therefore the substance of the past; (4) an effort to make sense of *selected* facts of the human past, that is, to explain and evaluate them.

Every historian is a collector of facts of the human past. Collecting these facts is so important that it is pursued by specific institutions, such as museums, archives and archaeological expeditions. But although they emphasize the fact-finding aspect of historical research, these institutions exist only in relation to the other aspects of historical research – namely, selection of the evidence and explanation and evaluation of the facts emerging from the selected evidence.

What we call 'historicism' is a situation arising from this process of selection, explanation and evaluation. More precisely, historicism is the recognition that each of us sees past events from a point of view determined or at least conditioned by our own individual changing situation in history. Raymond Aron and others have given good reasons to explain why historicism should have become an acute question in the early twentieth century. But its roots lie in the extension of historical interpretation to all aspects of human life (indeed of the universe itself) in the nineteenth century.

Historicism is not a comfortable doctrine because it implies a danger of relativism. It tends to undermine the historian's confidence in himself. True enough, Ranke who, among the nineteenth-century historians, is supposed to be the 'Altvater' of Historicism, lived very comfortably. He seems to have felt no difficulty in relating the individual facts disclosed by the opening of the archives to the march of universal history. But we suspect Ranke of some confidence tricks. If God is in the individual facts, why should we care about universal history? If God is not in the individual facts, how can he be in universal history?

In our more prosaic terminology, there is a question about the categories according to which events must be classified, correlated, explained and judged; but the question is complicated by the changing experience of the classifying agent – the historian – who is himself in history. This is not to accept the thesis very acutely developed by Hayden White in his recent book *Metahistory* (1973) that Ranke, or any other historian, classifies the facts according to rhetorical questions. Rhetoric does not pose questions of truth, which is what worried Ranke and his successors and still worries us. Above all, rhetoric does not entail techniques for the research of truth, which is what historians are anxious to invent. The question is, rather, how we stand nowadays in relation to this task of discovering facts and fitting them into a pattern in order to understand and evaluate them, *if* we ourselves are part of the historical process we are trying to understand.

If history-writing implies that we choose our facts according to certain criteria – or we try to discover new facts according to certain interests – these criteria and interests already imply a choice of universals or generalizations according to which we want to classify and understand the facts. We cannot understand and evaluate facts unless we relate them to general categories and values, but we would not be able to start to choose (or discover) facts unless we had in mind some value or general category to which we want to refer the facts.

To choose facts about the history of feudalism means having some idea of what feudalism is. Facts become meaningful only by becoming part of a situation or of a process, but the choice of the facts depends on the situation we envisage from the outset (call it a hypothesis or a model or an ideal type). Furthermore, to attach importance to certain facts in view of a certain situation or process is equivalent to attributing a value to these facts. History is always a choice of facts fitting into a static or dynamic situation which appears worth studying.

This characterization of historical research can be interpreted either pessimistically or optimistically. The pessimistic interpretation is that history-writing is selecting facts for a situation one envisages before having selected the facts. Consequently we shall find what we want to find because our initial hypothesis or model or idea will determine our choice of the facts to be studied. An extra dose of pessimism may be injected by the further consideration that between the moment we start our research and the moment we end it we ourselves shall be changed and therefore guided by different interests or presuppositions. But the pessimistic interpretation depends on the assumption that any initial hypothesis or model is arbitrary and unfalsifiable; and the extra-pessimistic dose depends in its turn on the further assumption that the human mind is incapable of consistency because of historical change. We have emphasized that the historian collects facts: his initial hypothesis or model is propounded in view of the facts he has before him and in order to test it against more facts. If I formulate a provisional hypothesis or model about feudalism it is because I know some facts which I connect with the feudal order.

I expect to modify my initial hypothesis or model as my research progresses; indeed the very selection of the facts will continuously be modified by the requirements of the research itself. Leaving aside for the moment the question of the relation between facts and evidence, historical research is controlled by the facts indicated by the evidence. In so far as evidence presents facts, facts are facts – and it is characteristic of the historian's profession to respect facts. The pessimist underrates the discipline to which the historian is submitted.

Even so there are two ways of going wrong. One is avoidable ignorance or error, the other is unavoidable ignorance. I may misinterpret a text because my knowledge of its language is faulty, but I may also misinterpret it because certain circumstances about it were not yet known when I studied it. In either case I am shown to be not only changeable, but fallible, and there seems to be a relation between my changeability and my fallibility, though the relation is neither clear nor perhaps necessary. It will be enough that we, being mortal and fallible, study change from changing points of view and can never boast of absolute certainty. If we were unchangeable and infallible, we might still be interested in change – as the ancient gods were supposed to be in relation to changing humanity (it saved them from boredom). But it would be a different interest, presumably with a different method.

We study change *because* we are changeable. This gives us a direct experience of change: what we call memory. Because of change our knowledge of change will never be final: the unexpected is infinite. But our knowledge of change is real enough. At least we know what we are talking about. Our knowledge of change is both made possible and circumscribed by our changing experience. All we can do is to produce facts which fit into our model or hypothesis and models or hypotheses which fit the facts. We shall soon hear from our colleagues (or from our changing selves) if the alleged facts are non-existent or if the facts, though existent, can be better interpreted by a different hypothesis or model.

There is no hope that structuralism will save us from the predicament of historicism. Structuralism has sharply reminded us that synchronic understanding is even more necessary than diachronic history-writing and has its own presuppositions and rules. On consideration, this was perhaps not such a revolutionary intimation. 'Altvater' Mommsen should have been enough to warn us that the diachronic history of 'Altvater' Ranke had no claim to exclusiveness. The *Römisches Staatsrecht* is essentially a masterpiece of synchronic history. Burckhardt wavered between synchronic and diachronic history. Looking more carefully, one might even discover that most of the important books of cultural and social history of the last 120 years (from Fustel de Coulanges to J. Huizinga and M. Bloch) are more synchronic than diachronic: that is, they are based on stereotypes, or ideal types. Structuralism certainly reveals deeper and more permanent elements of our human nature. It has taught us to seek new relations between diachronic and synchronic sets of events. But the reality of change, which is the reality of death, cannot be wiped out. In the future we may as historians have to study long-term changes which are for the moment hardly conceivable. But I cannot foresee history ever becoming a science of the permanent.

III

As we cannot do better than studying change from a changing point of view, there is a point in doing it well. But the determination to do it well depends on an extra-cognitive factor: the conviction that it is worth doing well. If we are never absolutely certain about the facts, we want at least to be absolutely certain about the purpose of our efforts.

Now this may become a troublesome requirement. What is the point of writing the biography of a good man if we feel that goodness is a historically conditioned value? What is the point of studying the phenomenology of freedom if freedom is a transient value?

It is easy to object that our moral conscience has nothing to do with the facts in question. If we study parliamentary institutions (this objection implies) we must see how they work, not whether they are what we think they should be: if anything, the desirability of a certain type of parliament will be a separate question. But this objection leaves out the possibility that the model from which we start and to which we ultimately return with modifications will be a morally desirable model: the good man, the good institution or the good society. Are we to exclude a morally coloured model?

We would have much to exclude. Present-day researchers who worry about the status of women, children, slaves and coloured people will be affected. True enough, they may not be looking for the good society, but for a better society emerging out of a bad society which exploited women and humiliated slaves. But the moral conscience which requires the historian to do research with a view to a better society must be able to resist the claims that its values are as historically conditioned as the values of a ruthless adult white male slave-owner.

The true answer, I believe, lies in a dilemma. Either we possess a religious or moral belief independent of history, which allows us to pronounce judgement on historical events, or we must give up moral judging. Just because history teaches us how many moral codes mankind has had, we cannot derive moral judgement from history. Even the notion of transforming history by studying history implies a meta-historical faith.

What history-writing without moral judgements would be is difficult for me to envisage, because I have not yet seen it. It would, however, be unwarranted to exclude *a priori* the possibility of a historiography inspired by mere intellectual curiosity or by interest in technical achievements while indifferent to any moral value.

IV

Having in any case made my choice in this dilemma – that is, having decided to use my moral judgement as a sign of my liberty in the face of history – I prefer to concern myself with the technicalities and actual trends of historical research in the age of historicism.

Here it will be enough to underline with H.-I. Marrou what was too easily forgotten in the golden age of the discussion on historicism (for instance by E. Troeltsch himself and by O. Hintze), namely that between us (as historians) and the facts lies the evidence. We can envisage borderline cases in which the historian looks straight at the facts. A contemporary reporter can write about what he has seen: an archaeologist can examine the features of a perfectly preserved buried city which he has discovered and excavated personally. In both cases there will be questions about the reliability of the writer's memory or notes; but his evidence and his facts will in practice coincide. However, the great majority of historians work on relics of the past – in the form of written or oral accounts, documents, material remains discovered by others, etc. The historian has to interpret the evidence in order to establish the facts and normally has to consider previous interpretations. All this implies that he has to write history not only from his personal (and changing) point of view, but also taking into account the points of view of previous witnesses and interpreters. Furthermore, he has to assess the value of his evidence not in terms of simple reliability, but of relevance to the problems he wants to solve. He may discover that much of his evidence is irrelevant or superfluous; but more often (especially if he is a historian of Antiquity or of the Middle Ages) he will find the evidence inadequate. Though every piece of evidence is a fact in itself, it is not necessarily the fact we need. We all know that what is a useless forgery to one historian is excellent evidence of intellectual trends to another. A historian employs much of his time in establishing the correct relation between the evidence before him and the hypothesis or model he has in his mind. Even in the case in which the relic is a fragment of the fact he wants to study (an incomplete text, the ruins of a city) there are basic questions about the relation between what is lost and what survives. Consequently the historian will worry less about his own inevitable situation in history than about the historical situation of his evidence, previous historians included.

Many of the difficulties in assessing the relation between evidence and events have become routine and therefore require less attention now than they did in the eighteenth or early nineteenth century. But the difficulties re-emerge in strength when new types of evidence are offered. Psycho-analysis or psycho-history, for instance, is a newcomer to historical research and therefore raises acute questions. Few will doubt that psycho-analysis has justified its extension beyond the abnormal and beyond the living. Its right to be treated as a tool for historical research has been asserted (for instance by H. U. Wehler, *Historische Zeitschrift*, 208, 1969, pp. 529–54 and by B. Mazlish, *Trans. Royal Hist. Society*, 5, 21, 1971, pp. 79–100). But the nature of the evidence psycho-history can offer is not very clear to me. If we are talking about the age of Julius Caesar, we may conceivably psycho-analyse Caesar and Cicero, about whom we have documents (though that too will create difficulties), but would that be enough? We ought to know what was going on in the subconscious of their friends and enemies, even of the opposed armies. I cannot see any *a priori* objection to incorporating the subconscious in the problems of historicism. The changing points of view of the psycho-analysts will take their place among the changing points of view of other historical observers. But the psycho-historian will have to justify his use of evidence like anybody else in the historical profession.

One of the curiosities of historiography is that the removal of restrictions on research does not necessarily make research easier. We have seen the theologians become increasingly indifferent to the results of historical research on the Bible. They have found other ways of knowing God. The first reaction of the historians was one of elation. Bible criticism (and patristic studies) flourished in such a climate; and the religious creed of the historian became largely irrelevant to his performance. But now we begin to suspect that by becoming irrelevant to theology, Bible criticism risks becoming irrelevant to everything else – or at least trivial. To call the Bible a historical document is to forget that the Bible used to be the foundation of more than one living creed.

On a different (perhaps lower) level, the disappearance of national history as a meaningful notion is embarrassing to historians. We Italians have been asking ourselves for a long time what Italian history is. But it was almost a shock to have to admit, on being faced with the first three volumes of the *History of Italy* recently published by Einaudi, that one did not understand why all these interesting, and often admirable, essays had to be collected under this title. Some chapters appeared to be fragments of a history of European culture, others were episodes of the history of the Catholic Church, others were descriptions of regional societies, etc. What is relevant here is that the virtual disappearance of the concept of nation as an elementary unit for historical research multiplies the points of view from which one can consider events that used to be taken as episodes of national history.

It is not surprising that in the circumstances biography should steadily progress towards the centre of historical research. While almost any type of political and social history is made more complex by the claims of historicism, biography remains something relatively simple. An individual has clear contours and a limited number of significant relationships: there are recognized techniques even for psychoanalysing him. Biography allows any kind of question within well defined limits: political history, economic history, religious history and art history become easier if confined to one individual. Even the biological factors can be brought to bear in controllable terms. It will be interesting to watch this development which is at least partly a function of the tiredness of the historians in the age of historicism.

The inevitable corollary of historicism is history of historiography as the mode of expressing awareness that historical problems have themselves a history. This, however, has produced books the sole purpose of which is to prove that every historian and any historical problem is historically conditioned – with the additional platitude that even a verdict of this kind by the historian of historiography is historically conditioned.

Such an expression of pure relativism, in my opinion, is not defensible. History of historiography, like any other historical research, has the purpose of discriminating between truth and falsehood. As a kind of intellectual history which purports to examine the achievements of a historian, it has to distinguish between solutions of historical problems which fail to convince and solutions (=hypotheses; models; ideal types) which are worth being restated and developed. To write a critical history of historiography one must know both the authors one studies and the historical material they have studied.

References

1. The excellent article by G. G. Iggers on *Historicism* in *Dictionary of the History of Ideas*, New York, II, 1973, pp. 457–64 gives the essential German, Italian and American bibliography, but is weak on the French contributors (not even H.-I. Marrou and R. Aron are included). We owe to G. G. Iggers and K. von Moltke a useful introduction to the *Theory and Practice of History* by L. von Ranke, Indianopolis, 1973. The following books may serve as introductions to other positions: J. W. Meiland, *Scepticism and Historical Knowledge*, New York, 1965 (mainly on Croce, Oakeshott and Collingwood); Th. Schieder, *Geschichte als Wissenschaft*, München, 1965 (for the German academic tradition of Historismus); M. Jay, *The Dialectical Imagination*, Boston, 1973 (on the Frankfurt School); P. Veyne, *Comment on écrit l'histoire*, Paris, 1971 (for the 'Annales' tradition). Nor should one forget H. Stuart Hughes, *Consciousness and Society*, New York, 1958, and A. Heuss, *Verlust der Geschichte*, Göttingen, 1959. For recent Italian developments (in which D. Cantimori has a central part: *cf.* the posthumous collection of essays *Storici e Storia*, Torino, 1971) N. Badaloni, *Marxismo come Storicismo*, Milano, 1962, may be a point of departure. F. H. Bradley, *The Presuppositions of Critical History* (1874) is now to be read in L. Rubinoff's edition, Chicago, 1968. Isaiah Berlin's essay on 'Historical Inevitability' (1953) is collected in *Four Essays on Liberty*, Oxford, 1969. New literature in *Wiener Beiträge zur Geschichte der Neuzeit* I, 1974.

Index

Paschalius, C., 207–18, 227, 228
Pasquali, G., 327, 353
Passerin d'Entrèves, A., 2
Passionei, D., 286
Patrizi, F., 91–2
Paul, Saint, 111, 315
  Apocalypse of, 152
Paulinus of Nola, 285
Paulus Aemilius, 67–8
Pausanias, geographer, 68, 80
Pausanias, regent of Sparta, 31–2
Pédech, P., 71, 201
Peithidemos, archon of Athens, 43, 62
Pericles, 25, 166
Perizonius, J., 231–5, 241, 244–5, 288
Perotti, N., 76, 86
Perret, J., 268
Perrotta, G., 327
Petavius, D., 271
Peter of Galatia, 154
Petrarch, 79–80, 279
Petronius Probus, 131
Pfaff, C., 289–90
Pflugius, C. [pseudonym], *see*
  Gruterus, Ianus
Phaedima, 26
Phaedrus of Sphettus, 40
Phainias, 172
Philinus, 85
Philip of Macedon, 47, 162
Philip of Side, 153, 155
Philippides, 42
Philiscus, 39
Philistus, 39, 50
Philo, 315–17
  Pseudo-, 114
Philochorus, 44, 46, 50–51
Philopoemen, 68, 70, 331
Philostorgius, 153, 155–6
Philostratus, 118, 144, 145, 148–9
Photius, 25–6, 81, 120, 153
Phylarchus, 69
Pibrac, G. de, 214–16, 228
Piccolomini, A., 211
Pichena, C., 219
Pighius, S., 220
Pindar, 56, 185, 191
Pirrone, N., 237

Pithou, P., 226
Plantin, C., 226
Plato, 18–20, 22, 39, 46, 48, 69, 172,
  183–4, 195, 258, 292
  Pseudo-, 19
Plautus, 13
Plessen, V. von, 93
Pliny the Elder, 19, 79, 102–3
Pliny the Younger, 131, 162
Plotinus, 20
Plutarch, 43, 80, 82, 86, 93, 102, 144,
  161, 169, 173, 209, 308
  and Timaeus, 47, 58–9
Pohlenz, M., 199, 299
Polemon, 39
Polenton, Sicco, 85–6, 96
Polet, A., 220
Politian, 88, 94, 279
Politica (journal), 351
Pollio, Trebellius, 146
Polyaenus, 172
Polybius, 15, 67–77, 79–98, 104, 130,
  136, 143–4, 161–8, 174, 177, 216,
  242, 308
  and time, 187–9, 192–3
  and Timaeus, 38–9, 47–50, 57–8,
  142
  Fustel de Coulanges on, 328, 331–3
Polycrates, 32
Polyperchon, 37
Pompey, 15
Pontano, G., 205
Porphyry, 20, 79, 111, 155
Port-Royal, school of, 4, 280
Posidonius, 15, 141, 143, 162, 174, 189
Post, A. H., 326
Potter's Oracle, 20
Pouilly, L.-J. Lévesque de, 271
Praetextatus, Agorius, 122, 132
Preen, F. von, 295, 299
Prezzolini, G., 348–50, 352, 361
Proba, 152
Probus, copyist, 152
Probus, Emperor, 147
Procopius, 80–81, 84, 115, 190
Prohaeresius, 149
Propertius, 221
Ptolemy, Claudius, 85–6